# DEMOCRATIC ELOQUENCE

# DEMOCRATIC ELOQUENCE

*The Fight over Popular Speech in Nineteenth-Century America*

Kenneth Cmiel

WILLIAM MORROW AND COMPANY, INC.
*New York*

Library of Congress Cataloging-in-Publication Data

Cmiel, Kenneth.
    Democratic eloquence : the fight over popular speech in nineteenth-
century America / Kenneth Cmiel.
        p.   cm.
    Originally presented as the author's thesis (doctoral—University
of Chicago, 1986).
    Includes bibliographical references.
    ISBN 0-688-08352-8
    1. English language—Spoken English—United States—History—19th century.
2. English language—United States—Usage—History—19th century.   3. Political
oratory—United States—History—19th century.   4. United States—Popular
culture—History—19th century.   5. English language—19th century—Rhetoric.
6. Americanisms—History—19th century.   I. Title.
PE2809.C57   1990
420'.973—dc20                                                    90-5412
                                                                     CIP

Printed in the United States of America

First Edition

1 2 3 4 5 6 7 8 9 10

BOOK DESIGN BY PAUL CHEVANNES

## TO ANNE

How can my muse want subject to invent,
Whilst thou dost breathe, that pour'st into my verse
Thine own sweet argument, too excellent
For every vulgar paper to rehearse?

WILL SHAKESPEARE

You knew the job was dangerous when you took it.

SUPER CHICKEN

# Acknowledgments

This was originally a dissertation, and my committee was exemplary. Neil Harris encouraged me to expand the project beyond the usual bounds of the dissertation genre, and his early criticisms made me acutely aware of some of the problems connected with writing about language. Over the years, Barry Karl provided more kindnesses to me than I can possibly remember, let alone acknowledge. And Robert Ferguson stepped in toward the end and gave of himself with truly inspiring generosity.

Friends also helped. An awful lot of this book I owe to discussions with Danny Bluestone. It probably wouldn't exist save for him. While doing her own dissertation, Lamar Murphy kept finding all sorts of stuff for mine, and various chapters are much stronger because of her. Beth Bailey I thank for coffee at the Medici and for telling me that women had problems with language too. (Beth, you'll see it's better than the dissertation but not nearly as good as it could be. I ran out of steam.) David Farber gave me a great reading, helping to solve a very basic conceptual problem. Steve Wheatley also provided support and insight. And Tony Martin and Linda Buchanan have, over the years, provided the kind of interest and discussion characteristic of all civic-minded gentlemen and ladies.

In Iowa, Sydney James, Allan Megill, and Kathleen Diffley all thoughtfully commented on the manuscript. My research assistant, Mark Meier, was indispensable. His sense of humor didn't hurt either. Typists Peggy Peach (Chicago) and Julie Scott (Iowa City) were great. At the last minute, Karen Anderson and Oscar King were gigantic help.

I'd like to thank my mother, Jean Cmiel, who knew I was going to be a historian since I was in the fifth grade. For a million reasons, I would have never started this project without her help. Finally, of course, Anne, Willa, and Cordelia. Without them I'd be nothing.

# Contents

# Introduction

It is commonplace to decry the level of political discussion in America. The banalities of advertised politics seem to overwhelm the political process, filling the air with slogans, "sound bites," and only marginally meaningful clichés. If "the dreaded 'L' word" was central to the campaign of 1988, "Where's the beef?" served in its place four years before. Professional handlers manage willing politicians, the mass media bores in on the horse race, and the public remains apathetic. The rhetoric of American politics is debased, reduced to bromides designed to soothe an audience into complacency or invective essaying to conjure up vague demons. In the process, the very possibility of the public's carrying on a spirited debate over its own future is undermined.

While I will argue that this overstates the case, it does contain a large grain of truth. Why is this so? One common answer is to blame the recent past, contrasting, for example, the rhetoric of a John F. Kennedy with that of Ronald Reagan. If only the right person (or people) were in place, all would be well. Others see the evil as technologically driven, with television as the prime villain. Modern mass media corrupts democratic debate; we are "amusing ourselves to death." Still another response claims fatalism, noting how such rhetoric is endemic to popular politics, citing perhaps the 1840 American presidential campaign or, taking the extremely long view, the invective of Cicero.

All these explanations selectively read the past, locating one *bad* strain of rhetoric and associating it with the complex whole (something to keep in mind before accepting my own first paragraph as a *complete* picture of contemporary rhetoric). These explanations also miss the ways that cultures actively *encourage* one style over another at given times. In the seventeenth century, the "grand style," heavily ornamented and taking a delight in the very way that words sounded, was taught to all Europeans who might communicate with the public. Today this style is, for the time being, dead. Contemporary students, thousands of them, turn to manuals like Strunk and White's *Elements of Style*, a book relentlessly devoted to simple, unadorned declarative sentences. Nothing would sound stranger to someone from the past than the utter plainness with which much of our serious discussion is conducted. Nothing would sound stranger to us than the past's delight in formal oratory.

This book is about the debates over linguistic usage in America from the time of the Revolution to the turn of the twentieth century. While I do not discuss contemporary rhetoric, this book is meant as a "prehistory" of our time, pointing out the decline of one way of encouraging public speech and the origins of the contemporary replacement. The kinds of language characteristically used in twentieth-century public discourse had their roots in the simultaneous effort to accommodate a more educated, assertive popular audience and to construct some kind of social authority for the highly educated in a modern, democratic, commercial culture. Part of this effort, I suggest, was the attack on older traditions of civic rhetoric.[1] The characteristic idioms of our time reflect the outcome—the culture of professional expertise, a depoliticized public, a mass consumerism.

Revolutionary Americans inherited neoclassical traditions of rhetoric (chapter 1). The best language was that of those gentlemen schooled in the literary arts. A gentleman's words were refined and not vulgar, well-suited for civic (and civil) discussion. While such presumptions were challenged in the eighteenth century, they were decisively upset by the arrival of mass democracy in the early nineteenth century. Distinctly nonclassical language entered the public forum with a vengeance. Populist rhetoric appeared in various guises, from rank demagoguery to a kind of humble nobility, and created what I call "middling styles" (chapter 2), idioms that

easily mixed the refined and the raw. Cultivated and vulgar cultural categories still existed but the clear sociological correlations of earlier times
eroded. Men like Andrew Jackson and Abraham Lincoln mixed together
high and low language to fit their needs. Their speech was at times refined
but at other times crude. They were often eloquent but they were also
often folksy.

The nineteenth-century debate over language pitted those trying to
accommodate the new styles of popular rhetoric against those who resisted.
These debates are recounted in chapters 2 through 6. I explore fights about
political oratory, conversational English, and newspaper rhetoric as well
as disputes over the teaching of grammar, the nature of biblical translation,
and the making of dictionaries. The outcome (chapters 7 and 8) was that
by the end of the nineteenth century, varied and conflicting idioms were
presented to the public as correct, a practice that continues to this day.
Thus my first paragraph needs qualification; a diversity of styles is the
norm.

At the end of the nineteenth century, defenders of refined literary
rhetoric still existed, but they were joined (and increasingly displaced) by
people with other ideas about English usage. In college composition classes
and in "serious" newspapers like *The New York Times*, a new respect for a
plain, unadorned, declarative prose emerged, a prose leaner than anything
traditional rhetoricians had favored except for the simplest of purposes.
Elsewhere, academic linguists, newly installed in America's growing research universities, suggested that colloquial English was the norm, a
standard so casual as to be inconsistent with formal eloquence but quite
compatible with certain strains of the middling rhetoric that had surfaced
earlier in the century. By the 1890s, colloquial English found favor with
political "spellbinders," divines pushing for a colloquial English Bible,
and in the "homely realism" of popular new magazines like *Munsey's* or
*McClure's*.

Finally, the late nineteenth century saw the birth of a new respect for
technical languages, the idioms of expertise. While eighteenth-century
rhetoricians had denigrated such language as tainted with vulgarity and
ill-suited for public debate, the late-nineteenth-century academic linguists
championed it, claiming that educated speech was in reality professional
and not civic. Educated adults, the linguists argued, were marked by their
command of technical vocabularies instead of their immersion in rhetoric
and literary English. Thus by the turn of the century, technical, plain,
and colloquial styles were all presented as alternatives to traditional rhe-

torical ideas about speech. Moreover, the rhetorical tradition itself atro-
phied, often becoming little else than a pedantic search for "correct"
speech.

Language debates are inevitably about more than words, and I have
connected nineteenth-century quarrels about usage to three critical issues.
The first is the relation of language to the self. Telling people to speak
one way instead of another is a way of telling them to be a certain kind
of person, of saying that certain skills and practices are valued while others
are not. The nineteenth-century debate over language was a fight over
what kind of personality was needed to sustain a healthy democracy.
Neoclassical notions of discourse assumed that the *homo rhetor* was a gentleman, that his ethos, or character, would guide his every act and word.
His refined taste, his avoidance of vulgar speech, was essentially tied to
his sense of self, that *humanitas* presumed to commit him to the public
good.

By the mid-nineteenth century, however, the very decorum that
"gentlemen of the old school" saw as essential to principled behavior was
viewed by large segments of the democratic public as "aristocratic." Audiences increasingly demanded that speakers know how to combine the
refined and the vulgar. They demanded middling styles. By the turn of
the twentieth century, the new linguists gave academic legitimacy to such
behavior, asserting that style did and should change for functional reasons,
and that the self was more "compartmentalized" than older rhetoricians
had assumed. The linguists actively accepted what John Pocock has called
"the specialization of personalities," something eighteenth-century theorists widely feared as detrimental to the public good.[2] It is a central
contention of this book that late-nineteenth-century linguistic theory gave
intellectual credence to popular styles that had dominated public debate
since the middle of the century.

I argue, moreover, that this was intimately connected to the redefinition
of the educated adult from the cultivated gentleman to the expert professional. For neoclassical rhetoricians, character was connected to a uniform
commitment to refined literary language. But for many late-nineteenth-
century social theorists the self was more flexibly organized, and they
often argued that educated speech was technical, that character related to
one's occupation as opposed to one's being. The new thinking about language was more closely connected to what contemporary sociologists call
"role theory" than to any classical sense of a "unified soul." With the self
thus split up, education became associated with a particular skill (a profes-

sion) instead of a whole way of life (gentility). One could then be educated and still participate in popular culture.

A second important theme is the relationship of language to social authority. Encouraging people to speak in one manner necessarily implies that something else is not valued; authoritative ways of speaking are enveloped in prestige and power. When eighteenth-century linguists located linguistic authority in the speech of gentlemen, this might or might not have been well suited to the creation of reasoned and civil public debate, but it certainly wrote off the language of at least nine tenths of the human race as "vulgar" and not to be taken seriously. And *no* woman, even one from the elite, was allowed to be an orator. This neoclassical standard was intimately connected to the traditional division between the few and the many, a division that excluded "the many" from any systematic contribution to public debate. The more raucous, "carnivalesque" atmosphere of the nineteenth century did, as we shall see, sometimes undermine serious discussion of important issues, but it also opened the forum to more people than ever before. Attacking gentlemanly decorum meant that you did not necessarily have to be refined to have your words count. And, I hasten to add, it was in the nineteenth century that women spoke in public for the first time.

Paradoxically, earlier ideas about social order were undermined by the spread of civil speech as much as by any new vulgarity. Mass democracy meant mass education; and by the 1820s, the diffusion of basic linguistic skills undermined all coherent efforts to exclude people of "middling culture" from public debate. Everywhere you looked—the popular press, political oratory, courtroom forensics, and religious homiletics—the story was the same: All combined the refined and crude. The stylistic *bricolage* made it maddeningly hard to divide the world into the few and the many, impossibly difficult to see which men were "truly" gentlemen, which women "really" ladies. Terms like *refined* and *vulgar*, which formerly had distinct sociological resonance, in the nineteenth century became vaguer allusions to cultural styles.

The variety of idioms used in contemporary life makes simple conclusions impossible, but one indisputable effect of the celebration of technical language that began in the last decades of the nineteenth century is that it helped create an aura of prestige around those who could lay claim to some specific expertise. Thus it supported the institution of a towering form of contemporary power and authority. Rhetoricians, both ancient and early modern, had explicitly diminished technical language and, consequently, diminished the social authority of professional expertise. This contrasts sharply with today, where in school and the workplace the message is clear—advancement is for those who know how to act (and *speak*) like a "professional."

My third major theme is the relationship of language to audience, or, more precisely, to the *assumed* audience. One can flatter, patronize, reason, trick, converse, or argue with an audience. Rhetoric can restrict the size of an audience (as much professional discourse does today) or expand it. The neoclassical canons of eighteenth-century Scottish rhetoricians placed a high value on that discursive, informal reasoning critical to the creation of an informed public opinion. They assumed an elite but rational public. The boisterous rhetoric of the nineteenth century, on the other hand, reflected the increased assertiveness of the popular audience. Today's political flattery, finally, with its roots in the mid-nineteenth-century idiom of Henry Ward Beecher, tends to be a way to "cool off" that mass audience. It is, as Kathleen Hall Jamieson has argued, a rhetoric of conciliation instead of conflict.[3] Serious discussion is then moved to places like *The New York Times* Op-Ed page and the *MacNeil/Lehrer Newshour*, where the audience is small, or to more arcane journals where experts discuss the future in language inaccessible to the public.

"Rhetoric," C. S. Lewis once wrote, "is the greatest barrier between us and our ancestors."[4] Traditions of civic rhetoric virtually disappeared at the beginning of the twentieth century. The moment should not be minimized for the consequences were large: "Crowds once gave thunderous applause in open fields, now we nod our tacit approval in living rooms."[5] Lewis thought this a change in taste but it was really much more. Linguistic styles are not simply personal idiosyncrasies, technological reflexes, or the by-products of specific political regimes. They are cultural practices that are encouraged, perpetuated, challenged, and discarded through time. The kind of rhetoric we get in our presidential elections says much more about ourselves than we care to admit. It is one indication of the way we have organized our lives.

I have imbibed enough rhetorical theory, from Cicero to George Campbell, to take to heart the advice to speak a common idiom. Throughout the book I have strenuously tried to avoid technical language of any kind and have removed my own contentious scholarship from the flow of the text. Specialists, therefore, are forewarned to refer to footnotes in order to see what secondary literature I have relied upon or challenged.

At the same time I have tried to use a "civic" idiom, I also want to accommodate those cultures of expertise that have guided me and cannot be willed away without loss. So at the outset, for those who are interested, let me make my methodological and scholarly presumptions as clear as I can.

Throughout this book, I expressly use the phrases "middling styles" and "middling rhetoric" to avoid saying "middle class." Certainly the middle class was critical to the triumph of the new kinds of speech. But there are reasons to resist such a tidy label. For starters, this book is first and foremost about debates over language and style and my terms help readers keep that in mind. But as important, when scholars casually use "middle class" to describe some cultural form (as in "middle-class speech" or "middle-class morality"), it is often a kind of intellectual laziness. Such phrases miss important divisions within the middle class and the precise ways that cultural forms operate in specific social settings. Nineteenth-century middling styles encouraged people to shift back and forth across linguistic registers, a process that confused social perception, at least at the middle and top of the social order. Also, middling rhetoric reached beyond the middle class at both ends of the spectrum. At the top, the rich often used it and liked it while the highly educated, in public at least, were forced to adopt it. And below, many people with less than middle class status enjoyed hearing it. Middling rhetoric, in short, was part of a popular culture.[6]

I realize that the word *popular* can seem maddeningly vague, but I believe it does serve a purpose. Recent cultural studies have challenged the word because it misses the ways that various subcultures decode mass culture for their own ends. To Roger Chartier, for example, *popular* lumps together far too much.[7] I do not disagree that classes, genders, regions, and ethnicities can each take the same piece of mass culture and interpret it in wildly different ways. The point *I* pursue, however, is about the *production* of culture. For a message to resonate with huge numbers of people it must be constructed in such a way that makes it available for all sorts of subcultural interpretations. As the communications scholar John Fiske puts it, mass culture must be polysemic.[8] And this is exactly what nineteenth-century popular styles of communication were. Middling rhetoric actively and happily adjusted its tone to appeal to as wide an audience as possible. This was, moreover, something very new. The conscious effort to reach out to the crowd, so explicitly discussed by Henry Ward Beecher (see chapter 2), marked a real change in the nineteenth century. It indicated how popular communication would proceed in a culture that no longer practiced classical deference.

Social scientists often treat language as simply a reflex of social class, as in "that is middle-class speech," or "that is elite speech." This thinking usually does not allow for good or bad speech, reducing language norms to configurations of authority, power, or social location. Other writers, however, casually treat language as if all issues of "good" or "bad" speech were divorced from any social order, effectively denying the possibility that many linguistic norms might be socially rooted aesthetic biases.

Throughout this book I have tried to combine the best of both strains of thought. Language, like all social practices, can be appropriate, inappropriate, civil, rude, insightful, evasive, liberating, oppressive, wise, foolish, rational, or crazy. But while I have freely commented on good and bad strains of rhetoric, I have also tried to separate good *criticism* from bad, which means, in this book, separating that linguistic criticism that is about the effective production of public debate from that which is about matters of social taste. I have tried to avoid sociological reductionism without ignoring the social dimension.

Jeffrey Stout has called this "criticism with both eyes open," attempting to identify the goods internal to embedded social practices while at the same time understanding how those same practices might be socially misused. This means, to use Stout's example, both understanding what is sublime about Don Mattingly's swing *and* realizing that professional baseball is big business. For my part, I have tried to respect the excellence that is possible in public speech and also see how language can turn into a badge of status or class. My approach has been influenced by the work of Alasdair MacIntyre, and in a more distant fashion, the dual approach to high culture envisioned by Theodor Adorno.[9]

By claiming that language can be either "good" or "bad" I obviously separate myself from some recent writing on language. While this book is about language, and while I try to take language very seriously, I want to align myself with scholars such as David Hollinger and Martin Jay who have expressed reservations about at least some of the directions that the "linguistic turn" has taken in intellectual and cultural history.[10] I do not see language as so opaque that it inevitably defeats critical reason, and would strongly contest Roland Barthes's assertion that language is essentially fascistic.[11] Responsible language, I would claim to the contrary, is central to the possibility of an antiauthoritarian politics. My own interest in language and rhetoric should not be associated with those poststructuralist theorists who, having decided that language is preeminently self-referential, then turn to rhetoric as the self-consciously playful alternative.

I would also separate myself from those who find us so enmeshed in language (or culture) that there is no way out of our hermeneutic circle, a position that can be broadly associated with such figures as Hans-Georg Gadamer, George Steiner, or Clifford Geertz. While I have learned much from all three writers, and largely because of them have tried to incorporate a hermeneutic moment into my text, I feel uncomfortable resting there. To say that language suffuses everything is not the same as saying that language *is* everything. To say that all social practices have cultural meaning is not to say that cultural meaning is all there is. Both Gadamer and Steiner have commitments to "taste" that I find incompatible with the best democratic politics. Geertz's anthropological hermeneutics is connected to an irrationalism that leaves us no effective room for critique.[12]

I remain committed to critical rationality, although I do not understand this in terms of objectivity, positivism, or scientific models. The alternatives are not between formal, instrumental, scientific rationalism and rank irrationality. In between is that informal, discursive reasoning associated with *praxis* rather than *techne*. This locates my own interest in rhetoric. Rhetoric, as Hans Blumenberg has noted, is rooted in the principle of "insufficient reason," but this "is not to be confused with a demand that we forgo reasons, just as 'opinion' does not denote an attitude for which one has no reasons but rather one for which the reasons are diffuse and not regulated by method."[13]

Ultimately, my sympathies are with those who have worried about the erosion of public debate in the twentieth century, people as diverse as John Dewey, Jürgen Habermas, Hannah Arendt, and C. Wright Mills. Spirited and contentious public discussion by no means assures social harmony or that all interests will be appropriately rewarded, but I do believe that a lively public is a critical element of a flourishing democracy. My own work is meant to adumbrate some (and only some) of the nineteenth-century forces that contributed to the twentieth-century decline of an effective public in the United States of America.

# A Note on the Terminology
# of Style

Since ancient Greece, rhetoricians and critics have used broad descriptive labels to categorize stylistic levels. Some rhetoricians claimed there were two basic styles; others that there were four. Most commonly, however, it has been asserted that there are three basic levels. Cicero, for instance, in *De Oratore*, divided all rhetoric into the plain, tempered, and grandiloquent. Over the years, the labels used to describe stylistic levels have been remarkably fluid. Terms like high, low, simple, tempered, florid, vulgar, Attic, Rhodian, Ciceronian, plain, middle, and grand have had various meanings, not all of them consistent. My own terms are constant, but because such terms have had such varied meanings and because many readers may not be familiar with rhetorical terminology, I will here explain my usage.

I have used four basic categories: the low (or vulgar), plain (or Attic), middle (or Rhodian), and grand (or Ciceronian). The low comprises that language falling below the standard dialect. Folk dialects, obtrusive regional idioms, and stark grammatical solecisms are low speech. Any language, in sum, that for whatever reason would be shunned by educated speakers is low or vulgar. Most ancient rhetoricians did not include this in their catalogue of styles because they shared with their readers the assumption that vulgar language would simply not be used.

The plain style uses refined syntax and avoids vulgar vocabulary. The plain style, however, is completely unadorned. It is straightforward and void of any figures of speech. It is the style of much contemporary newspaper prose. Cicero thought it was best suited for teaching, and indeed, the plain style is the idiom of the best school textbooks of our age. It has been said that the plain style is the official style of our time. It is important to remember how recent the rise of the plain style is. Swift should be seen as a pioneer, and one who was not particularly successful in his own day. Some ancient rhetoricians occasionally called the plain style the "low" or "vulgar" style because they thought it best suited for speaking with the vulgar. But I have avoided calling the plain speech "low" or "vulgar" because it confuses one refined idiom (the plain) with styles falling below the line separating the refined from the unrefined. When refined writers in the 1770s complained about Thomas Paine's "vulgar" language, they were not saying he used the plain style but that he was using substandard speech.

The middle style is that of Addison—elegant, copious, and containing a moderate number of figures of speech. It tries to strike a balance between a showy, obtrusive prose and the bland, plain style. Cicero said its aim was to please.

The grand, also called "lofty," style is that florid speech that impresses with sound. It delights in the play of words; it hopes to carry an audience with its power. Cicero said its end was to "bend" the audience to the speaker. It is the style of Cicero, of Johnson and Gibbon, of William F. Buckley. And just as the plain style has grown in importance in the last two centuries, the grand style has become remarkably unpopular.

# CHAPTER ONE

# The Best Speech of the Best Soul

There can scarce be a greater Defect in a
Gentleman than not to express himself well
either in Writing or Speaking.

JOHN LOCKE

The ancients knew the splendor of words. Homer spoke of "a certain kind of man" with "comeliness on his words" who people looked on as "a god." What else than eloquence, Cicero asked, could have "gathered humanity" out of "the wilderness" and given "shape to laws, tribunals, and civic rights?" For the "one point in which we have our very greatest advantage over the brute creation is that we hold converse with each other, and can reproduce our thought in word." To such people the splendor of words was palpable, almost tactile, a notion still alive in the mid-nineteenth century, as witnessed by one reaction to Daniel Webster's famous Plymouth Address: "Three or four times I thought my temples would burst with the gush of blood. . . . It seemed to me that [Webster] was like the mount that might not be touched, and that burned with fire." It is hard to imagine contemporary oratory evoking such a response. So let me begin by discussing humanistic traditions of eloquence in order to better understand the habits of thought that erode during the nineteenth century.[1]

# I

Eloquence was not simply equated with fine speaking or the ability to move crowds. The ancients well knew that there were flatterers and demagogues who used language to their advantage. More modern rhetoricians like Henry Peachum also were aware that verbal grace could be misused: "Much hurt it may doe, if like a mad man's sword, it be used by a turbulent and mutinous orator."[2] Eloquence implied far more than the ability to handle words deftly; it invoked larger concerns about audience, personality, and social order.

Eloquence was civic. The *homo rhetor* lived in the forum, actively pursuing public life. His oratory contributed to civil debate, hence the classic definition of rhetoric as "the facility to speak persuasively." Using language to manage human affairs was viewed as an alternative to violence. In Plutarch, Cicero banished Catiline from Rome by noting that he (Cicero) would govern with words while Catiline would use arms. There must be a wall between the two.[3] The civic nature of rhetoric meant that the truly eloquent spoke to a wide audience. Historians like John Pocock, Elizabeth Eisenstein, Hanna Gray, Jerrold Seigal, and Natalie Davis have all pointed out that rhetoric was so important to Renaissance humanists because of their belief that knowledge and wisdom had to be communicated beyond small eremitic circles.[4] The Middle Ages were "dark" not because they lacked learned men but because "barbarian philosophers" hoarded their learning within university walls. Vico, a key early-eighteenth-century defender of civic rhetoric, regularly inveighed against what he called "voiceless wisdom."[5] Rhetoric taught people to live in the world.

Rhetoricians, then, cared little for the dialogues of experts, secret societies, or aloof philosophers. They looked to the public. Indeed, the arrival of the printing press in the fifteenth century and the dramatic increase in the literacy rates of the nobility and gentry in the sixteenth century were the technological and sociological forces that sustained the cultural changes associated with rhetoric and refined eloquence. Yet it was really in the mid-eighteenth century that a well-defined and independent "public" appeared. Steadily increasing literacy rates, burgeoning published material of all kinds, as well as coffeehouses and salons that encouraged the exchange of ideas, all worked to create a "free zone" where opinion could be formed independent of the state. It should be no surprise that the term *public opinion* first appeared early in the 1700s; and by the

1780s, historian J.A.W. Gunn has pointed out, it had "slipped—more or less unheralded—into the everyday language of politics."[6]

In the rhetorical tradition, addressing the public required language that was refined. Eloquence was neither pedantic nor vulgar. Carving too many fine and subtle distinctions served precision but guaranteed isolation; the choplogic scholastic analyses of the medieval world had proven that.[7] On the other hand, the language of the common people lacked the breadth and perspicuity needed to house true eloquence. Rhetoricians argued vehemently about style, but with the exception of certain Christian writers, it was taken for granted that only educated, refined speech could be eloquent. Quintilian and Cicero said so directly. It remained a standard assumption in the eighteenth century.[8] Refined language moved between the Charybdis of the low and the Scylla of the technical, asking for something more than uneducated vagaries but something less than pinpoint accuracy. Between dull-witted vulgarity and arcane jargon lay lucidity. That was the goal of the *rhetor*.

Rhetoric's civic-mindedness also demanded a bracing moral probity: For the true orator, virtue was a necessity. Both Cicero and Quintilian had argued that one literally could not be an orator without moral wisdom. Aristotle, in his rhetoric, claimed that "moral character" constituted "the most effective source of persuasion," and writers after him repeated the theme. Thomas Elyot, for example, in *The Boke Named the Governour* (1531), claimed that eloquence should be studied not only for its glittering words but also for examples of noble virtues. Over two centuries later, Hugh Blair, after noting the "high virtues" of ancient orators, added that modern speakers must "cultivate habits of the several virtues," and "refine and improve their moral feelings." Again and again, writers on language stressed that eloquence was the marriage of wisdom and style. In Emerson's words, it was "the best speech of the best soul."[9]

To be an orator, then, was to be a certain kind of person. It implied an ethos, a character that pervaded one's whole self. This ethos was ideally embodied in the cultivated gentleman and was purchased through a liberal education, which Quintilian, Cicero and others after them stressed was necessary for the orator.

A liberal education, however, was not narrowly bookish; it shaped the whole self.[10] *Education*, in Samuel Johnson's dictionary, was defined as "formation of manners in youth; the manner of breeding youth; nurture." Ideally, liberal education created young men and women of character. All education aimed toward caring for the self, controlling naturally unruly impulses. Without learning to habitually control such behavior, people were inevitably slaves to their passions. Freedom was intimately tied to *humanitas* which in turn generated a liberating self-control. If successful, one's ethos, or character, defined his or her every action. In Aristotle's *Ethics*, one commentator has noted, the man of virtue is a "unified soul," the "whole body and soul pull him in a single direction, toward restraint." By the Roman era, Michel Foucault observed, there was a concerted search for a "morality of style," a refined way of life that would be "common to different areas of conduct." In the classical world, Foucault observed, "one's ethos was seen by his dress, by his bearing, by his gait, by the poise with which he reacts to events. . . ." Cicero claimed that decorum was "nothing more than uniform consistency in the course of our life as a whole. . . ."[11]

Early modern writers echoed these sentiments. Eloquence, decorum, art, learning, and even sport were allies, each reinforcing the others and contributing to the formation of a young gentleman or lady. Polite learning, according to John Henley, tended to "form the Manners" and "cure the Depravity of human Nature. . . ." Fine art, to Sir Joshua Reynolds, was "among the means of bestowing on whole nations refinement of taste; which, if it does not lead directly to purity of manners, obviates at least their greatest deprivation, by disentangling the mind from appetite. . . ." The sciences were similarly sanctioned by the eighteenth century, as were the sports of the gentry. Ice skating "is a fine Art," John Adams wrote his son in 1780. "It is not simply Velocity or Agility that constitutes the Perfection of it, but Grace. There is an Elegance of Motion, which is charming to the sight, and is useful to acquire, because it obliges you to restrain that impetuous Ardour and violent Activity. . . ." A refined taste, Hume thought, "enables us to judge of the character of men, of composition of genius, and of the production of the nobler arts." As with so much else, Addison sums up the cluster of ideas with the most grace and compactness:

> The very design of dress, good breeding, outward ornaments, and cere-
> mony, were to lift up human nature, and set it off to an advantage. Ar-
> chitecture, painting and statuary, were invented with the same design; as
> indeed every art and science contributed to the embellishment of life, and
> to the wearing off or throwing into shades the mean and low parts of our
> nature.[12]

Decorum was rooted in respect for the feelings of others; refined manner implied civility. Not talking with your mouth full signaled something about yourself (that you were a "civil" human being) but also showed a desire not to insult those with whom you dined. Refined decorum pushed inappropriate acts out of public view and created psychological distance between people. Behavior or words too offensive or "familiar" were made private. Civilized ritual interaction emphasized polite reserve, although grace, wit, and noblesse oblige tempered the formality. This "morality of style" meant that formality was emphasized in ways we might find offensive or priggish, but for classically molded ladies and gentlemen, informality was a sign of disrespect.[13]

To be sure, certain eighteenth-century writers worried that the self was breaking apart. Scottish philosophers explored the psychology of market behavior, wondering if the division of labor in commercial cultures destroyed civic-mindedness, with "citizens" replaced by "specialists." Rousseau worried that the conflict between bourgeois rights and citizens' duties pulled people in opposite directions. And Benjamin Franklin, in his autobiography, frankly presented the possibility of succeeding in life by donning different masks to meet the moment.[14]

What tied these writers together was the sense that *ethos* was giving way to *persona*, or, to use other terms, that character was disappearing for role playing.[15] The most sustained exploration of the possibilities of fragmentation was found in a work too daring for the times. Diderot's *Rameau's Nephew*, written in the 1760s, remained unpublished until after his death. It is a dialogue between a gentleman of conventional morality and the composer's nephew. The latter lives a jagged life, at times gracious in refined salons, at times coarsely roaming the streets, all frankly in the pursuit of self-interest. At one point the gentleman remarks on the "unevenness" of the nephew's "style"—"sometimes high, sometimes low." The nephew responds, "Can the style of the vice ridden be otherwise?"[16]

The answer reflected conventional wisdom. Whatever demons modernity might conjure, eighteenth-century elites comfortably clung to the old morality of style. Chesterfield was typical: "Vulgar, low expressions, awkward motions and address, vilify, as they imply either a very low turn of mind, or low education and low company." He also urged his son to read, "nay, get by heart," the chapter on decorum in Cicero's *Offices*, for it contained "whatever is necessary for the dignity of manners."[17] Similarly, in the famous Enlightenment *Encyclopedia* edited by Diderot, the term *character* was given a classical definition—"the most usual disposition of the soul." The *Encyclopedia* denounced the very kind of inconsistent self exhibited by Rameau's nephew: "Nothing is more dangerous to society than a man without character, that is, whose soul has no dominant disposition. We trust the virtuous man, we distrust the rogue. A man without character shifts from one to the other." The self, it contended, must have an all-embracing *ethos*, and this ethos was reflected in one's demeanor. Good breeding, Locke had said, was "a Disposition of the Mind that shows itself in the Carriage. . . ."[18]

Eloquent language, then, was just one part of a larger self that hung together as a whole.[19] Refined speech was one indication of character. Learning to behave with decorum meant that the truly eloquent would always speak or write like a "gentleman" or a "lady." There would be a stylistic unity to the performance.

Rhetoric implied a whole social order: Those who ruled were eloquent; those who didn't were not. Over the years, the specific language in favor varied greatly. There was an extraordinary mixture of refinement and crudity in the Elizabethan period, marking the point where the elite was just beginning to withdraw from popular folk culture.[20] By the eighteenth century, however, commentators casually made the distinction between "high" and "low" speech. "But it is no hard matter," it was noted in the early eighteenth century, "to discern between the depraved Language of common People, and the noble refin'd expressions of the Gentry, whose condition and merits have advanced them above the other." Scottish rhetorician George Campbell's 1776 definition of *vulgarism* was frankly sociological. Vulgarisms were the idioms of the "far greater part of mankind," Campbell wrote, "perhaps ninety-nine of a hundred," who because "of poverty and other circumstances" were "deprived of the advantages of education and condemned to toil for bread, almost incessantly, in some narrow occupation." In the 1740s, young George Washington wrote out for himself a set of prescriptions entitled *Rules of Civility and Decent Behavior in Company and Conversation*. He noted that his language must emulate "persons of quality" and not "the vulgar."[21]

By the mid-eighteenth century, language was just one of various kinds of experience divided into *refined* and *vulgar*, terms roughly corresponding to *gentlemen* and *commoners*. One knew Cicero; the other the traveling clown. One attended the opera; the other the pantomime show. One danced the minuet; the other watched dancing bears. As the gentry saw it, what was crude was common and what was common was crude. Samuel Johnson's broadest definition of *gentleman* was a "man raised above the vulgar by his character or post" and his definitions of *vulgar* were "plebian; suiting to the common people" and "mean; low; being of the common rate."[22]

In some respects, the simple contrast between high and low is misleading. Some bits of culture were shared across the spectrum. Also, the provincial gentry (as in America) often retained elements of folk culture. The sharp division also ignores the small tradesmen, shopkeepers, and yeoman farmers who were often referred to as "people of the middling sort." Since the numbers of this group were comparatively small and because it lacked a distinguishable culture, the middling people were often considered part of the vulgar. As we shall see, however, where to place this group became a troubling issue during the eighteenth century.

Whatever the limitations, the picture of two distinct worlds, the patrician and plebian, was often used by eighteenth-century commentators. Those were the terms in which the elite understood their *own* world. "The English differ from one another in their Humors, as they do in their Birth, Education and Profession," John Camberlayne wrote in 1707. "The Nobility, Gentry, and Scholars, as well as most of the Merchants and Chief Tradesmen, are extremely well polished in their Behavior; but the common sort are rude and even barbarous." The two groups seemed to have nothing in common. Early modern society was a sharply pitched pyramid, conceived by the gentry, at least, as a polished few gracing the top and clumsy hordes elbowing the bottom. In this setting, the inability to command refined English had serious consequences. Language was an instrument of power, deciding who would be admitted to authoritative discourse, what words would be taken seriously.[23]

Elite disgust with the low, however, does not explain all interest in refined language; eloquence also implied dextrous verbal skills. Most of us have no trouble accepting the idea that education (in an ideal world) should make students more articulate and that, a few natural geniuses aside, the highly educated possess richer verbal resources than the less educated. In the eighteenth century this was called "copious" language, linguistic breadth such that "every idea may have its mark." Contemporary linguists call it the "elaborated code."[24] It is too facile to explain all interest in language as a quest for easily recognizable class cues. Language and power are tied together in more than a crudely manipulative sense. Rich rhetorical skills give us the power to frame our thoughts. They allow us entry into the public sphere. Early modern refined English blended communicative competence and class pride, and few even thought of trying to untangle them.

Refined eloquence subordinated elite women as well as common people, but in a more complicated manner. Ladies were excluded from public speaking; they were not taught to be orators. As one historian has noted, learning Latin in the early modern period was a "puberty rite" for boys.

Yet from the Renaissance on, a few "learned women" communicated to the public through the written word. Such women had to run sharp gauntlets, having carefully to maintain a "ladylike" decorum. Nevertheless, by the eighteenth century, the political writings of women like Catherine Macauley and Mercy Otis Warren were read widely and taken seriously.[25]

Still, women at large were excluded. Through the eighteenth century women were not allowed to speak in public. Until the very end of the century, women were assumed to have no need for an "enlightened" education. Young girls were just not trained to command "copious" language.[26] Moreover, notions of decorum subtly worked to justify women's exclusion from the public sphere. Cicero differentiated between appropriate refinement and effeminacy, the latter characteristic of females and too soft to be taken seriously. Chesterfield, in the eighteenth century, thought women models of decorum but incapable of serious intellectual work. Compared to the "unified soul" of a refined male, he believed, women were incomplete beings.[27]

Such arguments had linguistic implications. Cicero, while wanting the orator to be refined and graceful, also cautioned against appearing too "sweet" or "charming," traits he associated elsewhere with female decorum. The historian Walter Ong has noted that in Renaissance educational and rhetorical theory, the "connection of literature (Latin) with toughness of moral fiber" was explicit, "and this toughness of moral fiber" was tied to "physical toughness as well." Women were presumed not to have it. While refined decorum was applauded for all, "serious" refinement was given a masculine edge.[28]

Rhetorical theories traditionally held that the eloquent address a wide public, be liberally educated and morally committed, and come from the refined elite of the culture. In other words, rhetoricians connected eloquence to a specific kind of audience, self, and social order. But complications arose, particularly between the ideal of the self and the realities of the world. The eloquent gentleman or lady was supposed to have the cultivated sensibilities, the *humanitas*, needed to check their own self-interest and encourage a humane but unsentimental concern for the common good. In the ideal world, humane sympathies and skills conferred social authority; behavior determined status. Sensitive observers, however, knew that was not always the case. Refinement could be used simply as a badge of class, an assertion of elite domination rather than an expression of refined sensibilities. Montesquieu tried to distinguish between politeness, derived from a prideful desire to distinguish oneself, and civility, based on genuine concern for others. George Campbell thought that without Christian virtue eloquence was merely a "painted bubble." Eighteenth-century critics of Latin and Greek, such as Benjamin Franklin, attacked not the classics but the misplaced hubris of those flaunting the classical tongues.[29]

Rhetorical traditions directly contributed to the opening of a public space where serious discussion could take place outside the control of the state, in "civil society." Yet at the same time they perpetuated inequalities by restricting entry to the "refined." While a rhetorical approach to civic affairs made republicanism possible, the elitism foreclosed any move toward democracy.

At the core of the theories of rhetorical eloquence and liberal education was a conflict between understanding culture as a superior way of life or as a social barrier. Was civil language truly eloquent or was it a badge of class? To what extent was the interest in language a genuine quest for clarity and to what degree was it a search for easily recognizable cues with which to set off a social elite? When did graceful prose stop aiding communication and start flattering pretension? In the sixteenth century, with the great chain of being taken for granted, no reason existed to ask if linguistic culture was a "mask" of social hierarchy. Even at the close of the eighteenth century, most of the refined took for granted the value of liberal education. By 1800, however, doubts were being raised. And as we shall see, trying to sort out which linguistic concerns were legitimate and which were not became a central issue in nineteenth-century America.

# II

Rhetoricians, both ancient and early modern, approached language conservatively. Refined language had to be watched, controlled, so that it did not turn harsh or vulgar. In the late sixteenth and early seventeenth centuries, France, Spain, and Italy created state-sponsored academies to codify authoritative usage. No such institution appeared in England. Little was done to codify refined English until the last half of the eighteenth century when quite a few texts—dictionaries, grammars, and rhetorics— were published that soon were so widely known and so well respected that they became *de facto* authorities on usage. Their rule was less tidily arranged than that on the Continent, but taken together, they served England as the next best thing to a national academy.[30]

Codification served three ends. Most important, it defined and recorded refined speech. Next, the new books tried in small ways to modify the boundaries between "refined" and "vulgar." They were tied to a contemporary movement to further distance elite from popular cultural forms. Third, however, codification made refined speech accessible to an audience other than the elite. The simple printing of these books in ever larger quantities made the subtleties of refined language more readily available to people whose social position was not that of a lady or gentleman.

Until Samuel Johnson published his *Dictionary of the English Language* in 1755, no good comprehensive English lexicon existed. Johnson's dictionary was an immediate critical success and became the standard reference text well into the next century. Others published lexicons: William Kenrick in 1773, Thomas Sheridan in 1780, and John Walker in 1795. Walker's *Critical and Pronouncing Dictionary and Expositor of the English Language*, next to Johnson's the best known, simply copied Johnson's definitions and usage markers and added pronunciation symbols. Sheridan in his *General Dictionary of the English Language* did the same. So no one displaced Johnson as master lexicographer; in effect, his text reigned.[31]

Until the last half of the eighteenth century, relatively little attention was paid to studying English grammar.[32] In the 1760s, however, new grammars began crowding the bookshops. James Buchanan's *The British Grammar* was published in 1760, Joseph Priestley's *The Rudiments of English Grammar* in 1761, Robert Lowth's influential *A Short Introduction to English Grammar* in 1762, and so on. The new books were far more detailed than earlier texts had been.[33] Moreover, the number printed rose exponentially: As the century drew to a close, instruction in grammar became more important in schools. Between 1586, when the first pamphlet on English grammar appeared, and 1759, almost two hundred years later, 54 grammars were printed 121 times. In just the last four decades of the eighteenth century, 157 different grammars were printed 531 times.[34]

Rhetoric too underwent changes in the closing years of the century. A new school of rhetoric, born in Scottish universities, slowly displaced the Ciceronian rhetoric long a part of British education. In the late 1740s Adam Smith expressed the new ideas in embryonic form in lectures he delivered at the University of Glasgow. Lord Kames, who had listened to those lectures, expanded on Smith's thoughts in his *Elements of Criticism* (1762), a crucial work in eighteenth-century critical theory. The two crowning works of the new rhetoric, George Campbell's *The Philosophy of Rhetoric* and Hugh Blair's *Lectures on Rhetoric and Belles Lettres*, appeared in 1776 and 1783 respectively. The new rhetoric (the content of which we shall discuss presently) travelled south to England and west to America.

Blair's *Rhetoric* was immediately successful and remained a standard text well into the nineteenth century.

Broadly speaking, the lexicographers, grammarians, and rhetoricians agreed that customary usage was the authoritative standard of polite English. Prior to 1750 it was widely believed that linguistic reformers could "fix" the language once and for all, but Johnson, reflecting the new attitude, argued in the preface to his dictionary that "the boundless chaos of a living speech" was intractable and that a lexicographer, like any practical linguist, should "record polite usage, not engage in far-reaching reform."[35] But if custom was the "sovereign arbiter of all languages," it was pointed out in a late-eighteenth-century textbook *The Art of Speaking*, no one intended "to put the sceptre into the hands of the populace." It was not difficult "to discern the depraved language of the vulgar from the refined expressions of the learned and polite."[36]

In a variety of ways the new texts noted the divisions between high and low culture. Johnson marked as "low" or "vulgar" words like *conjobble*, *nab*, *bedizen*, and *betty*, all outside the respectable speech of the day. A more important strategy was to simply exclude words too low or crude. Words like *piece* (for arse), *codger* (for old man), *prick* (for penis), *dustman* (for corpse), and *bloody* (not meaning "bloodied") were all widely used by the lower orders but were not included in a book entitled *A Dictionary of the English Language*. Grammarians and rhetoricians also encoded the speech of the elite. That it was "difficult, if not impossible to reduce common speech to rule," one wrote, was no matter since that was "beneath a grammarian's attempt." Another testified that he was without interest in vulgar errors: "My animadversions will extend to such Phrases only as People in decent Life inadvertently adopt. . . ." Adam Smith told his Glasgow students that although "perhaps nine-tenths of the people in England say 'I'se do't' instead of 'I will do it,' " it was "the custom of the better sort from whence the rules of purity of style are to be drawn."[37]

Besides being the customary usage of gentlemen, polite language was also contemporary. "Contemporary," however, had a more complicated meaning than might be expected. Contemporary language was that found in literature currently read, which made certain texts of the sixteenth century "contemporary" with the eighteenth. Despite this, both archaism and reckless neology were suspect. Odd and poorly understood old words hindered clear communication and taxed the cultural homogeneity of the polite world. Words not found since Shakespeare's time were suspect, Campbell thought, and should be avoided. On the other hand, words coined by popular orators, in daily papers, or in familiar letters were "the insects of a season." For Johnson, laboring and mercantile terms were "fugitive cant," which, since not "part of the durable materials of a language," should "perish with other things unworthy of preservation." In the end, Campbell took his illustrations "neither from living authors nor from those who wrote before the Revolution," with the King James Bible as the one exception. Johnson also cited no living author but he extended his net back to Sydney. Grammarians made similar decisions.[38]

Polite language was customary and literary. It was also national. And the refined tongue of a civilized society was under perpetual threat from many sides. Specialized vocabularies of all kinds were suspect. Technical, scientific, commercial, theological, and professional terms all had their rightful place but they were not refined usage. Communication broke down, it was said more than once, when a doctor asked a man with a headache about his "cephalick symptoms."[39] "In strict propriety," Campbell thought, "technical words should not be considered as belonging to the language, because not in current use, nor understood by the generality even of readers. They are but the peculiar dialect of a particular class."[40] Regional variation, the peculiar dialect of a particular place, also suffered disrepute. Cosmopolitan gentlemen frowned on the provincialism of dialects. The empire, after all, was English. London was the epicenter, not Edinburgh, Philadelphia, or the muddy banks of some Virginia river. Ministers were advised not to use provincial dialects, which had "a coarseness and vulgarity" that made them ridiculous "to men of taste."[41] Regional speech also threatened the common culture transmitted through standard English. David Hume drew up a list of Scotticisms to avoid; John Witherspoon did the same with Americanisms.[42]

The dictionaries, grammars, and rhetorics well complemented one another. The dictionary revealed acceptable vocabulary, the grammars defined standard and substandard syntax. Combined, they marked the baseline of polite usage. Rhetoric rested atop them, explaining the most elegant ways to manipulate the language.

The texts defined contemporary usage, but in very small ways they also tried to alter speech. Their authors, trying to further differentiate refined from unrefined culture, were part of a larger reform movement of the late eighteenth century. The elite withdrawal from low culture was never more complete. The enclosure movement physically insulated the country gentry from the public. In London, gentlemen stopped attending street fairs in the 1780s. E. P. Thompson has written that the "great gentry were protected by their bailiffs from their tenants, and by their coachmen from casual encounters." They "met the lower sort of people mainly on their own terms, and when these were clients for their favors; in the formalities of the bench; or on calculated occasions of popular patronage."[43]

The Scottish rhetoric mirrored this physical removal from popular culture. The old Ciceronian rhetoric taught popular oratory, explaining how to speak before large public assemblies that included many unrefined listeners. The Ciceronian grand style, with its elaborate and highly ornate turns of phrase, was meant to establish relationships of authority between speaker and listener. The highly figured language, Cicero thought, would sweep the common people along. Ornate language was not needed when speaking to more sophisticated crowds. Because the Senate was an assembly of "wise men," Cicero told us, there oratory "must appear with less Pomp." All "Ostentation of Abilities" should be avoided. Speaking to the public, on the other hand, required "all the Energy, the Weight, and the Colouring of Eloquence." Such eloquence was aimed at the "arbitrary Command of the Passions. . . ." By the eighteenth century, Ciceronian rhetorical textbooks often included lengthy lists of figures of speech, all intended to teach students how to "command the passions" of a popular audience.[44]

Unlike Ciceronian rhetoric, the new Scottish school rarely discussed how to speak to the common people. In the very subjects emphasized, Scottish rhetoric paralleled the wider gentry withdrawal from popular culture. Ciceronian rhetoricians, with their keen interest in popular eloquence, rarely discussed the written word. The new rhetorics, however, spent much time talking about the canons of *written* eloquence. Hugh Blair, for example, analyzed the appropriate styles of history, philosophy, and poetry and dissected Addison's essays as models of prose. Most of Blair's *Lectures on Rhetoric and Belles Lettres* was about the printed page, about communication that was assumed to reach only a refined audience.

And Scottish rhetoricians, even when discussing spoken eloquence, paid little attention to the common people. Blair's political oratory focused on parliamentary speaking at the expense of public speaking. And courtroom oratory centered on communicating to a judge; nothing about moving a jury. Popular oratory was treated historically, but Blair noted that it was not cultivated among the moderns with as much zeal as among the ancients. In short, with the exception of pulpit oratory (where ministers were cautioned not to cater to the vulgar), communication with the common people was paid little attention. The new rhetoric taught refined gentlemen and ladies how to communicate to each other.[45]

The audience it presumed explains in part the Scottish attack on Cic-

eronian style. The Scottish rhetoricians eschewed the manipulative goals of
the Ciceronians. They argued that rhetoric should teach how to forcefully
communicate one's reasoned arguments. Metaphor was frowned upon;
highly ornate passages suspect. Adam Smith contended that Shaftesbury's
baroque prose stemmed from his intellectual insecurity and "very puny"
constitution. Hugh Blair thought Cicero suffered from "too visible a parade
of Eloquence," was on occasion "showy rather than solid. . . ." Blair considered modern oratory in general "more cool and temperate" than passionate. This reflected the modern "advantage" in "accuracy and closeness
of reasoning. . . ."[46]

Scottish rhetoricians favored a modestly ornamented style, one that
could please and instruct at the same time. The epitome of this style was
Joseph Addison, whose early-eighteenth-century essays became key
models to be followed.[47] Addison's fluid elegance was preferred to the
"Asiatic" gaudiness of Cicero. The lean, neoclassic style was directly
related to the new attitude toward popular culture. It assumed little contact
with the common people. It was the idiom that gentlemen used to speak
with one another.

In small ways the new dictionaries and grammars tried to further refine
polite society, to create new verbal cues to distinguish high from low.
Johnson labeled words like *brazenfaced, damnable, lingo, flippant*, and
*acquaintance* "vulgar," when in fact they were commonly used by people
of fashion. Johnson hoped that refined speakers would soon eschew these
words. Grammarians, too, hoped to reform polite usage in small ways.
Few of their proposed changes caught on, but the successes were conspicuous. The best example is *you was*. In 1760 this locution was in common use. When speaking in the singular it was correct to say *you was going
to the opera*. But in 1762 Robert Lowth called it "an enormous solecism"
in his grammar, and many others followed suit. By the turn of the century
the phrase was no longer unambiguously acceptable; it now marked a
division within elite culture. Was the refinement a necessary step of the
civilizing process, as most grammarians claimed, or was it silly overrefinement, as Noah Webster asserted? By 1816 the locution had descended
a little further on the social scale: Jane Austen recorded a half-educated
character using the phrase. By 1830, the transformation was complete.
*You were* became correct in both the singular and the plural. *You was* had
become a definite vulgarity. The semantic meaning had not changed from
1760 but the cultural meaning surely had. The same words were heard
differently. The phrase had been abandoned to low culture.[48]

Although such changes pushed high and low cultural forms further apart, they could not restrict access to refined ways of life. Codification of refined speech in grammars and dictionaries was tied to another broad trend of the eighteenth century, the social diffusion of civil culture. While high and low forms were further differentiated, more and more of those of the middling rank were adopting genteel ways of behavior. Particularly important in this movement were the wives and daughters of tradesmen, shopkeepers, and wealthy yeomen. Toward the close of the seventeenth century those women who could afford servants stopped doing housework and with their extra time began affecting genteel accomplishments. But middling women were not alone in cultivating gentility. Gentry spokesmen heaped disdain upon "the honest tradesman who after accumulating a thousand pounds decided his son would be brought up for some genteel profession." After attending Oxford and taking the Grand Tour, the son returned "neither fit for a soap-boiler nor a gentleman, with too much pride for the former, and too little improvement for the latter." Many complained of the small infringements on the prerogatives of the gentry. Tradesmen who announced their weddings in newspapers disgusted Samuel Johnson. This was a practice for gentlemen and ladies; tradesmen were wrong to assume anyone cared about their marriages. Significantly, Johnson referred to the tradesmen not as middling folk but as part of the vulgar.[49]

J. H. Plumb has observed that the diffusion of genteel culture was large enough in the eighteenth century to support a professional culture industry for the first time. Novelists like Fielding and Richardson served the expanded reading public. Circulating libraries appeared even in the provinces by 1750. Decorative arts were known only to a small elite in the late seventeenth century, but Hogarth sold thousands of engravings in the middle of the eighteenth.[50] The spread of the dictionary and grammar should be understood in the larger context of this diffusion of refined culture. Learning to speak as the gentry did was one aspect of adopting their overall manner. By the 1790s Johnson's *Dictionary* was published in pocketbook form and that is where its real sales lay.[51] Many of the grammars, particularly as the century drew to a close, had diffusion clearly in mind. As early as 1763 John Ash noted in the preface to his *Grammatical Institutes* that even for those gentlemen "designed merely for Trade, an intimate Acquaintance with the Proprieties, and Beauties of the English Tongue, would be a desirable, and necessary Attainment."[52]

Still, it is very easy to overestimate the diffusion. Early in the century, the *Spectator* published only three thousand copies an issue. Even at its summit in the 1750s the *Gentleman's Magazine* printed just ten thousand copies each week. Between 1755 and 1765 Johnson sold only five thousand folio copies of his dictionary.[53] The circulation, though, was wide enough to cause concern. What did it mean? How would it affect England? All the confusion between civility as a superior way of life and civility as a badge of class surfaced. Some, like the provincial Benjamin Franklin, simply worked for more diffusion. Samuel Johnson, who like Franklin used his education to rise from the middling ranks (Johnson's parents were provincial bookshop owners), had a more complicated reaction. Although peeved by the common people's petty affectations of gentility, he thought the diffusion was beneficial in sum. "Merely to read and write was a distinction at first," he told Boswell, "but we see when reading and writing have become general, the common people keep their stations. And so, were higher attainments to become general, the effect would be the same."[54]

Others, though, lacked Johnson's long-range optimism. Hume and Pope were among those who feared the uplift. Many explicitly called attention to genteel speech. "It is certain, there is a distinction and sub-ordination of style, as well as rank, and a gradation to be preserved in point of phraseology, as well as precedency. . . . An affectation of talking above our level, is as bad as dressing above it." Philip Withers argued in the 1780s that grammar was becoming more important precisely because so many people were dressing above their station:

> In the present Period, all external Evidence of Rank among Men is de-stroyed. . . . The same Gaiety of Apparel, and the same System of Edu-cation prevail in all Orders of the Community. . . . Hence the Importance of early Attention to Purity and Politeness of Expression: it is the only external Distinction which remains between a Gentleman and a Valet; a Lady and a Mantua-maker.

The *Ladies' Monthly Museum* in 1798 capped off a century of such comment: "When I see a girl destined to weigh candles behind a counter or make butter in a dairy, learning to jabber a language she cannot comprehend, I consider it a manifest infringement upon the rights of gentlemen." In the 1750s, a writer in *The World* pushed the analysis furthest. Ultimately the diffusion would topple the social order: "The mere word genteel seems to have so singular an efficacy in the very sound of it as to have done more to the confounding of all distinctions, and promoting a levelling principle, than the philosophic reflections of the most profound teacher of republican maxims."[55]

Such a worry, in mid-eighteenth-century England, was premature, to

say the least. But it was not wholly fanciful. Some eighty years later—
and throughout the Western World—it would become not idle speculation
but a felt reality. Technology, education, and politics conspired to rob
genteel cultural forms of their class status. It was not in England, however,
that the problem was most acute. That honor went to Britain's former
colonies, the United States of America. It was in conjunction with republican maxims that gentility confounded all distinctions.

# III

To many of its defenders, the American Revolution seemed the ultimate
triumph of civil culture. Jefferson, Madison, Franklin, and John Adams
were among the leading *philosophes* of America. Men like Hamilton and
Washington were refined gentlemen with a healthy respect for learning.
Civilized gentlemen ruled, without a hereditary aristocracy to claim privileges they did not deserve.

Yet it was far more complicated. The increasing political participation
of the middling classes, the "semieducated," made refined gentlemen
worry about the fate of civil eloquence. The public sphere was being
corrupted by vulgar language. But Revolutionary gentlemen also thought
that *all* citizens in a republic needed some sort of basic education. While
gentry spokesmen feared the new political assertiveness of small farmers,
artisans, and shopkeepers, the long-term consequences of the gentry's own
educational agenda could only further the phenomenon.

Moreover, the republican distaste for aristocratic usages made Americans wary about showy language. At the same time that the broad diffusion of genteel speech became a political goal, the opportunity for the
elite to set itself off via the grand style was foreclosed. The combined
pressures, increasing participation and education below, and the distrust
of overrefinement above, threatened to strip from the gentry their cultural
distinctiveness. A republican discourse had to find the right pitch, refined
but not *too* refined, a gentleman's language but not an aristocrat's. Ne-
gotiating these boundaries became an issue that nagged well into the
nineteenth century.

Eloquent language, almost all agreed, was critical to the new regime.
Republicanism was government by discussion as opposed to force of fiat.
Speech was more important to a republic than to any other kind of polity.
The historian Charles Rollin furnished the title-page epigram of *The Co-
lumbian Orator*, a patriotic schoolbook published in 1797: "Cato cultivated

Eloquence as a necessary means for defending THE RIGHTS OF THE PEOPLE, and for enforcing good Counsels." Those attending the Harvard commencement in 1794 heard that public speaking flourished in republican Athens but "Demosthenes and the liberty of Greece together expired; and from this period we hear very little more Grecian eloquence." John Adams reminded the Continental Congress in 1780 that "eloquence is cultivated with more care in republics than in other governments." Republics "have produced the greatest purity, copiousness and perfection of language." Even British textbooks repeated that message. Eloquence was not as important as it had been "when the *tongue* of an orator could do more than the *sceptre* of a monarch, or the *sword* of a warrior," it was reported in *The Art of Speaking*, a British text reprinted in Philadelphia in 1780.[56]

Despite the upheavals in the college curriculum during the 1770s and 1780s, rhetoric was not attacked. Instead, the texts of the Scottish school swept into the nation's classrooms to replace (or at least balance) the Ciceronian rhetoric used earlier. In 1783 Brown University ordered Blair's *Rhetoric* from England; in 1784 the first American edition was published. Yale introduced Blair in 1785; Harvard followed three years later. By the turn of the century Blair's book was used in virtually every college in the nation. Henry May and Steven Lundberg have charted the extraordinary burst of interest in Blair in the last two decades of the century. First published in 1783, the book by 1790 was in 41 percent of the libraries surveyed by May and Lundberg. In the next decade the percentage climbed to 55; only one book, Locke's *Essay Concerning Human Understanding*, was more widely owned. As I have pointed out, Blair's *Rhetoric* essentially taught civilized men and women how to communicate with one another, the perfect picture of republican discourse.[57]

But this picture of enlightened civility is a superficial one. Nowhere was the triumph more complete; nowhere was the grasp less secure. American gentlemen fought a two-front war in the 1770s and 1780s: against British "tyranny" and against the withering away of the deferential order. The signs of the latter were small and large, from the Boston shoemaker who no longer tipped his hat when passing local notables to the radical Pennsylvania constitution of 1776 that had only the most minimal property qualifications for voting and holding office.[58] Most frightening to the elite, voters were electing people to office who were not gentlemen. "When the pot boils, the scum will rise," cautioned James Otis in 1776, and by the eighties the prophecy seemed to many dangerously close to reality. Men like Washington and Hamilton were deeply troubled by the "common sort" now populating the state legislatures. Sloughing off the hereditary aristocracy was supposed to inaugurate a rule of the wise and virtuous, but republican hostility to titles had led to a demeaning of all distinctions of talent and breeding. Academic education was attacked because "plain, unlettered" men could best communicate with the people. The leveling spirit did not bring equality, however, but a new, somewhat desperate and grasping search for power, distinction, and wealth. Talent was equated with mustering votes or amassing fortunes. It seemed clear that "in times of public confusion, and in the demolition of ancient institutions, blustering, haughty, licentious, self-seeking men" gained "the ear of the people."[59]

One way to get at the precise character of the elite's fears is by looking at the plays they wrote and watched during the 1770s and 1780s. Particularly illuminating is the comedy of manners. The comedies written by Americans were built on European conventions, but they also reveal a preoccupation with the social consequences of republicanism, a theme absent from Sheridan and only a bitter dream to Beaumarchais. The plays are especially useful here because they reveal just how conscious late-eighteenth-century ladies and gentlemen were of the political uses of every-day speech, of the subtle links between decorum and the social order.

One way the social order was challenged was through leveling. Low characters refused to defer to cultivated men and women. In Royall Tyler's *The Contrast* (1787) the time-honored terminology of subordination is refused and a democracy of white-skinned men is assumed. A servant is indignant that he is called such: "Servant! Sir, do you take me for a negger—I am Colonel Manly's waiter." But does he not blacken the colonel's boots? "Yes; I do grease them a bit sometimes; but I am a true blue son of liberty for all that. Father said I should come as Colonel Manly's waiter, to see the world, and all that; but no man shall master me." No longer was there master and servant, now there was—what?—master and waiter? The Revolution had emboldened men.[60]

Through the 1780s such low characters still provide comic relief, a convention reaching back to Elizabethan drama and suggesting that leveling was not yet a pressing concern. What loomed larger in the plays were the misuses of polite behavior. People reached above their station, adopting the forms of genteel culture to erase public distinctions between high and low. Yet forms were adopted without an honest commitment to civility; they were used merely to advance socially. Here were those self-interested opportunists the gentry worried about.

One good example is *The Blockheads*, a 1776 play usually attributed to Mercy Warren. Simple Blockhead, a farmer upset with the privation the war has brought on, supports the British with the hope of profit. His wife, Jemima, and his daughter, Tabitha, hope Tory sympathies will reap social advancement and they badger Simple to adopt genteel manners. When their pecking finally exhausts Simple, he angrily calls all women "she asses." His wife sternly rebukes him but the violence of her outburst indicates that she has not fully grasped civil ways: "No, I will learn you to treat your wife with a little more *good manners*—I wish you would become a little more polish'd, and go into the company of gentlemen and ladies—You would hear nothing of *she asses* and such filthy *farm terms. My dear* and *my honey* are the terms there made use of. . . . None of your language defiles their conversation—nothing but pure refinement." The family prepares to move to British Halifax and Simple tells his wife that she will cut "a miserable figure aboard the ship along side your polite company. . . . when what is in will come out, and perhaps at both ends." His wife again explodes at his coarseness, but her own breach of convention (the double negative) tells us of the woman's vulgarity: "Don't Tantalize me no longer. . . . I like no such coarse phrases: if I had *fifty ends*, my modesty should forbid any thing from coming out of either."[61]

Similar tensions run through William Hill Brown's *The Better Sort: Or the Girl of Spirit*, a play first performed in 1789. Mrs. Sententious hopes to entertain "the better sort" in order to ingratiate herself to them. Mr. Sententious, though, disapproves of her social climbing and counsels her to devote herself to learning the appropriate genteel accomplishments of a lady. After she says, "What fools *them is*!" he cautions her to study grammar. Mrs. Sententious, however, wants nothing that taxing: "The bettermost genii don't place the ton in mere words—it is in actions . . . the actions of high life and grandeur too—It is these that distinguish the better sort from the *canal*." "The *canaille*!" her husband explodes. "You ought never to use words you do not understand—say the vulgar, or commonality. . . ." Not only do the vulgarities of Mrs. Sententious reveal her essential frivolousness, her contention that the better sort care nothing for words is later disproved. Captain Flash, a British officer, makes fun of her by having her agree to ridiculous propositions that he has framed in language she cannot understand.[62]

Both Jemima Blockhead and Mrs. Sententious were stock literary characters of the same type as the more famous Mrs. Malaprop. (Sheridan's *The Rivals* was first produced in 1775.) Such characters had certain graces and were willing to affect any others that would help in polite society. Yet they had an imperfect command of refined forms, and they had no true character. Manners, dress, dancing, and speech had slipped away from their putative ethical correlates and were tied to a clawing drive for status. Similar characters are found in other American plays of the time. They could be men as well as women. In Robert Munford's *The Candidates* (1770), Sir John Toddy treats the hero Mr. Wou'be with gracious civility to secure the latter's political support. Toddy is a fraud, and Wou'be knows it. Toddy's first grammatical lapse comes at the moment Wou'be refuses him, as if to tell the audience what kind of man Toddy really is. In a Tory sketch, *The Americans Roused*, the rebel Puff tries to pass himself off as learned when in fact he mistakes Latin for French and cannot understand the language of "true" gentlemen. In still another American farce of the time a wealthy but rustic barber secures a seat in Parliament but his reward for not maintaining his station is financial ruin.[63]

The language and behavior of a Jemima Blockhead or Mrs. Sententious were suspect because they revealed a "moral void."[64] Humanistic discourse had long claimed that refinement should express character and had long observed that refinement was misused when turned into a badge of class. But by the 1770s, such behavior occurred in a cultural setting especially hostile to showy, aristocratic behavior. In all American plays from the early 1770s on, using refined culture for the express purpose of maintaining class distinctions was condemned as aristocratic.[65] Acceptable social cleavages could be based only on virtue, talent, and civil eloquence, not on luxury, fashion, or glib refinement. Jemima Blockhead and Mrs. Sententious committed two sins. They failed to adequately command refined linguistic forms and they had bad motives. They did not strike the pose of restraint necessary in a republican world.

Even when refined forms were successfully affected, they were unacceptable if adopted for the wrong reasons. Characters who affected refinement merely to set themselves off were found in many late-eighteenth-century plays.[66] Such characters, often called "fine" gentlemen, did not look like clawing parvenus; they rather resembled European aristocrats. They usually combined cynical glibness with an obsessive cultivation of polite forms. Often these characters pursued distinction through speech. Their use of *sir* was excessive ("Your appearance, Sir, bespeaks the gentleman of distinction, Sir.") and they piled politeness on top of politeness ("Sir, I have the honor to be, with the profoundest respect and esteem, your most obedient, most devoted, and most obliged humble slave, *foi d'Homme d'Honeur*.").[67] A variation on this theme is found in the *Debates at the Robin Hood Society*, a Tory dialogue performed and published in New York in 1774. Here the British are virtuous; it is the elegant but manipulative republican, Mr. Silver Tongue, who is the villain. Mr. Silver Tongue admits that despite his refined speech he cares nothing about the meaning of words; they are but manipulative tools. He uses his rhetorical skills to convince unlettered men to support the republican cause.[68]

Although in aristocratic characters politeness is so misused that it appears opposed to virtue, in no play written by an American during the 1770s and 1780s was there an unlettered hero. All were gentlemen. Refined, they were not coxcombs. Learned, they were not pedants. Americans were to be refined; the question was how. In answering, sexuality and politics met. In *The Politician Out-Witted*, the foppish Worthnaught not only apes British manners; his language is described as "effeminate cries." In *The Contrast*, the hero's name—Colonel Manly—says it all. Women were to avoid confusing gentility with card games, social calls, and gossip. Men were not to become womanly. ("He bowed so gracefully, made such a genteel apology, and looked so manly and noble.") Both had to avoid aristocratic, European demeanor.[69]

Connecting overrefinement with female behavior, I have noted, was a traditional practice. But in late-eighteenth-century America this traditional complaint was used to denigrate aristocracy. The American plays associated womanly overrefinement with aristocratic culture, something that writers like Cicero and Chesterfield had avoided. As a consequence, embedded in the very attack on aristocratic culture was the perpetuation of the assumption that eloquence was basically masculine. The Revolutionary critique of aristocratic language helped reconfigure patriarchy in a republican setting.

There was vocal opposition to aristocratic education in the Revolutionary years. Sending a young man to school in Europe, it was feared, would make him unfit for life in a republic.[70] In the same spirit, the aristocratic language of Britain was condemned. The late-eighteenth-century grand style was the most common target. The shift in British prose style from the plainness of Swift and the restrained elegance of Addison or Defoe to the more elaborate periods of Gibbon and the Latinate parade of Johnson jarred American critics.[71] The *American Museum* complained of the "turgid style" of Johnson and the "purple glare" of Gibbon. Noah Webster complained that Gibbon's *Decline and Fall* was "designed to show the author's talent in selecting words. . . ." Elsewhere Webster asserted that Gibbon's preoccupation with ornament made him forget that "he is writing for the *information* of the reader, and when he ought to *instruct* the *mind*, he is only *pleasing* to the *ear*." A writer in the *American Magazine* worried that Gibbon's prose dulled the intellect: "The ears are gratified at the expense of the understanding. The music of the language charms the mind from the *matter* to the *manner*. . . ." Still another critic complained that Chesterfield, Gibbon, Johnson, and Hume "were absorbed in the structure of sentences," that their "frothy manner" revealed a "corrupt taste." Such criticisms revealed a widespread preference for a more restrained prose style, particularly when writing history. The journalistic literary commentary closely parallels the shift in rhetorical theory from Ciceronian pomp to Scottish elegance.[72]

The fear of aristocratic overrefinement, of using civil forms solely to maintain social distinctions, surfaced in many ways. It reached the heart of the new government when the first Congress debated the President's official title. Some senators, arguing that the European style of formality was necessary to create respect for the office, urged that his title be "His Highness, the President of the United States of America, and Protector of their Liberties." The House of Representatives rejected this as aristocratic and the chief executive came to be called Mr. President, a title respectful and civil but without any European pomp. Trying to draw that fine line between true civility and aristocratic pride was an issue reaching even schoolchildren. Young boys and girls studying Noah Webster's *An American Selection of Lessons in Reading and Speaking*, published in 1789, found the following maxim: "*Excess* of ceremony shews *want* of breeding. That civility is best which excludes all superfluous formality."[73]

Caleb Bingham's *The Columbian Orator* (1797) was another schoolbook that attacked affected speech. In one dialogue, a farmer offers to sell fowl to a "Gentleman of the Ton[e]," fifty cents for a pair of ducks and seventy-five cents apiece for geese and turkeys. The gentleman petulantly tells the farmer he is a "numskull" for confusing fowl with geese and turkeys.

> Farmer: I crave your pardon, Mister. I begin to see that I never was larn'd the right use of language; for since I come among these fine gentlefolks, I don't understand one half that's said to me.

> Gentleman: So it seems. However, you have entered a good school to learn civilization. What I wanted, was, a pair of those creatures that lay eggs, wulgarly called hens.

Civilized speech presumes power and demands subordination. Yet the "fine" language is, in fact, bogus. Like today, in the late eighteenth century *fowl* referred to all birds and *hen* was not a vulgarism. The simple farmer was not wrong, the "gentleman of the tone" was overrefined. The refinement, moreover, was not rooted in civil respect for the farmer. To his face the rustic is called a "fool," a "blundering blockhead," and "almost savage." The overrefinement is cruelly imperious. Finally, very subtly, very ironically, the gentleman's refinement is shown to be imperfect. Putting a *w* sound where a *v* belonged was a common vulgarity of the later eighteenth century. Saying *wulgarly* instead of *vulgarly* tips us that the gentleman, like the farmer, has not "larn'd the right use of language." Left to himself, the farmer questions the manners of the gentleman ("I think this last chap to be of the race of coxcombs") but accepts the ethos of civil decorum. ("However, I don't despair yet of meeting with people of *real* civilization.")[74]

The aristocrat's obsession with genteel ornaments masked his neglect of humane learning, still one more way that surface forms paraded empty of any content. Elsewhere in the *Modern Orator* is a short piece entitled "Modern Education: Dialogue between Preceptor and Parent." The schoolmaster complains about parents who want their children to dance a little, flute a little, fiddle a little, and bow and curtsy. The parent enters demanding just such an education for his son. When asked about the basics, the parent coldly announces that his son "pronounces the English language genteely." The teacher denies that he is uninterested in dance or deportment but argues that they must be part of a more comprehensive education. Especially upsetting is the parent's contention that the son has learned oratory from an actor. In near despair the preceptor argues that to truly learn public speaking the boy must study contemporary rhetoric and the eloquence of the ancients. Manners, learning, and the arts were complementary pillars of a liberal education. Genteel speech and deportment, in themselves, were not the signs of the liberally educated.[75]

Literate Americans were preoccupied with the illicit uses of refined language. At the same time, however, it was difficult to find anyone who did not argue that the nation needed a refined, cultivated tongue. John Witherspoon, Benjamin Franklin, James Madison, Benjamin Rush, John Adams, James Wilson, and Thomas Jefferson were among those who emphasized the need for a refined language and literature in the new nation.[76] American critics praised the lean elegance of their own. The prose of the American historian George Minot was described as "of the pure, elegant, narrative kind," without any "pompous diction." Of Belknap's *History of New Hampshire* it was written: "No language could be better chosen for history." Although the bombast of contemporary British prose was under attack, the Queen Anne idiom became a model. Mercy Warren thought that Chesterfield's *Letters* were "dangerous," not least because of their style. She called the work "honeyed poison." But Joseph Addison, according to Warren, "did more to improve the English language and correct the style of the age than any other man." Similarly, Benjamin Rush praised Swift and Bolingbroke because they taught him "to prefer *Simplicity* to every thing in composition."[77]

Even radicals understood that entrance into public life demanded verbal felicity. William Manning, a barely literate New England farmer and no friend to gentlemen of any kind, still argued that schoolmasters should pay "purticuler attention to teaching the Inglish langueg." Robert Coram, while complaining that the legislatures were overstuffed with merchants and lawyers, admitted that most farmers were "unable to speak with propriety," meaning that they were inarticulate. Even if elected, he noted, a farmer would likely "see the dearest interest of his country basely bartered away" because he could not oppose it with any eloquence.[78] Indeed, as Gordon Wood has pointed out, poor oratorical skills had hurt anti-Federalists during the previous decade. In South Carolina, rural anti-Federalists rarely debated in public, and often complained about not being able to adequately express themselves. In other states the complaint arose that most of the educated were Federalists, "together with all the Speakers in the State, Great and Small." When anti-Federalists tried to speak in Conncticut, "they were browbeaten by many of these Cicero'es as they think themselves and others of Superior Rank." The power of speech was acutely felt. Its absence was bitterly remembered.[79]

Even as the Revolution heightened fears of the misuses of refined language, it also made the need for refined speech more pressing. As the Revolutionary years were left behind, a pronounced interest in vernacular usage was evident. To be sure, much of this simply followed the quickened British interest after midcentury.[80] In the United States, though, the fervor took on a patriotic cast. An educated populace guarded the republic and an educated people was an articulate people. Republicanism called for a diffusion of basic skills beyond all but the most radical dreams of the European *philosophes*.[81] "Too much pains cannot be taken to teach our youth to read and write the American language with propriety and elegance," wrote Benjamin Rush in 1791. For the first time systematic campaigns were undertaken to teach *girls* to read and write (public speaking remained forbidden). As the century closed, states began passing laws requiring schools to teach the vernacular. In 1789 the Massachusetts legislature required every town with at least fifty families to have a schoolmaster "to teach children to read and write and to instruct them in the English language. . . ." Delaware and Virginia enacted similar laws in 1796, Vermont in 1797. In 1793 the regents of the University of the State of New York pressed the state legislature to require lower schools to teach English usage, and in 1797 New York was the first state to explicitly require the teaching of English grammar.[82]

The increasing presence of grammars was another indication of the drive for diffusion, and during the 1780s a healthy market developed for them. Whereas only four grammars were published in the United States in the 1770s (nineteen different printings), in the 1780s ten different grammars were printed forty-five times. During that decade American schoolmasters like Caleb Bingham and Noah Webster began writing their own grammars (though still based on British models) to take advantage of the enlarged market. In the 1790s, the demand again more than doubled, a prelude to the truly phenomenal expansion in the early nineteenth century. Opposition persisted—some gentlemen still suspected that grammar bred frauds. In two plays of the 1780s grammarians were portrayed as ridiculous pedants. In 1788 Francis Hopkinson argued that grammatical study was "scholastic," arguing that parsing a sentence destroyed any appreciation of its grace.[83] At lower social levels parents still had to be convinced of grammar's utility. But in sum, in the closing decades of the century, the elementary grammar—a text relatively unimportant earlier in the century —was found in the hands of more and more people, and more and more people from modest backgrounds.

The same could be said of the dictionary, although its diffusion was slower. More systematic work would have to be done to chart out exactly who owned dictionaries and what they were used for in the early eighteenth century, but it is clear that the dictionary did not have the social role it occupies today. John Locke, Isaac Newton, and Jonathan Swift did not own an English dictionary. In the 1740s the Library Company of Philadelphia owned a copy of Bailey's *Universal Etymological English Dictionary*, a gift from Benjamin Franklin, suggesting that perhaps dictionaries were owned by printers more than by the general public. Harvard did not own an English dictionary in the early part of the eighteenth century and in the 1770s the New York Society Library did not have one. Only after Johnson published his did the generally educated begin to purchase dictionaries. Gibbon owned a copy of Johnson and in 1771 Jefferson urged his nephew to add that book to his library. Still, the process was gradual. As the New York library makes clear, even in the 1770s the dictionary was not yet a standard reference text. And although Adam Smith reviewed Johnson's dictionary in the *Edinburgh Review*, he did not keep a copy in his library.[84]

Only as lexicons were abridged and sold more cheaply in the 1770s and 1780s did the real diffusion begin. Daniel Drake, born in 1785, was the son of an illiterate Kentucky farmer. Only in the late 1790s, after a benefactor agreed to finance Drake's medical education, did the young man secure a dictionary—a pocket edition of Entlick's dictionary, which was derivative of Johnson. (In 1800, at age fifteen, Drake had still never studied grammar; his Yankee schoolmaster did not know the subject.)[85]

Elias Smith, the son of a modest Vermont farmer, recalled seeing his first dictionary and grammar in the mid-1780s when he was sixteen years old. At a church meeting when he was told to look up a word, Smith was lost. He simply did not understand how a dictionary was used or even what it was used for: "It appeared strange to me that the word used by the minister should be in that little book." Although his first contact with a grammar "fired me with zeal to gain useful knowledge," his father objected, arguing that arithmetic was a more useful subject for a farmer. After a heated family argument that included father, son, mother, and uncle and that lasted a whole evening, the father relented. The uncle then turned to the father and said, "You now consent to that which will be worth more to your child than all your farm." Smith went on to become a prominent Baptist minister.[86]

The spread of basic civil culture must be understood in conjunction with the concurrent fear of aristocratic misuse of civil language. Pressure was put on refined culture from two directions. On top, selfish "aristocrats" abused the forms of civility. Genteel speech without civic or civil responsibility was a traditional fear, but Americans became preoccupied with remaining free from baroque displays of eloquence. At the same time, however, civil language remained an important part of the republican gentleman's cultural baggage. Where should the line be drawn?

If fear of aristocratic pomp pressed from above, the educational demands of a republic pressed from below. The necessary diffusion of basic genteel accomplishments meant that refined culture, to some extent, was passing to the middling people. Given the two pressures, the restraint at the top and the diffusion below, how could gentlemen retain their distinction? How could refined language be defined? The breathing space of approved cultural forms was contracting in the late eighteenth century.

# IV

Although the Revolutionary era theater revealed the fears issuing from the gentry, there were more real portents of the future than Jemima

Blockhead or Mrs. Sententious. A small number of men pushed to the center of American culture who were neither refined nor crude, men who did not fit traditional cultural patterns. Far from being insecure social climbers, these men were aggressive and self-possessed. They had something to offer the Revolutionary public and they knew it. Three of these men, their language and their accomplishments, deserve mention.

In 1776 the nation was electrified by Thomas Paine's *Common Sense*. By best estimates one copy circulated for every five inhabitants of the American colonies. No single piece of political literature had ever come close to such popularity. Central to Paine's success, Eric Foner has argued, was the tone and style of the pamphlet. Paine avoided legal arguments and rarely invoked authorities. He assumed limited knowledge of the Bible and the little Latin he used was followed by an English translation. He made free use of *ad hominem* insult. His syntax was straightforward; his vocabulary simple. ("As is my design to make those that can scarcely read understand I shall therefore avoid every literary ornament and put it in language as plain as the alphabet.") As Foner notes, *Common Sense*, "written in a style designed to reach a mass audience, was central to the explosion of political argument and involvement beyond the confines of a narrow elite to 'all ranks' of Americans."

Many educated gentlemen, even those swayed by his political argument, were disturbed by the pamphlet's tone. John Adams thought calling George III the "royal brute of England" who slept with "blood upon his soul" was "suitable for an emigrant from New Gate, or one who had chiefly associated with such company. . . ." Others complained of Paine's "uncommon frenzy" and the lack of "decorous and reasonable" language. Gouverneur Morris called him "a mere adventurer . . . ignorant even of grammar." Benjamin Franklin apologized to a French correspondent for the "rude way of writing" in *Common Sense*. Yet despite the obvious incivility, the pamphlet was not the scratchings of an illiterate man. Paine's clear, simple prose and his clipped rhythms showed an uncommon feel for the language. So too did his striking metaphors and turns of phrase. The billingsgate was carefully crafted. In no conventional sense can *Common Sense* be considered either high or low culture. It was popular culture but it was not low culture. It was correct language but not refined language.[87]

Eleven years before Paine's pamphlet galvanized the country, a different newcomer burst on to the public stage. Patrick Henry's speech against the Stamp Act would have, in itself, assured him a place in American history, but through his eloquence Henry built an impressive career as a lawyer, Revolutionary leader, and governor of Virginia. If there was one thing contemporaries agreed upon, it was the bewitching character of Henry's oratory. Even at a time when rhetorical categories were commonly known, Henry's speaking proved difficult to classify. Jefferson called it "peculiar," Spencer Roane claimed it "baffled all descriptions." Edmund Randolph mentioned Henry's similarities to evangelical ministers but St. George Tucker recalled that Henry drew up short of such preaching: "He was emphatic, without vehemence or declamation, animated, but never boisterous, nervous, without recourse to intemperate language; and clear, though not always methodical."[88]

Henry's background and desultory education explains much of the confusion. The son of a backwoods planter, Henry was a lazy student (and a lazy lawyer) who cared little for liberal learning. He rarely read. Never bothering to shake off his provincial dialect, he spoke of "the yearth" and of "men's naitural parts being improved by larnin'." Edmund Randolph remembered his lapses of grammar. Patrick Henry was, his biographer tells us, a "rising Virginia planter who still retained a vestige of the manner and habits of the yeomanry." But only a vestige. Henry was a staunch defender of gentry rule, an Episcopalian who in the 1780s opposed disestablishment. When governor, he carefully dressed himself in an elegant wig, black small clothes, and brilliant scarlet cloak. His presence and demeanor were designed, as Moses Coit Tyler once observed, "to sustain, in the popular mind, the traditional respect for his high office." Much of Henry's speaking style, the tense antitheses, the rhetorical questions, was not derived from evangelicals but from those gentlemen who had studied the speeches of Demosthenes and Cicero. Henry had much of the gentleman in him but was disinclined to make up (or at least hide) what he lacked. Thomas Jefferson remembered him this way: "In private conversation he was agreeable, and facetious and while in general society appeared to understand all the decencies and proprieties of it; but in his *heart*, he preferred low society, and sought it as often as possible."[89]

Despite his rusticity, Henry's speaking was undeniably powerful. Gentlemen often recalled being moved by Henry almost in spite of themselves. Again Jefferson:

> When he had spoken in opposition to *my* opinion, had produced a great effect, and I myself been highly delighted and moved, I have asked myself

when it ceased, "What the Devil has he said," and could never answer the enquiry.[90]

Henry's genius is not hard to find. He meshed word, tone, gesture, and cadence in a way that transfixed people. He was proof of Cicero's dictum that natural talent was the most important attribute of a fine orator. What made Henry's eloquence difficult to describe was that he did not channel his talent into any recognizable cultural "slot." Classical cadences, passions verging on the evangelical, pronunciation that smacked of the rustic, and dress and deportment that were genteel—it all added up to a thoroughly sui generis public performance.

Both Henry and Paine jumbled symbolic and expressive cues that most men assumed would neatly cohere. Paine put his billingsgate into grammatically acceptable form. Henry's graciousness, on the other hand, was wrapped in syntax and pronunciation often falling below the line separating the educated from the uneducated. Both men challenged the commonly held assumption (found in both Cicero and Blair) that a liberal education was necessary to produce acceptable prose. It took another man, however, to explicitly challenge that assumption. It was Noah Webster who first suggested that gentry custom should not be the appropriate standard of the English language.

Noah Webster began writing about language in the early 1780s. At first, he offered nothing original. His first grammar, published in 1783, was derivative of Lowth and used standard British spelling. The radicalism of the Revolutionary years had affected Webster, though, and for a time in the 1780s he argued that society should allow no ruling elites. Late in the decade Webster applied his antiauthoritarianism to language. In *Dissertations on the English Language* (1789) Webster charged that most writers in Europe cared more for sound than words and argued that no class should be allowed to set the linguistic tone of a nation:

> When a particular set of men, in exalted stations, undertake to say "We are the standards of propriety and elegance, and if all men do not conform to our practice, they shall be accounted vulgar and ignorant," they take a very great liberty with the rule of the language and the rights of civility.[91]

Webster argued for a new principle of linguistic appropriateness, one based on the universal usage of Americans and analogy. Much of the language Americans used did not differ from class to class or from region to region. This language was not to be touched. Where differences existed, however, the internal logic of the language should be the appropriate standard. The language was to be made more regular, more predictable, more analogous. Much of any language is founded upon analogy (for example, since English generally forms plurals by adding *s*, that rule can be analogously applied when forming most plurals). Where regional or class differences existed, Webster argued that the language should be made more analogous. No elite, Webster argued, was to set standards. The authority would be removed from any custom save universal custom. Where differences existed, free-floating rationality would replace gentry custom.[92]

Webster's linguistic theory has often been described as nationalistic, which it was, but his sociolinguistic radicalism has rarely been noticed. Later in life, Webster gave up his political radicalism and became thoroughly disenchanted with the political drift of the nation. By the end of his life Webster longed for the rule of gentlemen. Yet he never jettisoned his linguistic theory. As he grew older, his attacks on gentry usage and his defenses of rude speech contradicted his political authoritarianism. But in 1789 there was, for a moment, sharp clarity in Webster's writings. All linguistic differences that threaten to create status hierarchy were to be destroyed. Provincial dialects, he recognized, were sources of tension between sections. Erase them and such tensions would be erased. Even Webster's advocacy of simplified spelling rested on political reasoning. Webster hoped to tie spelling to pronunciation, arguing that current orthography was so difficult that few conquered it. His reform would not only make orthography accessible to all, it would unify pronunciation: "All persons, of every rank, would speak with some degree of precision and uniformity. Such a uniformity in these states is very desirable; it would remove prejudice, and conciliate mutual affection and respect."[93]

Webster, though, did not direct the linguistic opinions of late-eighteenth-century Americans. Ironically, the book that made him famous, his blue-backed speller, was first published in 1783 before he had contemplated the wrongs of established linguistic thinking. By the end of the 1790s Webster's ideas were already considered "radical chic" by many of the literary and educational leaders of the nation. Webster complained that he could not receive a fair hearing in large towns but teachers and writers were fearful that Webster's reforms would alienate Americans from Shakespeare, Milton, Johnson, and perhaps even the King James Bible.[94]

Whatever the fears of Revolutionary gentlemen, old presumptions were not often strained. "The people, in all nations," John Adams wrote in his defense of the Constitution, "are naturally divided into two sorts, the gentleman and the simpleman, a word which is here chosen to signify the common people." Thomas Jefferson argued in *Notes on the State of Virginia* that three years of common schooling would sift the natural aristocracy from what he called "the rubbish." Even later in life Jefferson divided the citizenry "into two classes—the laboring and the learned." Both Jefferson and Adams argued that what separated the two groups was a liberal education.[95]

Such thinking was derived from standard educational theory and was even built into linguistic convention. Cosmopolitan American gentlemen readily thought with terms inherited from Europe. But they were also republicans, intent on molding an eloquent and civil citizenry. What would happen if refined culture, or significant parts of refined culture, became the property of a whole people? Wouldn't that contradict the social order implicit in the canons of civil decorum? A civilized man was known by his cultivated taste, his superior discrimination. Just as in Hegel's famous chapter on lordship and bondage in the *Phenomenology*, the gentleman could know himself only through an "other." Could any stable social hierarchy be sustained if civilized culture was the property of the common man?

# CHAPTER TWO

# The Democratic Idiom

The use of slang . . . is at once a sign and
cause of mental atrophy.

OLIVER WENDELL HOLMES

. . . his slang-whanging drew a considerable
crowd around us.

DAVY CROCKETT

The issue of social decorum dogs the liberal political state. Just what
unwritten social laws must be followed to participate in a government
ostensibly built on equal rights for *all*? In the United States, the issue has
usually revolved around assimilating outsiders—civilizing Indians, Amer-
icanizing immigrants. It is not, however, a peculiarly American problem.
In his study of Jewish Diaspora intellectuals, John Murray Cuddihy has
posed the problems in this way: "Is political emancipation tied to social
emancipation? Does access to the political *rights* of the *citoyen* hinge on
the prior performance of the social *rites* of the *bourgeois*? Must we prove
ourselves *gentle*men before claiming the rights of men?"[1]

The problems have not been better stated (and Cuddihy's answers
are among the most sensitive yet offered) but the experience of mid-
nineteenth-century America suggests another dimension. The dramatic
expansion of basic schooling and the concurrent breakdown of deference
to gentlemen—the highly refined—reordered the relationship of education
to leadership and pushed the problem of civility to the center of society.
By the Jacksonian era incivility was not only a problem for outsiders, a
question of their conforming to established standards. The issue was more

basic. How could there be any standard of decorum in a democratic culture?

The prominence of vulgar speech was much talked about in early-nineteenth-century America and often seen as a part of the general democratizing of culture. But more was at work in those years than simply the disappearance of decorum. Mass education was a countervailing force, and this chapter examines that phenomenon through early-nineteenth-century dictionaries and grammars. The dramatic increase in their production and use combined with their continued respect for the "old" themes of linguistic refinement was sharply at odds with the rough speech democracy supposedly demanded. Linguists struggled to maintain old attitudes toward public speech and behavior. When reformers appeared early in the century to challenge the refined literary language codified in grammars and dictionaries, they were sternly rebuffed. The educational establishment worked to save the old decorum in the face of the democratic threat.

It was a difficult fight. The spread of basic education created a group of men with enough useful knowledge and practical skills to challenge the authority of the refined. Nineteenth-century debates about linguistic decorum, however, were not simply reflections of a fight between a fading aristocracy and a new "middle" class, between gentlemen and self-made men. Issues of linguistic vulgarity and refinement cut through social divisions. Coarse stump speaking and "vulgar" conversational informality were part of meeting the *demos* on their own terms, and not only did men and women of middling culture engage in such behavior, so too did many refined ladies and gentlemen. Vulgarity was often a prerequisite to participation in a democratic world. On the other hand, even those of middling culture did not completely eschew refined speech. The gravitational pull of traditional assumptions was one factor; the seemingly inexorable impulse to create *some* social hierarchy another. Democratic sentiment created contradictory cultural pressures. It encouraged rough, familiar speech and widespread education. The popular grammars and dictionaries of the early nineteenth century appeared to be part of an educational movement that not only perpetuated and diffused refined cultural forms but *also* undermined the rule of the refined. The cunning of history seemed at work.

The contradictory push toward democratic rawness and pull to universal education created a kind of cultural vertigo. Even the traditional language of civil authority became unsteady. In the early nineteenth century, usage of *lady* and *gentleman* broadened to include all adults. The class character of the words was lost. James Fenimore Cooper complained that calling someone without "education, manners, accomplishments, tastes," or "associations" a gentleman was "just as absurd as to call one who is thus qualified, a fellow." The *Boston Quarterly Review* disagreed. "It is very important that our democrats should be taught good manners," it noted, but "universal education" was accomplishing that task. "We confess that we look with pleasure on the fact that footmen and cooks are rising to the dignity of gentlemen and ladies."[2] Who, indeed, had firm ground under their feet? Could there be a language of authority in a democratic culture?

# I

By the middle decades of the nineteenth century, divisions between the refined and the vulgar, the few and the many, were not aligned as neatly as before. There was vulgarity among the few and refinements amid the many. This was, of course, the result of forces long at work—increasing literacy and politicization of the public. Although the engaged public had been expanding for over a century, in the 1830s critical mass was reached. Popular newspapers, popular education, and popular political parties all attested to that. Mass democracy had arrived. And the mass commercial democracy of mid-nineteenth-century America demanded a new kind of rhetoric.

Cultivated language was still nurtured. It was not simply the concern of a few literary men. The oratory of Rufus Choate, Daniel Webster, Charles Sumner, and Edward Everett delighted the highly educated, whose diaries, letters, magazines, and newspapers are strewn with references to elegant prose.[3] At the other end of the spectrum, each rural region and outsider group had grammatical and lexical peculiarities that were recognized as the marks of an uneducated person.[4] In the nineteenth century, as before, distinct forms of high and low culture lived icily side by side. But although for every Boston Brahmin there was an Irish immigrant and for every cultivated Southerner a black slave or white dirt farmer, the situation became far more complicated. Increasingly, more Americans were able to command at least bits of refined language. Increasingly, the public culture taught citizens that some vulgar language was useful. Cultural *forms* remained constant, people continued to speak of "refined" and "vulgar" behavior, but the *uses* of the forms became more subtle. The men, and to a lesser degree the women, who challenged the gentry for cultural authority were not uneducated rustics. They were men and women of middling culture, people who cultivated refinements but who were not refined.

Extraordinarily complex mixtures of cultural styles defined middling culture. There was a fluid movement between the high and low, refined and vulgar. Speakers might shift from the formal to the folksy as the situation demanded or they might merge refined and unrefined behavior in a single moment. However accomplished, the middling culture easily roamed across traditional cultural borders. Henry Ward Beecher, a master of middling rhetoric, knew exactly what was involved. By the middle of the century, Beecher was one of the most popular speakers in the nation. Everywhere he spoke, huge crowds gathered. In 1835, at the outset of his career, Beecher confided to his private journal what is perhaps a perfect definition of middling oratory. "He is sure of popularity," Beecher wrote, "who can come down among the people and address truth to them in their own homely way and with broad humor—and at the same time has an upper current of taste and chaste expression and condensed vigor."[5]

Middling rhetoric married the high and low. It was part of a larger change in the cultural landscape. As one historian has put it, American doctors and lawyers "typically strove to appear not only folksy but also erudite."[6] European visitors were fascinated by the way Americans self-confidently slid from the refined to the coarse. De Tocqueville noted that "Americans often mix their styles together in an odd way, sometimes putting words together which, in the mother tongue [British English], are carefully kept apart." Especially intriguing were the strange farragoes within one person at a given moment. Language contradicted manner, dress belied deportment, one word jarred with the next. People appeared "half-formed."

> I remember still more vividly—the incongruity was so ludicrous to one unaccustomed to the fashion of the country—a Southern poet reading me some of his verses, with one large plug of tobacco in his mouth; and every now and then, when his mouth became too full, stopping in the middle of some beautiful line to squirt another mouthful of tobacco juice towards the grate.[7]

Henry Ward Beecher provides a very good example of one kind of middling rhetoric. Beecher preached at both revivals and refined churches and he criticized any minister (rustic or urbane) who thought one better than another. Even in his church sermons, however, Beecher merged the high and low. He studied standard rhetoric—his oratory reflected that—

but he also scoured popular romances to find what he called "gorgeous vocabulary." Most of all, Beecher wanted "colloquial and familiar" language. He advised ministers to use "homely words" and "plain language." Their "subtle charm," he thought, "rang out suggestions to the popular heart." Don't be afraid to illustrate a truth in an "undignified manner," Beecher said, and avoid using a "literary style." Beecher was not afraid of slang. "The man who slimes his way," "to cuff about the controversies of theology," "to make a man cotton to you"—all appeared in his published sermons. Beecher scoffed at what he called the "superstition of dignity." His sermonizing was casually informal, as informal as everything else in his church. Again and again he said that the best public speaking sounded like a familiar conversation.

Beecher's colloquial language was part of an effort to create a theology of feeling. In contrast to his father, who was also a minister, Beecher never discussed formal theological doctrine. And he advised others to do the same. "Do not *prove* things too much," he told prospective ministers. Instead of formal reasoning, Beecher stressed the importance of emotion and feeling. He wanted to pull his audience to him by "suggestions to the popular heart." An 1856 *New York Times* article spoke of Beecher's magic, although noting that "here and there he introduces a strange, odd figure of speech, or some startling simile which seems to clash with the solemnity of the moment." Still, the paper saw the logic of middling oratory: "The question is not how to impress one or other fastidious intellect, but how to impress the generality of a congregation."[8]

Abraham Lincoln provides an example of a very different kind of middling style. Unlike Beecher, Lincoln reasoned with his audiences. But no one would call him refined. Born in Kentucky, raised in downstate Illinois, throughout his life Lincoln used the provincial dialect of the rural Midwest. He said "howdey" to visitors, spoke of being "hornswoggled," of "staying a spell," and of coming from "out yonder." Lincoln was also an inveterate storyteller: He loved the tales of the backwoods that he first heard from his barely literate father. In the White House, Lincoln found relief from the pressures of the war by spinning a few yarns to whatever audience he might capture. Yet Lincoln was hardly a rube. Although he had little formal schooling, the young Lincoln assiduously studied, among other things, Caleb Bingham's *Columbian Orator* and Samuel Kirkham's *English Grammar in Familiar Lessons*. Before he married, Lincoln would one night trade bawdy tales with fellow lawyers and the next remain at home reading poetry—Burns, Byron, and Shakespeare. Lincoln never pretended to know more than he did but he also never thought that reading

*Macbeth* (his favorite Shakespeare play) was anything but natural—Shakespeare was as much "his" as the tall tales of the backwoods. The Whig hierarchy in the 1840s valued Lincoln for his oratorical skills. He was adept at communicating the thoughts of the party to large audiences. When speaking to farmers Lincoln slipped into their shared dialect, but, as the Gettysburg Address makes clear, Lincoln could pen words as elegant as any in the English language.[9]

Middling rhetoric appeared in political oratory, popular preaching, and daily conversation. Its true carrier, however, was the popular press. The number of papers steadily increased during the nineteenth century and the 1830s innovation of the "penny press" (papers costing one cent) made newspapers accessible to all. Penny papers like Horace Greeley's *New York Tribune*, Benjamin Day's *New York Herald*, the Boston *Daily Times*, and the Philadelphia *Public Ledger* quickly became the most popular newspapers of the nation. A weekly edition of Greeley's *Tribune* circulated throughout the rural East and Midwest. Earlier journalists had aimed at refinement: Addison's essays were stylistic models; common pseudonyms like Cato or Publius reflected assumed acquaintance with classical culture. The new journalism, however, catered to popular taste, with slang making the tone breezier. Stories of marital infidelity and bizarre crimes were introduced. The social activities of refined ladies and gentlemen were reported often with snide comments about "aristocratic" behavior. Personal abuse of politicians was also common.[10]

The popular press did not eschew genteel behavior completely. Horace Greeley promised that the *Tribune* would be "worthy of the hearty approval of the virtuous and refined," a promise he did not always live up to.[11] Penny papers also showed skill with some of the mechanics of high culture. Disrespect for refined language never extended to grammar. The slangy vocabulary was nestled inside a refined syntax.

Not all newspapers adopted this style. Each city had papers, always with much smaller circulations, that were known as "gentlemen's newspapers." Newspapers provided the most visible evidence of the contrasting expressive cultures of nineteenth-century America. Whereas Horace Greeley once bragged that "I can write better slang than any editor in America," the poet-editor William Cullen Bryant kept an *Index Expurgatorius* listing some one hundred vulgarities and imprecisions that were never to mar the New York *Evening Post*. According to one writer, *The New York Times* was "temperate, habitually restrained," and "scholarly," but the *New York Tribune*'s "stupid rusticity of diction" and "school-boy use of expletives" were "offensive to good taste." While the *Chicago Tribune* in 1870 discussed the coarseness of American speech the *Chicago Times* abused politicians and others in contemporary slang. In 1852 *Arthur's Home Gazette* advertised a product free from "VULGARITY, LOW SLANG, PROFANITY, or anything that can corrupt or deprave the mind"; the New York *Commercial Advertiser* of the 1880s promised a paper that was "NEWSY! SPICY!! SUCCESSFUL!!!"[12]

The rising popularity of middling rhetoric was directly related to the changing demands of the public. Increased education, combined with democratic sentiment, smashed neoclassical canons of speaker and audience. No longer could refined arbiters presume deference; no longer would the elite set the tone. In a democratic culture, all would contribute.

Newspaper editors were keenly aware of which papers were popular and which catered to an elite.[13] Of another milieu, Lawrence Levine has written how nineteenth-century theatergoers routinely spoke, whistled, and hooted during performances, often to express contempt for actors not meeting popular standards.[14] Public speakers also discovered they could not avoid audience demands. Timothy Flint, the Harvard-educated minister, found that even using notes while speaking was a sign of literary effrontery in the West. "A frothy and turgid kind of ready eloquence is characteristic of every public speaker," he wrote. "I have broken over all early habits . . . and against my own taste and feelings, have become all things to all people."[15]

Nor was such behavior confined to the West. In the next chapter we shall see James Russell Lowell adopting populist poetics to reach a New England audience in the 1840s. By that time all mainstream politicians accepted the new style. The new political oratory was pioneered by Jacksonian politicians and journalists in the late 1820s and early 1830s.[16] At first the Whigs resisted, but by 1840 they had capitulated. Party leaders sent Ohio blacksmith John Bear around the country insulting Democratic journalists. Abraham Lincoln, called "the rail-splitter" for populist appeal, drawled provincial wisdom in the rural Midwest. Refined Whig gentlemen, hungry for political victory, found themselves applauding the very invective they had previously condemned. Even Whigs of the highest culture went "down to the people" in the 1840 campaign. Daniel Webster, one of the nation's most eloquent speakers, was asked by the party hierarchy to forgo his elegant speech for the campaign. With an authentic devotion to classical eloquence, Webster was no fan of middling oratory. The Massachusetts senator brooded over the decision, but he agreed, and his vulgar demagoguery proved enormously successful.[17]

Ciceronian oratory dazzled its audience into submission. Scottish rhetoric taught the civilized how to communicate with one another. Middling oratory willingly slipped below the refined to win the audience. Henry Ward Beecher, perhaps middling oratory's best theorist, advised ministers to be "en rapport" with their audience, and in direct contradiction to the Scottish rhetoricians he argued that ministers should shift their speaking styles to the cultural level of the crowd. Beecher caught the spirit of much modern mass communication by developing strategies for communicating to large, diverse audiences without antagonizing anyone. The ultimate goal, Beecher argued, was not authority over the listeners but sympathy with them. Sympathy—or the illusion of it—was at the heart of the new idioms. Middling rhetoric of all kinds shifted tone to be "en rapport" with the audience. Conciliatory colloquial prose, Beecher thought, would make "your labors successful among the multitudes."[18]

Nineteenth-century popular rhetoric undermined refined decorum in a number of ways. There was, for example, its intrusive informality, which took two forms. One was the use of regional folk dialects. Since the Renaissance, education was associated with leaving behind provincial, familiar cultures and engaging in a larger, more formal and cosmopolitan world. That the untutored were locked in their small universe the educated took for granted. But the idea that those with some contact with refined culture would freely use folk dialects seemed an insult to cosmopolitan values and provoked remarks such as that provincialisms were "food for local prejudices," or "men of letters" ought to resist provincial dialects because they "corrupted" national sentiment.[19]

Familiarity was also expressed by very subtle forms of linguistic informality, an example of which is Henry Ward Beecher's colloquial language. By the middle of the century, the increased use of the word *slang* reflected the growing debate over this informal sort of rhetoric. The word dates from the 1750s but was little used until the 1830s.[20] In the eighteenth century, *slang* was a synonym of *vulgar*. Early in the nineteenth century, however, the word began referring to the informal, chatty language of all social groups. *Slang* became a reference to a free-floating cultural style rather than a bound description of a specific social stratum.[21]

Still, it was not until the 1830s that the word began routinely turning up in novels, magazines, the *Congressional Globe*, and newspapers across the nation. Most of the reported uses related to the rise of partisan politics,[22] for indeed both political parties introduced popular slang in the 1830s. Both British and American gentlemen complained about language such as *go the whole hog* (a Democratic phrase for radical reform), *loco foco*, and *Tippecanoe and Tyler too*. The Whig gentleman George Templeton

Strong was happy that the new style brought his party success, but he thought it a "pretty commentary" that "His Majesty the People" could be "bamboozled by the slang of *hard cider*, *log cabins*, and *Tippecanoe*." The populist Whig Horace Greeley, on the other hand, found nothing wrong with such language.[23]

By the middle of the century, the issue of slang reached beyond politics into all areas of life. The first slang dictionaries appeared in French and English in the 1850s. In 1870 an Irish priest visiting America noted that the Irish were giving up their brogue but were adopting American phrases like *right away*. This he saw as a sign of assimilation, for America was "a great place for slang." He did have reservations, though, being shocked that the *New York Herald* referred to eternal punishment as "perpetual roasting" and "eternal basting." And upon reading an article on "pulpit slang," he was dismayed that Protestant ministers spoke of "knocking the bottom out of hell."[24]

A second major feature of middling poetics was calculated bluntness. Like the informality, this took both a soft and hard form. The soft form was often called, by the 1820s, "plain speaking," which should not be confused with the classical plain style, that which in antiquity was commonly thought best for teaching. The ancient plain style was simple, unadorned, good prose, not unlike good textbook prose of the twentieth century. Nineteenth-century plain speaking, on the other hand, had its roots in the prose of Swift and Paine. It was direct and rough, valuing truth over politeness, no matter how hard the language might sound. It marked the difference between saying, "I think you're mistaken there" and "That's stupid and you're wrong." As late as the 1860s and 1870s, children's magazines warned against "plain speech," associating it with the rustic and half-educated, and encouraging the use of civil, polite English in its stead.[25]

The hard form of blunt speech was the deliberately insulting. It was a particularly masculine style. Paradoxically, the egalitarian familiarity was often tied to abuse of outsiders. Andrew Jackson, Stephen Douglas, Benjamin Butler, and Andrew Johnson were just the most prominent nineteenth-century politicians who built their careers around bitter personal harangues.[26] It is somewhat difficult to explain exactly what was "unrefined" about such speech. Oratory had always had its share of invective. Demosthenes's "On the Crown" and Cicero against Catiline contain violent personal abuse; and certainly Federalist and Republican debates of the 1790s were not short of the same. It appears that when the invective became associated with the "semieducated" it was less easily tolerated. No longer was the insult the prideful disdain of one gentleman for another. Coming from the outside, the invective seemed more charged, more taunting, directed against a whole class instead of an individual.

The 1830s was a turning point. Andrew Jackson's 1832 veto of the charter of the Second Bank of the United States was not only a landmark for the constitutional authority of the President, it also altered the tone of public debate. Previous presidential messages were addressed to Congress. Jackson's veto message (actually penned by Roger Taney) directly appealed to the public. While most of the language was civil, certain key passages (excerpted in Democratic newspapers) complained of "aristocrats" who had turned the Bank into a "Hydra of corruption." Political opponents like Henry Clay and Daniel Webster, although expecting the veto, were shocked by the tone and derisively condemned its *ad captandum* style. Jackson's continued assaults on the nation's "aristocrats" irritated gentlemen through the 1830s. Upon reading the President's December 1834 message on the Bank, Philip Hone recoiled: "The language . . . is disgraceful to the President and humiliating to every American." It smelled "of the kitchen," closer to that of a "scullion" than a "gentleman."[27]

Democrats, however, did not own the idiom. Horace Greeley was typical of all kinds of popular newspaper editors who freely insulted opponents:

The Express is surely the basest and paltriest of all possible journals.

We defy the Father of lies himself to crowd more stupendous falsehoods into a paragraph. . . .

Major Noah! Why *won't* you tell the truth once in a century, for the variety of the thing.

These were some of the opening lines of articles Greeley penned for the *Tribune* during the 1840s and 1850s. He was constantly involved in libel suits, well known for ignoring what an 1855 biographer called "editorial dignity." Greeley vigorously defended his approach, dismissing the more civil style of the elite papers as evasive and "mealy-mouthed."[28]

The third major device of middling poetics was inflated speech. This style exalted words over meaning, replacing content with sound. One sort of inflated speech was bombast or the spread-eagle style. Politicians, ministers, and newspapermen produced pompous and often meaningless language to impress their audiences with the importance of the occasion and the learnedness of the speaker. In 1855, the *Knickerbocker Magazine* reported a typical example from a speech delivered in Vernon, Ohio, entitled "Virtue will Triumph":

> Orators have exhausted their spacious fund of rolling genius in delineating the incomprehensible vicissitudes of Virtue! Wise and prudent philosophers, with tacit interrogations, have levied upon it the profoundest powers of the mind; while the world, in anxious numbers, attracted by inherent curiosity, turns to it a solicitous eye. Retrospectively wafting our mental visions back upon the stream of time, all along the regular routine of providential jurisdiction we behold the approximate exterminations of morality, the nefariously diabolical javelons of Satanic influence maliciously hurled upon the zealous vindicators of truth. . . .[29]

If rude stump speaking dominated the campaign season, "high-falutin" bombast was widespread on ceremonial occasions. It raised the eyebrows, if not hackles, of many American and European gentlemen. One American wondered how "these pompous gentlemen rule in society" and noted that if one looked closely, one would find "the awful charm" broken by some pure vulgarity. A German immigrant tried to parody the style in Kentucky, filling the air with all the glittering nonsense (in English *and* Latin) he could dream of. His audience loved it. Such pomposity showed a readiness to adopt refined language and the ability to manipulate many of its features. But it also demonstrated an inability to hit the right pitch, the absence of refined taste. Pomposity was a style of the half-educated.[30]

The same was true of the other forms of inflated speech, jargon and euphemism. Until the closing decades of the nineteenth century, introducing strange technical languages into public speech was usually associated with lack of breeding. Rhetoric taught people to avoid arcane language, as did most etiquette books. Jargon did not only function as an insider code, as it does with late-twentieth-century professionals. Entrepreneurial hucksters like P. T. Barnum and patent medicine salesmen used strange "technical" language to create a sense of awe, a phenomenon noticed by Addison more than a century before.[31] Radical intellectuals, on the other hand, created new descriptive vocabularies because they felt old language had bad associations and needed to be discarded. From very different perspectives, both transcendentalists and utilitarians provide examples of this. To those who defended refined speech, the new vocabularies of such intellectuals unwittingly contributed to the decline of linguistic deportment.[32]

The final form of inflated speech was euphemism, the effort to do away with sensually charged language. Victorian linguistic prudery, which Mencken suggested reached its peak in the 1830s and 1840s, is well known.[33] If the plain speech was a particularly masculine activity, euphemism was feminine, or at least designed to please the female audience. *Limb* replaced *leg*. The word *corset* was deemed an insult. Servant girls were no longer *seduced*; they were now *betrayed*. The word *cock* became an anatomical vulgarism. After more than two centuries of use, the word *haycock* was replaced with *haystack*. The role of euphemistic language in nineteenth-century America is quite complicated, but we shall see that there was an important strain of resistance to such speech by defenders of refined language. To them, euphemism created a sickly, anemic speech. Like other forms of inflated language, euphemism showed the desire to act refined but the inability to be refined. It reflected the rise of the half-educated.

The power of the audience to alter the nation's "tone" should not be confused with the rule of the common man. Once the new situation was grasped, very sophisticated editors and politicians used the new styles to bend public opinion. Motives varied greatly. Even old-fashioned gentlemen found it hard to resist, although they chafed about it more than mainstream politicians did. The new rhetoric reflected not so much the "rule" of the common man as the arrival of a new public idiom. But precisely because middling rhetoric encouraged widespread movement across previously firm cultural borders, it contributed to the vertigo. Who belonged and who didn't? Who should speak in public and who shouldn't? James Fenimore Cooper, posing as a European visitor in *Notions of the Americans*, put it this way: "There has been so singular a compound of intelligence, kindness, natural politeness, coarseness and even vulgarity, in many of these persons, that I am often utterly baffled in the attempt to give them a place in the social scale."[34]

# II

The arrival of middling styles led to a war over the soul of American life. From the 1820s and 1830s through the end of the century, there was continual sniping between those favoring a more refined decorum and those committed to the new idioms. Many books could be written on this conflict; here I will address only the specific issue of how the new middling styles came into conflict with refined notions of personal deportment. The new vulgarity rudely challenged neoclassical notions about the morality of style, and buried in the debate about language were other issues. How was character defined? What was civility? And part of the cultural vertigo was connected to the fear that moral rectitude would be impossible in a democracy. With the people in command, the critics feared, *ethos* would sink into *persona*.

First, the middling mixture of refined and vulgar speech conflicted with older ideas about the morality of style. Indeed, among the refined and in various kinds of social thought, inherited assumptions about gentlemanly and ladylike deportment remained common. James Walker, who taught moral philosophy at Harvard for almost two decades and was president of the college between 1853 and 1860, defined character as the molding of good habits "into a consistent and harmonious whole." As the historian D. H. Meyer has pointed out, this was typical of all mid-nineteenth-century American moral philosophy: "The consistency and harmony of this whole was crucial: good character meant integrity, the perfect and harmonious interaction of all one's mental and moral powers."[35]

With good character understood as a unified soul, it was easy to make the traditional connection between good taste and moral probity. Dozens of nineteenth-century etiquette books did so, just as Cicero had some two millennia before. According to an 1821 edition of Hugh Blair's Rhetoric (abridged for "schools and academies"), "Improvement of taste seems to be more or less connected with every good and virtuous disposition." (Blair's Rhetoric remained in wide use through the middle of the century.) Similarly, an 1857 introductory reader had, across from its title page, drawings of two boys reading. One was lounging, his slovenly body rudely inconsistent with the refined literature in the book. The other "correct" reader was upright in his chair, his posture as dignified as the words he read, illustrating that there was to be an integrity to language, manner, and dress. The logic of the connection between deportment and morality was laid out in an 1847 article on language in the *Ladies' Repository*: "As we become refined in our tastes and feelings, we will the more disdain the tame and the vulgar, and will aspire with fervor to the elevated and noble."[36]

With "good character" tied to a uniformly refined way of life, the roughness, informality, and easy provincialism of middling rhetoric violated moral standards of personal conduct. There is no better example of how a nineteenth-century gentleman could think that a few words of slang polluted the sanctity of civil character than one densely packed half page of an 1857 *Blackwood's Magazine*. It relates a momentary encounter between a group of British gentlemen and an American traveler. Upon hearing that the American has come from Florence, one of the Englishmen asks him, "Of course you were in raptures with the Venus de Medici?" but the American replies, "Well, sir, to tell you the truth, I don't care much about those stone gals." My "friends collapsed," the author reported, brimming with "anger" and "indignation." The next two paragraphs also bristle with choler, not so much an argument as a series of staccato outbursts of the sort one makes when reduced to utter stupefaction.

The article makes clear that the American's *tone* is a much more profound judgment on civilized life than his stated opinion of classical statuary. The Venus de Medici, "a thing Praxiteles might have touched with his chisel, or Pericles have looked upon, to be called a 'stone gal.' Had he doubted its genuineness, or spoken of it as a specimen of secondary art, he might have been deemed critical, hypercritical; but this was classic impiety, an irreverence, a profanity." The article then lunges into some comments on gentleness and politeness, the American's words are described as an "uncivism" and an "egoism." This assessment appears strange to our ears; why would calling the Venus de Medici a "stone gal" be evidence of naked selfishness? No explanation is given, but the traditional ties between refined words and civil character are clearly implied. Without transition the article then turns to "provincialism." The impious tone of the American is evidence of failed cosmopolitanism, of the inability to see "the good and the true everywhere." Again no explanation is given but again none is needed. Art and manners are by implication tied to the fate of civilizations. The article abruptly ends by discussing manners and "the hierarchy." The social order civility imposes has collapsed in America. Wealth, refinement, and prestige no longer cohere as they should.[37]

If many of the refined, both British and American, continued to connect refinement with morality, there were others, more comfortable with middling culture, who spoke about principled behavior without worrying about deportment. Late in the century, in a popular text for adolescents of both sexes, Samuel Smiles noted that a "man may be gruff, and even rude, and yet still be good at heart and of sterling character."[38] In the partisan frays of the 1830s, Abraham Lincoln found himself accused of being a liar. Lincoln answered the charge, contending he had "a character to defend. . . ." On that occasion and others, Lincoln associated good character with "consistency," with leading a life unified by principle. But Lincoln never linked this to refined language or deportment, thus implying norms quite different from those of Cicero, Chesterfield, or many of his more refined contemporaries.[39]

There were precedents for this. Christianity, particularly strains of primitive Christianity, was quite skeptical of classical ideas about the morality of style.[40] Jesus, of course, was a humble carpenter and the Apostles rough, simple men. Any Christian could be holy. Such thinking was alive in antebellum America. *The Friend*, an American Quaker magazine, variously bemoaned the crude vulgarity of religious oratory, claiming that language was directly tied to good character, but also calling grammar "a vain conceit" and unnecessary for a minister. Here language was connected to good character but not to refined syntax; questions of substance were severed from questions of style.[41]

If one difference between middling and refined culture was about the relationship between uniform refinement and unified soul, another concerned the nature of civility. To refined critics, the informality of the American language was insulting. Slang and other gestures of familiarity violated canons of civil behavior.

Now legendary, American informality, which Europeans continue to comment on,[42] was just being discovered in the early nineteenth century.[43] From lower classes, familiarity undermined deference. Servants ate at the same table with their employers. Carriage drivers chatted as if friends with their fares.[44] Gentlemen found themselves being referred to as "friend," "fellow," or "stranger" instead of "Sir" or "Mr.———."[45] Both gentlemen and ladies found their first names used indiscriminately;[46] the respectful distance the formal titles maintained was destroyed.

But the problem went even deeper. Even among men and women of the same ostensible social position (similar income, similar occupation), convention was tossed to the wind. From the 1830s through the close of the century one way the refined identified people of middling culture was through the latter's indiscriminate familiarity. Fanny Kemble wrote of "that odious Dr.———, who came into the drawing room without asking or being asked, sat himself down, and called me 'Miss Fanny.' I should like to have thrown my tea at him." When Charles Murray arrived at a New York farm in the 1830s he was struck that the owner immediately referred to him as "Charlie," something that "would doubtlessly appear very *familiar* to an English ear. . . ." (He was even more surprised when the hired help also called him Charlie.) Several decades later George Templeton Strong archly commented on the cloying familiarity of Henry Ward Beecher's Plymouth Church: "Verily they are a peculiar people. They all call each other by their first names and perpetually kiss each other." As late as the 1890s, J. H. Holland, the editor of *The Century* magazine, was asking, "How can a man lift his head under the derogation of being called 'Sam' by every man, young and old, whom he may meet in the street?"[47]

Traditional refined decorum was premised on dignified reserve. For the refined critics, politeness *was* distance, *was* reserve. It was how one was civil; one showed respect for people by *not* treating them familiarly. This is what George Eggleston had in mind when he contrasted William Cullen Bryant, who always called even the youngest men "Mr.————," with Grover Cleveland, whose greeting was a slap on the back and a "Why hello, Eggleston! How are you?" As Eggleston put it: "Had I been an intimate personal friend . . . I should have accepted his greeting as a manifestation of cordiality. . . . I was in fact only slightly acquainted with him and . . . his familiarity of address impressed me as boorish."[48]

Middling decorum, however, was just the opposite. Being civil meant being friendly. The slang, informality, and first names were all ways of being *nice*. Unyielding reserve implied not respect but a pose of superiority: It was acting like an aristocrat. A new kind of civility was arising. Middling ritual interaction was bent on creating mildly affective bonds between people (Beecher's oratory was emblematic of this). And central to middling decorum was the idea of a familiar conversation.

Confusions about standards of conduct led to another fight concerning language and character—women were speaking in public. The American Revolution had not changed the fact that women were not supposed to orate; it was only in the 1820s and 1830s that women began appearing on speakers' platforms. It was controversial behavior. In 1828, Fannie Wright gave a number of lectures in Cincinnati, the first lecture *series* given by a woman and certainly the first female oratory to capture the whole nation's attention. Newspaper hostility, while not universal, was at times intense. As the New York *Free Enquirer* put it, by speaking in public, Wright had "with ruthless violence broken loose from the restraints of decorum, which draws a circle around the life of a woman." The *Louisville Focus* argued that Wright had "leaped over the boundary of female modesty" and committed an act against nature. The New York *American* claimed that Wright "waived all claims" to courtesy since by speaking in public she "ceased to be a woman" and became, instead, "a female monster." Such criticism appeared despite the fact that all accounts, even the hostile ones, agreed that Wright's oratory was refined. She violated none of the linguistic rules of contemporary rhetoric. Her breach of decorum was simply that she—a woman—spoke in public.[49]

In the 1830s, female abolitionists faced similar assaults. Abolitionist women had been speaking in private houses to other women from the early 1830s. The oratorical power of one of these women—Angelina Grimké—gradually expanded her audience. First, husbands came to listen with their wives, but soon Grimké outgrew private parlors. By the middle of 1837, she was speaking to both men and women (called "promiscuous audiences" in the nineteenth century) in public forums. As with Wright, Grimké was attacked for violating feminine standards of decorum despite the refinement of her speech. The *Boston Reformer* argued that if men properly performed their duties there would be no reason for women like Grimké to do so. The *Boston Morning Post* stated that Grimké could reel off an antislavery speech with as much grace and style as if she were at a spinning wheel, which, the paper added, was where she should be. In 1837 the General Assembly of Congregational Ministers issued its "Brookfield Bull" affirming their belief that women should not speak in public. Grimké's oratory precipitated the split in the abolitionist movement between radicals and moderates. William Lloyd Garrison, the nation's leading radical abolitionist, defended the right of women to speak in public: "We allow our women liberty of the press—why should we deny them liberty of speech?"[50]

In one sense, the issue was resolved by the 1850s when the number of female orators expanded considerably. By the end of that decade, at least in the North and West, it was established that women would speak in public. Moreover, during the 1840s the women's styles of speaking became as diverse as the men's. While speakers like Lucretia Mott and Lucy Stone would continue to use "ladylike" English, others fell into middling idioms. Abby Kelley could be as abusive as any male editor, Ernestine Rose as flowery as any pompous politician, and Sojourner Truth had all the rustic dignity of Abraham Lincoln. By 1859, New York bureaus that booked lyceum lecturers around the nation advertised women speakers as well as men.[51]

In other ways, however, the issue was not closed by 1860. For one thing, Southern women did not begin to speak in public until the Civil War.[52] More important, women as a whole continued to hear that public speaking was not "ladylike." The number of female speakers remained small and there was far more pressure on them than on men to speak in a refined manner.[53] Even when not actively discouraged, women usually got no substantial encouragement. To this day, more men are comfortable speaking in public than are women, something clear to anyone who has taught a class in an American university. Residues of ancient taboos persist far beyond any "official" end to barriers against women speaking in public.

All the vulgarity, all the confusion about roles, refined critics thought, was connected to the new power of the audience. In a democracy, language served the crowd. American ladies and gentlemen made this criticism, but Europeans felt it more strongly, often being unprepared for the experience.

In 1864 Ernest Duvergier de Hauranne stepped off a train in Galena, Illinois, "a small village perched astride a valley," and by chance came across a speaker preparing to orate. Although Hauranne did not know it, the speaker was Richard James Oglesby, currently a Union general and after the war three-time governor of the state. Oglesby began "not without a little grace and dignity."

> Little by little, however, he grew heated; he frowned; his face got red; his expression became menacing, his eyes wild. He began to pound his fists, to stamp his feet, to twist backward, to lean far forward, to throw his arms about like an epileptic. . . . For two hours, he carried on without a halt, like a caged beast. From time to time his enthusiasm suddenly evaporated; he wiped his brow, sat on the railing with his feet dangling, and exchanged humorous remarks in a familiar manner with the audience; then he bounced up again, as if galvanized by an electric shock, and heaped on an imaginary adversary every insult known to the language of the barroom.

The curses, flattery, and inappropriate familiarity exhausted Hauranne as much as the audience response shocked him: "You should have heard the applause of the listeners and their delighted, prolonged cheers every time some great blasphemy fell from his lips. I almost thought I was in the midst of a pack of bloodthirsty wolves. . . ." This "strange scene" was far removed from French rural gatherings "where some elegant gentleman addresses our worthy peasants in that dignified and protective style" or even from meetings of the French proletariat where "decency" and "civilized manners" ruled more often than not. Still, Hauranne saw that the "wild use of language" was intimately connected to the desires of the audience: "These people deal and wish to deal only with their equals; one has to speak their language, to be even more vulgar than they are." The speaker was "only making concessions to popular taste: the American people, especially here in the West, love these raw, bloody slabs of butcher's meat."[54]

Refined critics argued that this demanding glare of the *demos* withered principled behavior. Political Jacksonians, Philip Hone bitterly confided to his diary, would "sell their souls" for victory with no regard for "the refined feelings of gentlemen." In an 1841 advice book a minister warned young men that politics was more detrimental to character building than any other career. Popular oratory was critical, for those men with "more than ordinary talent for talking" too easily fell to "seductive visions" of political power. The "convivial usages" of electioneering fixed bad habits and catering to the *demos* replaced moral probity: "The question . . . is no longer what is true and what is right, but what will be popular."[55]

For refined critics, then, middling lapses in taste were truly connected to the failure of character and the power of the crowd. Speakers often pretended to be "of the people" to reach an audience. Although well-educated, an old political foe remembered, Illinois governor John Reynolds "took great pains" to hide it. Although familiar with English literature, "he pretended to abhor books. He wished to be considered one of the people, and used intentionally on proper occasions the common talk of the backwoods settlers. . . . His speeches were in part grotesquely pathetic, in part ludicrously comical, always attracting great crowds."[56] To this more refined critic, Reynolds was "selling his soul" for popularity just as Daniel Webster had done in the campaign of 1840. Popular democracy was smothering the very possibility of moral rectitude in public affairs. To translate the critique into a contemporary idiom, the middling mix of refined and vulgar speech was interpreted as role playing, as donning masks (*persona*) instead of revealing character (*ethos*). Rameau's nephew now ruled.

Although this critique of popular oratory saw how much democratic rhetoric would pander, it missed many of the complexities of middling oratory. While some speakers and editors did "fake it" to humbug audiences, for others a folk dialect was simply a way to communicate in a shared idiom. Black ministers would speak to their flocks in Black English, not because they did not know the standard dialect, and not because they wanted to manipulate their audience, but simply because the idiom was "theirs."[57] When Lincoln spoke to farmers in a rural Midwest drawl, he was only slipping into the speech he had been brought up with. It by no means meant that all reasoning would stop. Middling styles eased social mobility. They allowed one to speak in public without having to master the gentry's tone.

Moreover, audiences *expected* such speech. There was cynical manipulation, but there was also the democratic sense that the public ruled. As Beecher had said, the orator must establish sympathy with his audience, not authority over them. Even when Horace Greeley sprayed invective throughout New York City, he was not simply manipulating his public, or pretending to be somebody he wasn't, he was relying on stylistic preferences *he shared* with his readers.[58]

There were many gentlemen and ladies, in fact, who realized this. Especially in the years before the Civil War, many of the refined tried to find ways to understand and accommodate the new styles.[59] Yet they were hampered by other commitments. Popular practices were changing but formal social thought was not. Being highly educated still meant acting like a "gentleman" or a "lady," even while the rhythms of popular life taught people to slide back and forth from the refined to the vulgar. The educated were caught between their commitment to refined language and the headiness of *vox populi vox dei*. Assumptions about gentlemanly or ladylike behavior had come into sharp conflict with the nation's idiom.

# III

It was not only refined men and women who listened to messages about language, education, and the morality of style; such thinking dominated *popular* textbooks as well. *All* educational thought collided with popular practice, which is revealed in no better way than by the elementary English grammar, a text that became phenomenally important in the early nineteenth century. Into the 1850s, popular grammars were written with the same informing premises that had been at work in the mid-eighteenth century. Refined language continued to be the goal.

This was the case despite the fact that in the 1820s and 1830s a host of new grammars were written challenging the tenets of the eighteenth-century texts. The new grammarians saw themselves as populists, tied to the concurrent social attack on gentry decorum. Drawing on strains of eighteenth-century radical thought, the radical grammarians suggested that rationality replace refined custom as the criterion of good speech, that gentry usage no longer guide. But the reformers' efforts fell short because the educational establishment overwhelmingly remained committed to refined custom. Moreover, populist politicians and editors did not want some "rationalistic" syntax. They remained wedded to customary language—they just wanted a plurality of customs, both refined and raw. Both the Horace Greeleys and the Henry Raymonds, for very different ends, remained committed to the study of traditional syntax. The reforming grammarians found no public.

The spread of elementary grammars that began in the late eighteenth century exploded after 1800. The number of grammars simply becomes impossible to count. One writer has counted more than 250 different grammars published in America in the first half of the century. He was surely conservative in his estimate.[60] Not only were grammars published in New York, Cincinnati, and Boston, the centers of educational publishing, but many others were written (or plagiarized) by local schoolmen and published in places as out of the way as Montpelier, Vermont; Norwich, Connecticut; and Cazenovia, New York. The number of grammars published gives no indication of the number of copies printed. Caleb Bingham's *Young Ladies Accidence*, first published in 1785, was estimated to have circulated about a hundred thousand copies by 1820. Samuel Kirkham reported in 1837 that he was selling sixty thousand copies of his *English Grammar in Familiar Lessons* each year. Such figures were probably hyperbole; they nevertheless do suggest the growing importance of the subject. Easily the most popular grammar of the time was Lindley Murray's *English Grammar, Adapted to Different Classes of Learners*. First published in 1795, this book has more than three hundred known editions published prior to 1850. Between 1810 and 1830 Murray was reprinted 195 times, an average of just under ten new editions each year for a twenty-year span. In the 1820s Murray was reprinted 85 times. By comparison, James Fenimore Cooper's most popular novel of that decade, *The Spy*, was reprinted seven different times and Sir Walter Scott's *Waverley* was issued in nine different American editions.[61]

Between the 1780s and 1820s grammar was firmly established as a basic subject in American popular education. Eighteenth-century diffusion was more limited. Elias Smith, the Vermont farmer's son, had not even heard of "grammar" until the 1780s, but by the time he wrote his autobiography in 1816 he apologized for that fact, indicating that there was something strange about not knowing what the subject was. In 1800, the schools attended by the sons and daughters of the Yale faculty did not yet serve up grammar, but by 1826 a writer in the *North American Review* was complaining that popular parental prejudice in favor of the subject stood in the way of any critical thinking about it. Parents forced teachers "to follow the beaten path."[62]

In rural areas parents were often uninterested. The school superintendent of Adams County, Pennsylvania, who reported that "none of the parents wish their children to study English grammar and geography," was not unusual. These parents found support for their views in the antiauthoritarian popular culture and from politicians and ministers who flattered them in their own dialects. Ruralites distrusted the cultural imperialism of grammar; they had no use for those small books that told them their folk speech was wrong.[63]

Yet even in rural areas grammar was studied by many. At age nine in the 1840s William Torrey Harris was introduced to Roswell Smith's grammar in North Killingly, Connecticut. At the same time grammar was "carefully and correctly taught" by Dartmouth students and "young women of the best education that the times afforded" in Salisbury, New Hampshire. George Eggleston recalled that Samuel Kirkham's grammar was studied in Vevay, Indiana, before anyone there had yet heard of Horace Mann.[64] Moreover, the subject was not only studied in schools: "The young Horace Mann followed his sister Rebecca about the house, holding a Noah Webster grammar in his hand, as she listened to his lessons while attending to her chores." Abraham Lincoln, Andrew Johnson, and Horace Greeley each studied the subject on his own. Each had rustic parents with little interest in education. Each was raised in a rural setting. Each had limited formal schooling. Greeley was reportedly unpopular with girls in the small Vermont hamlet he grew up in because he constantly corrected their grammar. That simple fact conjures up the tensions that must have been found within all rural areas as well as the imperatives felt by those with ambitions larger than the farms or small towns they hailed from. Even if refined syntax was not always spoken it should be known. In nonfiction print, the authority of standard grammar was never seriously challenged.[65]

Through the 1820s the most popular grammars were those first published in the 1780s and 1790s. Caleb Alexander's *A Grammatical System of the English Language*, Caleb Bingham's *The Young Ladies' Accidence*, and Noah Webster's *Grammatical Institutes of the English Language* were among the best known. Lindley Murray's *English Grammar* was the most popular among the dozens of others also published.

The grammars of Murray, Webster, Bingham, and Alexander were based on those published in the 1760s by Joseph Priestley, Robert Lowth, and John Ash. Format and terminology were largely unchanged. From one book to the next not much different was said about nouns, pronouns, the subjunctive mood, or irregular verbs. The description of appropriate English remained remarkably stable from the 1760s through the 1820s.[66]

In the 1820s, defenders of polite usage were shocked by newly written grammars that challenged the tenets of the earlier texts. Grammarians like William Fowle, James Gilchriest, William Cardell, and Joseph Wright claimed that polite custom was not grammatical English. Some of the most radical attacked the idea of politeness altogether; others merely stopped at calling for a standard of elegance removed from custom. All agreed, though, that reason must replace custom as the standard of good English.[67]

Many of the new books looked for philosophical ballast from a philological treatise entitled *The Diversions of Purley*. This was written in the late eighteenth century by a British nobleman, John Horne Tooke, whose philology was introduced to Americans by Noah Webster in his *Dissertations on the English Language* (1789). Inspired by Tooke's etymological speculations, Webster argued that eighteenth-century grammarians had soiled the purity of the English language. He said that grammarians like Lowth had tried to force the English language to follow Latin grammatical rules. Webster also argued that grammar should be analogous and rational instead of customary, although he did not directly cite Tooke on these points. In 1807 Webster published his *Philosophical and Practical Grammar of the English Language*, a text he explicitly based on Tookean principles. In that book, Webster threw out established grammatical terminology, argued against contemporary custom, and claimed his research was based on "pure" Saxon English. Webster hoped he could replace all the misguided grammars currently in use, including his own earlier text. The book was a financial failure and by the 1820s could not be readily found even in Boston. In 1828, Webster reprinted much of the grammar as part of the introduction to his *American Dictionary of the English Language*.[68]

The reforming grammarians of the 1820s followed the lead of Webster, all arguing that analogy should intrude upon and correct custom. Even refined custom, they rightly observed, was arbitrary. Theirs was the dream of a "rational" language, a language where principle and internal logic would be the final arbiter. The reigning grammars were likened to the science of the Dark Ages when "the earth was thought to be a platform." Rationality had to triumph over received wisdom. "Whatever is opposed to philosophical correctness," William Cardell thought, "will prove as mischievous and inapplicable in practice as it is incongruous in theory." These grammarians believed that there was a universal grammar that corrected the vagaries of custom and that English had to conform to it. According to John Lewis, the philologist will find "the true principles of language, and the materials of its formation combined . . . not arbitrarily, but by human reason—not understood by consent, but by the force of a law of our nature."[69]

The reforming grammarians defended some "low" speech. Noah Webster argued that the terms of the farmer, seaman, and artificer were legitimate and necessary. Just because the refined have "no concern with the workshop" does not mean they have the right to condemn what Webster called "vulgar words," words "used by the common people." Webster, in 1807, strongly attacked Lowth and Lindley Murray for condemning *you was*. It was not a solecism, Webster argued. The introduction of *you were* in the singular was a good example of the silly overrefinement of late-eighteenth-century linguists.[70]

It was, however, very difficult to find specific examples of "low" language favored by the reforming grammarians. It was rather their theoretical boldness that caused concern. The radicals argued that "common people" naturally tend toward a more rational language. According to William Cardell, "the nations of unlettered men so adapted their language to philosophic truth, that all . . . research can find no essential rule to reject or change." Webster, in his 1807 grammar, thought that nineteen out of every twenty linguistic errors were caused by literary men. Common people, on the other hand, tended toward uniformity—toward analogy. That "popular tendency," Webster asserted, "is governed by the natural, primary principles of all languages." William Fowle also thought that the common people naturally veered toward universal grammar. Many "of the vulgarisms which bring upon them the sneer of grammarians," Fowle wrote, "are only the use of the regular for the irregular form of verbs." To say "I breaked the pencil" was more rational than saying "I broke the pencil." The "vulgar" version was based on rational analogy (add *ed* to form the past tense) while the "polished" version was merely customary.[71]

Fowle and Gilchrest, the most radical, attacked all polite usage. They raged against fawning schoolmen who perpetuated gentry authority by teaching refined custom. They railed against an educational system that deified fat, pompous, self-satisfied Brahmins whose status was reinforced by whatever words dropped from their mouths. Fowle saw it as nothing less than a war between himself and the *North American Review*. Gilchrest scorned that "polite literature" containing "nothing but dull regularity and sickly exotics." Nothing was more important than overthrowing those "popular doctrines" that elevated "delicacy, elegance, propriety and such precious matters." Voltaire, Pope, and Johnson were all assaulted; Lindley Murray, Robert Lowth, and Hugh Blair abused. Even Virgil was "a dull versifier"; Tully, "a petty rhetorician." All their "*slabbery* nonsense about taste" now constituted a literary despotism, yet feeble contemporaries could not stand the light of reason, preferring the shelter of Addison, "like asses under a stately shrub."[72]

Cardell and Webster affirmed the expressive power of elegance but they were no gentler with their enemies. Johnson, Lowth, and Blair had scratched the purity of Queen Anne prose; their grammars, rhetorics, and dictionaries had done more harm than good. Webster and the Virginia schoolmaster John Lewis even felt kindly toward the usage of gentlemen but they still argued that analogy should correct custom.[73]

Their rationalism was yoked to etymological speculation that led these grammarians to claim they were recovering pure Saxon English. No conflict arose between reason and tradition. It was the established grammarians, the reformers argued, who had disrupted tradition—their Greek and

Latin rules had smothered Gothic English. It was Lowth, Murray, and the others who had destroyed the purity of the English language. It disgusted William Fowle that Shakespeare and the King James Bible were presented to children as examples of false grammar. (In his traditional grammar, Noah Webster had done just that.) Gilchrest argued that the first rule of composition was to be free and bold; the second to adopt no model of style. Freeing writers and speakers from the shackles of artificial grammatical rules was a recurring theme in their books. As William Fowle put it:

> There was a time, before grammars were invented to clip the wings of fancy, and shackle the feet of genius, when it was considered more important to express a thought clearly and forcibly, than, as now, prettily and grammatically; when genius would as soon have stopped to accommodate itself to a rule of syntax, as the eagle would to take lessons from the domestic goose.

History, reason, and genius all spoke powerfully against contemporary grammar.[74]

The specter of radicalism surrounded these grammars for more than philological reasons. John Horne Tooke was best known in America not as a speculative linguist but as a British Jacobin who in the 1790s went to jail for treason. Moreover, in the early nineteenth century Tooke's memory was cared for by British utilitarians like James Mill and Henry Hazlitt.[75] Finally, in the Boston area where the *North American Review*, the *American Journal of Education*, and the *United States Literary Gazette* debated the new grammar, the most vocal proponent of reform was William B. Fowle, a well-known traitor to the literary hierarchy of the city. Born in 1795 to a pump and block maker who had longed for a literary career, Fowle grew up in a home that valued education. Although money was not available for college, the young Fowle deeply impressed William Ellery Channing, who offered to pay the boy's way at Harvard. Fowle, however, refused, scorning the "artificial systems" taught at the university. He threw himself into common school teaching to bring basic education to the sons and daughters of the social strata from which he sprang. Later he coedited the *American Journal of Education* and served in the state senate. Throughout his life he remained on the edges of the Boston literary community, deeply interested in the doings of its lionized gentlemen but scorning their hubris and thanking heaven that "poverty prevented my receiving a collegiate education, which would have furnished me with a diploma to wrap and bury my intellect."[76]

Traditional grammarians feared the radicalism of the followers of Horne
Tooke. The "philosophical" speculations would set loose the language,
free it from refined customs built up over the years. To adopt such a
system, they felt, would guarantee barbarism. Were the reformers to
"recede into the native obscurity and barbarity of the ancient Britons,
Picts, and Vandals," Samuel Kirkham asserted, "the cause of learning and
refinement would not suffer." Whether or not the reforming grammarians
desired to undermine the literary language, they played into the hands of
those that did. One hostile reviewer called Joseph Wright "a grammatical
O'Toole" whose *Philosophical Grammar of the English Language* would no
doubt "signal relief to many a lazy urchin. . . ."[77]

The strident reviews, testy footnotes, and spirited prefaces all testify
to the import of the matter. Grammarians took their quarrels seriously.
Yet few others did. Although ferocious, the debates did not echo past the
tiny number of men actively engaged in writing grammars. The reformers,
whose books rarely went into a second printing, never made an impact
upon the schools because teachers remained overwhelmingly committed
to traditional grammar. Between the 1830s and 1850s, when New York
teachers reported to state officials on their teaching methods, not uncom-
monly they told of asking the best-read members of the community to
decide thorny problems of usage. Even in small towns in upstate New
York teachers deferred to the customary usage of the best read. In over
twenty years of reporting, rarely did a teacher speak about "rational"
grammar.[78]

Textbooks multiplied in the twenties and thirties. Murray, Bingham,
and Alexander slowly fell from favor, and a host of newcomers swarmed
into the schools. By 1840 Roswell Smith's *English Grammar on the Productive
System* was the most popular grammar in Massachusetts and Connecticut
and was also widely used in Ohio. In New York, Samuel Kirkham's *English
Grammar in Familiar Lessons* was most in demand and he was not unknown
in Indiana and Illinois. *The Institutes of English Grammar* by Goold Brown
also circulated widely. In Vermont and New Hampshire, William Well's
*A Grammar of the English Language* was recommended and used.[79] Dozens
of others competed. Yet all the successful grammars repackaged the "traditional" wisdom. Amid the widespread complaints by educational reformers of bad teachers, the new textbooks innovated in presentation but
not content.[80] Again the grammarians emphasized the humble nature of
their calling. Again they cautioned that they were simplifying old texts,
still alluding to the genius of Lowth and Priestley.

Old messages about usage and cultural authority were repeated. Grammarians continued to be committed to a refined way of life. They continued to argue that grammar should inform all speech acts; grammar's ties to civil decorum continued to be stressed. Without English grammar, one wrote, "it is presumptuous to expect an appearance in good society free from embarrassment. . . ." Goold Brown asserted that grammatical study dignified the "whole character." "How can he be a man of refined literary taste," Brown asked, "who cannot speak and write his native tongue grammatically?" Avoid low and technical speech, the grammarians cautioned. Samuel Kirkham's *English Grammar* included samples of rustic speech to be avoided. The *Institutes of English Grammar* advised against using "low and provincial expressions" such as "says I," "thinks I to myself," or "to get into a scrape." There was no pity for those reckless minds "lamentably careless of what they utter. . . ." Grammarians were not unaware of the raucous political oratory that had become popular. They condemned those sequacious politicians who used "local phrases" sweet only to those "whose ears can revel in low epithets and vulgar phrases." Hooker, Milton, Johnson, Byron, and Scott constituted the standard of good English, not "those whose lips are eloquent in party slang and political cant."[81]

If educators defended traditional syntax as a part of a unified refined decorum, many Americans happily used the grammars for different ends. While the refined grammarians wrote the books to outlaw folk dialects, the grammars were often used by people like Horace Greeley, Abraham Lincoln, or Southern black ministers to become bidialectal. Such people felt that grammar could be studied without ever needing to be consistently refined, without ever associating refined syntax with character. Grammars of genteel syntax could be used instrumentally, to develop skills needed for specific occasions.

The philosophical grammarians viewed themselves as populists, but they misread the nature of the middling style. Popular speakers and editors did not want to master a "rational" syntax. To be a popular speaker, as Henry Ward Beecher noted in 1835, one had to know *both* refined and unrefined ways of talking. Middling writers and speakers did not want to transcend custom or "deconstruct" the lines separating refined and raucous; they wanted to make many customs legitimate. The philosophical grammarians tried to reintroduce a style of thought derived from late-eighteenth-century radical intellectuals, but nineteenth-century popular rhetoric ran along completely different paths.[82]

Consequently, what Robert Lowth had presented to university students, refined Londoners, and country gentlemen in the 1760s was by the

1860s being passed to millions of American schoolchildren. Whoever picked up Peter Bullions's *Analytical and Practical Grammar of the English Language* (1853) still read the precepts about good usage first worked out in the second half of the eighteenth century. The usage that gives law to the language was derived from widely read authors. Good English was reputable, national, and contemporary. Bullions drew his thoughts directly from George Campbell's *The Philosophy of Rhetoric*, first published in 1776. When Abraham Lincoln opened Samuel Kirkham's *English Grammar in Familiar Lessons* in New Salem, Illinois, in the 1830s, he too was informed that the best English was that of "speakers, distinguished for their elocution and other literary attainments, and writers, eminent for their correct taste, solid matter, and refined manner."[83]

# IV

Tensions similar to those underlying antebellum grammatical debates also informed the pre–Civil War discussion of the English dictionary. The eighteenth-century model, that of Johnson, reigned unchallenged until the 1820s. Then Noah Webster's dictionary was published. Like the reforming grammarians, Webster championed rationality and analogy over the lure of custom. Like the reforming grammarians, Webster failed with the public. Popular dictionary makers, like successful grammarians, were interested in the wide diffusion of refined language.

The dictionary of the English language never rose to the popularity of the English grammar, but it did come close. The dictionary spread by shrinking. In the 1790s lexicons about the size of mass-market paperbacks were widely published for the first time. These "pocket" dictionaries, or dictionaries "in miniature" as they were called, quickly became big sellers, followed closely by octavo-sized texts. Dictionaries, first printed in the United States only in the 1790s, by the early years of the nineteenth century rolled off the presses of American publishers with great regularity. Traveling book salesmen sold dictionaries everywhere they went, and hasty notes to their suppliers asking for more were not unusual.[84]

Clearly by the early nineteenth century merchants kept dictionaries in their offices. Country lawyers and doctors also felt the need for a handy reference text.[85] The common school movement also contributed to the spread of the dictionary. By the 1830s school administrators were teaming up with publishers to pry money from state legislatures to purchase dictionaries. One dictionary in each of the nation's schoolrooms was their goal and by the 1850s Northern and Midwestern state assemblies were complying. In rural areas, school dictionaries served the same purpose that a public library's dictionary serves today. In the midst of an argument parties were known to stop and check disputed meanings at the local school.

Schoolmen encouraged students to own a dictionary. Dictionaries "in miniature" were also packaged as dictionaries "for the common school student." Over twenty of these dictionaries were written and published in the United States in the first half of the century. And others, such as Samuel Johnson's dictionary, continued to be printed in miniature form in the United States until the 1830s. As more students purchased dictionaries, parents became accustomed to the idea that each home should have its own dictionary. By the 1850s, dictionaries were common fixtures in homes of those with even moderate educational credentials. One hundred years before, owning a dictionary of the English language was odd even for the best educated.[86]

As they had with grammars, American schoolmen and scholars rejected radical new approaches to lexicography. Until the 1820s, the dictionaries most often seen in America were John Walker's *A Critical Pronouncing Dictionary of the English Language* (1791) and Thomas Sheridan's *A General Dictionary of the English Language* (1780). In 1828, though, Noah Webster published *An American Dictionary of the English Language*. The product of twenty years' work, it was the first major challenge to the hegemony of Johnson. Webster had a genius for defining words and his new vocabulary was well received. Though among scholars Webster's etymologies caused considerable debate, for the general public clearly the most controversial feature of the new dictionary was its simplified spelling.

Webster's interest in simplified spelling went back to the 1780s. It was a concern he shared first with Benjamin Franklin and later with several followers of John Horne Tooke.[87] Some of Webster's spellings merely lent authority to changes that were under way: Americans already had begun to drop the *u* from words like *honour* and *neighbour*, leave off the *k* in *musick*, *publick*, and *logick* and turn around the *re* in *metre*, *theatre*, and *spectre*. Webster's respellings, however, did not stop there. *Ieland* "is the genuine English word," he argued, *island* "an absurd compound." Although *tongue* was accepted, Webster argued that "the true spelling is *tung*." *Women*, he declared, should be spelled *wimen*. *Chemist* was an error; properly it was *chimist*. Wrong also were *bridegroom* and *hammock*; the correct spellings were *bridgroom* and *hammoc*. Webster also defended *lether, groop, steddy, thum, soe, ake, aker, ribin, nightmar, bild, spred, turky, fether, nusance,* and *nehbor* as well as many others.

By the 1820s, Webster had moved beyond any direct reliance upon John Horne Tooke. His own etymological research had convinced him that Tooke was wrong on almost all particulars. There were, however, lingering effects of Webster's earlier contact with the British philologist. The revised spellings in the 1828 dictionary were based on analogy and etymology, the same principles that underlie the reforming grammars of the 1820s.[88] Though the dictionary was praised in many quarters as a soaring achievement of American scholarship, Webster also suffered the same obloquy that was handed to the reforming grammarians. In Boston, the *Courier* raised questions about Webster's spellings. Lyman Cobb, a rival textbook author, published a pamphlet attacking Webster, which was sent to members of Congress and educational leaders throughout the country. The New York *Evening Post* condemned Webster's tendency to unsettle the language. Lexicographers were to codify polite usage, it was argued, not create it. In July and August 1829 the *New York Morning Herald* ran seventeen articles attacking Webster's orthography and in numbing detail the scholar's inconsistencies were pointed out. For example, if analogy dictated that the *k* be dropped from *publick, physick,* and *garlick,* why was the letter left in *lock, stock, attack,* and *traffick*? If etymology suggested *thum* and *crum* without the *b,* then why did Webster keep *dumb, limb,* and *numb*? All Webster's reforms underwent similar scrutiny. He had not systemized spelling; he had done more to unsettle the language than any author of the past fifty years.[89]

Webster, moreover, faced subversion from within. He hired Joseph Emerson Worcester, a schoolteacher who had previously edited an edition of Johnson's dictionary, to abridge the giant dictionary into an octavo edition affordable to schools. Since Webster was ill, he asked his son-in-law, Yale professor Chauncey Goodrich, to oversee Worcester's work. Upon viewing the completed book, Webster was astounded. Most of the reformed spellings were gone and the dictionary looked unlike the larger book with his name on the cover. Disgusted, Webster sold the rights of the book to Goodrich and also wrote the Yale professor out of his will.[90]

Webster's *American Dictionary of the English Language* was a commercial failure. It cost twenty dollars, which was too expensive even for most institutions. The first edition of twenty-five hundred copies lasted thirteen years.[91] The octavo edition carrying his name was more successful but it did not carry his orthographical reforms. Like the new grammars of the

1820s, Webster's linguistic reforms were ignored and would have remained as unknown today as the grammars were it not for the entrepreneurial talents of two Massachusetts publishers, George and Charles Merriam.

When Webster died in 1841, his publisher sold the rights of the dictionary to the Merriams. The Merriams felt the dictionary had great potential because, thanks to the speller, Webster's name was nationally known. But the brothers were also aware of the strange spelling and the terms of their contract were such that the family had to approve any changes in the lexicon. The Merriams immediately hired Chauncey Goodrich to edit a new edition. Goodrich had far different ideas about linguistic propriety than those of his father-in-law. For years he taught rhetoric at Yale and into the 1850s he used Hugh Blair's *Lectures on Rhetoric and Belles Lettres* as a textbook. He published two volumes of British eloquence that included Pitt, Sheridan, and Burke. Altogether, his beliefs about elegance, literary language, and the transmission of culture were utterly orthodox.[92]

With the consent of the Merriams, Goodrich withdrew most of Webster's bizarre spellings. He kept those toward which the language was naturally evolving, such as replacing *re* with *er*. At first, Goodrich had hoped to keep the whole family happy, but his efforts split the family apart. As work on the book progressed, it became clear to other family members that the radical orthography was being jettisoned. William Fowler, another of Webster's sons-in-law and a professor at Amherst, tried to stop the changes. He demanded a say in the revised dictionary, joined by his wife and Webster's son William. If the spellings were sanitized, they argued, Noah's name should be taken off the cover.[93]

For nearly a year, the Merriams, Fowler, Goodrich, and the other family members tried to find common ground. In the end, there was none. The executor of Noah's will was called in, and he interpreted the documents so that Fowler lost. The Goodrich edition of Webster's dictionary was published in 1847.[94] Paradoxically, the family battle prefigured the "war of the dictionaries" that raged across America and Britain in the forties and fifties. One year prior to Goodrich's *Webster*, Joseph Worcester, then living in Cambridge, published *A Universal and Critical Dictionary of the English Language*. Worcester's spelling was conservative; he had intended to provide an alternative to Webster.

For the next two decades newspapers, magazines, school boards, and even state legislatures argued loudly about which dictionary was superior. Both publishers fueled the debate: They reprinted newspaper and magazine articles in pamphlet form and sent them to educators and journalists. The latter would reprint them again thus further spreading the controversy. The nation's leading literary men all took an interest in the debate as well as teachers and scholars. Lawyers and jurists too took a keen interest in the battles. Since Goodrich came from Yale and Worcester from Cambridge, Massachusetts, the debates were also perceived as between competing universities. As Oliver Wendell Holmes observed, "The war of the dictionaries is only a disguised rivalry of cities, colleges, and especially publishers."[95]

The debates merely recapitulated the earlier debates about grammar and Webster's 1828 dictionary. By pressing analogy too far the Webster dictionary "has unsettled what before was fixed," it was claimed. Without some restraining authority, "if one has a right to make an innovation, all others have an equal right." In a short time language "would become hopelessly corrupted by barbarisms and vulgar slang."[96] Webster was referred to as "a vain and plodding Yankee, ambitious to be an American Johnson without one substantial qualification for the undertaking. . . ."[97] Again and again, Webster's linguistic "radicalism" was alluded to. His detractors felt if used in schools, his dictionary would have catastrophic effects; at the most impressionable age bad habits would be formed. They felt the transmission of culture would lapse, and that it was already happening. The New York state legislature was told of the student who insisted on writing *bild* and, "upon being permitted by his teacher to go to the library . . . returned, bearing Webster open at the place, in triumph, to prove himself right."[98]

While those in the Webster camp did defend using analogy to occasionally correct custom, they also emphasized the modest nature of the reforms. Webster's defenders correctly pointed out that their opponents compared Webster's 1828 dictionary with Worcester's 1846 dictionary. They contended that "Worcesterians" misled the public by ignoring Goodrich's modifications. The 1847 Webster had fewer than one hundred innovations in a lexicon of some eighty thousand words—hardly a radical document. Defenders of Webster also claimed that their dictionary was in fact the best record of contemporary usage. Worcester's orthography, one observed, was "neither American nor English, but . . . a mongrel, vacillating complication." Ignore the claims of the Worcesterians, it was urged, and look at actual usage. Webster's *Dictionary*, as edited by Goodrich, was the actual standard.[99]

Most American authors followed Worcester. Literary kings like Melville, Hawthorne, Bryant, Bancroft, Irving, and Emerson all used Worcester. In Boston and Cambridge there was not an important voice raised against him. The literary community in New York and the South also favored Worcester. In monthly literary journals and refined newspapers the defenses of Worcester were most often sounded.[100] However, the opinion of university professors was more mixed. Worcester enjoyed some influence by association with the prestige of Harvard, but Yale graduates, important partisans of Webster, spread out in the antebellum years to found colleges throughout the Midwest. In the South, few professors defended the Connecticut lexicographer.[101]

The battle, though, was to be won elsewhere. Most dictionaries would be purchased for common schools. It was there that popular loyalty would be built. Publishers of both dictionaries employed agents to buttonhole administrators, flatter teachers, and lobby state legislators. By the 1850s, some states were providing funds to purchase a dictionary for every school-room. It was there that the Merriams were most successful. Despite the opposition of William Cullen Bryant, Washington Irving, Nathaniel Haw-thorne, and George Bancroft, in 1851 the New York state legislature purchased three thousand copies of Webster for the state's schoolrooms. One year earlier, the Massachusetts legislature had debated the issue. When it looked as if the Boston area literati would prevail, the Merriams wired Yale professor Noah Porter, who left his New Haven house at 5:00 P.M., arrived in Boston at midnight, and the next morning testified as to the superiority of the Webster tome. The legislature then purchased three thousand copies of Webster for Massachusetts schools. New Jersey also purchased three thousand copies of Webster's dictionary.[102]

The same drama was played in the Midwest. William Swan, Worces-ter's publisher, spent considerable energy to recapture ground lost in the East. In Ohio and Indiana he checked the progress of Webster. In 1852 Swan was elected an honorary member of the Ohio State Teacher's As-sociation. But the Merriams triumphed in the end. Wisconsin in the mid-1850s adopted Webster as its standard and ordered three thousand copies. In 1856, Iowa did the same. In the 1860s, a hundred copies of Webster's *Dictionary* (unabridged) could be sold in one year in Crawfordsville, In-diana, and a Davenport, Iowa, bookseller could report that Webster out-sold Worcester thirty to one. Although in 1870 the Chicago literary journal *The Western Monthly* condemned Webster and praised Worcester, in 1868 the former superintendent of Chicago public schools wrote the Merriams that it "will be difficult hereafter for an American to die before he becomes thoroughly Websterized."[103]

Only in the South did Webster's dictionary fail. As sectional contro-versy heightened, Southerners took seriously the charge that Webster was a Yankee reformer. The Southern public school system was in a rudi-

mentary condition, with state legislatures appropriating no money for
dictionaries. Even the testimonial letters in the Merriam-Webster Company files indicate that the dictionary was not widely used in the South.
They report allegiance to Webster in the face of hostility from superiors
and other teachers.[104]

In 1859 Goodrich published a new *Webster's*, and in 1860 Worcester
issued a new edition of his work. It appeared as if the debate would
continue. New Yorkers in particular still appeared riled. In New Haven
and Boston, however, the intensity was gone. By the 1860s both camps
realized that the differences of the two books were minimal. Preferences
remained and publishers still pushed their books but each side was willing
to admit that the other was a fine dictionary. The debate wore itself out
during the 1860s.[105]

The battle of the dictionaries has usually been interpreted as a debate
between Anglophiles and nationalists. This interpretation misses the essential similarities in the two books; for example, the spellings differed
very little. Worcester never opposed American words; in fact, he included
many in his dictionary provided they were neither regional nor vulgar.
Chauncey Goodrich was not hostile to British English. Both men were
committed to upholding an Anglo-American literary language. To be
complete, Worcester wrote, a dictionary "must contain all the words of
the language" with their definitions "exemplified in their different meanings by citations belonging to different periods of English literature. . . ."
According to the *Methodist Quarterly Review*, Goodrich's "well-known literary tastes" and "his long and familiar acquaintance with English literature" were what qualified him to revise Webster's dictionary. Both sides
agreed that Anglo-American literature, broadly meaning prose published
in books, was the foundation of a solid English dictionary. Vulgar, low,
provincial, and technical words were strictly marked. To be sure, some
of Webster's Western defenders like I. W. Andrews in the *Marietta (Ohio)
Intelligencer* condemned the tendency of metropolitan areas "to make fac-
titious distinction by dress, deportment and language" and to abandon
linguistic fashions when they passed to the middle and lower classes. Yet
there was authentic elegance, Andrews argued, and Webster's dictionary
was that used by men of "the highest literary culture."[106]

The passions raised by the dictionaries were real; the differences perceived were not. Did Webster's dictionary cater to the rootlessness of the
democratic culture? Would the new spellings contribute to the drift away
from high culture? Would the radical new spellings eventually make

Shakespeare, Addison, and the King James Bible as alien to readers as was Chaucer? Was Webster really a "radical" Yankee, bent on reforming the language and undermining its graceful clarity? Both sides had their own answers but both also agreed that such prospects were noxious. Like the grammarians, those who wrote and cared about dictionaries expressed indurate pride in the established canons of usage. Refined language contributed to elevated conversation, firm character, and civil behavior. "There are thousands of words used colloquially, or in newspapers, or belonging to the repository of slang, whose incorporation in a work claiming to be an *arbiter elegantiarum* of speech would be either needless or positively objectionable," wrote a defender of Webster in *The New York Times*. Worcester's dictionary, noted the *Christian Examiner*, "has all the words in the language which any gentleman ever uses, or any lady," and the thousands marked "low," or "vulgar," or "regional" allow us to understand "the newspapers, without danger that we shall be contaminated as we do so." Dictionaries continued to be thought of as important carriers of accumulated knowledge and wisdom:

> We can scarcely conceive of a more valuable contribution to the literature of a country, than a good dictionary of its language. He who prepares such a work is . . . identified with the preservation of the language in its beauty and vigor, and its transmission as a correct vehicle of thought, from age to age.[107]

The Webster dictionary succeeded for a variety of reasons. The entrepreneurial skill of the Merriams should not be underestimated. Yet the Merriams were successful in large part because they convinced the public that the dictionary was *not* a radical document, that it recorded the refined literary language of the mid-nineteenth century.

The antebellum dictionary wars have much in common with the 1820s and 1830s disputes about English grammar. In each case reformers introduced "reason" as a linguistic standard superior to that of refined custom. In each case defenders of refined custom accused the reformers of catering to the vulgar in American life, also arguing that the reformers themselves were half-educated. On the other side, the reforming grammarians and lexicographers associated reliance upon custom with illegitimate elitism.

Finally, both the reforming grammarians and Noah Webster moved at odds not only with the refined linguists but also with middling communicators who cared nothing about linguistic "rationalism." Popular speakers and writers of the mid-nineteenth century were not guided by analogy and etymology but by widespread code switching—refined and unrefined customs mixed. Rational orthography, like philosophical grammar, was rejected.

## V

A long string of writers, from de Tocqueville through Mencken to Daniel Boorstin, have contended that only a few alienated literati still nurtured refined language in nineteenth-century America, that folk speech was the prevailing patois. The popularity of grammars and dictionaries, however, suggests something else. Americans were pulled in contradictory directions. The new expressive decorum encouraged informal speech, and slang, dialect, and familiarity all contributed to moments of egalitarianism. Popular education, however, encouraged refined and elegant prose. The demands of the audience pushed against the educated way of life. The result was middling culture.

How far did middling culture spread in America? No doubt answers are to some degree speculative, but the recent scholarship of Lawrence Levine and Cathy Davidson suggests that for both men and women the popularization of refined culture went far beyond what it was in the eighteenth century.[108] My own assessment of the spread of the dictionary and grammar suggests something similar. Good reasons still existed to cultivate refinements. It is "easy enough to see," reported the self-help book *How to Educate Yourself*, that a "mastery of English has a decided pecuniary value to its possessor." Standards had changed but they had not collapsed. Standard syntax in print was never challenged. Since Andrew Jackson could not write grammatically, nearly all his prose was written (or amended) by someone else. Although Davy Crockett claimed to be proud that he knew no grammar, that "big men" had more important things to learn, when he wrote his autobiography he handed the manuscript to someone who could fix the syntax.[109]

Moreover, contact with educated prose not only made one "refined," it also made one "articulate." The grammars, dictionaries, and elementary readers all aided in cultivating a child's public voice. The millions of Americans who studied these books did not necessarily wish to cultivate expressive verve (folk speech of all sorts often is more metaphorically vivid than standard dialects) but to nurture an expressive breadth that could easily withstand the demands of any subject. Many examples could be cited but few are more powerful than that of Frederick Douglass.

Douglass purchased Caleb Bingham's *Columbian Orator* for fifty cents while still a slave. Impressed by a story in which a Negro *convinced* his master that slavery was wrong, Douglass became determined to be as articulate as the fictional slave. He pored over the words of Pitt, Sheridan, Burke, and Fox:

> The reading of these speeches added much to my limited stock of language, and enabled me to give tongue to many interesting thoughts, which had recently flashed through my soul, and died away for want of utterance.

The study had literally transformed him, making him a different person, giving him the voice he had not had. Studying those old speeches had transferred to Douglass that "copious speech," that "elaborated code" that is needed for effective entry into the public sphere.[110]

The prestige of refinement was by no means gone. Despite his attacks on "aristocrats" like Nicholas Biddle, Andrew Jackson still urged his ward to be liberally educated and become (in Jackson's words) a "polished gentleman." Andrew Johnson, notorious for his violent stump speaking which was anathema to gentlemen throughout the nation, still urged his daughter to avoid "low and vulgar acts or expressions." As a country lawyer and despite his addiction to rustic humor, Lincoln thought both "Abe" and "Abraham" were vulgarly familiar. He preferred the refined "Mr. Lincoln" and only as a campaign tactic did he agree to "Honest Abe."[111]

Throughout the nation, everybody demanded to be called a "lady" or a "gentleman," which was another sign of the continued interest in refined culture. The words lost their substantive meanings, referring neither to a member of a ruling class nor to a refined person, yet they retained their emotional pull. "We Americans are all gentlemen by self-appointment," *Harper's Monthly* not too happily reported in 1857. "You may find even a black washerwoman advertising herself as a 'colored lady,' " one European was startled to learn. "The negros are a long way behind," he added, "but with white servants the change is not a mere change of words." The sociologist Lester Ward grew up in modest circumstances in rural Pennsylvania. During the Civil War, he served the North as a sergeant. Although as a young man he praised the moral superiority of the common man and condemned "that more polished and affected class of society commonly called the literati," during the war he was insulted when not introduced to the sister of a superior officer. He bitterly noted in his diary: "It was not that I have any desire to make her acquaintance but I wish to be treated as a gentleman." In 1846, after a lawyer wrote to the *New*

*York Tribune* about the spread of slaughterhouses throughout the city, a butcher responded, "We think we have the right to be gentlemen and Christians in this land of freedom." To Europeans, the contempt for *true* gentlemen coupled with the appropriation of prestige by sergeants, doormen, butchers, and scrubwomen was one of the most startling disjunctions of the new nation. The festivals of misrule had become the decorum of everyday life.[112]

The social order civil refinement had supported collapsed, but the way of life it supported merely eroded. While most intensely felt in America, the fear lived throughout the Western World. Each country had its own disturbing forms of popular culture; each its own enemies of popular culture resisting the undemanding informality of so much bourgeois leisure. "An epileptic dance, a delerium tremens, which is to proper dancing what slang is to the French language . . ." wrote a French dancing master about the cancan, which first appeared in the 1830s.[113]

Far from being a uniquely American dilemma or one experienced only in the mid-nineteenth century, alternating between the refined and the coarse, between public reserve and public informality, touches the heart of modernity. So too does separating education from leisure, the ethos informing work from that informing play. The issues agitating grammarians, lexicographers, newspaper men, and educators of mid-nineteenth century America were those that have roused the West's leading social thinkers. Ever since Rousseau argued that the rights of man conflicted with a citizen's duties, intellectuals have feared that modernity fragments man. Work, state, leisure, and neighborhood all pull in their own directions, rewarding human beings with numerous identities but robbing them of a single coherent identity. As one contemporary social scientist puts it:

> The fact is that people do have choices on how to identify themselves, they will choose different identities to emphasize in different settings, and identities they choose over time will also change. Ethnic identities are alternatives to occupational, regional, religious, neighborhood, and other identities.[114]

Such a description will today strike few as remarkable. Modernity leaves us with a multitude of expressive choices.

Since the eighteenth century, the likes of Adam Smith, Herbert Spencer, Max Weber, Talcott Parsons, Erving Goffman, and Clifford Geertz, whatever their differences, have either embraced or preached stoic resignation to modernity's inexorable fragmentation. A different tradition, however, has resisted. Rousseau, Hegel, Coleridge, Marx, and others both of the left and the right have exhibited what Peter Gay has called a "hunger for wholeness," the dream of reintegrating man into a unified whole. By the early nineteenth century, American democracy rewarded both refined educational skills and expressive gestures of familiarity. Those gentlemen who read and took seriously the messages of *The New York Times*, Boston *Daily Advertiser*, New York *Evening Post*, and all the rest of the gentry literature pressed to maintain a coherent and all-embracing identity, that of the Christian gentleman. As *The New York Times* once editorialized about the *Tribune*:

> As a manner of personal taste, we do not believe Mr. Greeley enjoys hearing men calling each other liars, or d——d liars, or any other epithets, more or less ornamented with theological adjectives. . . . Why, then, does he put them into his newspaper? . . . We see no reason why the language of a newspaper should be very different from the language of decent society, from the language used by gentlemen in their daily intercourse.[115]

Nineteenth-century refined gentlemen exhibited that hunger for wholeness that has characterized so many of modernity's discontents. They were buoyed in the first half of the nineteenth century by an inherited ethos that told them that education *was* a discriminating sensibility that informed decorum, work, and leisure—a whole way of life. The grammarians' opposition to dialect, the lexicographers' wariness about slang—these were more than matters of expressive choice. They were questions of character.

# CHAPTER THREE

# Saxon Eloquence:
# The *Sermo Humilis*

I hope the farmer may sing snatches of Scripture at his plough, that the weaver may hum
bits . . . to the tune of his shuttle.

ERASMUS

*Guts* is a stronger word than intestines.

EMERSON

From the beginning, Romanticism was about words: Herder on the origins
of speech, the Grimms on the language of the common folk, and, of course,
the *Lyrical Ballads*:

> The majority of the following poems are to be considered experiments.
> They were written chiefly with a view to ascertain how far the language
> and conversation in the middle and lower classes of society is adapted to
> the purposes of poetic pleasure.[1]

Romanticism came late to the United States, reaching full force only in
the 1820s. From its arrival, it was bound up in all the efforts to come to
terms with the vulgarity of American democracy. Romantics seemed to
praise popular folk speech, but what did that mean in a nation that was
so rootless as to seem to have no "folk" and so new as to have no past?
Cooper provided a model, but Natty Bumppo smelled of the lamp, harking
back to European salons and theories of the noble savage. More frequently,
when American Romantics looked for an appropriate idiom, they turned
to that English derived from Teutonic sources. "It cannot be denied," one

typical observer commented, "that the most expressive, picturesque and national parts of our complicated language are the remains of the Anglo-Saxon." Emerson hit it directly. "*Guts*," he wrote in his notebook, "is a stronger word than intestines."[2]

The sentiment was based on knowledge of the language that now only specialists possess. Because English borrowed thousands of words from Latin, French, Greek, Spanish, and Italian (the Latinate languages) between the twelfth and the seventeenth centuries, it is the least "pure" of the Indo-European languages. Even today, English vocabulary is extremely complicated, with thousands of synonyms, one derived from a Teutonic language and the other from a classical source. Almost invariably the Saxon word is shorter with more punch, while the Latinate word is longer and more formal. To *lie* is Saxon, to *prevaricate* Latin. In a panic we shout, "*Stop!*" We leave *desisting* to the lawyers. With Saxon English we *end* something; with Latinate English we *terminate* it.

Saxon eloquence was presented as a turn from the elite standards of the eighteenth century; English was to be steered from the Latinate cadences of Johnson, Hume, Gibbon, Jefferson, and others. But Saxon English was valued for another reason. By the mid-nineteenth century, Saxonists argued, the pompous diction of the eighteenth century had become one of the popular styles of the day. Half-educated editors and politicians made Johnson's style their own. Recovery of our folk roots signaled not only a shift in *high* culture (classic to Romantic), but also a defense of an animate literary language against vulgar popular imitators. Traditional Saxonism sustained pride in the common Anglo-American heritage of humane learning.

Romantic eloquence conjured up a democratic version of the sublime by merging the lofty with the rustic. The dignity of the commonplace, the blessedness of the humble—such were celebrated by Romantics as surely as breezy newspapermen and pompous politicians were denounced. Saxon eloquence was a middling style at war with other middling styles, or perhaps I should say, a middling style trying to transcend itself.

Whatever, its lure was strong at midcentury. Saxon English colored all sorts of American Romanticism. It virtually defined, as we shall see, Romantic philology. It contributed paeons to the English Bible. It taught gentlemen how to use a vulgar voice. At times it moved too close to gentry speech, but it also braced some of the nation's finest oratory. Romantic eloquence created a very special kind of middling style, evoking the only sort of nobility suited to a democratic regime.

# I

The problems of mediating high and popular culture were not new to the nineteenth century. They were deeply rooted in Christianity. The Old Testament was the literature of tribesmen. The New Testament, of course, was not originally written in classical Greek and was riddled with numerous Hebraisms that cultivated pagans found barbarous. The Bible as a whole was a huge, sprawling compilation of tales about shepherds, fishermen, and a mystic Hebrew carpenter. For educated Romans to admire the Bible was to admire a primitive literature. When Rome adopted Christianity as the state religion in the fourth century, the classically educated Church Fathers did not recast the Bible into refined Latin. Instead, led by Augustine, they developed the notion of the *sermo humilis*, the humble style, in which the most sublime matters could be treated in the most matter-of-fact manner, with the humblest prose, and through the lowliest characters. Christianity's contention that all were equal in the eyes of God was distinctly egalitarian, even if the equality was "only" spiritual. The fourth-century fathers developed their own version of the middling style, moving back and forth from the refined to the crude to pay homage to the spiritual egalitarianism of the faith.[3]

The King James Bible, completed in 1611, was another of many attempts to reach the common people. The translators noted in the preface that they wanted a Bible that "may be understood even of the very vulgar." Without a vernacular Bible, they added, "the unlearned are like children at Jacob's well (which was deep) without a bucket or something to draw on. . . ."[4] And the translators were remarkably successful. For over two hundred years, the Bible was the one book read by high and low, rustics and scholars, ladies and their maids. Generation after generation memorized its words and turns of phrase.

Writers in the nineteenth century knew that the King James Bible was successful because, as the *Bibliotheca Sacra* noted, it had been designed "to instruct the illiterate and uncultivated as well as the scholar," because it mediated high and low culture. Its translators had chosen only those words "which find a ready response in every heart."[5] Indeed, the English of the King James Bible is at times a rough, hard language, one in which *piss*, *dung*, and *bowels* stand uncensored. Yet it can also soar, and passages like the opening of Genesis and of John's gospel arch to the sublime. The King James Bible cuts through many of the sociocultural divisions that refinement and civility had built.

Nineteenth-century writers also regularly claimed that the poetry of the Common Version was due in large measure to its overwhelmingly Saxon vocabulary. The "old Saxon Bible" was what one called it. It preserves the language's "original Saxon purity" thought another. The Bible was the "standard of language as well as faith," noted Fisher Ames. Even Catholics heard its music: "Who will say that the uncommon beauty and marvellous English of the Protestant Bible is not one of the greatest strongholds of heresy in this country? . . . In the length and breadth of the land, there is not a Protestant with one spark of righteousness about him, whose spiritual biography is not his Saxon Bible."[6]

The Authorized Version's Saxon beauty and common touch were its strengths. It had weaknesses. First, sectarianism pulled apart what the Common Bible drew together. Some distrusted the book's Anglicanism. Second, the canons of civility made others uncomfortable with its vulgarities. Third, two centuries of scholarship had accumulated and it was commonly known in scholarly circles that the Greek texts used by the seventeenth-century translators were defective. Finally, changes in the English language caused problems. Certain words in the Common Version were archaic. Based on these shortcomings, in the 1820s, agitation began for a new popular Bible. By the 1850s, the celebration of the Authorized Version had become a defense of it.

Efforts to revise the King James Bible took two paths. On one side were the sectarians. Baptists in the 1830s, Mormons in the 1840s, and others revised the Bible to comport with specific theological principles.[7] On the other side were linguistic modernizers. In the 1820s Noah Webster tried his hand at revision, hoping to bring sacred diction into the nineteenth century. He completed the job in 1833. At about the same time, the idiosyncratic Alexander Campbell tried to blend a sectarian and modernized version. These early efforts, however, were stillborn; there was not yet any public interest. That was not true in the 1850s, however, when the most talked-about modern revision of the King James Bible to date appeared. Leicaster Sawyer published a complete New Testament in 1858 and portions of the Old three years later. The books themselves were failures, important only for the discussion they generated. Sawyer's revisions were a lightning rod for opinion of all sorts on biblical English. He had thoroughly modernized the Bible. His was not, he told readers, a work of compromises.[8]

Sawyer was born in 1807, the son of a wagonmaker. Intent on raising himself in the world, Sawyer attended Hamilton College and the Princeton Theological Seminary. Between 1832 and 1859 he was pastor of various

Congregational and Presbyterian parishes in the Northeast and Ohio, serving from 1840 to 1843 as president of Central College in Columbus. In the 1840s he became an abolitionist and produced a widely read anti-slavery tract. He began to work on a new translation of the Bible in the 1850s. At the same time, Sawyer began to drift from evangelical Protestantism, and in 1859, between his New and Old Testament publications, he left the Congregational Church and became a Unitarian. Then in 1860 he gave up the ministry altogether. Still later, he became a skeptic, arguing that Jesus was merely a social reformer. And from 1868 through 1882 he worked as the night editor of the *Utica Morning Herald*.[9]

Sawyer's 1858 translation of the New Testament was a product of his early training as well as his drift away from it. American biblical scholarship of the early nineteenth century focused almost exclusively on language. Both conservatives like Moses Stuart and progressives like Andrews Norton followed German biblical scholarship only so far. While they scoured ancient texts to determine the meaning of sacred words, and while they argued about the canons of interpretation, neither would question the authority of Scripture. The Holy Word remained inviolable. Radical critics of the Bible like the German David Strauss were almost uniformly condemned by biblical scholars in antebellum America.[10]

In 1836 Sawyer published a popular introduction to biblical interpretation, a gloss on the system of Johann Ernesti, a founding father of biblical hermeneutics. In the mid-eighteenth century, Ernesti explored the subtleties of the figurative and allegorical uses of language in the Bible. But he made no critical exploration of the social context of the texts. His philological studies were to uncover the true meaning of the Scriptures, not to render the Scriptures "historical." Hermeneutics should explore only the meaning of words, not their truth-value. The strict limits of Ernesti's philology gained him few followers in Germany; his work was assimilated and then passed by. In American biblical criticism, however, Ernesti remained quite important. In 1822 Moses Stuart translated Ernesti's *Elementary Principles of Interpretation* into English, although more advanced works like Johann Herder's *Lectures on Hebrew Poetry* were not yet available in English. Following Ernesti, Sawyer argued that language was figurative and allegorical as well as literal. But also following Ernesti, he argued that words were never ambiguous, that they always had only one meaning (that is, a word was either figurative or literal, but never both), and this unambiguous meaning was always available to the careful interpreter. He claimed that no interpretation could explain away any of the Bible's truths. The Bible was "an exposition of religious science."[11]

Ernesti brought eighteenth-century ideas about language into the America of the 1830s. He fit well with the common sense rationalism shared by figures as diverse as Stuart and Norton. In the 1850s, when Sawyer grew skeptical of the Scriptures, he remained faithful to his linguistics. To him, language was a body of custom, but hermetic, self-contained. Words were explained by other words and not by their relation to any "external" reality. The modern diction of Sawyer's Bible was possible because he ignored the bonds between the original Greek and its cultural milieu, and it was the eighteenth-century hermeneutics of Johann Ernesti that encouraged him to do so.

Sawyer's most important changes were relatively simple. *Ye* and *thou* became *you*, the old *th* plural became *s*, the subjunctive *be* was turned to *is*. These small bits of archaic diction appeared in hundreds of places throughout the Bible, and cumulatively these changes did more to modernize the tone of the Scriptures than anything else Sawyer did. Passages like John 1:25, which read in the Common Version:

> And they asked him, and said unto him, Why baptizest thou then, if thou be not the Christ, nor Elias, neither that Prophet?

became in Sawyer's version:

> . . . And they asked him, and said to him, Why then do you baptize, if you are not the Christ, nor Elijah, nor the prophet?[12]

Other changes clearly revealed Sawyer's new theological leanings. His rendering of Matthew 3:2 sapped the fierce righteousness of the prophet. The Authorized Version's "Repent ye: for the kingdom of heaven is at hand" became "Change your minds, for the kingdom of heaven is at hand." Sawyer's modern diction, however, was not colloquial. He carefully removed words that he felt lacked dignity. *Fables*, he thought, had a tinge of vulgarity to it, so he used *myths* instead. *Damsels* belonged in fables, Sawyer held, not in the Bible, and he replaced them with *little girls*. Sawyer justified changing *brethren* to *brothers* as "giving to the language of religion an improvement which belongs to the common language, and which constitutes one of its graces." Sawyer thought *folk* was too folksy and instead used *persons*. The word *folk* since the early eighteenth century had been thought unrefined, but Romantics of the early nineteenth century were working to resuscitate it. Sawyer's distaste for the word is one indication of his indifference to Romantic currents of thought.[13]

Sawyer went even further, carrying refinement into the realm of euphemism. Various strategies were devised to rid the Scriptures of *wombs*.
"Conceive in thy womb" (Luke 1:31) became "shall be with child." A man
"impotent in his feet, being a cripple from his mother's womb" (Acts 14:8)
became a man "infirm in his feet, lame from birth." Perhaps most egre-
giously, what in the Common Version is "the deadness of Sarah's womb"
(Romans 4:19) in Sawyer's Bible is Sarah's "incapacity for child bearing."[14]
The King James Bible's *to conceive seed* was rendered *to become a mother* by
Sawyer. *Dung* became *manure*, and the healthy Saxon *fleshly lusts* became
*carnal desires*. (Elsewhere *lusts* was changed to the clumsy latinate *inordinate
desires*.) Some euphemisms injured meaning as well as tone. Sawyer sacrificed clarity to refinement when he replaced *damnation* with *eternal mistake*. Damnation we know, but what is an eternal mistake?[15]

Euphemisms attempt to remove sensate concreteness from language.
Denotation remains the same but the sensual connotation is hidden. A
large part of the beauty of the Authorized Version is its sensual concreteness, its palpable morality, the feel of the tangible magnifying the spiritual.
Sawyer worked hard to strip such language from his Bible. In the Common
Version *unclean* referred to a spiritual state, but the physical implication
lent power and immediacy to the description. Sawyer, though, removed
the word and used *impure* instead. While *impure* might mean the same as
*unclean*, it is a more abstract, spiritual term. Similarly, Sawyer threw out
*filthy* when describing a spiritual state and replaced it with *lewd*. *Uncleanliness* became *corrupt desires*.[16]

Sawyer removed the sensate at all costs. *Swelling* was replaced with
*extravagant*. "Purged from his old sins" became "purification of his former
errors" (*errors* instead of *sins*, again diction betrayed theology). Sawyer too
thought nothing of snapping the cadences of King James Bible. In the
Common Version, 2 Peter 2:18 reads

> For when they speak great swelling words of vanity, they allure through
> the lusts of the flesh.

The rhythm of the first phrase slopes down, leading to a natural pause at
the comma and allowing the second phrase to build to the last four words.
Rhythm contributes to meaning. Sawyer, however, would neither *swell*
nor *lust*: "For speaking extravagant words of vanity, they entice with carnal
desires." The rhythm is jagged. The sensuality blunted. The alliteration
lost.[17]

Sawyer was heir to an eighteenth-century movement to refine the Bible.

In 1764 Quaker Anthony Pulver spoke of "obsolete, uncouth, clownish" expressions in the King James Bible. James Worsley in 1770 translated the Scriptures "according to the present idiom of the tongue." Some went beyond merely turning the prose into refined English. Edward Harwood, a Presbyterian minister and friend of Joseph Priestley, attempted to refine the cultural milieu. "A certain man" (Luke 15:11) became in Harwood's Bible "a gentleman of splendid family and opulent fortune." The "damsel who is not dead" (Mark 5:39) became the "young lady" who was not dead.[18] Benjamin Franklin's suggestions along similar lines were even more ludicrous. He turned Satan and his minions into British country gentlemen.[19] Most writers, however, did not want to modernize the characters, just the language, as Pope had done with Homer, as Warburton had done with Shakespeare. Prominent scholars such as Robert Lowth, the author of the famous eighteenth-century grammar and the Bishop of London, Alexander Geddes, a Catholic Bishop, John Symonds, Cambridge's first professor of modern history, George Campbell, the Scottish Presbyterian minister and rhetorician, and William Newcome, an Anglican divine, each argued that the Bible's vulgarities must be purged, that the language had been refined since 1611 and the Scriptures had to be brought up to date. In his grammar, Lowth included passages from the Authorized Version as examples of false syntax. John Symonds argued that terms like *blockhead*, *sneered*, and *bawled out* had no place in the English Scriptures. A sentiment "is often lessened, and even utterly destroyed," he wrote, "when a writer deviates into a meanness of language." Dignity preserved the sacred.[20]

The budding reform movement was stopped by the French Revolution. Opponents of revision argued that the reformers were "too fond of innovation" and addicted to "dangerous French principles." The death of Lowth, a nationally respected scholar, also dampened the movement. Alexander Geddes's proposals for a new Bible were greeted enthusiastically in the 1780s but in the 1790s Catholic authorities pressured him to give up the cause. Changing the Bible would undermine the faith of the common people, it was argued. Thus interest in a new Bible dwindled.[21]

Though heir to the eighteenth-century Bible revision, Sawyer's specific refinements were distinctly of his own day. The eighteenth-century revisers wanted to root out language that they associated with the common people. Their aim was primarily sociological, to create a Bible whose English matched that of cultivated ladies and gentlemen. No eighteenth-century reviser worried about *lust*, *whore*, *whoredom*, *suck*, or *damnation*. Leicester Sawyer's changes, however, were designed to reform the language. His main interest was in cultural style, in rooting out any words

that conflated the spiritual and the sensual. We see in Sawyer the traditional search for refinement tipping over into Victorian prudery.

Sawyer had explicitly built on Alexander Campbell's (1826) and Noah
Webster's (1833) euphemized Bibles. Although both books were ignored
in their time, they were the first to shift from Enlightenment elegance to
Victorian prudery. The change, however, was not seen as a break in
continuity but as the next step of the civilizing process. The language
and logic of reform was no different from Lowth to Webster. Webster
argued in his preface that euphemisms (he frankly termed them such)
were necessary because the King James Bible was made when society
was "half-civilized." But "in the present state of refinement," he added,
"such offensive language, in the popular version" was "injudicious, if not
unjustifiable. . . ." Webster concluded: "Purity of mind is a Christian
virtue that ought to be carefully cherished; and purity of language is one
of the guards which protect this virtue."[22]

Those working to refine the Bible felt the Authorized Version's crudities undermined its authority. To be respected, they thought, the sacred
must be dignified. Grammatical structures deemed vulgar and words like
*piss, suck, whore*, and *shit* chipped away at the Bible's dignity. Since in
common parlance they were clearly unacceptable, how could they be used
in the Bible? It is difficult to assess how successful the euphemistic movement was in general, but it is worth pointing out that from the beginning
there were those who thought it needless overrefinement. For example,
one opponent of revision argued that it was the less moral and pure who
"exhibit the greatest amount of false delicacy." He felt there was no word
in the English Bible that did not belong there. Euphemisms were unnecessary.[23]

Defenders of the King James Bible associated euphemisms with mod-
ernisms and they did not want a modern Bible. To update the Bible, they
held, would not dignify it but reduce it to the commonplace. Partisans of
the Common Version also believed that the sacred must be dignified.
They argued, however, that religious dignity was maintained by keeping
us aware of its "specialness." Archaisms like *hath, doeth*, and *maketh* should
remain, argued R. C. Malan in his widely read *Vindication of the Authorized
Version* (1856), because "the style of the Bible ought to be more solemn,
and it ought to speak with more gravity, than that of any other book in
the language." To command authority the sacred diction should be English, but not common English. Leicaster Sawyer's biblical prose was
described by one critic as "hasty and crude." Another thought his "thor-

oughly modernized style" had "vulgarized" the Bible. Sawyer's dialect was a "hard and meagre" one, editorialized the *British and Foreign Evangelical Review*. He made "the language as bare and lifeless as a May-pole or an awning post." The point was true of all revisers according to *The Church Review and Ecclesiastical Register*. Revisers degraded the style of the Bible "to a level with the language of society." According to one minister, the change from the Common Version's "Nay, verily" to one reviser's "No, indeed," was from the true stern dignity of Paul the Apostle to the frivolity of "a petulant school girl." Perhaps, he sarcastically added, the "No, indeed" should be changed to "No, Sir'ee" so the "common people" would better understand.[24]

Arguments about the need for a "special" religious diction were derived from Romantic translation theory. Many of those ministers who defended the King James Bible had firsthand knowledge of Romantic Biblical scholarship. The seminal proto-Romantic work, still in print one hundred years later, was *The Sacred Poetry of the Hebrews* (1753), written by Bishop Robert Lowth. Lowth was the first to stress the tribalism of the Hebrews: "Not even the greatest among them esteemed it mean and disgraceful to be employed in the lowliest of rural labor." The vulgar diction, he held, and barnyard metaphors, contributed to the Old Testament's "natural force and dignity," its "vivacity and boldness of figure."[25]

*The Sacred Poetry of the Hebrews* was known by all key British Romantics and influenced Germans such as Herder and Hamann. From Lowth's starting point new ideas were developed about how to translate the Bible (and indeed, how to translate anything). Emphasizing the intimate bonds between language and the larger social order, it was argued that one must translate not only words but the whole cultural milieu. In his 1778 translation of *Isaiah*, Lowth asserted that he must not only find the right words for the original author's, but also "imitate his features, his air, his gesture, and, as far as the difference of language will permit, even his voice." This was not a "free" translation but a higher species of literalism. "Flatness and insipidy will be the consequence of a deviation from the native manner of the original. . . ." The same insight was brought to bear on the New Testament. George Campbell, the author of *The Philosophy of Rhetoric*, published a translation of the Gospels in which he tried to capture the tone of the original. Nothing could be more misleading, he noted, than to think the Evangelists spoke the dialect of "gentlemen," of "men of fashion." They used "the barbarous idiom of a few obscure Galileans," not "the politer and more harmonious strains of Grecian eloquence." It was all, to Campbell, part of God's larger plan: "That it might appear, beyond contradiction, that the excellency of the power was of God, and not of man."[26]

Germans such as Herder, Hölderlin, and Schleiermacher broadened the insights into theory. Translation should not recapitulate contemporary idiom but find a way to edge toward the original in new dress. It should be *in* the new language but not *of* it. There should be a "peripheral opaqueness" exposing the cultural gap between original and translation.[27] In the late eighteenth century this did not conflict with modest revision of the Common Version. But by the mid-nineteenth century it had hardened into a staunch defense of the Anglo-Saxon King James Bible. It was a blessing of incalculable scope that the translation had been done in the early seventeenth century, for it was then that the English language was best able to recapitulate New Testament Greek. By the eighteenth century, however, our language had become too "copious," too "specific," too Latinized to "have any true correspondence with so simple and inartificial a diction as that of the Christian Scriptures."[28]

Although the old Saxon English predominated in the early seventeenth century, it was still a time of some refinement and learning. Translated earlier, the *Bibliotheca Sacra* argued, the Bible would have been "clothed in the forms of an obsolete language," but later, "decked out in the . . . garb of a Latin and French philosophical style." The King James translators worked in the Golden Age of scholarship, thought Alexander McClure in *The Translators Revived* (1853). The opening years of the seventeenth century were seen as the moment when scholarship, literary sensibilities, and sensitivity toward the common people fell into a perfect fit. The Common Version was "removed from vulgarity and pedantry," felt Richard Chenevix Trench. Its words were neither "too familiar" nor "not familiar enough." *Harper's Monthly* agreed: There was no better representation of the tongue than the "Anglo-Saxon English" of the Bible. It was "pre-eminently the language of the people, refined by the advance of learning, and not yet made scholastic by writers whose only world was the student's closet." *Harper's* doubted that such a tender balance could be repeated.[29]

Theology meshed with sociolinguistics. We were fortunate that Shakespeare and the King James Bible crystallized the language "precisely at its freshest and most vigorous period." A writer in the *North American Review* argued that the King James Bible was done "early enough to escape those influences which have made our language at once more ductile and varied to the purposes of modern usage, and less fitted for the highest offices of eloquence, poetry, devotion."[30] Defenders of the Authorized Version worried that its muscular Saxon prose would be lost in revision. The defense of the King James Bible was an important part of the nineteenth-century movement away from Latinate English.

The defense of the Common Bible was not only a part of the stylistic evolution of high culture (classicism to Romanticism), it was also a defense of the integrity of high culture in the face of the new middling customs of the nineteenth century. Defenders of the King James Bible regularly linked the revisers with the vulgar middling. Phrases like "sophomorical performances" and "ruthless hand of innovation" were used to describe the reforming efforts. Words like "shallow adventurers" and "half-learned advocates" described the reformers. The "idea of modernizing the language of the Bible is one of the follies of shallow thinkers," said one satisfied with the King James Bible. In every "civilized nation," wrote another, the newspaper press destabilized the language by mindlessly coining new words. An important counterweight was "the continuous circulation of old English books"—Shakespeare, Milton, the Book of Common Prayer, and the Saxon Bible.[31]

Ancient fears of overrefinement reappeared but associated with middling vulgarity instead of desiccated aristocrats. One critique of Sawyer's euphemisms deserves special mention, for it best sums up the themes of Romantic linguistics:

> It is neither the unsophisticated common reader, nor the man of true culture and refinement that stumbles at [the King James Bible]. It is chiefly men of low associations, men of corrupt minds and prurient imaginations, or half-learned smatterers, or ill-bred upstarts—*the real vulgar*, in short—who are afflicted with the excessive sensitiveness of delicacy.[32]

High and low were "organically" yoked together against the destabilizing vulgarity of the "half-learned smatterers." The Bible's *piss* and *damn*, its occasional archaisms and lapses of grammar lent it power, recapturing the tonal idiom of the original, exemplifying the best of English prose, preserving the dignity of the sacred, and defending against the vulgar half-educated.

The Bible would not be modernized in the years before the Civil War. The reaction to the American Bible Society's (ABS) effort to correct the King James Bible shows the depths of hostility even among the more educated Protestant ministry. The ABS was an interdenominational Protestant organization created in the early nineteenth century to distribute Bibles all over the world. In 1848, it delegated a committee on versions to check various editions of the King James Bible and create one uniform text. The hundreds of editions published since 1611 included an unknown quantity of printers' mistakes and editorial licenses that gradually corrupted the original. The committee reported some twenty-four thousand discrepancies between the Authorized Version of the nineteenth century and that of 1611 (the overwhelming majority of changes were of punctuation). In 1854 the ABS published a "purified" edition which came under attack in 1857 when A. Cleveland Coxe, a Baltimore Episcopal bishop, published a pamphlet entitled *An Apology for the Common English Bible*. All the negative arguments about Bible revision were applied to the ABS's corrected version: It challenged Protestant comity, Saxon dignity, the organic ties with the past. It encouraged capitulation to fashion, which encouraged disrespect for a public standard (". . . would become as untrustworthy as an old-town-clock, continually corrected by private watches."). It all pandered to new destabilizing popular culture: "In a day when the *New York Tribune* is the Bible of thousands of our countrymen; when Magnetism is the highest spiritualism of thousands more; when gigantic elements of evil, which have no name, are visible in our Great West . . . can it be wise to insert the sharp end of the critical wedge into the Standard Bible?"[33]

Coxe's pamphlet created an enormous stir among Protestant ministers. Up and down the East Coast and in the cities of the West, members of the ABS clamored for the board of managers to discard the Bible of the Committee on Versions. Presbyterians—old school and new—threatened to defect from the ABS. Hundreds of Methodists and Quakers wrote to the New York headquarters demanding change. In vain did the committee argue that its work was textual *correction*, not textual *revision*. In 1858 the managing board of the ABS bowed to the uproar of the membership and threw out the uniform edition. For Protestants, there was *no* tampering with the common Bible. The Common Version, with all its faults, was untouchable.[34]

# II

Americans took to Romantic philology for the same reasons they clutched the Saxon Bible. In the United States, the ideas of Rasmun Rask, Friedrich Schlegel, Franz Bopp, Jacob Grimm, and William von Humbolt were seen as one way to reconfigure lines between high, popular, and low culture.

Already in 1822 John Pickering welcomed the "new science" in the *North American Review*. Already in 1831 that journal published a lengthy article on the Anglo-Saxon language based on the work of Grimm.[35] Sustained penetration, however, was more difficult. In the thirties and forties Eastern European immigrants like Charles Kraitsir, Karl Follen, and Maximilian Schele de Vere introduced the new ideas to American college towns, but it wasn't until the fifties that a series of books on the principles of philology appeared in English.[36] Despite Robert Latham's groundbreaking *The English Language* (1841) (which the *North American Review* said "revolutionized" thinking about the language), it was only in the fifties that the new Anglo-Saxon scholarship was made widely known. Books like William Fowler's *The English Language* (1852), Richard Chevenix Trench's *On the Study of Words* (1851) and *English: Past and Present* (1855), and George Perkins Marsh's *Lectures on the English Language* (1859) introduced literate audiences to the new interpretations of English. By the fifties, writers like Emerson and Thoreau were devouring the books and themselves becoming amateur philologists. How the new philology provided an escape from contemporary cultural dilemmas can best be seen through the poet James Russell Lowell.[37]

Lowell, whose grandfather and father were both ministers and had gone to Harvard, was born and raised in Cambridge, Massachusetts, and attended Harvard as well. In the 1840s, this young Brahmin became involved with radical abolitionist movements. In 1846, he wrote a poem in New England rustic dialect, an account by (the fictional) Ezekiel Biglow of his son Hosea's trip to Boston, a satiric comment on the efforts to raise troops to fight the Mexican War. Over the next few years Lowell wrote nine of what came to be called *The Biglow Papers*, the tales of various inhabitants of a mythic New England town. All attacked the war effort (which Lowell thought a ruse to extend slavery) and satirized theories of Anglo-Saxon superiority. The sentiments of one character, Birdofredum Sawin, were those Lowell made light of:

> Afore I come away from hum I hed a strong persuasion
> The Mexicans worn't human beans, an ourang outang nation
> A sort of folk a chap could kill an' never dream on't arter
> No more 'n a feller'd dream o' pigs he hed to slarter;
> I'd an idee they were built arter the darkie fashion all,
> An' kickin' colored folks about, you know, 's kind of
>     national . . .

Enraged by the Mexican War, Lowell wanted to shape public opinion. Originally published in newspapers, the Biglow poems were reprinted throughout the Northeast. Lowell himself was astonished by their success: "Very far from being a popular author under my own name," he wrote, "so far, indeed, as to be almost unread, I found the verses of my pseudonym copied everywhere; I saw them pinned up in workshops: I heard them quoted and their authorship debated."[38] Although there were positive reviews, most literary journals ignored the poems. The *New Englander* apologized for discussing them. In 1848, Lowell wrote to Mary Peabody Mann defending the "husks of Hosea Biglow" against the more "ambrosial diet" of his refined poetry. The "practical," he argued, took precedence over the "beautiful." "But I assure you that Mr. Biglow has a thousand readers for my one, and that he has raised the laugh at War and Slavery and Doughfaces to some purpose."[39]

Lowell was not creating a genre. Humor born of dialect had become a staple part of American popular entertainment in the 1830s. Davy Crockett, Sam Slick, and Jack Downing were the same kind of household names in the 1830s and 1840s that popular television stars are today. Lowell writing such poetry in the 1840s would be as if today Saul Bellow (a *young* Saul Bellow) felt strongly about some public issue and wrote a made-for-TV movie on the subject.

Lowell was immediately uncomfortable with the success of his popular poetry. In 1847 he wrote to his good friend Charles Briggs that he was sorry he had made Hosea such a bad speller and toyed with the idea of having his protagonist win a scholarship to Harvard. ("They are admirable, very good indeed," Charles Sumner said to Longfellow of the poems, "but why does he spell so badly?") When he published the collected Biglow poems in 1849, Lowell introduced a fictional editor, the Reverend Homer Wilbur, who, although humorously pedantic, was still Harvard-educated. Lowell feared his deeply held opinions would be vulgarized if only recorded in dialect. Wilbur, the epitome of staid Whig respectability, lifted the sentiments. To the end of his life Lowell was ambivalent about the success of his popular poetry. In 1859 he wrote to Charles Eliot Norton about those "who like my humorous poems best. I guess they are right —up to date—" but they ignored his serious side that combined "the results of life with those of study." Lowell's wife detested the Biglow poems, and Lowell once wrote that he loved her all the more for her opinion.[40]

Lowell was caught in a dilemma facing many highly educated Americans in the middle of the nineteenth century. On the one hand, to be popular often meant having to be "vulgar." On the other hand, civil social thought taught that the educated were not vulgar, that to be educated was to be a lady or a gentleman.

In 1846 Lowell could do little except be uncomfortable with his success. But during the late forties and the fifties, he became acquainted with the new philology, and it gave him a new way to think about rustic language. Language is vitalized from the folk, Lowell argued. Left alone, literary languages turned pallid: "No language after it has faded into *diction*, none that cannot suck up feeding juices from the mother-earth of a rich common-folk-talk, can bring forth a sound and lusty book. True vigor of expression does not pass from page to page, but from man to man. . . ." Lowell praised the "life, invention, and vigor" of American "popular speech." He felt that words like *bogus*, *chowder-head*, and *loafer* had an elemental ring to them. Phrases like *to go under* (to die) or *to be nowhere* (to fail) were vivid popular metaphors. He feared not rustic vulgarity but the "universal Schoolmaster" who "wars upon home-bred phrases," championing English that is "faultlessly correct" but stale.[41]

All this was not to deny literary language but to keep it alive, to make sure that literature did not stray too far from speech. Lowell was preeminently a man of books, or more precisely, one of the last to assume the connection between humane learning and disinterested public spiritedness. To maintain that connection book language could not become "bookish." He quoted Ascham: "Ye know not what hurt ye do to Learning, that care not for Words, but for Matter, and so make a Divorce betwixt the Tongue and the Heart." Lowell found the early seventeenth century propitious for the same reason the Common Bible's defenders did: "Shakespeare, then, found a language already to a certain extent *established*, but not yet fetlocked by dictionary and grammar mongers." He defended refinement, but a refinement free of prissiness or pedantry. His own speech and prose bore no resemblance to Hosea Biglow's, but it did have occasional touches of homeliness. Rustic poetry contributed but was not mimicked. "Familiar dignity" is how he summed up the prose of Dryden, and it was Lowell's ideal as well—a prose elegant, free of pedantry, and "juicy with proverbial phrases." Lowell's motto for poets he adapted from Aristotle: "The tongue of the people in the mouth of the scholar."[42]

In the 1830s and 1840s, various young Harvard-educated men took up various sorts of radicalism: abolitionist (Lowell), philosophic (Emerson), egalitarian (Bancroft). But each brushed up against the inherited assumption that the educated man was the gentleman and that gentility should be an important social marker. Even during the 1840s Lowell distrusted the common man; indeed, his radicalism nurtured it. The "saddest part" of the country's indifference to slavery, he argued, was "that the moral sense of the mass of the people should be so dead. . . ." The opening motto of *The Biglow Papers* (prudently written in Latin) also reveals his disdain: "*Margaritas, munde porcine, calcâsti: en, siliquas accipe.*" ("Oh, swinish world, you have trampled pearls; so, take the husks.")[43] In the 1860s Lowell became more convinced that civil refinement was necessary to correct the "errors" of democracy. He slowly shed his radicalism, evolving into an unambiguous defender of the morality of style, regularly complaining about popular linguistic habits.[44]

The drift toward conservatism coincided with a new series of Biglow poems. In late 1861, with a new war on, Lowell began producing new poems in rustic dialect and wrote eleven of them through 1866. When republishing the book in 1870 he included a seventy-five-page preface. Literate, scholarly, and urbane, he explained his forays into rustic speech with his own familiar dignity.

Lowell drew heavily on all the Romantic philology published in the previous three decades. What he found was that Yankee dialect, the dialect of Hosea Biglow, was actually a pure form of Anglo-Saxon. The Englishmen who had come here in the seventeenth century had been provincials whose speech had not been affected by the Latinate vocabulary of the humanists. Moved to America and cut off from the progressive refinement of English speech, Yankee dialect was the product of arrested development. But that made it attractive, not vulgar. Since the opening of the nineteenth century, British travelers (and many refined Americans) had contended that Yankee speech was a vulgarization of standard English. It was a new provincial dialect whose use marked a declension and bore witness to the vulgarity of the new democracy. Lowell disagreed. He thought Yankee dialect was, in truth, the purest Saxon speech left in the world. *Humans* used for *men* was commonly condemned, for example, but Lowell found it used in Chapman's translation of Homer.[45] Using *progress* as a verb was condemned as a Yankee vulgarism by Coleridge among many others. Lowell, however, found it in Shakespeare ("doth progress down thy cheeks"). The double negative, common in the sixteenth century, also was frequently used by Shakespeare. *Barfoot* instead of *barefoot* Lowell discovered in the Coventry plays. Using *out* at the end of a sentence for emphasis (as in "it was the biggest thing out") Lowell found in John Glower's fourteenth-century poetry. Glower also said "there's a sight of flowers" as naturally, Lowell wrote, "as our upcountry folk would say it." And when a Yankee skipper says "boun' for Gloster" the New England poet noted that "he but speaks like Chaucer or an old ballad singer."[46]

For Lowell, the Saxon language proved that Americans were not devoid of traditions, that they had a cultural and ethical heritage stretching back hundreds of years. Language, wrote Richard Trench in *English: Past and Present*, was fossil-poetry, fossil-morality, and fossil-religion. It revealed the past in the present, and the history of our keywords revealed our ethical heritage.[47] To Lowell, Yankee dialect was no sign of cultural decay, as had been thought earlier in the century. It was a sign of a thriving organic connection with the best Saxon traditions.

Lowell may have praised American rusticisms, but he attacked other idioms. The poet had hard words for the American newspaper, whose language he thought vulgar and pompous. Newspapers were "dangerous," a subtle poison sapping the vigor of American prose. From them people would learn bad habits. And for those whose chief reading matter was the daily paper, as was the case with most Americans, the final result would be disastrous. Lowell cited some examples of the bloated prose he had culled from the press. "A great crowd came to see" was rendered "A vast concourse was assembled to witness." Newspapers could not say "great fire" or that the "house burned," they had to report that the "disastrous conflagration consumed the ediface." He found a "man who fell" described as an "individual who was precipitated." Instead of saying "began his answer" one newspaper had made it "commenced his rejoinder." Lowell pointed out that what simply could be "The mayor in a short speech welcomed" had been recorded as

> The chief magistrate of the metropolis, in well-chosen and eloquent language, frequently interrupted by the plaudits of the surging multitude, officially tendered the hospitalities.

And he found a man hanged described as one "launched into eternity."[48]

The pomposity stems from two sources, using more words than necessary and using non–Saxon English (*concourse* for *crowd*, *conflagration* for *fire*, *individual* for *man*, *commenced* for *began*). Lowell praised folk dialect not only to set himself off from earlier men of letters—the Johnsons and the Gibbons—but as well to set himself off from the new form of popular writing he found in newspapers.

Along with bombast, Lowell also attacked slang. Despite his defense of Yankeeisms, he drew a sharp line between "provincialism properly so-called and slang. Slang is always vulgar," Lowell wrote, "because it is not natural but an affected way of talking."[49]

Here again Lowell was one of many Americans and Europeans who in the middle of the nineteenth century began worrying about slang. Slang was "that evanescent, vulgar language, ever changing with fashion and taste," according to John Camden Hotten in his 1859 *Dictionary of Modern Slang*. It was associated with nineteenth-century innovation and challenges to cultural tradition. People used slang, he held, "from a desire to appear familiar with the transient nick names and street jokes of the day."[50]

With such fears abounding, provincial dialects, or at least their literary remains, could be put to good use by people like Lowell. In the middle of the century, provincial dialects began to lose their subversive tinge, which in turn passed to slang. Bartlett's 1848 *Dictionary of Americanisms* was the last to call Americanisms vulgar. In 1859, Alfred L. Elwyn's *A Glossary of Supposed Americanisms* attempted to prove how much American speech was actually derived from the old Anglo-Saxon. By 1870, *The New York Times* editorialized tongue in cheek that recent scholarship had taken away America's sense of verbal ingenuity: All "our" words were really Anglo-Saxon. These commentators shared with Lowell his distaste for American slang and bombast, saying that those half-educated politicians, editors, and businessmen were alternately breezy and informal, or bloated and pretentious. They were the new vulgarians. Linguistically, they had lost touch with the culture's folk roots. James Russell Lowell's alliance of the folk and the refined was a literary alliance. Folk speech was not to be aped; it would provide memory and verve. Philology sanctioned folk speech, but only as a buffer against a "rootless" popular culture.[51]

# III

Saxon eloquence explored the possibilities of the common touch. Lowell's poetry and the King James Bible were both seen as helping to fashion a democratic rhetoric, one that would be popular but not crass, that would bring together the highest sentiments with the lowest language against the vulgarity increasingly associated with other middling cultural forms. The same can be found elsewhere, in American prose, linguistics, and rhetoric. Let us look briefly at each, through the thought of Ralph Waldo Emerson, the philology of George Perkins Marsh, and the oratory of Abraham Lincoln.

Very early on, Emerson's Romanticism and radicalism drove him from neoclassic aesthetics. "I embrace the common, I explore and sit at the feet of the familiar, the low," Emerson wrote in "The American Scholar." And indeed, Emerson was captivated by the new popular literature of the 1830s. The Jack Downing tales first published in that decade readily assaulted all standards of refined prose. Emerson was interested, as he was by all sorts of vulgar speech. "The language of the street is always strong," he confided to his journal in 1840. "I confess to some pleasure from the stinging rhetoric of a rattling oath in the mouth of truckmen & teamsters. . . . Cut these words and they would bleed; they are vascular & alive; they walk & run. . . . It is a shower of bullets, whilst Cambridge men & Yale men correct themselves & begin again at every half sentence."[52]

Despite this, it would be a mistake to press Emerson too close to American popular culture. There is the obvious: Emerson was not easy to understand. When he lectured, listeners easily misunderstood his point.[53] In print, his transcendental terminology was as important as any borrowings from backwoods literature. Emerson did not write a popular idiom.

This was related to his own more complicated attitudes toward language. For as Emerson pointed out in "Nature" (1835), common, earthy language was useful only if it embodied a spiritual, transcendental truth. This idealist strain could lead Emerson into a stratosphere of abstraction far removed from the language of teamsters and popular literature:

> The world proceeds from the same spirit as the body of man. It is a remoter and inferior incarnation of God, a projection of God in the unconscious. But it differs from the body in one important respect. It is not, like that, now subjected to the human will. Its serene order is inviolable by us. It is, therefore, to us, the present exposer of the divine mind.[54]

In fact, during the 1830s and 1840s, Emerson expressed many different ideas about language. His interest in contemporary popular culture was actually quite minimal.[55] Alongside his praise of teamster talk was discussion of Milton, Plutarch, and Montaigne. Alongside his transcendental speculations were casual asides about linguistic analogy that made him sound very much like the philosophical grammarians of his day.[56]

Finally, as every major commentator on Emerson has noted, there was a basic modulation in his outlook after the 1830s that moved him in a more "respectable" direction. Emerson, like Lowell, became more conservative. And when this happened, the lure of gentility was strong. One can already see this in his 1840s essay on manners, as tame as any product of the genteel tradition. By the middle of the 1860s, Emerson was writing in his journal of an American "aristocracy," of the "best men" at West Point. He was commenting favorably on the reserve of fine manners and expressing complicated thoughts about the distinctly vulgar Mr. Lincoln.[57] Emerson's Romanticism more and more became a gentleman's version. Tension remained in his thought, but he had been educated to refinement. His own language reflected it. His essays became examples of what Lowell had called "familiar dignity."

Many Romantic philologists lacked even Emerson's hesitations. A very good example is George Perkins Marsh, whose *Lectures on the English Language* (1859) was greeted with almost unanimous critical acclaim in both America and England. Marsh was a Vermont gentleman who in the 1840s had served in Congress, and who was a leading spirit in the creation of the Smithsonian Institution. His father served on the Vermont Supreme Court and his cousin was James Marsh, who in 1829 edited the first American edition of Coleridge's *Aids to Reflection*.

Like Lowell, Marsh defended civil refinement. One year after he published *Lectures on the English Language* he told graduates of West Point that their education had gained them entry into "the intellectual and morally-progressive class in civilized nations." They would enjoy a rank in life giving them "universal access to the highest circles of refinement and intelligence." In his study of the English language Marsh also defended refinement. He argued that English was kept vital through its Saxon heritage. "Many of our seemingly insignificant and barbarous monosyllables are pregnant with the mightiest thoughts." The "advocate who would convince the technical judge, or dazzle and confuse the jury, speaks Latin; while he who would touch the better sensibilities of his audience . . . chooses his words from the native speech of our ancient fatherland." Marsh did a statistical analysis to prove that the greatest authors of the English language overwhelmingly used Saxon-derived English: Eighty-five percent of Shakespeare was Anglo-Saxon, 83 percent of Addison, 89 percent of Swift. The King James Bible was a full 97 percent Anglo-Saxon English. But in the course of the eighteenth century, there was a dangerous drop in such vocabulary. Only 65 percent of Hume was from the Anglo-Saxon side of English, only 75 percent of Johnson. Gibbon fell to a shockingly low 58 percent.[58]

Marsh blamed the drop on "French principles of philosophy" that encouraged "rootlessness." Like Lowell, he also worried about the vulgarity of current American speech. The newspapers were a dark force, Marsh contended, potentially brutalizing us. Mass education may have spread civilization but it also created its own form of tyranny. "Popular literature in all its forms," Marsh argued, "is in the ascendant." He continued:

> The novel of society, the magazine story, the poetic tale of easy rhyme and easy reading, the daily sheet, and especially the illustrated gazette, these are the bazaars where genius now offers itself for sale. The aim of a numerous class of popular writers is to reproduce, in permanent forms, the tone of light and easy conversation, to make books and journals speak the dialect of the saloon, and hence the pungency of expression, . . . the dialect of personal vituperativeness, . . . the billingsgate of vulgar hate, . . . combined with a certain flippancy of expression.

Then he concluded: "The influence of the periodical press upon the purity of the language must be admitted to have proved hitherto, upon the whole, a deleterious one."[59]

For Marsh vital civilizations were inevitably balanced between barbarism and sickly decay. Eighteenth-century social theorists had made the same point but with one important difference. Hume, Adam Ferguson, and William Robertson argued that what was unique about the West was chivalry. Even in the barbarous Middle Ages, chivalry was the first sign of civility, which was introduced in the Renaissance. Marsh, though, dismissed chivalry. What was important about Saxon England was its energy, its power, in short, its barbarism. Yet this was not a celebration of barbarism so much as of its domesticated remains. A refined Saxon English kept us strong and virtuous. The period from 1300 to 1650 was the subject of Marsh's second book. That period showed how a profound literature could arise "organically" from barbarous roots. Other writers of the 1860s also paid special attention to the passage from Saxon to English. The Scottish scholar George Craik highlighted it in his study of English language and literature. *The New York Times* reported in 1863 that the period showed the shift from a language "still rude, elementary and imperfect" to one of "magnificent richness and flexibility," a "fit medium for the genius of Spencer, Bacon or Shakespeare." It was not folk language that was praised, but the folk roots of the refined language.[60]

Romantic philologists were not alone in trying to yoke together the high and the low against the middle. Leonard Richards has shown that the same dynamic lay behind antiabolitionist riots of the 1830s. "Gentlemen of property and standing" led mobs of the lowest sort against the abolitionists, who were seen as exemplars of a new and threatening middle class.[61] Philologists like Marsh were not rioters, but the similarity does suggest how broad-based were antebellum fears that the middle was a destabilizing force undermining "organic" connections between the high and low. We have already seen these sentiments appearing in the defense of the King James Bible. In the hands of a philologist like Marsh, Saxon eloquence became an effort to reconstruct a social order torn apart by a rootless and voraciously vulgar popular audience.

For men like Lowell, Emerson, and Marsh, Saxon eloquence all too often slid into a reformulation of the gentry ideal. Late-sixteenth- and seventeenth-century prose was too close to older forms of social authority, perhaps even closer than such gentlemen realized. It might be that the highest potential for Saxon eloquence can be found in someone *not* educated to be a gentleman, someone with deep roots in rustic life. Some of the greatest romantic eloquence ever produced came from one such person. It is in the Civil War oratory of Abraham Lincoln that Saxon eloquence displayed all its possibilities as a democratic *sermo humilis*.

Lincoln's prose is saturated in Saxon eloquence. He knew the Common Version well, particularly the Psalms and Gospels. And Lincoln loved Shakespeare, declaiming from the tragedies and histories as a provincial lawyer and as a president of the United States. Scholars have long appreciated the nobility of Lincoln's rhetoric and have carefully scrutinized its power. To Roy Basler in 1939, Lincoln's oratory suggested "comparison with the cadenced prose of the seventeenth century." Edmund Wilson, in *Patriotic Gore*, emphasized the scriptural phraseology of Lincoln's rhetoric. But as early as 1864 James Russell Lowell had summed up Lincoln's style with the same words he used to praise Dryden: "familiar dignity."[62]

At times, Lincoln's borrowing is direct. "Four score and seven years ago" explicitly echoes the Psalms' "three score and ten," the common life of a man. Lincoln also knew the power of Saxon English; no one would confuse his rhetoric with eighteenth-century prose. One very good example of this is the First Inaugural Address, reworked from a draft by William Seward. Over and over again, Lincoln cut the flab from Seward's version. Seward's suggestion:

> "We are not, we must not be, aliens or enemies, but fellow-countrymen and brethren."

Lincoln changed to:

> "We are not enemies, but friends. We must not be enemies."

The latter's virtue is its very simplicity. Lincoln cuts four nouns to two, allowing for the evocative repetition of "enemies" (repetition being one of

Lincoln's standard rhetorical techniques). Moreover, one of the nouns Lincoln erased is especially formal and Latinate ("aliens"), and he has replaced the complicated and partially Latinate "fellow-countrymen" with the simple Saxon monosyllable "friends." (Elsewhere, too, Lincoln found the Saxon where Seward had not.) Seward's nouns are an undistinguished mix, adding nothing to his prose. Lincoln, on the other hand, successfully dramatizes his sentences by reducing the counterpoint's complexity. It is quite simple—"friends" or "enemies."[63]

As important as any direct borrowing, however, was the borrowed tone. Lincoln's most famous oratory has all the dignified nobility of the Psalms, the *Areopagitica*, or Hamlet's soliloquy. There is, for example, his Second Inaugural Address:

> With malice toward none; with charity for all; with firmness in the right, as God gives us to see the right, let us strive on to finish the work we are in; to bind up the nation's wounds . . . to do all which may achieve and cherish a just, and a lasting peace, among ourselves, and with all nations.

Dignifying the occasion also accounts for the opening of the Gettysburg Address. "Four score and seven years ago our fathers brought forth" could, after all, have been rendered more prosaically: "The revolutionary leaders declared Independence eighty-seven years ago." Lincoln himself, in 1857 in a more informal setting, spoke of the Declaration being written "some eighty years ago." This as Garry Wills has pointed out, is much closer to the standard idiom of a twentieth-century politician, but it is not characteristic of Lincoln's most formal speech.[64]

But perhaps this overstates it. Lincoln very consciously strove to ennoble his prose, but not only with archaic language. More striking is how the sublime appears in the simplest dress, through words like "friends" and "enemies." Every "four score" in Lincoln can be offset by more familiar dignity: "that government of the people, by the people, and for the people, shall not perish from the earth."

The power of Lincoln's eloquence begins with his cadence, not vocabulary. Strategic repetition, antithesis, and parallelism lend mood far more than lofty diction. Take the Second Inaugural: "With malice toward none; with charity for all. . . ." The antithesis does the work here, the vocabulary is commonplace. So too at the close of the Gettysburg Address: the "government of the people, by the people, and for the people" is ruled by repetition, not diction, although the plainness of the idiom is given just the slightest touch of dignified formality when Lincoln uses "perish" instead of "disappear."

In the end, of course, Lincoln's rhetoric succeeded because he could bring it all together. He knew how to mesh the humble, rustic, and lofty better than all the second-raters. Nor should Lincoln's evident sincerity be ignored. Lincoln's pain over the war was obvious; his ruminations on political principles genuine. Lincoln's was a form of middling rhetoric that never pandered to the crowd. He did not so much play roles in public as reveal an *ethos*. His manner was, as Locke said of all good breeding, "a Disposition of the Mind that shews itself in the Carriage."

But this said, the simple and the rustic cannot be forgotten. They were critical to Lincoln's oratory, indeed to his whole self. Lincoln was not the bumpkin that Carl Sandburg once made him out to be, but he was a provincial all the same. He was notorious for his homely metaphors and his Midwest idioms. But less often understood by contemporary gentlemen was the way that these very bits of homely prose contributed to the dignity of his rhetoric, not by themselves, but with other, more formal cadences and turns of phrase. There was nothing simple about the way Lincoln mixed refined and vulgar styles, but the bits of vulgarity were not unimportant. In the democratic age, the noble would be bound to the humble. Lincoln's rhetoric exemplified the democratic sublime.

This should not be confused with the Ciceronian sublime. In fact, Lincoln's oratory reflects changes in the concept of the sublime that had occurred after the middle of the eighteenth century. Cicero had argued that style must match subject matter, which meant that the loftiest matters needed the loftiest prose. Samuel Johnson reflected this sentiment by defining *sublime* as "the grand or lofty style." But the meaning began changing with the publication of Edmund Burke's *Philosophical Enquiry into the Origins of Our Ideas of the Sublime and Beautiful* (1757) and the subsequent rediscovery of Longinus. The sublime came to be associated with terror, and awe, and, by the nineteenth century, with Christian revelation. It had lost its connection to lofty prose.[65]

Hugh Blair's *Lectures on Rhetoric and Belles Lettres*, still very influential in the middle of the nineteenth century, explicitly associated the sublime with very simple language.[66] For Blair, what was sublime was the object itself. Lofty language was unnecessary. "God said, Let there be light; and there was light." *That* was sublime. (Note that just as with Lincoln, it is the repetition rather than the vocabulary that is important.) According to Blair, nothing illustrated the sublime better than Hebrew poetry.[67]

For Blair and later Romantics, the sublime was connected to genius, and genius moved beyond any rules of decorum. The idea was culled from Longinus' *On the Sublime* and was one way that Longinus differed from Cicero. "Taste" was the first substantive chapter in Blair's rhetoric. Like Cicero, he considered good taste a moral as well as aesthetic good. For the genius, however, Blair thought good taste irrelevant: Geniuses broke the rules, especially when dealing with matters sublime.

For Blair, genius marked a special case. Refined taste and the morality of style was the usual run of things. By the 1850s, however, Blair's ideas could be used in ways he had never expected. With the public stage open to far more homely speakers than ever before, Romantic concepts of the sublime became ways to dismiss "taste" as a relevant political category. Kant had moved in this direction by subjectivizing the sublime, but Blair, who was far more important in mid-nineteenth-century America, did just the opposite. He dismissed "taste" by *objectifying* the sublime. Certain *things* were sublime; for them good taste was irrelevant. The awesomeness of nature, the power of the Almighty—these followed their own rules with no regard for the dictates of polite decorum.

Blair's path was the one taken by Lincoln. Lincoln did not get past issues of refinement by making everything subjective ("It's all just a question of taste"—a now familiar but thoroughly un-Kantian form of subjectivity). Lincoln moved past polite decorum by holding that the Union was sacred in and of itself. Many commentators have noticed Lincoln's increasing faith in the power of God after the mid-1850s. Just as important for Lincoln's sublime, however, was the political regime. A government "conceived in liberty and dedicated to the proposition that all men are created equal" had a grandeur to it that made all issues of refined taste secondary. Lincoln's political sentiments were expressed through his oratorical style. Both, in turn, revealed how the romantic sublime could be democratized, invoking a dignity beyond refined decorum.

A noble character that was vulgar. A unified soul without unified style. Lincoln's Romantic sublime suggested an alternative to neoclassical moralizing about taste. Even sympathetic gentlemen could be apprehensive or confused. "He is a barbarian, Scythian, yahoo, or gorilla," wrote the New Yorker George Templeton Strong after meeting Lincoln in the White House. Significantly, Strong pointed to a linguistic lapse to make the point: "He uses 'humans' as English for *homines*." Strong, however, was a fellow Republican and tried to soften his judgment by calling Lincoln "a sensible old codger," adding that the President's "evident integrity" would "compensate for worse grammar than his, and for even more intense provincialism and rusticity." Ralph Waldo Emerson expressed similar reservations: "Lincoln. We must accept the results of universal suffrage & not try to make it appear that we can elect fine gentlemen." Lincoln's taste could not be refined, Emerson thought, nor his horizons broadened. Lincoln would continue to "cheapen himself" by petty squabbling. "But this we must be ready for," noted Emerson, "and let the clown appear, & hug ourselves that we are well off, if we have got good nature, honest meaning, & fidelity to public interest, with bad manners, instead of an elegant roué & malignant self-seeker."[68]

St. Augustine's fourth-century *sermo humilis*, I have noted, was grounded in the spiritual egalitarianism of the Christian message, that any believer, no matter how humble, could be holy. Augustine's own move away from classical rhetoric reflected this. As Erich Auerbach has noted, Augustine's oratory mixed classical and popular styles. His rhetoric had all the cadenced subtlety of Cicero, but also included homely talk about "gobbling" up food and belching. But the important thing, as Auerbach notes, is that under the impact of Christianity, such vulgarisms ceased to be vulgar, as they now were connected to the most sublime truths. "Humble everyday reality," Auerbach writes of Augustine's style, "takes on a new *gravitas*."[69]

Nineteenth-century democracy brought Christianity's spiritual egalitarianism down to earth. All men were created equal. No doubt, as Auerbach notes of the Christian *sermo humilis*, the sentiment could be stale and false; but just as often, he adds, new life could be breathed into it.[70] What made Lincoln's rhetoric so powerful was its dignity, sincerity, and its willingness to take the audience seriously, *combined with* exactly that which made gentlemen apprehensive—its lack of couth.

The Christian *sermo humilis* appeared throughout the Middle Ages, in all forms of literary expression, and culminated in *The Divine Comedy*.[71] So it is with the democratic version. From *Huckleberry Finn* to *The Color Purple* it informs some of the best American fiction. It is there in the photography of Lewis Hine and Dorothea Lange, and in oratory, having guided the bravura performances of Martin Luther King, Jr., as it did Abraham Lincoln. It is certainly not the only valid democratic style. Nothing would have sounded sillier than FDR trying it. But it is one of the finest. The democratic *sermo humilis* draws on the commonest culture, not to pander or flatter, but to call us back to our best possibilities as human beings and citizens.

# IV

In the years prior to the Civil War, the inherited grammar, dictionary, and Bible had all come under attack. In each case those proposing reform argued that the incumbent texts were corrupt, obscurantist, and aristocratic. In each case the defenders of the texts associated the reformers with the newly assertive half-educated. It was clear who won. In 1860 the same Bible was used as had been found in the nation's pulpits in 1780. The names on the grammars and dictionaries were different, but the ideas inside remained essentially the same. All celebrated the literary language that was vital to the cultural health of a civilized nation.

What, though, had the victories accomplished? The debates over the grammars, dictionaries, and Bibles were strangely hermetic, about the messages *in texts* rather than the cultural and social problems raised by popular democratic rhetoric. Reforming grammarians, lexicographers, and Bible translators had been fought off, but middling politicians, editors, and businessmen still ran the country. Even as the defenders of civil English were winning all the battles they felt themselves losing the war.

The diffusion of civil culture raised problems never dreamed of in the eighteenth century. Now the small number of cultural creators had to find not only a refined audience but a popular audience as well. Moreover, access to that public was not direct. Each cultural elite found that popular success depended on winning the support of key groups of cultural mediators. The grammarians had their schoolmasters, the lexicographers their administrators, and the Bible translators their ministers. All had to argue through—and with—the periodical press. No longer was anyone sure that each voice speaking was one of informed taste.

Saxon eloquence was one effort to reharmonize the elements. Yet Romantic linguistics would ultimately encourage disrespect for the grammar, dictionary, and Bible. By the 1850s, it was common for writers to complain that grammar was excessively "rationalistic," a product of the worst of the eighteenth century. It imposed Latinate forms on idiomatic Saxon custom. George Fitzhugh thought grammars thwarted the "natural growth and development" of language. Edgar Allan Poe, George Perkins Marsh, and Samuel Goodrich expressed similar thoughts. Grammar was a "procrustean bed" to one writer, a "shrivelled skeleton, held together by such contrivances as the anatomist uses, rather than by the natural ligaments which give grace and elasticity to the whole body." Grammar was inorganic.[72]

As Romantic currents encouraged research into a culture's folk traditions, they uncovered new information that undermined the authority of the dictionary and Bible. In the 1850s, Richard Chenevix Trench, the author of *English: Past and Present*, published two short but influential works: one on the dictionary and the other on the Bible. In the first he argued that all English dictionaries did not take into account the importance of the new historical philology. He advocated a major new dictionary based on historical principles, one that was a true record of the nation's language and soul. This pamphlet reshaped ideas about dictionary making, eventually inspiring the *Oxford English Dictionary*.[73]

Trench's second book contained a qualified plea for Bible revision. The interest in the historical Bible had uncovered hordes of new information that could not be ignored. The limits of the King James Bible, despite its profound beauty, had to be addressed. The weight of accumulated historical information bore down on the Common Version. Trench knew that this was not the time for revision, but he told scholars to press on with their work, for sometime in the near future revision would have to come.[74]

Romantic philologists thought language was the soul of the nation, the record of the ethical heritage of the Anglo-American people. Such thought encouraged cultural conservation rather than reform. In the late 1860s, new currents of thought emerged attacking the idea that language was a privileged cultural form, holding that it was merely an instrumental tool for passing information back and forth. When the Civil War encouraged the highly educated to attempt to recapture their cultural authority, the stage was set to play out Trench's drama. In the years after the Civil War, it would be the "best men" who tried to reform the authoritative texts about the English language in the hopes of reasserting their authority in America.

# CHAPTER FOUR

# Bad English Exposed

> In the past on the contrary, in any ordered society, maintaining one's rank was a form of dignity, a kind of virtue. Ridicule and condemnation were reserved only for those who flaunted the symbols of a social rank to which they were not entitled.
>
> FERNAND BRAUDEL

Language can be bruised in many ways. Attacked by pedantry, strangled by euphemism, beaten by rant—the ways language can be defeated seem limitless. In the years after the Civil War, conservative language critics began arguing that English was being "bruised" by thousands of small errors creeping into everyday speech. These postwar critics no longer feared the harsh, abrasive rhetoric associated with stump speaking, although, to be sure, such rhetoric continued to exist. Instead, they focused on the pervasive informality and imprecision they saw all around them.

The practice of making fine discriminations about the meaning of words was known since the late eighteenth century as "verbal criticism." Verbal criticism had been a minor part of the British literary tradition since the sixteenth century, but between the 1860s and 1890s it turned into a thriving industry. The differences between *shall* and *will*, *lay* and *lie*, and *differ from* and *differ with* were issues that cultivated Victorians took quite seriously. Books such as *Vulgarisms and Other Errors of Speech*, *The Verbalist*, *Words: Their Use and Abuse*, and *Bad English Exposed* were read widely in those years.

A handful of educators, journalists, and ministers formulated opinion on verbal etiquette. Their impact cannot be fully appreciated by merely citing the books they wrote. Teachers at all levels incorporated their ideas into the English curriculum. Magazines like *Godey's Lady's Book*, *The Atlantic Monthly*, and the *North American Review* discussed and usually approved their work. "Gentlemen's" newspapers, like the New York *Evening Post* and the Boston *Daily Advertiser*, also published verbal criticism. And the critics' prescriptions were collected into numerous handbooks described as guides to good usage. With titles like *Verbal Pitfalls: A Manual of 1500 Words Commonly Misused* or *The Handbook of Blunders: Designed to Prevent 1000 Common Blunders in Writing and Speaking*, these books were shorn of the elaborate literary references favored by verbal critics. No discussion of Johnsonian vocabulary or Shakespearean syntax complicated the simple lists of dogmatically presented prescriptions. The handbooks were packaged as complements to the etiquette books popular in those years.

The vogue for verbal criticism first surfaced in the 1860s. Like many intellectuals of the time, the language critics were buoyed by the Civil War. They thought the mass discipline the war imposed made it possible for the "best men" to reassert their dominance in American society; that the post-Jacksonian "festival of misrule" would end. Postwar efforts by the highly educated to claim a place of pride in American life took many forms—civil service reform, independence from party politics, new publishing ventures like *The Nation*, the creation of social scientific organizations, and the quest for tougher professional standards.[1]

Verbal critics hoped to contribute through linguistic criticism. Like their "soulmate" Matthew Arnold, who began writing about the function of criticism in the 1860s, these critics wanted to re-create the cultural and social atmosphere of the late eighteenth century,[2] reiterating a vision that was humanist at its core. They hoped to maintain the traditional civility of refined decorum. Polite language was "reserved," not "familiar." The prestige of gentlemen and ladies had to be reasserted. The essential morality of style must not be forgotten. The habits of thought that drove the late-nineteenth-century critics were, in a very real sense, ancient, echoing Cicero's division between the *liberales* (gentlemen) and *sordidi* (the vulgar).[3]

Verbal criticism was designed to help redraw the lines between the few and the many that had seemingly collapsed in mid-nineteenth-century America. Disgusted by the aggressive vulgarity of American life, verbal critics, like humanists for centuries before them, tried to "withdraw from popular culture."[4] Victorian verbal criticism was meant to be both an analysis of what was wrong with American language and a way to correct it. It would reintroduce habits of deference into everyday speech.

Yet that was not so easy to do in the 1870s. In a world where literacy was the rule and where traditional forms of deference had disintegrated, anyone could affect the trappings of gentility. The public had expanded, and it did whatever it wanted. A home library, a parlor piano, or the passing acquaintance with art and literature were no longer the preserve of the highly educated. The "vulgar" were not so obviously "crude" as in earlier eras. The old lines between the few and the many were gone; attempts to redraw them required an exacting hand.

# I

What did the critics find wrong with American speech? Americans spoke too much and without enough care. Words were losing their moorings, the fit between signifier and signified was not as tight as it had been. *Calculate* had formerly meant "to ascertain by means of symbols" but it was now vaguely used for "believed," "supposed," or "expected." *Mad*, which meant "crazy," was distended to mean "angry." The new meanings needlessly muddied previously distinct terms.[5] Americans also created too many new words. Although critics paid lip service to the legitimacy of neologisms, they primarily worked to compress the resources of the language. Why use *rubbers* when the perfectly good *overshoes* was available? With *point of view* in the lexicon why add *standpoint*? But as important as the linguistic reasoning were the cultural fears. The critics maintained that casually adopted neologisms inflated the vocabulary and undermined the mutual understanding needed for a society to cohere. The language would not collapse under the weight of the new vocabulary, but accuracy and precision would suffer. The massive influx of new words clouded the semantic field. The vocabulary grew too large for any individual to handle; the idea of a common tongue was in danger.

The linguistic errors revealed a deep cultural illness. The unstable tongue was indicative of the American ethos. Americans were restless, hostile to the tempering influence of tradition, almost mindlessly committed to innovation. According to the critics, all this was due to the pervasive influence of commercial values in American life. Narrowly utilitarian self-interest bred linguistic sloppiness. Richard Grant White blamed "a class of men which increases among us year by year—men whose chief traits are greed and vulgarity. . . ." Engaging repartee was no longer cultivated, another thought, since "even the pettiest joke has a cash value." Professional humorists had replaced conversational wit. Even a defender of slang spoke of the pragmatic necessities of the commercial world. The shortening of *gentlemen* to *gents*, he claimed, resulted from "the rapid requirements of business. . . . Doubtless the average shopkeeper does not realize the violence such a change does to the significance of words. . . . But business is business, and word clipping may be essential to it, in these hurried days."[6]

According to the critics, the all-consuming self-interest contradicted the manner in which educated men and women were expected to behave. Language was so important because it was more than a tool used to describe the world. Language also revealed the inner character of the speaker. Echoing traditional humanistic canons, the critics associated style with ethos. Words were the "image of our soul," the "sounds of our heart." Not *what* we said but *how* we said it occupied the attentions of the post– Civil War language critics. The "cunning reader" looked "between the lines" to chart a writer's character. Subtle stylistic choices, as between *good* and *swell*, had portentous implications; such decisions were essentially ethical, externalizing our moral being. A consistently refined idiom implied a unified soul: "If a man is clear-headed, noble-minded, sincere, just and pure in thought and feeling, these qualities will be symbolized in his words; and on the other hand, if he has a confused habit of thought, is mean, grovelling and hypocritical, these characteristics will reveal themselves in his speech." Whatever might be said on the surface, style exposed the deep structure of our character.[7]

The promiscuous usage of American speech was at odds with the refined self-control of the educated gentlemen and ladies. Universal literacy had created a huge mass of half-educated adults, and political democracy had placed them at the center of American life. Grasping politicians and entrepreneurial hucksters had a smattering of knowledge, but not enough to teach them humility. This left a mass of people with pretensions but no real education. The bad language was due to

> the wide diffusion of just so much instruction as enables men to read their newspapers, write their advertisements, and keep their accounts, and the utter lack of deference to any one, or of doubt in themselves, which political equality and material prosperity beget in people having no more than such education.[8]

It was because of this that criticism was so necessary. Previously the educated had set the standards of linguistic usage. But now the semi-educated simply let the language drift. Criticism was a rudder, needed to guide the language through the waves of presuming half knowledge that threatened to engulf it.

Other worries of the verbal critics made more explicit their fears about the decay of civil language. They brooded over the growing informality of American usage and inveighed against the increasing indifference to precise meaning. Both problems reflected declining standards of personal conduct. Popular linguistic habits, the critics thought, showed that the self-interested "go-getter" was replacing the civic-minded gentleman at the center of American life. Moreover, the everyday errors of speech also contributed to the collapse of social hierarchy. Informality was leveling, denying deference to the cultivated; sloppy usage made accurate perception more difficult. It was becoming harder to tell who was who.

The offensive informality took many forms. The common use of contractions and the continual failure to pronounce the final *g* in words ending in *ing* were condemned. Henry James claimed that the general elision of consonants left "a mere helpless slobber of disconnected vowel noises." But most of all, the critics recoiled from the excessive use of slang. Slang, "always low, generally coarse, and not unfrequently foolish," was burrowing its way into American speech. Almost all writers, for example, worried about using *gents* for *gentlemen* and *pants* for *trousers*. Richard Grant White noted that *gents* and *pants* belonged together because one always wore the latter. One writer hated *gent* so that he claimed "if I were naked and starving I would refuse to be clothed gratis in a 'Gent's Furnishing Store' or accept a complimentary dinner in a 'Gent's Saloon'."[9]

Similarly, in 1885, *Good Housekeeping* published an editorial about the vulgar informality of *thanks*. Although the word was used in the attempt to be "proper," the effect was "strangled by the belief that there is not time enough in which to say so appropriately, or else not culture enough to recognize the fitness of things." The editor continued: "*Thanks* is cold, careless and uncivil. It is heartless, meaningless and harsh to the sensitive listener." *Thank you*, however, was "warm, considerate and polite."[10]

The critics believed that slang had to be severely restricted, even among men of similar status. It thrust a familiar speech register into settings demanding more formality. As Georg Simmel once pointed out, every human being has a core of beliefs so important to him that they simply must be taken seriously. An acquaintance cannot treat this "intellectual private property" lightly without offense being taken. As Simmel noted, penetration of this core "effects a lesion of the ego at its very center." Slang did just that. It was associated with "low" behavior. It was "the riff-raff of language." The untouchable core of a gentleman's self was his cultivated reserve, exactly the kind of day-to-day behavior that he interpreted as "civilized." The familiarity of slang signaled disrespect even from a social equal. Words like *gents* and *pants*, phrases like *blame it on* or *in our midst* rang with a familiarity rebarbative from the pulpit or in the newspaper, out of place while dining or at work. As one critic put it, "Familiarity is insulting and slang is familiar."[11]

Slang was tinged with a sensuality that made it especially improper in public places. White described it as "racy" at one point, "pungent" at another. Henry Alford, a British clergyman whose *A Plea for the Queen's English* (1863) was reprinted eight times in the United States, complained about couples using "unmeaning and ridiculous . . . terms of endearment." Alford offered a hypothetical example of the offense. After dinner, "after the departure of the ladies from the dining room," he begins conversing with a man whose "age and experience make him a treasurehouse of information and practical wisdom." But Alford develops some reservations about his companion, although he cannot exactly locate the source of his dissatisfaction. Then at 10:00 P.M., when the party is breaking up,

> a shrill voice from the other side of the room calls out, "Sammy, love!" All is out. He has a wife who does not know any better, and he has never taught her better.

Alford cautioned that we should never "let the world look through these chinks into the boudoir." The informal register thus slips into the still more private world of intimacy. "A more offensive habit cannot be imagined," he wrote.[12]

The anecdote captures the importance of seemingly trivial acts for the nineteenth-century bourgeoisie, their disgust with casualness, their presumed patriarchy. But it also suggests how easily such norms could be ignored. *Loveys* and *Dearies* might have been the "drivelling nonsense" that Alford claimed, but they still effortlessly invaded his dining room. The vulgar were not a distantly removed social class, but his own dinner guests. The battle for decorum was quite literally fought on the home front.

Beyond that, the informality that blanketed the nation threatened social distinction. The critics feared slang as a subtle leveling device. One way subordinates defer to superiors is by not treating them familiarly, by "keeping their distance"; informal speech indicates such deference is unnecessary. Slang forces a moment of egalitarianism on listeners by treating them with no special respect. Josiah Holland, the editor of *The Century*

*Magazine*, heard *"Bien! Monsieur"* from clerks, waiters, and cab drivers in Paris, but "All right, boss; you can bet on 't" from their counterparts in New York.[13] Another writer, complaining about boys who used *posish* for *position*, added that if "the *posish* of one of them should be that of a hotel-runner, and he should meet you as you step from a train, he will be certain to call you a *gent*." Many commentators observed that informality was a form of vanity, aggressively denying the force of social distinction.[14]

But to the critics such behavior was fulsome, another form of that "rude familiarity assumed by conscious inferiors." Hostility to slang rested on a broader opposition to the excessive casualness of American civilization. To the cultivated bourgeoisie, loud laughter, winking, whispering, and swaggering were all depressingly common acts of familiarity. Using first names indiscriminately was another American vice.[15] So too was gossip. All were attempts to erase social distinction, but all were evidence of the opposite, for the "first proof of lowness is seen at once in undue famil-iarity."[16] To the highly educated, such behavior was more than a mark of ignorance; it was an affront. Idle curiosity about others was an example of that vulgar "incursion on the personal" which "increases every day." One writer praised "reserve" in conversation because it saved us "from the vice of familiarity, which in an inferior is offensive, in a superior uncomfortable, in either case distinctly vulgar."[17]

Despite the basic opposition to slang, there were exceptions. Men, in small private gatherings, were generally allowed slang. This was not the case for women. "Girls don't talk slang," read one newspaper column. "If it is necessary that any one in the family should do that let it be your big brother. . . ." There was no respite for women.[18]

The leading critics were all men, yet they generally saw refined women as their allies. The male critics attacked vulgar women with the same zeal with which they criticized men, but they also took note of exemplary women who produced elegant and refined prose.[19] Women's magazines like *Godey's* or *Peterson's*, in turn, were friendly to the male critics. The women's periodicals cautioned against slang, excerpted the men's verbal criticism, and called attention to the special role women had in maintaining the language. As one magazine put it in 1868: "If it were not for our women there would be danger of having our English smothered in slang. They seldom use it—a well-bred woman never uses it . . . That is why, in all enlightened countries, women, scarcely less than scholars, are the conservators of the purity and beauty of their language, as they are also the conservators of religion and morals."[20]

The absolute injunction against women using slang directly relates to nineteenth-century cults of domesticity. One typical critic claimed that hearing a "young lady" answer a question with the "flippancy" of a "*Not Much!*" surrounded her "with the rougher associations of men's daily life" and brought "her down from the pedestal of purity. . . ." Women's language was presumed to be better than men's, and maintaining purity depended on remaining shielded from the toughness of masculine public life. "*I bet* or *you bet* is well enough among men trading horses or land," but "positively shocking" from "the lips of a young lady."[21]

Complaints about women's use of slang existed, but they were few. The scattered criticisms almost always cite adolescent girls as the offenders. When *The New York Times* in 1881 editorialized about the vulgarity of girls from "good homes" saying things like "What a cunning hat," the paper was making a complaint not unlike 1980s fears about "valley girl" talk. The next generation of "ladies" was falling sway to the tyranny of popular idioms.

That the women's magazines of the day accepted such dictums reflects their own effort to maintain traditional standards of decorum, to honor refined ways of life. The women's magazines were just as worried about popular vulgarity as were the male language critics. The position taken on language by the women writers also reflects their own uneasiness about their status. Writers like Catherine Maria Sedgwick and Susan Warner, despite their efforts to give women a public voice, were ambivalent about women's public role. They tended to be drawn in two directions—to open up more space for women but also to see women as fundamentally nurturing, caring, "mothering." While these editors and writers pushed for the end of *coverture*, they never unequivocally pressed for the vote, nor, especially important here, did they feel it particularly important that women *speak* in public. They viewed with awe those few women who were public orators but were also reassured when such women could be described as "feminine" or "refined." That the women's magazines saw women as essential guardians of the language should not be missed, but this was to be accomplished largely through the written word and conversation. Men would be the primary public speakers.[22]

In all of this, the male verbal critics could readily agree. Refined ladies had a special place, but one that did not aggressively challenge the prerogatives of public men. It should not be surprising that Richard Grant White thought women's special contribution was in letter writing.[23] This was a faint echo of Chesterfield's eighteenth-century argument that women were models of deportment but not suited for serious learning: Women would guard the language but they guarded it for use by men.

Despite the gender complications, the basic point was the same. America's public language was decaying. There was too much slang, too much informality of all kinds. And this decay revealed an appallingly low level of cultivation, the decline of the gentry, and the disappearance of social deference.

The pervasive indifference to precise meaning provided critics with more evidence that Americans lacked sensibility and taste. One handbook, published pseudonymously by "Critic," was simply entitled *Discriminate*. Lively discussion occurred among the verbal critics over the relative merits of *differ from* versus *differ with*. Edward Gould even complained about the phrase *blew his brains out with a pistol*, insisting that current pistols— revolvers—did no such thing. Musket shot, he contended, "placed within a few inches of a man's head, would literally blow his brains out; but pistol bullets destroy life in a much more neater and more cleanly style [*sic*]." Using *sociable* for *social*, *can* for *may*, *shall* for *will*, *avocation* for *vocation*, *proposition* for *proposal* along with hundreds of others were similarly proscribed.[24]

Imprecise usage was not only crude, it was dissembling. Habitual indifference to precise meaning had a "very bad moral bearing," according to Harvard professor Andrew Peabody. It often led one

> to distort facts, to misrepresent conversations and to magnify statements, in matters which the literal truth is important to be told. You can never trust the testament of one who in common conversation is indifferent to the importance and regardless of the power, of words.

Fuzzy language, according to Peabody, revealed a lack of commitment to honesty.[25]

Critics focused on two sorts of deceptive language. The first was what Richard Grant White called "squeamish cant." Genteel euphemisms such as *limb* for *leg*, *rooster* for *cock*, and *confined* for *pregnant*, invaded American vocabulary in the first half of the nineteenth century. This language usually surrounded biologically related phenomena with more circumspect associative meanings. Like the antebellum defenders of the King James Bible, the Victorian critics attached no opprobrium to speaking openly about biological facts. At the very least, euphemism had a contradictory effect, for the very use of *limb* was a flag that the speaker was thinking of the "indelicate meaning" associated with *leg*, leaving a "slight stain" on a "conversation intended to be perfectly pure."[26]

Although verbal critics might easily be called part of the genteel tradition, they in fact cautioned their readers not to use *genteel* in a positive sense.[27] *Genteel* and *gentility* slowly took on negative connotations after 1850, at least to the cultivated segments of society. The terms referred to false and pretentious efforts at refinement, or attempts of "low" people to affect cultivation. Women were often cited as the main offenders. As a youth Richard Grant White boarded for a time with a rural family who never "helped" him to anything on the dinner table but always "assisted" him to it. When the hostess once offered to "assist him to some sass" the cultivated White could not help from bursting into laughter, a lapse of civility he regretted in his later years. White also remembered the maid who told her employer "she and her chil'n hed ben awful sick; but they went into the country, and they resuscitated dreadful." The woman meant to say they had recovered. Genteel language, then, deceived in two ways. In the basic sense of naming the object, a word like *limb* surrounded a part of the anatomy with false airs by attempting to remove its sensate connotations. On the level of social interaction, such language was an assertion of refinement, although critics realized that in truth it revealed just the opposite.[28]

Bombast, the other common variety of deceptive usage, was proscribed for similar reasons. Choosing a long word where a short one would do incensed verbal critics. "The newspaper writers never allow us to *go* anywhere, we always *proceed*," Henry Alford wrote. "A man going home is set down as *an individual proceeding to his residence*." Using *predicate* for *say*, *transpire* for *happen*, *initiate* for *begin*, even *donate* for *give* were all condemned. William Mathews recalled the pedagogue of Kennebec County, Maine, who observed that a farmer was "excavating a subterranean channel." ("No, sir," replied the farmer, "I am only digging a ditch.") When Richard Grant White asked a policeman what a certain building was used for he was told, "That is an institootion inaugerated under the auspices of the Sisters of Mercy, for the reformation of them young females what has deviated from the path of rectitood." Such glaring contrasts between grammatical error and strained efforts at elegance were comically bathetic, but critics feared such language was rapidly becoming the habitual style of the American people. Like slang, stilted language was at odds with the verbal restraint of a true gentleman. Like euphemism, such usage was pretense, falsely inflating the importance of the commonplace. And like both slang and euphemism, bombast skewed perception of social status. Of course critics recognized that such language reflect a lack of "mental vigor" and "good taste," but they also saw it was the "fruit of a pitiful desire to seem elegant. . . ." Such language was affected to give the speaker "the air of a cultivated man."[29]

To Victorians, simple lack of elegance was not the only criterion of vulgarity. Illiteracy was not vulgar provided people did not inflate the importance of their actions. "The essence of vulgarity is pretense," one verbal critic wrote, and many echoed him.[30] In the eighteenth century, as I noted in the first chapter, *vulgar* meant "unrefined" but it also had close connections to "popular." Johnson, as I also noted in chapter 1, defined *gentleman* as "a man raised above the vulgar by his character or post," and *vulgar* as "plebian; suiting to the common people" or as "mean; low; being of the common rate." In the course of the nineteenth century, however, *vulgar* was slowly liberated from its connection with a specific social class. It drifted from a description of a social group to a more free-floating allusion to a cultural style. By the 1860s, commentators disavowed any tie between vulgarity and class. "There is no connection between vulgarity and humbleness of birth," one writer asserted. "Day laborers are less liable to exhibit vulgarity than other classes. . . ." Crudity in itself was not vulgar:

But when to a deficient sense of the beautiful is joined the pretension to possess it, there is the beginning of vulgarity, which blows out into full grossness when there follows a vainglorious display of the pretension.

In the 1871 edition of *Lectures to Young Men* Henry Ward Beecher also denied that vulgarity was connected to social rank. "A man's occupation is not vulgar simply because it is coarse, because it is low, or because it is unremunerative," Beecher wrote. Vulgarity was an "internal moral state." It was acting "from your animal and passional nature . . . under circumstances which require that you should act upon a higher plain. . . ." That Beecher, himself a symbol of middling vulgarity to many, should discuss the issue was just another example of how difficult it was to draw sharp lines in late-nineteenth-century America.[31]

Yet if the connection between vulgarity and social class was denied, the work of the verbal critics suggests some broad sociology. The lowest classes were *not* vulgar, thought Richard Grant White, their "simple and unpretending ignorance is always respectable. . . ."[32] Vulgarity was associated with the broad cultural middle, which should not be confused with the middle class. Verbal critics explicitly identified particular errors with policemen, maids, waiters, clerks, shopkeepers in the Bowery, en-

trepreneurs in general, rural schoolteachers (male), farmers, wives of farmers, popular editors, labor leaders, politicians, the young of virtually every
social class, and the nouveau riche both male and female. Some of the
very wealthy were condemned right alongside some people of very modest
means. It is wrong to suggest that the criticism was aimed at any easily
identifiable social group like the middle class, the new rich, or rustics.
The criticism cut across most class lines to all those who, as White put
it, set off little thoughts with "enormous phrases."

The combination of coarseness, pretension to sophistication, and ob-
tuseness about the resulting disjunction were the elements making up late-
nineteenth-century vulgarity. The late-nineteenth-century critics attacked
linguistic habits that seemed to be prevalent everywhere. They were looking for language that undermined deferential attitudes toward the gentry.
Imprecision and informality were doing just that, denying social distinction and pandering to the public. Moreover, by cavalierly changing, inflating, and confusing meanings of words Americans were not only
deceiving other Americans, they were rapidly destroying English as a
medium for seeing the world as it really was. The ceaseless motion of a
democratic commercial society threatened language itself. All that was
solid was melting into air.

# II

The arch villain, according to the critics, was the popular press. White
entitled his chapter on bombast "Newspaper English. Big Words for Small
Thoughts." Every verbal critic decried the vulgarity, coarseness, pomposity, and incivility of the popular press. Henry Alford argued that
linguistic debasement "is mainly owing to the vitiated and pretentious
style which passes current in our newspapers." Edward Gould commented, "Among writers, those who do the most mischief are the original
fabricators of error, to wit: the men generally who write for the newspapers."[33]

Although historians have often noted contemporary criticism of the
press, rarely have they analyzed the character of the anxieties caused by
the newspaper. When in the 1830s newspapers became widely accessible,
many quite correctly saw them as fundamentally reshaping the flow of
authoritative information. "The ascendency in literary and philosophical
questions which belonged to the writers of books is manifestly passing in
a very great degree to weekly and even daily papers," wrote William Lecky

in his *History of European Morals* (1869).[34] The newspaper was as important to the nineteenth-century mind as television is to ours.

Today complaints about newspapers usually stress their liberal bias, but through the nineteenth century the animadversions were more fundamental—that the medium by its very nature debased the culture. Such criticism was common by the 1830s and continued through the century. Newspapers sensationalized. They had an unhealthy monopoly on public opinion. Readers were overstuffed with information while their capacity to judge was dulled. "The effect cannot be but bad," said Henry Ward Beecher. "Rome had her gladiators; Spain her bull-fighters; England her bear-baiting; and America her newspapers."[35]

The reaction of the most literate sections of the community was not uniform. As with television today, some of the highly educated took pride in avoiding newspapers; others argued they should be read in moderation; still others claimed there was nothing to worry about. And just as contemporary professionals monitor their children's television viewing, nineteenth-century ladies and gentlemen worried about children feeding exclusively on newspapers. The first lists of "great books" were compiled to wean young Americans from their overreliance on daily journalism.[36]

Verbal criticism was part of the nineteenth-century movement to come to terms with the daily newspaper. Many of the critics, it should be noted, themselves worked for newspapers—Gould and White for the New York *Evening Post*, William Mathews for the *Chicago Tribune*. Such papers, however, were the aristocracy of the press. They aimed at refinement. Their vulgarities were errors of judgment, not matters of policy.

Papers that wanted to reach a broader audience, however, had a far different tone. Critics were not wrong to complain of the vulgarity of much of the popular press. In the New York *Sun* in 1870 one could still read articles with titles such as "Judge Woodruff's Court—Air That Would Kill a Hog" and "Is Secretary Fish a Fool or a Scoundrel?" When a murderer repented on the scaffold, the *Chicago Times* ran the memorable headline: JERKED TO JESUS. Such papers still reported (as the *Chicago Times* here) that there was "no more conceited ass, and a more useless member of society generally, than the college graduate." The "highly educated man" was given to "speculative theories that confuse the masses." He should be kept from government. These papers defended their provocative style as direct and truthful. They were plainspoken. Responding to the charge that he was unnecessarily abusive, Horace Greeley called *The New York Times'* refinement "mealy-mouthed." Similarly, in an article entitled "Dignity in Expression," the *Chicago Times* made fun of refined scruples.

Of course, there is no doubt that Grant will get drunk, and will lie, and will accept bribes, and will persist in saddling upon the people of this and other countries all of the insignificants in the Grant and Dent families, and that Senator Sumner told the truth when he said, "there is no weight, nor standard of weight or measure, by which Grant's stupidity can be estimated," but the courtesies of journalism will not permit these facts to be plainly stated.[37]

That the popular newspaper was the primary villain underlines a key point—the critics primarily complained about other men. While the Victorian linguistic criticism noted the ways that women abused the language, the overwhelming emphasis was on the vulgarity of men. The initial impetus for the craze of verbal criticism, I have argued, was a move by refined gentlemen to reassert their cultural authority over popular editors and politicians. The critics just did not fear women. New popular styles were associated with new kinds of male leadership. Women who were criticized were generally viewed not so much as uppity women claiming equality, but as the wives and daughters of the offending men.

Newspapers were just one of the many prominent institutions in which the expressive informality surfaced. They were even teaching slang songs in the schools, reported one who had heard "A Broadway Toff" sung in a New York classroom.[38] One could step into any number of restaurants throughout the nation that catered to "gents," which were not dives for the lower classes but informal spots for the middling sort. For example, in the center of Chicago there was Schlenker's Ladies' and Gents' Hotel and Restaurant on State Street, and the popular Vienna Café, which advertised itself as a "First Class Restaurant for Ladies and Gents." Just a few steps away, however, was the elegant Palmer House restaurant, which catered explicitly to "gentlemen." *Baedecker's*, the famous travel guide, cautioned European visitors to avoid American restaurants that served "gents."[39]

The contrasts between formal and informal language worked their way into everyday life. These were keenly observed by the novelist William Dean Howells. Having grown up in rural Ohio and been accepted into refined Bostonian circles, Howells was in the unique position of having firsthand knowledge of both ways of life. His ambiguous commitment to gentility and his superb eye for detail contributed to sympathetic interpretation of all parties. As an ethnographer of middling and refined life in late-nineteenth-century America, Howells is unsurpassed.

In the opening pages of *A Hazard of New Fortunes*, the shrewdly entrepreneurial Fulkerson converses with the cultivated Basil March in the latter's insurance office. Fulkerson attempts to convince March to leave his current employ and edit a new magazine. Fulkerson's speech is littered with grammatical solecisms ("You ain't an insurance man by nature."), slang ("such swell quarters"), and informality ("My dear boy! What are you giving me?"). There is also bombast:

> "I tell you March, this is the greatest idea that had been struck since"— Fulkerson stopped and searched his mind for a fit image—"since the creation of man."[40]

At one point Howells creates a wonderfully ironic moment by embedding a dignified sentiment in crude speech: "I do cotton to a Western man when I find him off East here, holding his own with the best of 'em, and showing 'em that he's just as much civilized as they are." In contrast to Fulkerson, the speech of Basil March is scrupulously correct. He leaves Fulkerson with these words: "I thought I might walk your way but I shouldn't have time. Good-bye." ("Ta-ta," Fulkerson says.) It is not only the textbook grammar and lack of slang that makes March's words more dignified than Fulkerson's. Consider a more informal statement of March's farewell: "I'd walk with you but I don't have the time. Good-bye." Both versions are syntactically correct but March uses "might" and "shouldn't" where "would" and "don't" would have sufficed. These subtle vocabulary changes blunt the direct impact of the statement and make it more reserved. So, too, does substituting "walk your way" for "walk with you." The second indicates a common activity that the first refuses to explicitly recognize. March's words create a psychological distance that the casual version lacks.[41]

Such contrasts run through many of Howells's novels. The stylistic differences between the Laphams and the Coreys in *The Rise of Silas Lapham* and between Dickerson and Ludlow in *The Coast of Bohemia* are similar to those separating Fulkerson and March. On the one side was the informal speech verbal critics disliked; on the other the reserved language they favored. Occasionally cultivated characters act as verbal critics, admonishing others for their bad English. Basil March's wife has to reconcile herself to Fulkerson's "graphic slanginess." In *A Hazard of New Fortunes*, the daughters of a Pennsylvania Dutch farmer are cautioned by their New York governess to say *allowable* and not *rulable*. In *The Coast of Bohemia*, the cultivated Ludlow is disturbed that the country-bred Cornelia Saunders does not distinguish between *that* and *as*, although he realizes that "ninety Americans out of a hundred, lettered or unlettered," could not have made the discrimination.[42]

Not only do speech habits reveal a character's degree of cultivation, they also indicate larger cultural identities. Informal language is associated with characters who are wed to narrowly entrepreneurial values and are comfortable with rural manners. Characters who use cultivated speech, on the other hand, usually feel that such commitments should be softened. Basil March works for an insurance firm, but he is proud to be cultivated and not crass. He earns a comfortable income, but he also keeps up with current literature and lacks the aggressiveness shown by some of the other employees. March grew up in the West, but he has assimilated Bostonian manners to the extent that he is a respectable member of the community (the parallel with Howells himself is obvious). Fulkerson, although living in New York City, is more demonstratively proud of his Western background. And March looks with some distaste on Fulkerson's cheerful scheming.

Similar associations prevail in *The Rise of Silas Lapham*. Lapham is a successful paint manufacturer born and raised in Vermont. Now living in Boston, Silas and his wife are uncomfortably out of place, not exactly understanding the folkways of Bostonian society and wistfully remembering their rural past. After the Bostonian gentleman Bromfield Corey first meets the Laphams, he tells his son Tom that he wished the family was "grammatical." His son responds: "How can you expect people who have been strictly devoted to business to be grammatical? Isn't that rather too much?" And the son adds that he rather liked Lapham "in spite of his syntax." When Tom Corey marries Lapham's daughter Penelope, his father forces himself to make "a sympathetic feint" of appreciating her "way of talking."[43]

Uncultivated characters did not view relaxed speech as rude or presumptuous. Fulkerson genuinely likes Basil March and shows it by adopting a camaraderie in speech. What informal characters encoded as normal behavior, educated characters decoded as lack of cultivation. Speech acts also affirmed bonds stronger than friendship. The mutual "pshaws" and nicknames that passed between Silas Lapham and his wife created brief moments of intimacy between the two. After one such exchange, Howells describes Mrs. Lapham as "insensibly" moving "a little closer to her husband." This style, which Howells called "blunt," was, according to the novelist, "the New England way of expressing perfect confidence and tenderness." The intimate language, exactly what Henry Alford inveighed against, periodically reaffirmed the couple's commitment to each other. What to Alford was "drivelling nonsense," to the Laphams was a tender act of reassurance.[44]

Here then we get a hint of the meaning "uncultivated" Americans attached to familiarity. Informality created its own kind of civility, one based on mildly affective bonds rather than on deferential reserve. Especially outside the workplace, friendliness was valued over formality. E. L. Godkin caught the shift when ruminating on the morals of the future. Every civilization had its own ideal character type, Godkin thought. The warrior served feudal Europe and the gentleman Greece, Rome, and the early modern West. But now democracy was creating a new ascendant personality—the kindly man, who is "ready to help everybody" and "shuts his eyes to other people's faults," avoiding "distinctions, moral or otherwise, between men." Combining "success in trade or commerce" with "the power of displaying his kindliness," he was becoming the "real paladin of our day . . . the good man of the twentieth century." Ritual interaction was now bent on creating sympathetic bonds between people.[45]

# III

What were the critics trying to accomplish? In the 1860s, they thought their attack on popular language could help reestablish the authority of refined ladies and gentlemen, redraw the lines between the few and the many. It was an effort to withdraw from popular culture. During the next decade, however, verbal criticism became just one more way to bring refined culture to a popular audience. By the 1880s, the books and handbooks of verbal criticism were being used by people with middling cultural credentials to assert social status. The very success of verbal criticism was undermining the original goals.

In part this was due to the critics' own uncertain attitudes toward the public.[46] At times they echoed eighteenth-century Scottish rhetoricians, claiming that they were teaching the refined how to communicate with themselves. At other times, however, the critics appeared to be looking for a wider and more diversified audience in the hopes of improving the public taste. But if the social goals of verbal criticism were undermined in part by confusion about the relevant audience, far more important was the inability to *control* the audience in any way at all. No one could stop the verbal criticism from being packaged in cheap handbooks and sold to a mass audience. No one could stop popular newspapers from publishing their own word critiques. Conspicuous emulation of the critics became a reality by the 1880s. In a democratic commercial society, controlling cultivation was a losing proposition.

Historians have differed over whether there existed a sharp division between high and popular culture in late-nineteenth-century America. Van Wyck Brooks is representative of a whole school of thought emphasizing such a split. Writing early in the twentieth century, Brooks also applied his analysis to the immediate past: "What side of American life is not touched by this antithesis? Between university ethics and business ethics, between Good Government and Tammany, between academic pedantry and pavement slang, there is no community, no genial middle ground."[47] Other historians, though, have argued that the broad diffusion of civil refinement in the nineteenth century made such divisions less meaningful. Writers like Harriet Beecher Stowe, Longfellow, and Dickens had large audiences in the nineteenth century, and that "which we would regard as 'high' culture was characteristically undifferentiated in the Victorian world. . . ."[48] At first glance it may seem that the language habits described by the verbal critics conform to the picture drawn by Brooks. Vulgar bombast stands opposed to restrained correctness, the slang of Fulkerson against the measured cadences of Basil March. This simple split is misleading; the worries of the critics were more complicated. They recognized that the half-educated who dominated American society easily affected the trappings of gentility and in doing so blurred the old lines between high and popular culture. The problem was not that high and popular culture were so different; the problem was that they were so much alike. The critics' analysis of popular speech was aimed at showing just how much of the diffusion was a sham. However fashionable the dress, however up-to-date the parlor, the details of everyday speech exposed the absence of genuine cultivated deportment. Verbal criticism worked to maintain the lines between high and popular culture in an increasingly confusing period of time.

The diffusion was real and palpable. As the nineteenth century progressed, many traditional and obvious symbols of gentility became accessible to increasing numbers of Americans. In 1800, few Americans had any knowledge of the fine arts. Copies of important paintings were costly and time-consuming; museums did not exist; travel to Europe was prohibited to all but the rich. Art itself, in fact, was suspect as potentially subversive of Republican virtue. But attitudes toward art gradually changed. After the War of 1812, when hundreds of Americans began traveling to Europe each year and absorbing its high culture, art took on the cast of a civilizing force. Various forms of art reproduction were developed, and after 1840 chromolithography spread thousands of copies of artworks through the nation every year. Women were urged to decorate their homes with these reproductions. By 1876, the enormous popularity of the art exhibition at the Philadelphia Centennial Fair was the final confirmation of the widespread popular interest in the fine arts. A passing acquaintance with the best of the world's painting and sculpture was no longer the private preserve of a small elite.[49]

A similar democratization took place in women's dress. Although in the early part of the century European observers were already noting how difficult it was to tell an American's social position by his or her dress, as late as the 1850s making clothes was still a laborious, time-consuming task, resulting in the prevalence of simple and coarse clothing. But the introduction of the sewing machine in the 1850s and the emergence of the dress pattern industry in the late 1860s changed that. By taking advantage of new marketing techniques, pattern makers like Ebenezer Butterick nationalized the industry. Fashionable dress then became accessible to huge numbers of American women.[50]

Universal education and the explosion of printed material in the nineteenth century also contributed to the diffusion of civil culture. By the mid-nineteenth century it was standard for native whites to be able to read, and printed matter of all kinds was produced in quantities unheard of in the previous century. Nineteenth-century novels generally extolled the virtues of cultivated living. Didactic women's magazines appeared, telling their readers how to cultivate themselves. Even newspapers paid some lip service to the value of civil and refined speech.[51]

Universal literacy, improved technology, and new marketing techniques all served to extend the trappings of gentility. Urbanization also contributed to the process. As increasing numbers of Americans moved to cities rural manners were gradually discarded. Chewing and spitting tobacco, popular prior to the Civil War, were afterward actively discouraged in cities, where the effects were more unsightly and more unsanitary. Recent rural arrivals who had the means took to cigar smoking, itself a male symbol of status and cultivation. The less fortunate took to smoking cigarettes, a practice associated with urban poor and decadent aesthetes until the First World War.[52] Etiquette books, whose production increased dramatically after the Civil War, also inveighed against many rural manners. Virtually nonexistent prior to the war, handbooks of linguistic etiquette increased somewhat in the sixties and seventies but reached their apogee of output in the 1880s, the same time that the eastern and mid-western countrysides virtually emptied into the cities, and thus enabled recent rural arrivals to speak in ways appropriate to the city.[53]

One important aspect of this was that many popular cultural forms *looked* more like refined culture as the century progressed. From the 1840s to the 1870s, popular culture underwent a slow change that mitigated the harsh vulgarity so prominent early in the century. Dress was just one example. In the 1870s, the popular stories about Davy Crockett were transformed: The mythic hero lost his thirst for violence and became a more benign, folksy hero. In the 1860s, minstrel show characters began toning down the extravagance of their dances and took to dressing in refined stage costumes. In chapters 2 and 3, I discussed the preoccupation with slang beginning in the 1830s. The fear of slang developed in contrast to worries about more exotic provincial dialects. Now it was not a whole way of talking that was troublesome, it was just a question of subtle vocabulary choices that violated refined decorum. And in chapter 6, I shall explore a similar transformation in the popular urban press during the 1870s. Although vulgarity by no means disappeared, it was toned down in important ways, and the gap between refined and popular mid-dling culture shrank.[54]

As important as civility was to the critics, the dispersal of its trappings made the line between the cultivated and the uncultivated harder to draw. "It is easy to put on the exterior of a lady," said a women's magazine as early as 1847, "but to *be* a lady is a very different thing."[55] As the larger more obvious symbols of civil culture opened up to many people, they threatened to lose their meaning. The diffusion of civil culture, the dream of eighteenth-century republicans like Jefferson, was proving to be subtly corrosive. What had been signs of moral character, literally fraught with ethical import, were rapidly becoming—in the most trivial possible reading of the phrase—mere status symbols.

As I noted in chapter 2, in the early nineteenth century the meanings of the words *lady* and *gentleman* broadened to include all adults; the class character of the words was lost. And the assertion that the broadened meanings of *lady* and *gentleman* were illegitimate was prominent in *every* book of verbal criticism. Critics still understood the words in their earlier sense; the extended meaning carried all the marks of assumed egalitari-anism they despised. They said it was vulgar pretense. Moreover, it was deceptive at its very core. American speech was insultingly informal, without the reserve of authentic cultivation. Popular language habits belied the claim that all were gentlemen and ladies. Here the elitism shone through most clearly. "There never was and there never can be a nation wholly composed of ladies and gentlemen," one wrote. "The sooner the fact is realized and tacitly acknowledged, the sooner will the titles be raised from the morass in which they have been trampled by a multitude of pretenders."[56]

The verbal critics were not alone in complaining about false affectations of refinement. Trained architects in the closing decades of the nineteenth century complained of self-taught builders, "mere" builders, who cited Ruskin but who in fact did not adhere to the values of discipline and restraint inherent in traditional architectural form. One major complaint was that builders had appropriated the term *architect* for themselves, a practice the trained architects thought pretentious and confusing. Political writers complained about politicians who claimed to be heirs of Jefferson and Washington but who had only a superficial understanding of the founders. And music critics told of women who claimed cultivation on the basis of a piano in the parlor and a few lessons. E. L. Godkin, in his now-famous essay, "The Chromo-Civilization," argued that cheap periodicals, lyceum lectures, and small colleges spread "a smattering of knowledge, a taste for reading and art" which "pass with a large body of slenderly equipped persons as culture. . . ." Although this "pseudo-culture" gave people "unprecedented self-confidence," its end result was "a kind of mental and moral chaos" which threatened "many of the fundamental rules of living, which have been worked out by thousands of years of bitter experience."[57] Here again, the theme is sounded—diffusion is ultimately corrosive.

Democracy might have been killing refined culture, but it did not kill its forms. Traditional symbols of cultivation were distended beyond recognition, yet they retained their emotional pull. It was still important to be called an *architect* and not a *builder*. To tell someone he was no gentleman was still an insult. What exercised verbal critics above all was their inability to control such symbols. Only through careful usage could the iconic value of these symbols be saved, but critics had no way to police their dispersal. In the late 1860s, the *Round Table*, a New York journal which had recently serialized George Washington Moon's *Bad English Exposed*, ran a critique of Horace Greeley. To postwar critics, Greeley embodied the essence of American rootlessness. The writer in the *Round Table* complained that Greeley's scurrilous language was "such as to unfit him for the society of gentlemen, inasmuch as it is the sort commonly confined to blackguards." It lacked that "self-control which is among the gentleman's first attributes." Yet just a week before in the *New York Tribune*, Greeley had argued that two New York politicians had ignored those "ideas of delicacy sacred to every gentleman." The *Round Table* critic could marvel at Greeley's temerity, but he could not stop the editor from appropriating the terms for himself. Whatever restriction on the usage of *lady* and *gentleman* the critics might have called for, the words had simply lost the specificity they had in previous times.[58]

Whatever the difficulties associated with the dispersal of civil culture, verbal critics never jettisoned their belief that certain forms of behavior were indications of civilized living. Their faith in the morality of refined style held firm. As the larger signs of civil culture became readily accessible, interest turned to the smaller points of deportment. Analysis of minute vocabulary choices would expose vulgarity. *Donate* or *give*? *Shall* or *will*? *Numerous* or *many*? The correct answer separated the educated from the half-educated. When critics emphasized the importance of fine discrimination they, to be sure, were not exaggerating. In the fluid world of nineteenth-century America these trifles had become the most important markers of cultivation.

Verbal critics were no different from other highbrow critics of the mid- and late-nineteenth century. Ornament and decorative detail were enormously important to Victorians. Highly wrought architecture and elaborately cluttered parlors are part of what leaps to mind when the word *Victorian* is heard today. Etiquette, the ornament of interpersonal behavior, is similarly remembered as strategically complicated. In the 1870s, *Godey's Lady's Book* ran a monthly column on the ornaments of dress. Appropriate ornamentation was now the means of distinguishing the "truly" educated from the mere *poseur*. Often only gaudy ornament or flagrant disregard for the details of appropriate cultural forms differentiated the cultivated from the uncultivated. The same observation was made about dress, etiquette, and architecture. The word *gentleman* was misused, one critic observed, when applied to people with "outlandish watch-chains hooked in the lowest button hole of their vest, Brazilian diamonds in their shirt bosoms," or "big-seal rings on their little fingers." Character was even revealed "through the tips of men's fingers" or the "quick sweep of an eyelash," another wrote. "Try to play the dainty lady, when you are not, and the clumsy way you hold your teacup will betray you." The major source of contention between architects and builders was over the appropriate degree of finial decoration to be included in new houses. Builders interpreted varied and extensive ornamentation as an expression of individuality, but to the architects it was gaudy vulgarity.[59]

Yet could detail really distinguish the educated sensibility? The verbal criticism was shot through with confusion on this point. To verbal critics the ability to make fine verbal distinction was a sign of cultivation. Yet verbal criticism was also meant to reestablish the old decorum, to restrict the meaning of *gentleman*, to build deferential gestures into the language. Yet for this latter to succeed all would need to become verbal critics able to distinguish between true and false civility. This in turn would mean that everyone would develop an educated sensibility, that all would have the verbal dexterity of a lady or a gentleman. Ultimately, verbal criticism could not be both a marker of cultivation and a method of building deference into the social system.

There is some indication that the verbal critics realized this. The vulgar were vulgar precisely because of their refractory pretentiousness. They could not be reached. The problem with the misuse of *gentleman*, Richard Grant White once pointed out, lay with people who would not do him the honor of reading his book.[60] Early verbal critics, in fact, were not interested in popular didacticism but in elite didacticism. White, for example, refused a lucrative offer to write a school textbook. His intended audience was the refined themselves, his work a means of separating the cultivated from the "semi-cultivated." The criticism was occlusive, not meant to reorder the world so much as to safely enclose a small part of it. Essays of verbal criticism appeared in the 1860s in publications with small but literate audiences. *The New York Times, The Galaxy*, and *The Atlantic Monthly* were not exactly the popular reading matter of the day. And the casual allusions to Addison's style, Milton's syntax, or Pope's translation of Homer in the verbal criticism presupposed an acquaintance with the English literary tradition. The books of verbal criticism are not overly didactic, but have the tone of one gentleman speaking to another. Together the cultivated would search for slang and bombast in the speech of others to reassure themselves of their own superiority. The very activity of verbal criticism would be a sign of cultivation.

All of this was an echo of eighteenth-century Scottish rhetoric. The presumed audience was refined. Distance from popular culture was the order of the day. It should be no surprise that it was the Scottish rhetorician George Campbell who made the phrase "verbal criticism" widely known to Anglo-American writers; the appropriate standards of "verbal criticism" figured importantly in his *Philosophy of Rhetoric* (1776).

In the years after the Civil War, social divisions in America seemed to grow harder. Everywhere Americans looked for ways to set themselves off from other Americans. Class lines, never absent, seemed to solidify, and the bitter labor disputes of 1870s and 1880s awakened many to the fact that European-like divisions were entering American life. Many of the trappings of conspicuous consumption—sumptuous private railway cars, exclusive suburban country clubs, and so on—appeared in the years after 1865. In Northern cities, Negro ghettoes appeared for the first time. Whites physically removed themselves from blacks. The nascent movement for professional standards was also an attempt for a small group to distinguish itself. Verbal critics searched for distinction by reaffirming the contribution of civil language to civil order. In keeping with old humanistic traditions, they strove to distance themselves from popular customs. In this way they were at one with those political mugwumps who withdrew from electoral politics.[61]

Yet even as verbal critics struggled to prove their superior sensibilities they were pulled by the desire to upgrade popular education. How could popular culture be ignored in a democracy? Verbal criticism seeped into the schools. Thousands of children were taught that educated people made fine verbal distinctions, and by the 1880s, verbal criticism was a part of popular adult education. L. T. Townsend's *The Art of Speech* and Adams Sherman Hill's *Our English* were originally Chautauqua lectures. When published, the books were used in the Chautauqua reading course, reaching some sixty thousand people every year. And thousands of handbooks of verbal etiquette were printed. Their extensive lists of the do's and don't's of good usage were more explicitly didactic than the cultivated criticism, clearly intended for an audience that lacked social assurance. And the same advice in truncated form was offered in the thousands of etiquette books floating around the country in those years. By the eighties mothers were overheard on trolleys cautioning their daughters not to use slang phrases like *by the skin of our teeth* and readers wrote into newspapers on the subject of linguistic purity. But if the audience was to be a *mass* audience, then how could verbal criticism succeed in distinguishing "true" refinement from the vulgar pose? The New York *Evening Post* in the eighties inveighed against the popularity of the handbooks of verbal criticism. These manuals (the *Post* sharply distinguished them from literary verbal criticism) were no substitute for an adequate education. Assimilate the classics of English literature, the *Post* urged, don't study lists of vulgar words. Even C. W. Bardeen, the compiler of *Verbal Pitfalls*, one of the handbooks, agreed that verbal criticism had become "almost a disease." Too much of the criticism was "puerile," he thought; most critics simply parroted what they had picked up from one book or conversation. The half-educated had become verbal critics.[62]

The linguistic criticism of the late nineteenth century had some value.

It was particularly good in pointing out newspaper bombast. But overall, the criticism did not serve the culture well. By invoking gentlemanly notions of taste and decorum, the criticism perpetuated the notion that refined style was somehow connected to good prose. The lessons of Saxon eloquence were forgotten. Far too much of the criticism was simply designed to set off a social elite—*Donate* or *give? shall* or *will?*—the "taste" involved in such discriminations was more precious than civic.

As troubling was the emphasis on single words. By writing long books about good and bad words, the critics helped undermine some of the values they hoped to preserve. Verbal criticism had long been a minor part of the rhetorical tradition because it was a *minor* part of discourse. The critics forgot this, magnifying out of all proportion the import of verbal nicety. To be sure, the leading critics knew rhetorical theory, but it should not be surprising that those reading their books began to think getting individual words "exactly" right was the sum of good speech. The critics' preoccupation with the social prestige of taste together with their relentless focus on single words almost guaranteed that verbal criticism would get hooked into popular cycles of conspicuous emulation.

Just as the cultivated critics of the late nineteenth century could not control the other symbols of status and cultivation, they had no way to keep verbal criticism their own preserve. By the 1880s, the activity itself became just another symbol of cultivation to be affected at will. The critics were helpless to redraw the lines between high and popular culture that they felt were so desperately needed. So despite their hunger for exclusion, the critics became arbiters of middling taste. And because their prescriptions were taken to heart, spread via the schools, through thousands of handbooks, and no doubt through innumerable conversations, their efforts to sharpen the differences between high and popular culture were defeated. In the process, the critics watched the traditional symbols of civility rot. The very diffusion of the symbols was emptying them of their substantive meaning. Fashion, manners, and verbal criticism could now be affected without the cultivated reserve that such symbols had traditionally been a sign of. Civilized forms no longer meshed with civilized living. Beneath the verbal critics' haughty injunctions and abrasive condemnations of vulgarity lay painful *Weltschmerz*. As they stridently defended the civilizing process, the critics watched the iconic value of civility drain out of its forms. The irony, of course, was that their work contributed to the end.

# CHAPTER FIVE

# Scholars Versus Critics

Behind all the present discussion of the foundations
of the educational system, the struggle of the "specialist type of man" against the older "cultivated
man" is hidden at some decisive point. . . . This
fight intrudes into all intimate cultural questions.

MAX WEBER

In the middle of 1871 Richard Grant White took up pen to respond to
one critic of *Words and Their Uses*. The book had been widely reviewed
and the response was overwhelmingly favorable. The sales were remarkable, surprising White as much as anyone else. Success, though, had not
tempered White's touchy hubris. Fourteen pages he devoted to an assault
on X, the anonymous author who had published a ten week broadside on
*Words and Their Uses*.

In one way White's essay was counterproductive. X's articles were
published in the *College Courant*, a magazine directed at Yale graduates
and without any national reputation. Responding in the prestigious *Galaxy*,
White rang attention to obscure criticism. Yet if White's instincts for
literary politics were questionable, his sense of important intellectual ad-
versaries was keen. X, White knew, was Thomas Lounsbury, a professor
of English literature at the Yale Sheffield School of Science and a budding
authority on the history of the English language. White also knew that
Lounsbury had collaborated on his essays with William Dwight Whitney,
another Yale Sheffield School professor and the author of *Language and
the Study of Language*. The latter, first delivered as lectures at the Smith-

sonian Institution in 1864, then published in 1867, was even more critically acclaimed than White's book. These Yale men were no half-educated journalists. That Lounsbury called *Words and Their Uses* "reckless," "gross," and "dangerous" must have stung White as much as it rankled him.[1]

The exchange was an early sign of cultural tensions opening up in the 1860s. Through the seventies and eighties sniping between verbal critics and scholarly philologists intensified as philologists like Lounsbury, Whitney, Francis March, and Fitzedward Hall published books castigating the critics. The two sides debated in *The Nation*, *The Galaxy*, *The Atlantic Monthly*, and *The New York Times*. The number of recognized authorities was tiny, but other authors, journalists, educators, and scholars quickly chose sides. Hundreds of pages in newspapers and magazines were devoted to the debates. As White and Lounsbury argued in 1871 about Latin accidence, Anglo-Saxon etymology, and Elizabethan prose style, they were only dimly aware of the full implications of their differences. The next years made them plain. By the 1880s, the critics and scholars were at war.

Yet there were common origins. Both groups were part of a remarkable debate over education that took place in England and America during the fifties and sixties. John Henry Newman, Herbert Spencer, Charles Dickens, Matthew Arnold, F. W. Farrar, Thomas Huxley, and John Stuart Mill were just the most prominent Britons who wrote enduring works on education during those years.[2] They were read immediately in America, and Americans made their own contributions. Abraham Lincoln and Horace Greeley defended the sufficiency of a common school education,[3] while Harvard professors Thomas Hill and Frederic W. Hedge cautiously advocated reform within the framework of the established curriculum. Francis Wayland called for more specialization, Henry Tappan for more professionalism, John Draper for more science. Charles Eliot vaguely asked for all three; Noah Porter emphatically demanded none.[4] The verbal critics, in sympathy with Matthew Arnold, looked for broad, humane, critical Hellenists to leaven the unrelenting philistinism of American life. The philologists grew from the concurrent movement for higher professional standards and more precise specialization.

In the 1860s, educational reform was tied to a broad movement of the college-educated, the "best men," to reassert their leadership in America. Inspired by the heady years of the Civil War and early Reconstruction, the highly educated felt the time was right to reestablish their preeminence over the "half-educated."[5] All the educational reformers worried about the vulgarity of American life in general, and American popular speech in particular. The study of the native tongue figured prominently in Charles Eliot's famous "The New Education." English literature should be studied, Eliot contended, "so that no child's knowledge of his native tongue should be left to the chance influences of his home, the street, and the newspaper." The academic president who veered Harvard to the elective system voiced the same concerns as did verbal critic Andrew Peabody, who opposed Eliot for the presidency of Harvard in the name of the old-style education. William Dwight Whitney, the philologist who championed scientific scholarship and vigorously fought the critics, also conveyed similar sentiments in his 1867 book: "The low-toned party newspaper is too much the type of the prevailing literary influence by which the style of speech of our rising generation is moulding. A tendency to slang, to colloquial indulgence, and even vulgarities, is the besetting sin against which we, as Americans, have especially to guard and struggle." In the early years, differences between scholars and critics were masked by common fears.[6]

As the critics and scholars squabbled during the 1870s, it slowly dawned on them how much they actually differed. Scholars in the 1870s began to defend slang, dialect, and other forms of "unrefined" English. By the 1880s, it appeared to a critic like Richard Grant White that the new science of philology was in collusion with the vulgarians in control of American life.

But the scholars went even further. Not only did they portray verbal critics as wrong about the dangers of popular language. The scholarly philologists, particularly William Dwight Whitney, edged toward arguing that technical vocabularies were the heart of educated language and that a refined literary language had no special standing. Verbal critics saw themselves as defending traditional standards threatened by populist democracy. The new philological experts began to see verbal critics as elitist blowhards.

The battle over linguistic norms was at bottom about something else —about fundamental attitudes toward education and the self. The defense of literary language was part of a commitment to the model of the civic-minded gentleman, hungering for a unified soul, defending the morality of refinement, and needing to communicate to the public. The scholarly celebration of slang and technical talk was part of an emerging commitment to the "expert," happily dividing life experience into various roles, valorizing knowledge over taste, and defining the relevant audience as fellow specialists. No one involved in the debate would have put this so starkly. The period from the 1860s through the mid-1880s was the time when all involved were just beginning to sort out these issues, but the currents of thought introduced then would have large impact in the ensuing years.[7]

Historians of the English language regularly portray the late-nineteenth-century linguists as partisans of a democratic idiom. Yet they were not nearly as populist as they are usually seen. Historians have constantly pointed out the philologists' new attitudes about slang and everyday usage but have missed the scholarly celebration of expertise. The language norms presented by late-nineteenth-century linguists were part of new ideas about the educated adult. The linguists were among the vanguard of a movement that would establish the forms of social prestige that we continue to live with today.

# I

Most of the leading verbal critics and scholars were born in the twenties and early thirties.[8] In many cases their American heritage could be traced back to the first half of the seventeenth century. Most of them came from refined backgrounds and were college-educated. But even though they had similar backgrounds, in the 1860s each group turned in a different direction. Most critics were actively interested in the arts. Thomas Osmun (who under the pseudonym Alfred Ayres published *The Verbalist*) was a drama critic. George Washington Moon wrote poetry. William Mathews wrote literary criticism. Richard Grant White and Richard Meade Bache wrote novels. White was also a music critic, a performer in a New York string quartet and an editor of a complete edition of Shakespeare. Of the major philologists, however, only Thomas Lounsbury showed an outside interest in the arts. The scholars were interested in science. Before he attended Harvard, Fitzedward Hall was an early graduate of Rensselaer Polytechnic Institute. The philogist William Dwight Whitney, after whose brother, Josiah, Mount Whitney is named, was keenly interested in geology and accompanied his brother on several expeditions. On two occasions William authored the geological reports of the trips.

Verbal critics were journalists, educators, and ministers. Often they moved from one to the other in the course of their adult lives. With the exception of Fitzedward Hall, who became a British civil servant, the scholarly philologists spent their lives teaching college. Whereas the critics were essayists who dabbled in scholarship, the linguists were scholars who dabbled in essays.

Although the geographical origins of the critics and scholars were similar, the former lived their adult years in urban areas while the latter did not. White, Gould, and Osmun lived in New York, Bache in Philadelphia, and William Mathews in Chicago and Boston. Even the critics who taught college were at the edge of major cities. Andrew Peabody and Adams Sherman Hill both taught at Harvard (Hill worked in New York before he came there). The experience of the philologists, however, was different. Lounsbury and Whitney spent their adult lives in New Haven, which in the late nineteenth century still had a small-town feel. Francis March taught at Amherst. Fitzedward Hall moved from Troy, New York, through Cambridge, Massachusetts, to several British outposts in India, ending up in the English countryside. Apart from his brief stay at Harvard, Hall did not live near a major city.[9] Verbal criticism was an urban phenomenon, born of the anxieties caused by the confusing mix of peoples in nineteenth-century cities. In rural retreats, such urbane anxieties hardly affected the scholarly philologists.

More than anything else, the philologists complained of the critics' ignorance. In general, one reviewer wrote of White's *Everyday English*, there was "too great an abundance of assertion for the supply of facts." The critics were "intuitive philologists," Fitzedward Hall thought. Hall indeed was one of the great polymaths of the time, displaying a stunning knowledge of English literature. He had read the works of every major figure and almost every minor figure in the pantheon of Anglo-American letters. His erudition was monstrous, with footnotes and citations often crowding the text off the page. Hall contributed more to the *Oxford English Dictionary* than any other single individual. The less the critics' knowledge, Hall thought, the more their daring: "Tell a person of this class, that he can with no more safety pronounce, intuitively, on a philological matter than on an astronomical or a chemical, and his answer is ridicule." Dean Alford's *Plea for the Queen's English*, Whitney thought, showed "ignorance of the history of English speech, inaccuracy, loose and unsound reasoning, and weakness of linguistic insight." Even in the 1860s, when Whitney still admitted that critics scored some telling points, he emphasized the triviality of their work.[10]

Philologists felt they were creating a science of language. The immense study of Indo-European languages that Sir William Jones had inaugurated in the 1780s unmasked mythic ideas about language and language history. The patient work of Bopp, Rask, and Jacob Grimm had uncovered hordes of invaluable information. Now with the strange residues of the Romantics swept away, observation and insight would be able to proceed to the scientific level. Whitney wanted to get the study of language "out of its mythological and into its positive stage."[11]

The most important philological idea was one that appears utterly banal—that language is a social convention. Written symbols and phonetic clusters were arbitrary signs that societies collectively agreed would denote certain concepts. Although old, in the 1860s the idea needed restating. Romantic theorists like Richard Trench and Max Müller had challenged the idea, contending it undervalued language. Far from being an arbitrary convention, language was intimately tied to reason. Words and ideas were inseparable. Complicated concepts did not exist without verbal representation. Man could not reason without language. Whitney rightly pointed out that theorists like Müller were combatting phantoms of their own creation. All that was meant by the conventionality doctrine was that one sign was as good as another, that I called my neighbor *you*, and not *vous*, *dog*, *clummock*, or anything else because English custom favored that particular set of sounds.[12]

Locke had argued that language was a social convention in his *Essay Concerning Human Understanding*. The idea was the foundation of the rhetoric of Campbell and the dictionary of Johnson. The Victorian linguists, however, pushed the doctrine in radical directions, claiming that it obviated the need for *any* verbal criticism. As a set of conventions evolving through time, the linguists argued, language had the inherent ability to regenerate itself. Change was inevitable, customs always in a state of flux. Language was naturally unstable. But flux should cause no alarm. It reflected the natural sway of any living tongue. Language did not decay; it merely changed. Language, as Whitney put it, had both "conservative" and "alternative" forces built right into it, creating custom that slowly evolved and inevitably reflected the needs of the community. Philologists argued that language was a cultural epiphenomenon. Inferring cultural decay from linguistic evolution put the cart before the horse. Verbal critics' "mournful complaints" of present degeneracy were idiotic, Thomas Lounsbury asserted, "the real truth is, that the language can safely take care of itself. . . ."[13]

Both verbal critics and scholarly philologists conceded that the language was imprecise. But what critics keened over, the philologists shrugged off. Usage was God and verbal criticism sinned against usage. How could White complain about *militate*, Fitzedward Hall asked, when the word was used by Smollett, Burke, Paley, Southey, Coleridge, De Quincey, Landor, and Newman? Although White called *tenantry* "of very low caste" it had been used by Burke, Landor, Macauley, and Ruskin. And the progressive passive (*is being built*) was used for some seventy years before writers like George Marsh and White inveighed against it. Southey, Lamb, Landor, Pitt, Shelley, Arnold (the father), Arnold (the son), Newman, Ruskin, and others had already used the form. Criticizing it was criticizing refined usage.[14]

The critics often did deny the ultimate primacy of custom. As White put it:

> The truth is, that the authority of general usage, or even the usage of great writers, is not absolute in language. There is a misuse of words which can be justified by no authority, however great, by no usage, however grand.

Philologists in the 1870s were already citing such passages to prove the critics' indifference to the hard facts of language, and historians have continued to do so until the present day.[15] Yet the critics were more complicated than historians have realized; the philologists more polemical than normally admitted. Edward Gould, for example, although he wrote that the "final proof of accuracy cannot be established by usage" also added that as "a general rule, the usage of good writers is held to be the common law of a language. Such usage, therefore, is *prima facie* evidence of the accuracy of a disputed word or phrase." And elsewhere in *Words and Their Uses* White noted:

> Within certain limits usage has absolute authority in language. To assert this is not to lay down a law, or to set up a standard, but merely to recognize a fact.

The critics never hoped to run roughshod over custom, but neither did they think that broadly accepting literary usage precluded all criticism. They believed that language was conventional but they worried over the quality of the conventions. Merely to cite Addison using a word did not prove its legitimacy. Words changed their meaning over time and this was cause for caution, not passivity. White wrote to Whitney that there was "no question" that usage determined speech:

> But as to what is usage, whether all usage is of equal weight and significance, whether they may not be temporary uses which would justly be regarded as fitful, abnormal caprices in language—it seems to me that there is at least a question. And it seems to me that the example of a great, i.e., gifted writer, or half a dozen, does not completely justify such uses.

As journalists, the critics knew well that in the course of producing hundreds of pages of text mistakes were inevitable, that no writer was perfect. Usage cannot be the final arbiter, Edward Gould wrote, "because the writer, in any particular instance, may have been guilty of carelessness. . . ." Custom, after all, was habitual behavior, not idiosyncratic.[16]

The scholars knew they bruised hoary sentiments. Polymath that he was, Fitzedward Hall was aware that Elyot, Milton, Dryden, Swift, Gray, Godwin, Hazlitt, Coleridge, Wordsworth, Macauley, De Quincey, Arnold, Ruskin, Leslie Stephen, and dozens of others had contributed verbal criticism to the stream of British letters. Hall also knew that what he called the "habit of denouncing new words indiscriminately" was an ancient practice. Cicero, Quintilian, and others had regularly caviled about linguistic propriety. Hall called the Victorian critic an "Aristarchus the Little," after the Alexandrian Homeric scholar famous for his exacting standards.[17]

The critics built on a long tradition that both celebrated cultivated usage and accepted the necessity of criticism. Quintilian was an early proponent of the doctrine of usage but although he defined correct language as the consensus of the educated (*consensus eruditorum*), he still engaged in verbal criticism.[18] First to voice the usage doctrine in Western letters was Horace, who in the *Ars Poetica* spoke of ". . . Usage, with whom there rests / The right of deciding what forms our speech shall take." Yet also in the *Ars Poetica* Horace repeated the standard classical dictum to fit style to subject matter and he told poets to "Show nice judgement and care / In threading your words together." Horace argued that verbal criticism was essential to fine writing:

> . . . A man
> Who is honest and wise will censure unskillful lines,
> Find fault with those that are harsh; of those lacking polish
> He'll daub a black mark with a cross-stroke of his pen;
> He'll cut out showy embellishment, force you to throw
> Daylight on what is not clear enough, charge you with writing
> A doubtful expression, mark what he thinks should be changed.

"Be a real Aristarchus," Horace told the critic.[19]

The moderns often repeated similar sentiments. Locke argued in his *Essay Concerning Human Understanding* that language was conventional but he also spent pages probing the imperfections of linguistic customs and the ways that careless speakers undermined clarity. Late-eighteenth-century grammarians, lexicographers, and rhetoricians also valorized polite usage, but as I noted in the first chapter, this did not preclude any criticism. Although George Campbell chided Robert Lowth and Samuel Johnson for defending polite usage and then criticizing it, he did so to put verbal criticism on solid foundations. Instead of random criticism, Campbell listed nine principles that philosophically sanctioned the activity.[20]

Like Horace, Quintilian, Locke, and Johnson, Victorian verbal critics asked educated men and women not to deny custom but to probe its contours, to see where it failed, to find where accepted usage blurred meaning. And they asked—and this is what is hardest for twentieth-century readers to comprehend—to see where custom sinned against elegance. Critics knew that contemporary custom, precisely because it was *custom*, could be imprecise, confusing, contradictory. They recognized what Wordsworth called "the sad incompetence of speech." And they believed that for a culture to use its language wisely it must be neither low nor pedantic, neither passionate nor bloodless. Refined concision preserved civilized discussion.

Although the philologists undermined certain long-standing ideas about language, they primarily saw themselves as reacting against early-nineteenth-century Romanticism. By emphasizing the conventional nature of language the scholars returned to a social compact theory of language. Whitney frequently decried the application of organic metaphors to language. The linguists emphasized that language was a mediating cultural form, passing information from one source to another. Whitney defined language as "instrumental." The contention that words were arbitrary and instrumental symbols led the American philologists to restrict semantic discussion to the external core of meaning. Meaning according to them was social, what speaker and listener agreed upon. If that was to some degree vague, so be it, for that was simply the way language worked. To explore beyond that point was silly if not pernicious. Philologists saw the critics holding the Romantic assumption that style could be read to uncover the character, or soul, of individuals and nations. The linguists did not agree that significant meaning was revealed through unconsciously adopted style. The "impulse to speak", they held, came "not from within, but from without, not from the desire of expression, but of communication."[21]

The linguists lost interest in what Coleridge had called the "tonal valuation" of words, the subtle ways that words ring differently in different ears. Yet although the Romantics had prominently displayed their belief in a correlation of style and character, the idea was by no means unique to them. It was Robert Burton who wrote, "It is most true, *stylus virum arguit*, our style betrays us"; Buffon who claimed that "Le style, c'est l'homme"; and Condillac who observed, "Everything confirms that each language expresses the character of the people who speak it." In their zeal to overthrow the Romantics, the Victorian linguists undermined attitudes about language that had persisted for centuries through the various fluctuations of the history of ideas.[22]

Nothing better shows the Victorian philologists' alienation from literary sensibilities than their tone deafness. From repeated contacts with the verbal critics the scholars developed a hard-boiled indifference to the semantic dimension of style. For Whitney it was not so much congenital as forced upon him by the logic of his theory. In the 1860s he still complained about newspaper prose and rusticisms such as *I expect* or *I calculate*. But gradually such comments were dropped as Whitney developed his contention that linguistic signs were invariably loose, arbitrary tools used to express thoughts to others. Lounsbury showed that the study of English literature need not lead to an appreciation of stylistic grace. In his biography of James Fenimore Cooper for the "American Men of Letters Series," Lounsbury called *The Pathfinder* and *Deerslayer* "pure works of art." Mark Twain shrewdly disagreed, calling *The Deerslayer*, "literary *delerium tremens*." Twain cited 18 literary offenses Cooper committed (and claimed he knew of 114). High on the list was Cooper's English. His dialogue was absurd; he had no ear for precision. Cooper, according to Twain, "was not a word musician." He used *verbal* for *oral*, *precision* for *facility*, *phenomenon* for *marvels*, *necessary* for *predetermined*, *unsophisticated* for *primitive*, *preparation* for *expectancy*, *rebuked* for *subdued*, *dependant on* for *resulting from*, *fact* for *condition*, *fact* for *conjecture*, *precaution* for *caution*, and so on. "There have been daring people in the world who claimed that Cooper could write English," Twain asserted, "but they are all dead now—all dead but Lounsbury."[23]

Fitzedward Hall too had little sense of tone. He often repeated that he was no literary man and was unqualified to pass literary judgment. As he bludgeoned opponents with footnotes, piling citation on top of citation, Hall demonstrated little sense of how words echoed differently in differing settings. He never recognized that Samuel Johnson writing *I calculate* in the middle of the eighteenth century had a far different cultural meaning than a Midwestern farmer uttering the same phrase in the 1870s. He did not sense that even if Cowper, Elyot, and Burke used *splendid* legitimately, the word could still be overworked and turned into cant by women of thin culture in Victorian America.

Setting was central to verbal critics. Incongruity was the cardinal sin of vulgarity. It was a small sign of lack of character. Refined decorum was connected to morality. "To say that every person who aspires to be esteemed a gentleman should carefully shun all barbarisms, solecisms, and other faults in his speech, is to utter the merest truism," one critic wrote. "The man who habitually deviates from the custom of his country in expressing his thoughts, is hardly less ridiculous than one who walks the streets in a Spanish cloak or a Roman toga." Yet the scholars could not understand what linguistic propriety had to do with tone, style, or decorum. Fitzedward Hall recast correctness to free it from considerations of congruity. "Language may be at once perfectly correct and ludicrously inappropriate," he wrote. "Experience and tact instruct us when it is appropriate; but scholarship alone can enable us to estimate its correctness." No verbal critic could have made such a distinction. To the verbal critic, appropriateness was a key aspect of correctness.[24]

Philologists distrusted literary language. Like the critics, the scholars viewed the educated classes as the conservative ballast of a language. But while the critics worried that the half-educated had set the language adrift, the philologists argued that the educated threatened the language's health. The danger was not drift, but catalepsy. Separated from popular support, Whitney contended, a cultivated dialect "at once" begins to "lose its vitality"; no language "can remain alive which is not answering the infinitely varied needs of a whole community. . . ." Whenever cut off from vital popular wellsprings, Whitney continued, "a learned or priestly caste has become the guardian of the tongue in which it was written; while to the masses of the people both have grown strange and unfamiliar." Whitney drew on a profound range of history to prove his point—Egyptian hieroglyphics, Zoroaster's Old Iranian, Brahmin Sanskrit, and Christendom's Latin. His examples, however, were more suggestive than incisive. He slid across centuries of relatively stable aristocratic rule to prove that aristocratic dialects "at once" lose their vitality if not in touch with the populace, that "aristocracy and exclusiveness tend to final overthrow, in language as in politics. . . ."[25]

One sign of the scholars' association of the written word with aristocratic culture can be gleaned through their interest in simplified spelling. Through the 1860s, calls for phonetic spelling were associated with cultural outsiders often described as "half-educated." During the 1870s, however, the scholarly philologists took over the movement, with practically all the leading names involved.[26] The written word, they argued, should follow the spoken; phonetic spelling was necessary. While scholars argued that linguistic conventions should not be tampered with, they did not extend this courtesy to orthography. Customary English spelling was "much more an aristocratic luxury than a popular benefit," wrote William Dwight Whitney. Its success over the years was not due to "its instructing effect upon the general public" but to "its tendency to call up pleasing associations in the minds of the learned." Verbal critics were amazed that such scholarly men could undertake to unsettle the language in this way. Richard Grant White argued that it was precisely language's connection with literature that made established spelling so important.[27]

For centuries humanistically educated Westerners had feared the vagueness and incivility of popular speech. Now philologists argued that decorum was irrelevant and that popular speech actually kept the cultivated dialects alive. Linguistic creativity, scholars contended, came from many sources outside the literary language. Mistakes, for example, enriched the language. "The history of language is the history of corruption," wrote Thomas Lounsbury, the "blunders of one age become good usage in the following." Returning to practices "theoretically correct would seem like a return to barbarism." Fitzedward Hall noted that *mob* was a vulgarism in Swift's time, that *ancient, pennant,* and *truant* were created by misusing Latin endings and that *rightwise* had become *righteous* "probably from mere slovenliness of pronunciation. . . ." Such examples were powerful arguments against verbal criticism, for too rigid a view of mistakes might choke off the healthy evolution of the language. "Every dialect which is made the subject of literary culture," Whitney darkly concluded, "is liable to the fate of Latin."[28]

Scholars also looked on Americanisms with tolerant eyes. Whitney praised Twain's fiction, comparing the author to the Vedic poets who drew on the language of the pasture and cattle yard. Scholars agreed with critics that most so-called Americanisms were misnamed. Words like *Congress, President,* and *Senate* were English words describing American institutions. Many other supposed Americanisms were really old British folk dialect. But true Americanisms, those words used only in America, the scholars did not object to. Lounsbury noted that it was only in the area of technology that the two dialects were splitting. Railroad terminology in particular was different. Our *car* was their *carriage,* our *conductor* their *guard,* the American *engineer* was the British *engine-driver,* and our *freight-train* was their *goods train.* Yet such differences were minor. There was not the "slightest prospect of serious divergence" between American and British speech.[29]

Finally, the philologists developed a grudging respect for slang. If slang was defended in the 1860s it was not through a scientific linguistic theory but as an anti-intellectual defense of popular customs.[30] The word *slang* does not appear in a positive sense in the early work of Lounsbury and Whitney. By the mid-seventies, however, linguists were acknowledging slang's power. In *The Life and Growth of Language* (1875), Whitney praised slang for liberating speech "from the oppressive conventionality" of worn-out words. The year before, the British anthropologist E. B. Tyler, in "The Philology of Slang," told scholars that many "a philological hint may be gleaned from the talk of factories and stables, music halls and thieves' kitchens and pawnbrokers' shops." In a review of Fitzedward Hall's *Modern English*, Francis March pointed out that although old philologists made "much of the difference between folk speech and classical idiom," Hall rummaged through "low comedy and familiar letters, as well as rare tracts of forgotten pedantry, to catch every fugitive form of expression." In 1877 John Bartlett published the fourth edition of his *Dictionary of Americanisms* and for the first time praised and included slang. In 1880, Lounsbury, echoing Whitney, asserted that speech always weakens "in the literary language, just as, unfortunately, the individual in the process of becoming civilized is too apt to gain gentleness at the expense of vigor." Slang was "the great feeder of vigorous expression." Those who indulged in slang were "simply performing a proper and indispensable office." Those who complained about slang misunderstood its character and function.[31]

Distrusting literary language, advocating simplified spelling, and tolerating mistakes, Americanisms, and slang all pointed to new attitudes toward popular customs. Not surprisingly, the scholars showed none of the ambivalence about popular education that racked the verbal critics. To them, popular education demonstrated democracy's success: "The cultivated speech now in use is in an entirely different position from that occupied by the language in any previous period in its history. It is no longer confined to a small class . . . but is the language of entire communities."[32] There were outsiders. Whitney worried that Catholic schools insulated the Irish. Their brogue and peculiar locutions might endure. But other groups were learning the English language even if they still spoke in their original tongue. Linguists were unworried that the old lines between the few and the many could no longer be drawn. Hall agreed that mass education had made too many "who are but barely qualified to read books" undertake to write them. "Yet the result, though repulsive enough, is not in the least serious. Penny-a-liners and such parcel-learned adventurers have had their fellows in every age; but no known language has ever suffered from their escapades perceptibly."[33]

Philologists not only defended many forms of popular language, they also used arguments that earlier in the century most refined men and women dismissed as ill-thought-out. This must have especially perplexed the verbal critics, many of whom began their careers attacking such ideas. Distrust of the literary canon was a theme of the reforming grammarians between the 1820s and 1840s. The philological scholars took it up after the war. Simplified spelling was a scheme of Noah Webster and the followers of John Horne Tooke. In the 1860s, critic Edward Gould regularly assailed such a rank, democratic notion. In the next decade, however, the philologists adopted it. Until the 1870s, only populist editors like Horace Greeley had good things to say about slang. Many ideas that the critics in the 1860s dismissed as vulgar and eccentric were in the next decade espoused by the philologists as simply the scientific view of language.

To be sure, the rapprochement with popular culture was merely an intellectual one. The scholars showed no signs of abandoning refined culture. "God forbid that the grand old name of gentleman should ever be dissociated from the name of scholar," Francis March proclaimed. Whitney argued that *Bildung* was a necessary prerequisite to philological study. His home, a former student recalled, was "filled with all the symbols of a broad, refined culture. . . ." Whatever the theoretical value of slang, none of the linguists had any intention of diving into such icy waters themselves. Lounsbury and Hall still claimed that the best English was that of "the refined and educated class, represented by the spoken and written speech of the most cultivated members. . . ." The best Whitney could muster was to call slang a "necessary evil."[34]

Yet if evil, it was still necessary. And that moved Whitney miles from the verbal critics' camp. Of all the philologists Whitney pushed his theory furthest; he alone discarded literary language as a standard. Language, Whitney thought, was essentially the spoken dialect, the written word merely a subordinate variation. Proper language was the spoken conversational dialect of the educated class. In his 1828 dictionary Noah Webster had made exactly the same argument. Both men came from the New Haven community and enough of the smoke remained from the dictionary war to connect Whitney and Webster. One early reviewer called Whitney's spoken language argument "radical." It was a radical argument. Until Whitney, few would have thought to make such a sharp division between spoken and written language. The two played off each other, informing each other, dialectically contributing to the stability of a refined language. After Whitney both Ferdinand de Saussure and Leonard Bloomfield forcefully argued the point and it has become one of the staples of twentieth-century linguistics. Whitney took the first step toward intellectually discarding the literary language.[35]

The Yale linguist at times argued that no language was better or worse than any other. He emphasized that literary languages were derived from regional dialects. Standard English was originally the East Midland dialect, Italian at first the "popular idiom only of Tuscany," and Latin some twenty-five centuries before was merely the vernacular idiom of "a little isolated district in middle Italy." He held that it was wrong to call literary speech a "language" and regional folk speech a "dialect"—strictly speaking, all were dialects. "The science of language has democratized our views on such points as these; it has taught us that one man's speech is just as much a language as another man's; that even the most cultivated tongue that exists is only the dialect of a certain class in a certain locality." Written English was that dialect "used by the educated class for certain purposes." It was only the "alleged superior" of other forms of English.[36] This view, now commonly held by linguists,[37] reduced all dialect differences to questions of status. This was a monumental challenge to the humanistic view that self-conscious care produced a language superior in breadth and flexibility. Although long recognizing that refined forms could be abused and turned into badges of status, defenders of literary English were also convinced that they contributed to clear and civil discourse. Whitney at times asserted that all linguistic pride was simply a form of class hubris. Elsewhere, however, he also wrote that literature was "one grand test of the worth of the language" and he routinely spoke of dialects being savage, barbaric, and civilized. Whitney did not come to terms with his contradictory feelings, but in his most "radical" moments he pushed very close to characteristically twentieth-century academic opinion.[38]

# II

The philologists' attack on verbal critics had to do with more than language. In the course of their arguments, the scholars smuggled in new ideas about higher education. Critics and scholars locked horns over the relative importance of expertise and liberal culture, over fundamental issues of education and authority. The philologists were part of a group of Victorian "positivists" who dealt a series of hammer blows to traditional humanism that the latter still reels from.

First, scholars stressed the importance of learning over breeding. They called themselves "experts" and "specialists" whose command of the English language must be bowed to. To write verbal criticism, the linguists argued, would take a degree of specialized knowledge the critics did not possess. Refined sensibilities and broad acquaintance with English letters no longer were sufficient to settle questions of usage. Fitzedward Hall's redefinition of correctness not only freed it from considerations of decorum, it tied correctness to erudition. In short, knowledge was pitted against taste.

In the 1860s, then, differing ideas appeared about how the educated should reestablish their authority in American life. The critics looked to the traditional canons of civility and humanism. The scholars urged expertise. In so doing, they rearranged time-honored attitudes. Humanistic canons placed specialized skills and knowledge below general culture.[39] Humane learning had long been associated with opening up the mind, with creating a sympathetic and socially responsible ruling elite. From Cicero through Erasmus, Locke, and Jefferson, it was meant to breed men of virtue and character, a stratum of humane leaders. "Let it be our hope to make gentlemen of every youth who is put under our charge," James Russell Lowell told a Harvard audience in 1886, "not a conventional gentleman, but a man of culture, a man of intellectual resource, a man of public spirit, a man of refinement, with that good taste which is the conscience of the mind, and that conscience which is the good taste of the soul." While philologists did not deny the importance of broad, humane culture, they did slide the accent from civility to expertise. As Francis March proclaimed in an 1868 Phi Beta Kappa address: "Under the old philosophy the highest word was CULTURE, under the new philosophy the highest word is PROGRESS." Montaigne once noted that it was more important to teach a young man virtue than how to decline *virtus*. Victorian linguists were not so sure. They emphasized the ultimate social rewards of declension over cultivation, unintentionally taking one large step toward withdrawing moral authority from high culture.[40]

Arguing that common language was inevitably vague, the scholars asserted that only technical vocabularies could purchase precision, that specialized vocabularies bore witness to the advance of civilization. Here was another hammer blow to humane literacy. In antiquity and since the Renaissance, rhetoricians, orators, and writers had contended that technical vocabularies impoverished civil conversation. The most dreadful blunder of eloquence, Cicero had said, was "to deviate into abstruse expression, and out of the beaten track of common sense." Nineteenth-century verbal critics agreed. Technical talk was neither civil nor civic.

Pedantry, the "too frequent or unreasonable obtruding of our own knowledge in common discourse," had been commonly condemned by nineteenth-century critics. Richard Grant White, echoing the Scottish rhetorician George Campbell, asserted that scientific terms were not part of the language: "They belong to no language. They are part of the terminology common to science and scientific men of all tongues and nations."[41]

The scholars, however, did not believe that a "refined" common language was possible. It was inevitably vague. On the other hand, the technological and scientific cornucopia of the nineteenth century had undeniably enriched the language: "In these days of railroads, steamboats, and telegraphs, of sun-pictures, of chemistry and geology, of improved wearing stuffs, furniture, styles and buildings, articles of food and luxury of every description, how many words and phrases are in every one's mouth which would be utterly unintelligible to the most learned man of a century ago, were he to rise from his grave and walk our streets!" The Whitmanesque lyricism of the passage is highly uncharacteristic of its author—Whitney—but it reveals exactly what warmed his passions. Whitney praised the new technical vocabularies of geology, botany, and mineralogy. "Even the bigoted purist cannot object to them: conservatism here would be the conservatism of ignorance, opposing itself to the progress of civilization and enlightenment." But he misrepresented the critics' position. They did not oppose scientific vocabulary, only its introduction into common conversation, a practice critics thought would undermine conversation and make the uninitiated passive hostages to the experts. Nevertheless, Whitney reached the heart of the issue: Did the immense educational, technological, and political changes of the nineteenth century create the need for new ways to think and care about language and discourse?[42]

Turning to expertise also facilitated the scholars' rapprochement with popular culture. They recast the relationship of education to popular customs. For the critics, education informed a whole way of life. Culture bred gentlemen of character, and character was not put on the shelf in the evening hours. Moreover, emphasizing refined taste, the morality of style, inevitably pitched the cultivated against the less cultivated. Those who were most educated were those with faculties more discriminating than the rest. Expertise, on the other hand, did not inform a whole way of life. It was a specific skill or body of knowledge to be used as necessary. Honor shifted from "being" to "function." What made Whitney, Hall, and March feel more educated was not so much their "culture" but their profound knowledge of linguistic theory and their detailed acquaintance with the history of English. Knowledge was more important than "taste." A specialist could be educated and—in theory at least—still comfortably participate in popular culture. The linguists did not oppose popular culture, they sidestepped it.

The philologists dealt another hard blow to *humanitas* by rending academic from literary culture, learning from literature. They called themselves experts in the scientific study of language and not men of letters. March sharply separated truth from beauty; one was scholarly and the other literary. He himself called the insight historic: "Heretofore the masters of language have been workers in literature—that is, in language as shaped by the aesthetic faculty—the poets, the orators, the prose poets, like Plato or Bunyan, whose speech is most carefully wrought to harmony." There was no question where March's sympathies lay: The identification of "thought and speech which was so favorable to the poet and orator, is a grievous hindrance in the pursuit of truth." Truth "is more beautiful than beauty," March wrote, and "power is more graceful than grace."[43]

The philologists were part of a larger cultural shift separating literature from learning. The birth of academic culture together with positivist social theory wrenched apart the felt connection between literary grace and scholarly zeal. Now for a scholar to be a man of letters became a matter of decision; one no longer assumed that the two should be the same. This separation is shown in the changed meanings of *literature* and *belles lettres* in the second half of the nineteenth century. In the early part of the century, *literature* denoted *all* learning. As Webster defined the term in 1828: "Literature comprehends a knowledge of the ancient languages, denominated classical study, history, grammar, rhetoric, logic, geography, etc, as well as the sciences." Chauncy Goodrich, in his 1847 revision of *Webster's*, drew in the meaning. In its "distinctive and usual sense" *literature* "excludes the positive sciences," though it still referred to the complete range of human learning. But by the close of the century dictionaries opposed the "usual" sense of *literature* to scholarship and science. In its "strictest sense," the *Standard Dictionary of the English Language* reported, *literature* "belongs to the sphere of high art and embodies thought that is power-giving, or inspiring or elevating, rather than merely knowledge giving (excluding all forms of scientific writing)."[44]

The term *belle lettres* underwent a similar transformation. First introduced in the early eighteenth century, *belles lettres*, at that time referring to all humane learning, was a term of high ethical seriousness.[45] By 1828

Webster noted that the word was "vague," although all agreed it included poetry and oratory. Worcester, more definite, defined it as "polite literature; the fine or elegant department of learning as rhetoric, poetry, criticism, and philology; classical authors." But as with *literature*, at the end of the century dictionaries contracted the term to mean imaginative literature such as poetry, drama, fiction, and the essay. Oratory was dropped, history gone. There was no mention of philology. Learning was separated from fancy.[46]

Hall, Lounsbury, and March roamed through English literature, but only to find evidence about the history of the language. Prose style was irrelevant; earlier opinion on usage "unscientific." Setting and context being ignored, literature was studied only to get at the history of the language. Fitzedward Hall cited Addison twenty-six times in *Modern English*, but not once did Hall consider an opinion of Addison's. Twenty-five of the citations merely reported particular words that Addison had used (never in context); the last reference condemned those who still used Addison as a model for style.[47] With Hall we step very close to a social science that obliterates any living connection with the past.

Yet that presses it all too far. Victorian philologists would have been astounded by the charge that they lacked historical sensitivity. March studied Anglo-Saxon. Lounsbury wrote a history of English. Hall contributed mightily to the *Oxford English Dictionary*. Whitney defined linguistics as in essence a historical study. Indeed the philologists were evolutionists (Whitney corresponded with Darwin, who in turn cited the American in *The Descent of Man*). The Victorian philologists' emphasis on history most clearly sets them off from the rigorously ahistorical linguistics of today. Yet Ferdinand de Saussure's famous shift from the diachronic (historical) to the synchronic (present-minded) was prepared for by Whitney. It was Whitney's assertion that language was an arbitrary social convention that, according to Saussure, put linguistics "on its true axis." Yet if language was custom, Saussure asked, why study past custom at all? Rather than immerse oneself in the evolution of the language, he posited, the linguist should simply observe contemporary speech. Whitney unwittingly undermined the necessity of historical study even while he championed it. His theory shriveled the husk; Saussure merely pulled it from the stalk.[48]

Traditional humanism was built on the idea of a universal human nature. All civilized voices were contemporary because all shared the same starting point. Evolutionary linguistics, however, treated each succeeding period as *sui generis*, which inevitably cut the past off from the present. The implications are best seen through the career of Francis March. In the 1860s interest in the Anglo-Saxon language was high. The books of Richard Chenevix Trench and George Perkins Marsh had piqued curiosity, and the Romantic rejection of Latinate diction further encouraged the study of medieval Anglo-Saxon. The young March undertook to map the field in a thorough and scholarly fashion. He published a grammar of Anglo-Saxon and selections of Anglo-Saxon literature in 1870. But March found that his intensive study of the subject had cost its relevance to the present. Interest in the subject survived only as long as it was studied as "fossil-poetry," the past encased in the present. Trench in the 1850s swooped through centuries to find the importance of Anglo-Saxon to the nineteenth century. The history of the word *religion* showed the progressive alienation of the English people from the trap of Rome. The word *kind* was descended from *kinned*, which revealed that our sense of humanity was originally tied to our sense of family.[49] March, though, patiently studied the Anglo-Saxon language itself. His diligence and thoroughness with the medieval sources left him no time (or inclination) to explore the relevance of Anglo-Saxon to modern times. March contributed much less to the arguments on usage than was expected in the 1860s because he locked himself in the past. He had become an expert.

Yet only March approached being an expert in our sense of the word. None of the other philologists came close. Lounsbury, Hall, and Whitney called themselves specialists, but they used the term in no way known to us. No simple label, in fact, can be used without qualification. *Professional, scholar, specialist*—all must bend to accommodate not only a different setting but also fundamentally different conceptions of intellectual work. Lounsbury, March, and Whitney grew into much between the 1860s and 1880s, but we would not recognize them as "typical" late-twentieth-century academics.

For experts, the range of these men was remarkable. Lounsbury wrote pioneering scholarship on Chaucer, Shakespeare, and Cooper as well as writing a history of the English language and numerous magazine articles. Fitzedward Hall published a number of monographs on Sanskrit culture before he took up his study of the English language. Hall's knowledge of English literature was immense; in this field he was no specialist. Whitney wrote on Sanskrit, linguistic theory, Hindu astronomy, current events in India, Darwin, the origin of language, mythology, ethnography, and paleography. He dabbled in geology. All this dwarfed his work on the

English language, which included a school grammar and various essays on usage, spelling, pronunciation, and Anglo-Saxon. Whitney also edited the seven-thousand-page *Century Dictionary*, published in 1889. And he taught linguistics, French, and German at Yale.

The term *professional* has its own limits. Hall held a university post for only a brief period of time. His sinecure in the British Civil Service allowed him to pursue his scholarly research. Moreover, if the term *professional* is set against *gentleman* it can mislead. The major philologists would have taken umbrage at the assertion that they were not gentlemen. The scholars praised expertise, but they did not feel that it would undermine gentility. Nor did they think that it should. In the 1860s and 1870s the scholars could not yet imagine Max Weber's "specialists without spirit." They all thought that a liberal education was a necessary prerequisite for the productive study of language.[50] The philologists often published in general interest magazines like *The Nation*, the *Academy*, the *North American Review*, and *Scribner's Monthly*. They did so not only because scholarly resources were meager (which they were),[51] but also because of a genuine commitment to the enlightenment of the educated public. Specialization, in their eyes, would nourish the cultivated mind, directly and with minimal time lag. It was still possible to ingenuously argue in the 1860s and 1870s that specialization would stimulate instead of fragment the educated public, feed the general culture instead of starve it.

It would be tempting to see the philologists as transitional figures, but that would be but a half-truth. Victorian linguists were not straining to "break through" to modern professionalism. They suffered no failure of nerve. Everywhere their differences with verbal critics were over different stress on common values. Civility and learning, culture and expertise, art and science—neither group completely threw away any of the elements. If there was one firm difference that separated the verbal critics from the scholarly philologists it was method. The linguists displayed a methodical approach to their work that the critics were incapable of, and the end result was a far more productive discussion of the history of English words. One might feel that Fitzedward Hall (or any of the other philologists) had a simplistic theory of language, lacked an ear for tone, or suffered from any number of other shortcomings. Yet no one could deny his profound knowledge of the English language. The scholarly philologists simply knew more about English than anyone else had ever known before them. To ignore them while writing about the language was to risk sounding ignorant. The Victorian scholars were instrumental in reshaping our sense of what it meant to be informed on the subject of the English language.

# III

The stirrings of cultural life in the 1860s had one social purpose—to reassert the authority of the best educated. The differences between Charles Eliot and Noah Porter should not mask their many similarities. The plea for culture was heard in many quarters in the late 1860s and usually there was no sense of its opposition to specialized learning. E. L. Godkin, for example, strongly praised the program of the Yale Sheffield School of Science where Whitney and Lounsbury taught. It would teach young men to be practical, Godkin thought, but it would also teach them character. *The Galaxy* in 1871 asked that a "[leader] of thought" have both "a marked and practical excellence" in some special field and "that general culture which will enable him to sympathize and appreciate his co-workers in every other department." Charles Eliot called for the same combination in his inaugural address at Harvard in 1869. A few sensed what would come—Noah Porter was far more perceptive than historians have usually painted him—but most, Charles Eliot, E. L. Godkin, Charles Norton, Thomas Lounsbury, Francis March, William Dwight Whitney, Andrew White—the list could go on—only gradually became aware that they were divided by more than what banded them together.[52]

In the early days Whitney corresponded with everyone who wrote. Patiently he explained the new field of linguistics to many who would not or could not possibly contribute to the field. To a traditional classicist high school teacher in rural New Jersey, Whitney sent off copies of the *Transactions of the American Philological Association* (Whitney was a cofounder of the association in 1869). To Richard Grant White, Whitney explained how language *really* worked. (White broke off correspondence upon learning that Whitney had collaborated with Lounsbury on the *College Courant* articles.) To Maximilian Schele de Vere, the author of a collection of Americanisms, Whitney offered avuncular encouragement, despite de Vere's obviously second-rate mind. All this was done partly from kindness, partly out of the desire to further the understanding of the science of linguistics. The number of talented people in the 1870s who studied philology was tiny, the number who applied its insights to the English language was minuscule. Whitney needed converts who would spread the message if not do any scholarly work themselves. Whitney was half scholar and half publicist because he worked from a position of extreme weakness, facing a popular culture that distrusted arcane learning of any kind and a traditional literary culture that needed to be persuaded of the value of scientific linguistics. It was a narrow path and Whitney hesitated to push anyone lest he himself crash to the ground.[53]

On the other side, the best-known defenders of liberal culture welcomed the new specialists. When James Russell Lowell and Charles Eliot Norton took over the moribund *North American Review* in 1863, they immediately recruited Whitney to write for them. They had no sense that scholarship was not necessarily a literary activity. As Norton wrote to Whitney: "We wish to raise the standard of criticism as high as possible—and to have both authors and publishers reached with an independence of spirit and frankness of tone rare in American literary criticism. . . . And I trust that we shall have such help as may enable us to do something in this way for the progress of American letters." Similarly, upon founding *The Nation* in 1865, E. L. Godkin wrote to Whitney asking him to contribute. In the sixties and seventies both Godkin and Norton turned to Whitney to assess articles on philological subjects. Both wanted the Yale scholar to suggest other qualified writers.[54] Whitney, of course, had no objection to their queries. He needed the literati as much as they needed him, so he wrote to Norton that he was glad the *North American Review* had "fallen into such good hands." The periodicals gave Whitney a forum to advance his ideas and the careers of his colleagues. He encouraged Norton and Godkin to publish Francis March, Fitzedward Hall, and Eugene Schuyler, another graduate of Yale.[55]

The early years of Charles Eliot's presidency at Harvard also reflect the congruence of culture and expertise in those years. His essay "The New Education" explicitly praised the work of the Yale Sheffield School of Science, the academic home of Whitney. Yet Eliot's early efforts to upgrade Harvard's faculty did not lead him only to the new experts. Eliot was almost random in his search for excellence. Among others, he hired Charles Eliot Norton, Oliver Wendell Holmes, Jr., and the verbal critic Adams Sherman Hill, he offered a chair in history to E. L. Godkin, and gave the disgruntled Francis Child more time for research. Working diligently to hire Whitney, although the philologist had no desire to leave New Haven, Eliot persisted as only Eliot could, flattering and cajoling Whitney, urging him not to make a final refusal, asking him to try Harvard for just a semester. Whitney came to Cambridge in January 1870 to teach for a term, but even there the program he taught in shows how unformed intellectual lines were in 1870. The course was experimental and entitled "Language and Literature." The teachers were Whitney, lecturing on linguistic theory, Francis Child, teaching English literature of the thirteenth and fourteenth centuries, William D. Howells on recent Italian literature, and E. J. Cutler on the principles of criticism. Scholarship, literature, and criticism still shared the same podium.[56]

By the mid-seventies, however, there were strains showing. Norton and Lowell had grown tired of Whitney's acidic attacks on Max Müller's Romantic linguistics. "Yes, you are correct about Müller, you have shown his faulty scholarship, his bad reasoning," Norton wrote Whitney. "You have only now to show your superiority as a Christian, as well as a scholar, by the studied gentleness of your tone. . . ." Eight months later Norton again asked the Yale scholar to be "reserved" and not descend to "personalities." Whitney would have none of this, but what annoyed him above all was Norton's assertion that certain of Whitney's points were "too small game to be worth hunting." Norton, thinking about the audience of the *North American Review*, found some points just too pedantic for publication. Whitney, worried about the possibility that linguistics might take a wrong turn, did not agree. Norton thought in terms of pleasing the cultivated public, Whitney of the evolution of the discipline.[57]

The exchange was far more important than either man realized, for it indicated a conflict about basic attitudes toward audience. Norton remained committed to addressing the public, although he shared with so many late-nineteenth-century gentry the confusion about whether a refined or mass audience was most appropriate. (Certainly the *North American Review* was aimed at an educated few.) The commitment to the public, though, was directly connected to Norton's sense of self as a civic-minded gentleman, the *homo rhetor* in the tradition of Cicero, Quintilian, and Vico, among others. Whitney, however, was beginning to think that his key audience was the relevant body of linguistic specialists. This too should be seen as part of an emerging sense of self, in Whitney's case, the philologist as scholarly expert. Although Whitney never stopped writing for refined magazines even after professional journals became available in the 1880s, the 1876 dispute with Norton reveals a subtle shift in preferred audience. For Whitney, civic considerations were being edged aside by the professional.

By the 1880s, there was a major rift between scholarship and liberal cultivation. Real fears surfaced that the two had different aims. Many critics and essayists were growing disenchanted with scholarship. At Harvard's two hundred and fiftieth anniversary James Russell Lowell complained about the fragmentation on campus. E. L. Godkin by the eighties worried about the overweening drive of science. Charles Eliot Norton, too, feared the collapse of liberal culture in the face of the new utilitarian university. All three men, born in the 1820s, took the lead in American cultural life in the 1860s complaining about the sorry state of art *and* scholarship. Lowell had helped found the Modern Language Association. Norton was a founder of the Archeological Institute of America. In the pages of *The Nation* Godkin had championed specialized knowledge.[58] By the eighties, however, these men feared the experts' strange but potent combination of imperial claims to authority and restricted intellectual vision. The scholarship they had originally encouraged had taken on a life of its own and threatened to smother culture. The scholars saw themselves as anatomists, coolly dissecting human culture with the scalpel of science. More and more, however, men like Godkin, White, and Lowell saw them as madmen, hacking humane culture to pieces and then insanely distributing its remains.

Academics of all kinds of faced this issue. In engineering schools such as that in which Whitney and Lounsbury taught, a vocal minority began asserting that liberal culture was useless. Specialization was sufficient for the engineer. Still others argued that the humanities should be replaced with the new social sciences as supplementary studies for engineers. By the 1880s Charles Eliot could no longer blithely assume that there were no tensions between the electoral system and general culture. In the mid-eighties Eliot published a series of essays trying to explain the "new" meaning of liberal education under the elective system. As universities broke up into departments, outsiders worried about the impact on culture. Reverend Joseph Cook lectured on "Fragmentary College Culture," claiming that the new system destroyed Cicero's *humanitas*, that "vision of the inner universe and its harmonies." The New York *Evening Post* in 1882 argued for a middle ground between the undifferentiated college and the departmental system. Too narrow a division of studies, the *Post* contended, "tends inevitably to intellectual narrowness and bigotry." Nevertheless, the seemingly inexorable drive toward specialization continued. By the 1880s, Eliot was deeply worried about the growing reputation of Johns Hopkins University as the premier institution of higher learning in the United States. In the previous decade, Hopkins had aggressively hired research-minded Ph.D.s. To keep up with Hopkins, Eliot reasoned, he could no longer hire the same number of men of broad culture that he had in the seventies. Harvard had to have experts.[59]

Discussions of language reflected all these tensions. By the 1880s there was no question that verbal critics and philologists were on opposite sides of the fence. Although in 1871 White had quoted Whitney approvingly and argued that scholarship and criticism were complementary, by 1881 he complained that the philologists were "sublimely indifferent" to linguistic perversion. "Pilate could not have washed his hands with more serene disregard for the consequences," wrote White. In his presidential address to the Modern Language Association in 1889, James Russell Lowell worried that the "purely linguistic side" of the modern languages "seems to be getting more than its fitting share" of attention. Literature was superior to mere linguistic study and Lowell called on the association to "rescue" itself from what Milton had once called "these grammatical flats and shallows."[60]

Lowell's speech only capped off a decade-long discussion on the issue. When the *Transactions of the Modern Language Association* first appeared in 1885, the debate was ongoing, and the pages of the *TMLA* contained every possible shade of opinion. There were those who complained about the "growing" disregard of artistic grace among "scholarly oracles." The "democratization of our style" was blamed on the linguists, whose barbaric jargon was a front for "syntactical license masquerading in the guise of liberty."[61]

But there were just as many who defended the new linguistics. By the mid-eighties the number of scholars working on the English language swelled. Although Whitney's stature remained secure, he no longer was the epicenter of all English study in the United States. The younger men—Oliver Emerson, Brander Matthews, W. F. Allen, Gilbert Tucker, James Garnett, and others—were often even less committed to the literary language than were Whitney, Hall, Lounsbury, and March. L. A. Stager quoted the British philologist Henry Sweet to the effect that "spoken language is the only source of the literary language." To Stager this meant that "the living spoken form" of language should be "the foundation of its study."[62]

The debates of the eighties showed just how much the traditions of civil education had unraveled. Humanistic education had tied together learning, art, and decorum, each reinforcing the other, each contributing to the formation of the cultivated man or woman. The philologists, though, argued that scholarship had little to do with style. They separated learning from art and decorum. To them, correct language was known through a study of custom, preferably spoken custom. Correct language had nothing to do with context (decorum) or literature (style).

The philologists never discarded refined culture, yet their linguistics subtly contradicted the presumptions of civic rhetoric. The philologists, by accenting expertise and celebrating jargon, were rethinking the nature of the educated self. The new linguistics, stressing the separation of learning from breeding and literature, meant that the old notion of a unified soul had no "scientific" standing. And just as important, the contention that all linguistic custom was adequate to its task implied that public discourse needed no critical care at all. The late-nineteenth-century linguists are often portrayed by historians of the English language as liberals, scholars who began to recognize the validity of everyday popular usage. Yet the scholars were deeply interested in reconfiguring authority, not democratizing it. Their intellectual acceptance of popular speech was not unrelated to their own belief that authority would be confirmed by expertise instead of civil refinement.

The new scholarship was not alone in tugging apart the cultural webs of refined English. What we can call "literary modernism" for lack of a better name pulled from another direction. Running as a countercurrent to the genteel tradition, modernists argued that a literary language should shatter decorum, expose its vulgar conventionality. Only by constantly assaulting linguistic decorum could we preserve our vitality. Language should be freed from the binds of history and experience, Emerson argued in the 1830s, and tied to the untamed energy of "Providence and Nature." We could not find truth with a vocabulary "in a clean shirt and white neckcloth of a student of divinity." Whitman went further, demanding that the language be not only vitalized, but also eroticized:

> A perfect writer would make words sing, dance, kiss, do the male and female act, bear children, weep, bleed, rage, stab, steal, fire cannon, steer ships, sack cities, charge with cavalry or infantry, or do any thing, that man or woman or the natural powers can do.

Even a writer like Howells claimed that slang is "sometimes delightful and forcible beyond the reach of the dictionary" and he could wax enthusiastic over the Russian of Turgenev: "What a luxury it must be to have a great big untrodden barbaric language to wade into." And later, early in the twentieth century, H. L. Mencken praised the American language for being uncritical of "the difference between a genuine improvement in succinctness and clarity, and mere extravagant raciness."[63]

Like the scholars, the literary radicals separated the English of literature from the English of social convention. Yet there were differences. The radicals argued that literary language should bruise convention, assault it. Literary English had to be kept vital or else we would surrender to dull placidity. Dull placidity, however, was just what the philologists hoped for. The scholars wanted to make the educated relax with their language, not assault it in the name of verbal purity or in the name of authenticity, vitality, or erotics. To Whitman, slang was the "lawless germinal element" of language, the source of language's sinewy might. Whitney called slang a "necessary evil." Although both unraveled civil attitudes toward language, disentangling learning from literature from convention, it was the philologist who had the larger impact on American life. The scholars most visibly tangled with the critics. The scholars would soon begin to reconstruct the English dictionary and the English Bible. The scholars would soon devise new English programs for the schools. At each point the new scholars combatted defenders of the old traditions. At each barricade the cry of "science" was flung at the banner of "civility." Let us now turn to see how this battle of ideas worked itself out in the last decades of the century.

# CHAPTER SIX

# Gentle Speech in School
# and Street, 1865–1885

Learning once made popular is no longer
learning; it has the appearance of something
we have bestowed upon ourselves.

SAMUEL JOHNSON

The war over language was fought on many fronts. But nearly everywhere in the years after the Civil War, verbal critics dominated. In books, magazines, and schools, the philologists found little favor. Rhetorical ideas also increasingly turned up in popular urban newspapers, etiquette books, household encyclopedias, and other literature for the socially insecure. Interest in refined language was not shrinking, it was spreading.

Many historians have written about the slow fade of the genteel tradition in nineteenth-century America. In fact, the tradition remained quite important into the 1880s and even grew in stature after the Civil War. It was the tradition's very attractiveness that caused problems. The diffusion of refined ways of life made genteel language a less effective elite social marker. If you understood "taste" as a *moral* as well as aesthetic category, and if you judged taste by its outward manifestations, it was simply becoming harder and harder to tell who was who.

Historians writing about modern professionalism often take an understandably Whiggish view of their subject. "Where did it all begin?" seems a natural question. But this can obscure how long other ways of understanding social personality lingered on late in the nineteenth century. Into the 1880s, the primary identity of highly educated men was the gentleman and not the professional. Rhetoric and verbal criticism were understood as part of that way of life, helping to keep alive a refined public opinion. By the 1880s, the fear that "taste" could no longer divide the world pressed against the survival of rhetorical culture, but civic ideals associated with gentlemanly deportment kept it alive.

# I

In American colleges, the fight was directly between rhetoricians and philologists. Each understood language differently. Rhetoricians saw language as tied to literature, character, and civic life. Rhetoric was devoted to the production of public speech. Philologists, on the other hand, increasingly shifted attention from the noble and civic to the simple and everyday. For them, the core of language lay in the resources available for daily use. Built into their very theoretical premises, the new philologists asserted that any "scientific" study of language would have no interest in civic rhetoric.

The ties between verbal critics and college rhetoricians were strong. A number of critics spent time teaching rhetoric, and in their various books, critics and rhetoricians exchanged praise.[1] Not surprisingly, the philologists had little use for college teachers of rhetoric, distrusting their "foggy, aesthetic" ideas about language. Rarely did the philologists attack rhetoric, more often they ignored it. Still, the rhetoricians sensed the problem. In 1874, Theodore Hunt noted that despite the dignified history of rhetoric, "the whole department is on trial. . . ." When they bothered, philologists drew on traditional arguments to denigrate rhetoric. They contended that rhetoric taught verbal trickery. Francis Child studied philology in Germany in the 1850s, and at Harvard he taught courses in Anglo-Saxon while working on his monumental collection of early English ballads. As early as his senior oration in 1846, Child drew on Plato's *Gorgias* to argue that rhetoric taught the skills of manipulation. That argument was tied to the late-nineteenth-century hope that scientific philology could simply obliterate considerations of style, that science, being antiliterary, had no idiom of its own. An 1875 Harvard debate over rhetoric spilled onto the pages of *The Nation*. E. L. Godkin, strongly influenced by Whitney, claimed that rhetoric was unnecessary; the country needed not "glibness" but "well-ordered brains." Richard J. Dana, Jr., responded that thought and style lived in union and that neither could be neglected. Godkin, however, had the last word: Rhetoric only promoted style without thought, he asserted, just look at the "trash" in the *Congressional Record*.[2]

Opponents of rhetoric also argued that the subject was empty and formal. Students were taught the definitions of narrative, prosody, metaphor, ellipsis, catachresis, and trope but they did not study English language or literature. Philologists argued that *they* were introducing English studies into the college curriculum, a claim that has passed from late-nineteenth-century philologists to contemporary historians, who have tended to equate the rise of English studies with the appearance of English departments.[3] That view, however, needs reconsidering.

Pre–Civil War rhetoricians *did* teach English language and literature. Blair's text, for example, contained analyses of Addison, Johnson, the English Bible, and Hume's philosophical style as well as discussions of the oratory of both the ancients and the moderns. Students were likely to study Blair first in secondary school and then again in college. There were, of course, poor teachers who turned the subject into rote memorization (as there are soporific lecturers today), but for the best teachers the subject was a lively analysis of English literature and language.[4]

Post–Civil War rhetoricians also saw their job as cultivating the language. As one glowing reviewer of John Hart's rhetoric said in 1870, "A knowledge of the principles, the uses, and the powers of our own noble vernacular, . . . must assuredly form an essential part of the education of every cultivated, not to say of every civilized, member of Society."[5] These rhetoricians were also intimately interested in literature. The leading ones—John Bascom, Theodore Hunt, John Hart, Alfred Welsh, and Henry Day—all wrote companion texts on English literature to supplement the formal rhetorics.[6] They were full of citations, allusions, and commentary on the English literary tradition. Classical culture remained present in English translation. Teachers like Theodore Hunt of Princeton and John Genung of Oberlin berated mediocre teachers who taught the subject as a set of empty, dry, formal principles.[7] They, as well as Adams Sherman Hill, emphasized that rhetoric should be taught in conjunction with literature.

Philologists did not introduce the study of English language and literature into the American college system. Their differences with the rhetoricians were over *how* language and literature were studied, and *how much* they should be studied. Here let me look at the former issue, in chapter 8 the latter.

Rhetoricians still believed in the interplay of language and literature and in the fluid distinctions between the spoken and written word. A language, they argued, was known through its literature. "The student is to put himself in constant contact with the best authors," wrote Princeton's Theodore Hunt, maintaining that good literature contained "the best and fullest forms which language is capable of taking. . . ." Hunt then cited William Mathews and Samuel Johnson on the importance of studying the best models. "Of all the arts none outranks literature," wrote another teacher of the subject. Rhetoric, being based on the works of the greatest authors, "educated our taste to enjoy the treasures of thought and the graces of style of those authors." (Rhetoricians between 1865 and 1885 continued to use the term *literature* broadly to include poetry, essays, history, oratory, and philosophy. Even letter writing was a literary activity.[8])

Rhetoricians also stressed the interconnection of thought and language. "Form and substance, indeed, coexist, and to know the laws of one we must consider the nature of the other. . . ." Rhetoric, according to Brainerd Kellogg, taught "how to find the thought, and best express it in words." When philologists were cited, they were usually Romantic philologists: "As Müller has it," wrote one rhetorician, "speech is thinking aloud, and thought is speaking low."[9]

Like the verbal critics, rhetoricians evoked the connection between language and morality. Theodore Hunt repeated the old dictum that eloquence and republicanism flourished and perished together. William Mathews was skeptical of this, but he too suggested that oratory should be an ethical pursuit. *Eloquence a Virtue* was the name of a well-known mid-century rhetorical text. It was also a sentiment that had a distinguished history. Learning rhetoric—when tied to the cultivation of wisdom—was both a personal and public good. Theodore Hunt quoted Quintilian: "Discourse reveals character; and not without reason did the Greeks teach that as a man lived so he would speak." Another rhetorician cited Goethe: "The style of a writer is a faithful representation of his mind; . . . and if he would write in a noble style, let him first possess a noble soul."[10]

Philologists denied that language was intimately connected with literature, thought, or morality. Like the rhetoricians, philologists spoke of studying "language and literature," but to scholars like Thomas Lounsbury and Francis March, "language and literature" indicated two separate subjects. Language—etymology, syntax, inflection, and so forth—was one subject. Literature—the great authors—was another. In the 1860s and 1870s, James Hadley, Hiram Corson, Francis March, and Thomas Lounsbury rewrote the history of the English language to reduce the literary emphasis prominent in George Perkins Marsh's *Lectures on the English Language* and George Craik's *History of English Literature and Language*. For the earlier historians, literature made the language: Shakespeare, Chaucer, and Johnson, each in his own time, had actually shaped a language then used by countless English-speaking people. For the postwar scientific historians, however, language was a social convention that literary men used: Shakespeare did not create language, he merely used what was available at the time.[11]

Philologists also denied that language and thought were somehow connected. To them, language was an arbitrary social convention, not reducible to reason. As Whitney put it:

> Language is not thought, nor is thought language; nor is there a mysterious and indissoluble connection between the two. . . . There can hardly be a greater and more pernicious error in linguistics or metaphysics, than the doctrine that language and thought are identical.

Whitney's arguments were deep and philosophical, born of his disputes with the Kantian Max Müller. Whitney discussed the ways we thought without using language and noted that Darwin had shown that animals could think without speaking. Drawing from his metaphorical repertoire, Whitney contended that language was "the instrument of thought, the machinery with which the mind works. . . ."[12]

When philologists spoke of studying the language, they meant studying the history of the language. All were firm evolutionists, advocating that students be able to trace the growth of English syntax, etymology, and vocabulary. Rhetoricians studied the language but understood it in the framework of rhetorical categories which were timeless. To the philologists, that appeared as if it were no study of the language at all. "Sympathetic reading," thought Francis March, induced a love for neither literature nor language. Here is how he described the philological approach:

> The best students regularly look up the etymology of every word, and prepare for questions of its history and its relations to kindred words in other languages, the phonetic laws which govern the changes of form, the laws of thought which govern the changes of meaning, historical inferences to be drawn from it, and similar matters. They prepare for comparative syntax, to give the forms in other languages of expression each relation of thought, and their history.

March thought that studying Anglo-Saxon would improve the student's English. Whitney, on the other hand, downplayed the immediate practical benefits of linguistic study. Language, he contended, was known through habit and imitation. Linguistics was studied for the mental discipline it offered the student and the intellectual insight it offered the scholar.[13]

Just as distinctions between verbal critics and philologists were blurred at first, so too were the divisions between rhetoricians and philologists. Most rhetoricians advocated the study of Anglo-Saxon. In the 1860s, Francis March still taught a philology that mixed literature and language; only in the early seventies did he rigorously separate the two. The limited resources of many colleges also contributed to the blur. Although Francis Child intensely disliked rhetoric, he taught it at Harvard through the 1860s, only freed from the chore in the mid-seventies after Charles Eliot hired Adams Sherman Hill to teach the subject.[14] Institutional specialization helped clarify differences. By 1882 Indiana University had both a "Professor of English Language and Literature" and a "Professor of Elocution." In 1876 the University of Wisconsin created two departments— one of English literature and language and another of rhetoric and oratory. The first safely housed philology; the second ignored it, a common solution in the late nineteenth century.[15]

By the mid-seventies, the split was becoming apparent. Rhetorician John Hart observed in 1874 that philology, "in the strict sense of German *sprachwissenshaft*, or science of language, has nothing to do with literature as such." It is no matter to the philologist if an expression is "elegant or clumsy, profound or trivial and commonplace, as long as it throws some light on the growth of human speech. The philologist learns to disregard style as the botanist learns to disregard scent." Hiram Corson, who pioneered the study of philology at Cornell in the 1860s, in the next two decades decided that the approach was hollow. By the eighties, the division was clear. John Genung pointed out in 1884 that philology had emerged in the sixties as a new way to teach the English language but that its antiliterary bias vitiated its insights:

> Seeking power to write, men were fed with philology. And thus the attitude of the student was determined in the contra-rhetorical direction. English was pursued as an acquisition, not as an art.[16]

Although the differences in approach became well known, in practice philology and rhetoric continued to mingle. Only the true believers were

convinced that one excluded the other. In between, there were hundreds
of teachers who experimented with eclectic mixes. Rhetoric and philology.
Rhetoric and literature. Philology and literature. Literature alone. All were
tried at various schools after the Civil War. There were simply too many
teachers to expect any clean divisions.[17]

Despite all the discussion of Anglo-Saxon and the historical study of
the language, through the mid-eighties philology did not win many
friends. True, the Yale Sheffield School of Science had firmly implanted
linguistic studies in its curriculum. And true, the subject was introduced
at Harvard, Cornell, Lafayette, and the University of Pennsylvania in the
1860s and continued to grow in the 1870s. Yet for several reasons, philology's appeal was limited.

First, there was much inertia on college campuses. Most colleges did
not enthusiastically embrace the new curriculum in the 1870s. Rhetoric
continued to be the dominant English language subject so long as the
elective system was not adopted, and the elective system did not become
widespread until the mid-eighties.

Second, the small number of philologists limited the spread of the
subject. Even when someone did become a philologist, there was more
prestige in studying a language other than English; and even the new
research-oriented universities could not always find an Anglo-Saxon
scholar. At Johns Hopkins, Daniel Coit Gilman tried for over a decade
to find "the man who had both literary and philological aptitude—a future
Child or Lounsbury." Between 1876 and 1879, however, Gilman could
find no one to teach English. In 1879, Gilman hired Albert Cook, a
philologist who refused to teach anything past Shakespeare. In 1881, Cook
was not reappointed, perhaps because Gilman thought he could entice
the philologist Henry Sweet to come over from England. Sweet, however,
could not be lured to the States, and Gilman hired Henry Wood to teach
philology. Wood, an American with a Leipzig Ph.D., taught the history
of English for three years. In 1884, he asked to be transferred to the
German department because he enjoyed that language more than English.
Unable to find an English philologist, Gilman turned to literary figures.
He tried to convince the novelist Howells and the poet Browning to come
to Hopkins. Both turned him down. That left Gilman with William Hand
Browne, an M.D. who had edited the *Southern Review* and *New Eclectic
Magazine* and who began teaching English literature and composition in
1882. Browne opposed "swamping literature in philology" and told Gil-
man the "thoughts of great men, and not the laws of Teutonic vowel-
change, move and mould the world." Gilman's early efforts to find a

scholar combining philological and literary study were frustrated by the small number of philologists and by the growing disregard of philology for the literary arts and the emerging hostility of literary men for scientific philology.[18]

Finally, philology suffered because many felt that it did not contribute to a command of the English language. Whitney argued that philology should be studied for the mental discipline it offered, not for the practical benefit it would have on the student's speech or writing. That argument was used by opponents of philology to urge that it not be included in the school curriculum. The interest in Anglo-Saxon was born through men like Richard Chenevix Trench and George Perkins Marsh who in the 1850s and 1860s directly connected the study of Anglo-Saxon with contemporary English. When the postwar scholars produced textbooks on medieval English, however, outsiders just could not see the utility of it all. Hiram Corson's *Handbook of Anglo-Saxon and Early English* was a fine work, according to the reviewer in *The New York Times*, but what was it for? "The study of old English is no more practical . . . than that of Greek and Latin."[19]

Rhetoricians and philologists taught students to gain command of their language in fundamentally different ways. Rhetoricians urged students to take the language apart, to analyze how it was best used, to unlock the secrets of the best models. For them, language was self-consciously wrought, a medium we struggled to control. Rhetoricians had both a reverential respect for the importance of language in human affairs and a strong sense of Wordsworth's "sad incompetence of speech."[20]

For the philologists, however, style was mere fashion. "It is not the adoption of peculiar rhetorical devices that contribute either to the permanent well-being or corruption of any tongue. These are mere accidents of speech, the fashion of a time which passes away with the causes that gave it currency."[21] Linguists told students that language was learned not by studying the various ways it could be crafted, but by acquiring an ever more detailed empirical understanding of the conventions of vocabulary and grammar. Rather than challenge the sufficiency of customary usage, the philologists encouraged students to more deeply immerse themselves in a language's folk rhythms.

The same distinction can be put another way. One of Ferdinand de Saussure's most important contributions to linguistic analysis was his distinction between language (*la langue*) and speech (*la parole*). Language, Saussure pointed out, was the sum of grammatical, lexical, and phonetic possibilities in any given tongue. Speech, however, was what people actually wrote or uttered. Speech was made with language, but it was not the same as language. Late-nineteenth-century philologists and rhetoricians both taught English, but philologists taught about language and rhetoricians about speech. The linguistic scholars studied the grammar of the tongue; rhetoricians analyzed public discourse. Since Saussure's distinction was not yet recognized, each side poached on the other's grounds just as each poorly understood the other's terrain. In sum the two sides differed markedly.

Understanding this difference, however, makes even plainer how thorough was the linguists' attack on rhetorical culture. For the linguists, there was no room for any analysis of public discourse. As long as a "science" of language could be *only* about *la langue*, then no rhetoric, nothing associated with the production of speech (*la parole*) could have "scientific" status. Rhetoric, of course, was not meant to be scientific in the philologists' sense of the word; it was meant to preserve that public sphere where an informed public opinion could be discursively spun out via informal reasoning. Such an understanding remained evident into the 1880s, but it would soon disappear. Much was involved here—the culture of expertise, post-Victorian mass culture, new forms of electronic media—but the small part played by theories of language should not be forgotten. Increasingly, people would think about language in different ways. Through the influence of the new linguistics, many informed people would decide that *any* effort to monitor public speech was a betrayal of science.

# II

In the lower schools, the same disputes were played out with different terms. In academies, high schools, and common schools, the debate was over grammar. Rhetoricians and critics reiterated old arguments *contra* grammatical study. Philologists, though, defended the pursuit.

The wave of disgust with grammar that Romantics had stirred before the war swelled in the 1860s and 1870s. There were few verbal critics or rhetoricians who did not denigrate grammatical study. Henry Alford claimed that most grammatical rules were not contributions to the purity of the language, but in fact the "main instruments of its deterioration." Quoting Montaigne, William Mathews asserted that "they that will fight custom with grammar are fools." Little was original in the postwar attack on grammar; the subject, critics argued, was dull and inconsequential.

Grammars tried to force English syntax into unnatural Latin shapes. Moreover, studying grammar did not contribute to a command of literary language. Quite the opposite: "Had John Bunyan been taught to parse, in all probability *Pilgrim's Progress* would never have been written. Had Shakespeare spent five years diagramming sentences, his plays would have been lifeless and cold." Teacher after teacher complained about students who could recite grammatical rules but who could not speak properly.[22]

Most critics wanted grammar deemphasized. A few wanted it eliminated. Richard Grant White, with his indefectible feel for controversy, made the most unusual argument. He claimed that English had no grammar. Grammar, in White's eyes, was inflection, and since the Middle Ages English had steadily shed its inflectional forms. By the nineteenth century, English had little in common with highly inflected languages like Latin. It was, in White's terms, "a grammarless tongue."[23]

Educators, writers, and newspapermen drew on the antigrammar arguments to call for the removal of formal grammar from school curricula, or at least to push the study of it into the background. In 1878 *The New York Times* editorialized against the overabundance of "dry grammatical material" in the nation's classrooms. In the late seventies that paper also opened its columns to Richard Grant White, who expanded on his argument that English had no grammar and that its study in school was counterproductive. The *Chicago Tribune* also ran editorials against grammar in the late 1870s. Most postwar teachers' manuals encouraged the deemphasis of grammar. It was the "most important reform" in language study in the past thirty years, wrote Emerson White in his *Elements of Pedagogy* (1886). "Grammarians have dealt with language as if it were a game of chess," whereas "language is a game of life" it was reported in an 1883 teacher's guide. Francis Parker, in his *Talks of Pedagogy*, thought that grammar must be studied but conceded that English was basically "a grammarless tongue."[24]

To the philologists, nothing could be sillier than to claim that English had no grammar. By the 1870s they had firmly grasped an insight now a linguistic commonplace—all languages have grammars. Critics of grammar, however, held to the assertion that it appeared only in literary (advanced) languages. White's argument was a further refinement, suggesting that on a higher plane grammar again disappeared. Critics were skeptical of the grammars of Anglo-Saxon produced by the scholars; they felt the medieval language was just too lawless for such elaborate syntax. When the British philologist Edwin Abbott claimed to have worked out the grammar of Shakespeare, White and his friend Horace Furness were appalled. Furness, America's leading Shakespearean scholar, wrote to White: "Shakespeare wrote as he d——d please [*sic*] guided by nothing but an ear innocent of grammar." After White took on the British philologist in print, Furness wrote to him: "Lash Abbott well, and spare not. I loathe and detest and abhor the idea that Shakespeare wrote by rule."[25]

The philologists and their allies, however, were not persuaded by what they saw as fuzzy, aesthetic thinking. The "anti-grammatical frenzy" was fading, asserted the *Massachusetts Teacher* in 1873; the "new philology" would lead the subject back to favor. Philologists urged that the study of grammar be retained. March argued at the 1872 National Educational Association meeting that students entering high school should know the definitions, rules, and paradigms of syntax by heart. William Dwight Whitney also inveighed against the antigrammar trend. He urged that the subject be retained not for any practical benefit for speech or writing but for the mental discipline it offered. According to Whitney, grammar was studied not to attain "correctness of English speaking, but rather a systematic apprehension of the facts of English speech." Others agreed with March that there were subtle benefits to grammatical study. One of the few teacher's manuals of the 1880s that unambiguously defended grammar pointed out that there were many "fine points of construction in which the ear and memory will not serve as a guide." To learn those fine points, grammar was essential.[26]

In the two decades after the Civil War, few schoolmen listened to the academic philologists. By the seventies, a student did not usually start studying grammar until the fifth or sixth grade. And unlike before the war, students studied little grammar in high school, rarely beyond what today we would call the freshman year. In many places grammar disappeared completely from the high school curriculum in the 1870s. The decline was apparent all over the nation.[27]

In a few places, grammar was dropped altogether. In 1879, the Texas legislature voted to have the schools stop teaching the subject. In 1891, the Connecticut school board voted to end all grammatical requirements in the state's schools. Few went this far, but in the years after the Civil War technical grammar clearly declined in importance. In 1876, the principal of the Lewiston, Maine, high school summed up the feelings of many: "Of technical grammar little need be said except that it is possible for a smart boy or girl of fourteen years, in a single term, to learn all there is in it of value to the majority of persons."[28]

As powerful as the antigrammar campaign was, the subject was not run out of the nation's schools. There were still many schoolteachers in the 1870s and 1880s who defended old-fashioned grammar. In 1877, two reliable observers noted that although grammar was being "desperately assailed" by men "of high literary culture," the majority of "thoughtful, practical teachers have never doubted the utility of grammar."[29] Magazines for teachers continued to print some defenses of the subject, although usually with the lament that they were swimming against the tide.[30]

The subject also survived because outside the schools, by the middle of the nineteenth century, faith in grammar had become a part of middle- and upper-class folklore. Whatever the quarrels within the teaching profession, outside the small ranks of "informed" opinion and inside the broader categories of middling and refined culture, belief in grammar's utility was almost magical. As early as the 1820s a writer in the *North American Review* was saying of grammar: "There is a certain mystery hanging about it, to the eyes of most parents, it is true; they have not the slightest conception of any use there can be in it; but there is a vague and indefinable impression on their minds, that grammar is something very important, and indeed essential." Evidence for this is by nature scattered, but we do not have to look hard for it. From the beginning of the antigrammar campaign in the 1850s, casual middle-class comments on the importance of grammar indicated both ignorance and indifference to the "advanced" educational opinion of the day. There is, for example, the Harvard-educated lawyer and future justice of the California Supreme Court, who in the 1850s wrote his daughter that she should not neglect her grammar. In 1858 there is Mrs. Sigourney, who in *Lucy Howard's Journal* has the protagonist worry about her grasp of grammar. Just over a decade later there is the daughter of a wealthy Chicago businessman who in her diary feared that she did not parse as ably as she might. Although *The New York Times* occasionally expressed skepticism about grammar, when in 1879 the Texas legislature abolished the study of the subject, the *Times* recoiled, calling it the work of the "half-educated."[31]

The antigrammar campaign rarely reflected a barbarian assault on the schools. More often it indicated the revival of old literary arguments against grammatical pedantry, that studying the rules of syntax did not contribute to refined literary grace. Teachers emphasized the importance of "practical" language studies. Mental discipline was not enough; language study must directly contribute to good usage. Grammar did not.

The success of the antigrammar campaign also showed how unappetizing the ideas of the philologists were to primary and secondary school teachers. Despite the philologists' commitment to grammar, the subject fell into disrepute. Even when grammar was studied, the books used were usually the old-fashioned (Pestallozian) grammars. Into the eighties, Whitney's grammar for high school students was remarkably unpopular, and during the early and mid-eighties, high schools in Boston, Chicago and San Francisco did not use Whitney at all. In 1881, thirty-seven towns in Rhode Island reported on the English texts used in their high schools: Twenty-seven used the analytical grammars of Samuel Greene; only one high school used Whitney. Four years later, still only one town used Whitney. The postwar philologists had made little impact upon the lower schools.[32]

As grammar declined in schools, teachers and administrators turned to the ideas of the critics and rhetoricians. Superintendents began to encourage verbal criticism in the classroom, believing that as opposed to the dry-as-dust grammatical rules, verbal criticism would have practical results. In New York in 1876, it was reported that English was becoming "more popular" with students. "The correction of common errors of speech, as required in all the grades, has had much to do in making this branch . . . less dry and uninteresting than formerly." Similar comments were made by officials in San Francisco and New Haven.[33]

In the 1870s, authors began producing textbooks known as "language lessons," generally published in a series of two or three and designed as a course in the progressive study of English. Grammatical study was included in these texts, but not systematically. A "language lesson" course could begin in the first or second grade and continue into high school. Each lesson was meant to teach the student something practical about refined English usage. The important point was to focus each lesson on the actual speech patterns of the student, with all "abstractions" and "science" subordinated to the practical art of expression. These language lessons were recognized as part of the drift away from formal grammar. As one of the texts told teachers: "No rule need be given. The child should learn good English, as he learned bad, by imitation."[34]

Language lesson programs became quite popular in the late seventies and early eighties. In Rhode Island, two of thirty-six high schools used language lesson texts in 1876, but by 1881 those in sixteen towns did. The high school in Utica, New York, did not use the language lesson approach in 1875 but did by 1880. Lewiston, Maine, used the texts by 1876, Boston high schools by 1877. In San Francisco, Columbus, Ohio, and New Haven, the books were adopted in the early eighties. In April 1880, the Albany, New York, Committee on Textbooks urged that William Swinton's *Language Lessons* replace William Bullion's *English Grammar*.

In 1886, New York City began calling the whole subject Language Lessons instead of English, one sign of the approach's success.[35]

Also in the years after the Civil War, high schools began increasing their attention to English literature. In the first half of the century, students read snippets of great English writers in books such as *The Columbian Orator*, Scott's *Lessons in Elocution*, or the sixth *McGuffey's Reader*. Beginning in the 1840s, educators began calling for more systematic training in the English literary tradition. In 1846, Thomas Shaw wrote the first textbook on the subject of English literature. Many others soon followed.[36] Boston was the first place to introduce the systematic reading of English literature as a subject in 1848. Then John Hart, who in 1870 wrote a popular rhetoric, brought English literature to Philadelphia schools in 1850.

In the 1860s, there was a quantum leap in the amount of literature studied in the nation's schools, at least those in the East, Midwest, or in large urban centers.[37] While administrators were making these decisions on their own, colleges soon added more pressure on secondary schools. Until the post–Civil War period, no knowledge of English literature was required for entrance into college. In 1873, Harvard decided that prospective students would have to write a composition in English, answering a question that would be drawn from a list of seven to ten English classics. In 1879, representatives of most of the New England colleges agreed to use Harvard's entrance requirements as a model, and in the next twenty years, most colleges around the nation followed Harvard's lead. College preparatory schools now had to train students for the exam.[38]

What was an English classic in the late nineteenth century? Chicago's high school 1883 curriculum is a representative example. There was heavy emphasis on poetry, classical literature, Shakespeare, Milton, and the nineteenth century. On the other hand, the eighteenth century had virtually disappeared and the novel did not exist. Laughter, moreover, was clearly suspect. Literature was a serious business.

In four years, Chicago students read thirty-four works. William Cullen Bryant's translations of the *Iliad* and the *Odyssey* were included, as was *Antigone*, *Alcestis*, and the *Aeneid*. (But no comedy. Richard Jenkyns has pointed out that despite the enormous Victorian interest in ancient Greece, Aristophanes languished in general oblivion.)[39] Shakespeare was prominent, but the Shakespeare of history and tragedy, not the ribald Shakespeare. Students read *Julius Caesar*, *The Tempest*, *Macbeth*, *Henry IV*, and *Hamlet*. The only comedy was the relatively tame *As You Like It*. Also included were Milton's *L'Allegro*, *Il Penseroso*, and *Paradise Lost* and a sampling of Bacon's essays.

The eighteenth century was represented by only three poems. Two were Gray's *Elegy* and Burns's *The Cotter's Saturday Night*. Burns and Gray were, of course, two of the most "nineteenth century" of the eighteenth-century writers. The third poem was Oliver Goldsmith's *The Deserted Village*, his account of the deleterious effects of the enclosure movement on rural life. But the Chicago curriculum included no Johnson, Burke, or Pope; no Fielding, Swift, or Addison.[40]

The Chicago curriculum had much nineteenth-century literature, but it excluded the novel. Scott's *Lady of the Lake*, Tennyson's *Elaine* and *In Memoriam*, and several essays by Macauley appeared, as did William Morris's *Life and Death of Jason*. But Dickens, Hawthorne, Austen, Melville, and Cooper were not taught. American literature was represented (and in fairness it should be pointed out that in other cities some of Hawthorne's short stories were part of the curriculum) by Daniel Webster's orations "Bunker Hill Monument" and "Adams and Jefferson," Bryant's *Thanatopsis*, and Lowell's *Vision of Sir Launfel*. Emerson was read, but the domesticated Emerson of "The Conduct of Life," not the unhousebroken Emerson of "The Divinity School Address."[41]

The soberness of the curriculum reflected the ethical seriousness with which Victorian educators viewed their task. But studying literature was to cultivate more than appropriate moral values. A constant theme from the 1840s through the 1880s was that literary study would improve the linguistic habits of the students. One of the early textbooks of English literature informed readers that "the topic handled in the Philological Chapters is quite as important as those that occupy the literary ones." Thomas Shaw, in his *Outlines of English Literature* (1846) also discussed literary language, grossly contradicting himself trying to explain Chaucer's crudities, reporting that the time was past to worry about Shakespeare's vulgarities (the time was not past—in the 1840s even Shaw was reading Shakespeare in bowdlerized versions), and seeing Addison's prose as a brilliant exception to the coarseness of early-eighteenth-century language and manners.[42]

Those championing English literature in the 1860s and 1870s also emphasized the ties between literary study and linguistic skills. In 1873, when Charles Eliot decided that entering Harvard students must know some English literature, he did so because he felt too many Harvard students did not have a sufficient command of the English language. In an influential 1869 essay entitled "When and How Shall the English Language Be Studied?" Elbridge Smith spent the first three pages discussing the literature that ought to be read. He then paused:

> I do not forget that you have asked me to state how the *language* should be taught, and, I answer, by means of its literature. "Expression is the dress of thought" and the thought and expression are consequently so intimately connected that they cannot be separated. Let both be taken into the mind together."[43]

Rhetoricians were prominent in the drive to increase the attention to English literature in the secondary schools. But that is not to say that they were alone in spreading the subject. The antiformalistic arguments that so battered the grammarians were occasionally leveled at the rhetoricians. Literature should be studied alone, these schoolmen argued; rhetorical definitions were as soulless as grammatical rules. Literature taught us history, morality, and literary grace. We needed no rhetoric.[44]

To the postwar schoolmen, a literary program became so important because it covered so much ground all at once. Grammar, language lessons, composition, rhetoric, philology, and literature were all somehow supposed to become part of the program, and each school district tried to fit them together in whatever way it could. But just as in the colleges, there was much confusion about the makeup of the program. Expansion did not mean order; indeed, in some ways it encouraged chaos. But despite the confusion, one thing was clear. There was little talk of using the principles of scientific philology to create English programs in the lower schools. The debates took place among those committed to a view of language and literature akin to the verbal critics. There was no doubt that a key purpose of studying literature was to transmit the literary language to students.

# III

Moreover, all the evidence indicates that interest in refined language was spreading during the 1870s and early 1880s. Verbal criticism, by the late 1870s, was turning up in popular urban newspapers, in etiquette books, and in other media addressed to the socially insecure. Verbal criticism was becoming a part of middling culture. Thousands for whom the name Richard Grant White meant nothing tried to put his ideas to use. Fitzedward Hall found no such following.

It was very clear that the critics dominated among the highly educated. Book production provides one source of evidence. Between 1865 and 1885, twenty books of verbal criticism were published while only thirteen books of the new philology surfaced. Such a comparison, however, grossly underrates the verbal critics' success. The editions of each book listed in the *National Union Catalogue* indicate the comparative strength of verbal criticism and the new linguistics. By 1885, the *NUC* lists ten reprints of Whitney's *Language and the Study of Language*. White's *Words and Their Uses*, on the other hand, was reprinted seventeen times by that date. Hall's *Modern English*, the 1873 clarion call against verbal criticism, was reprinted only two times in the course of the century, his *Recent Exemplifications of False Philology* only once. At the same time, however, books like Alfred Ayres's *The Verbalist* or William Mathews's *Words: Their Use and Abuse* came out in edition after edition.[45]

A similar story is told in the journalistic media. Both women's magazines[46] and children's magazines[47] ignored the insights of the new philology. Literary monthlies, although less uniform in outlook, also favored the critics. In the 1860s, literary journals led the crusade for verbal purity. Much of *Words and Their Uses* first appeared in *The Galaxy*; Chicago's *Lakeside Monthly* originally published William Mathews's *Words: Their Use and Abuse* in the early 1870s; and the *Round Table* (actually a weekly journal) serialized George Washington Moon's *The Dean's English*. Despite the generally favorable attitude toward the critics, however, the literary journals did on occasion report the work of the philologists. One magazine, *Scribner's Monthly*, consistently supported the philologists over the critics, opening up its pages to Fitzedward Hall. *Scribner's* was the exception.[48]

Finally, in the late sixties and early seventies the verbal critics were received favorably by the nation's refined newspapers. Much of Edward Gould's *Good English* and bits of White's *Words and Their Uses* were originally published in the New York *Evening Post*. The *Chicago Tribune*, run by the educated mugwump Horace White and with verbal critic William Mathews on staff, condemned Yankee slang and thought *The Handbook of Blunders* a humorous guide to the speech of the Irish. The most conservative of all was the Boston *Daily Advertiser*, with its close connections to the Harvard community. While papers like the *Evening Post* and the *Tribune* had made peace with the fictional use of rustic dialect, the *Daily Advertiser* had not. In 1869 the paper ran articles complaining about the language of Mark Twain, Josh Billings, and the minstrel show. In an editorial on January 29, 1870, the paper assailed the vulgar insults dominating American politics. Rhetoric, the paper said, must replace billingsgate.[49]

*The New York Times* reported on both critics and scholars until the midseventies, when the paper tilted toward the critics. No doubt having in mind the intemperate attacks of Hall on White and Whitney on Müller, the *Times* editorialized in 1874: "To the casual observer, and every one is a casual observer who does not observe professionally, the science of philology is simply an excuse for the development of a malicious and bellicose temperament." Such comments set the prevailing tone. And although in 1874 the paper reported dispassionately on the philologists' new interest in slang and in 1879 editorialized in favor of usage over criticism in the making of dictionaries, comments such as these were drowned in the critical tide. Editorials were printed condemning the shoddy language of the *Chicago People's Journal* and the *New York Tribune*. From June 1877 through March 1880, Richard Grant White published over thirty articles of what was later to be *Everyday English*. In an 1874 editorial entitled "The Slang of Corruption" the *Times* argued that levity in serious matters, the common "making light of the distinction between right and wrong" is a sure sign of "moral corruption." In July 1881, the paper editorialized against women's cant ("Such a splendid day") and slang ("What a cunning hat").[50]

Yet all this does not mean that the philologists floundered alone. Allies there were, but they were usually restricted to a very specific audience. Darwin made use of Whitney in *The Descent of Man*. Charles Peirce's semiotics used instrumental metaphors similar to those of Whitney. In his discussion of language, Henry Morgan, the American anthropologist, also used such metaphors. The British anthropologist E. B. Tyler expounded a doctrine of linguistic conventionality similar to Whitney's. So did the American Spencerian E. L. Youmans in *The Culture Demanded by Modern Life* (1871), a book more hostile to literary culture than Whitney's work had ever been.[51]

Two magazines consistently favored the scholars over the critics, *Scribner's Monthly* and *The Nation*, a weekly. It was the latter that provided the philologists their most valuable medium for enlightening the public. Founded in 1865 by a consortium including Frederick Law Olmstead and E. L. Godkin, *The Nation* was one sign of the new assertiveness of the educated classes in the mid-1860s. In the first issues, Godkin, the editor, ran a review favorable to Alford's *A Plea for the Queen's English*. Another article sympathetic to the verbal criticism followed shortly. But the tone soon changed. Beginning in 1867, Godkin delegated philological commentary to Whitney, Hall, and March. Through the 1870s, *The Nation* hammered away at White, Ayres, Gould, and the other critics. Godkin himself soon came to share the views of his experts, in 1873 pronouncing the *odium philologicum* of the critics more foul than the *odium theologicum* of evangelicals.[52]

Godkin's defense of scientific philology seems at odds with his hostility to middling vulgarity. Why didn't Godkin remain faithful to verbal critics who were repulsed by many of the same things that he was? Godkin provides a good example of how later-nineteenth-century men and women *drifted* from genteel culture. There was no single decision that made a man stop being a gentleman and begin being an expert. There were countless decisions about small areas of life that were made by countless people over the course of several decades. Godkin was persuaded by the arguments of Whitney and Lounsbury, but he felt no need to press the implications very far. He could oppose verbal criticism and still remain hostile to the thick vulgarity of American life.

Even *The Nation*, as important as it was, could not offset the massive influence of the books, children's journals, women's magazines, refined newspapers, and literary monthlies in which the critics predominated. Godkin's efforts kept philology respectable in the eye of the literate public, but little else. For the most articulate, those we would call the intellectuals, philology jostled with criticism. But the new linguistics was less successful in percolating down to the broader refined public. The consumers of refined literature—the literate doctors, lawyers, merchants, teachers, and homemakers—read literature that was saturated with verbal criticism but almost dry of scientific philology. In journals like *The New York Times*, *The Atlantic Monthly*, the Boston *Daily Advertiser*, and *Godey's Lady's Book* the new philology rested in the background.

Verbal criticism also spread to that literature addressed to the socially insecure and upwardly mobile. Hundreds of thousands of etiquette books floated around the nation in the 1870s, each with short but unmistakably "unscientific" views of language. *The Ladies and Gentlemen's Etiquette* (1877) noted that only the uncultivated and coarse would "soil their lips" with slang. The *Bazar Book of Decorum* (1874) cautioned against words like *quiz* and *awful*.[53]

Home encyclopedias were another genre of popular literature that began including linguistic advice after the Civil War. Such books, farragoes of information on creating a refined home, first appeared in the early part of the century. Recipes, phrenological advice, business forms, and tips on letter writing were mixed with ideas about home decoration, choosing a mate, raising children, learning to swim, and social etiquette. And beginning in the 1880s, advice about refined language was included. James McCabe's *The Household Encyclopedia* (1881) contained about thirty pages of verbal criticism. Julia Wright's *Practical Life* (1881) repeated the common injunction against an inconsistent public presence: "The finest dress and the most dashing turn-out, accompanied by *you bean't* and *you ain't*, by singular verbs wedded to plural nouns, or by double negatives, proclaim 'shoddy' as promptly as if we had seen the transformation to the millionaire performed."[54]

It was, moreover, in the early 1880s that the small handbooks of verbal criticism, clearly designed for a socially insecure audience, were most popular. Unlike the elaborate literary criticism of White or William Mathews, the handbooks were simple lists of good and bad words. By the eighties, such works as Harlan Ballard's *Handbook of Blunders: Designed to Prevent 1000 Blunders in Writing or Speaking* (1880), Alfred Ayres's *The Verbalist* (1882), and C. W. Bardeen's *Verbal Pitfalls: A Manual of 1500 Words Commonly Misused* (1883) were all selling briskly.[55] By that time, verbal criticism seemed to turn up everywhere—even health manuals were not immune. John Harvey Kellogg's *Ladies' Guide in Health and Disease* (1882) included several pages on the "moral disease" of verbal impurity.[56]

Finally, during the 1870s and 1880s popular urban newspapers began taking more of an interest in refined life in general and verbal criticism in particular. In the late 1860s, papers like the *Boston Herald*, the New York *Sun*, the *New York Tribune*, and the *Chicago Times* were still dominated by a populist mentality hostile to the highly educated. But during the next ten years, most of these papers underwent a transformation. Horace Greeley distrusted the college-educated and tried not to hire them. But Greeley was pushed out of the editorship in 1872, shortly before he died, and the paper was taken over by Whitelaw Reid, who was himself college-educated and who hired college-bred men as reporters. Reid also introduced a regular column of literary intelligence, opening the paper to Edmund Clarence Stedman, John Hay, and Henry James. The tone gradually rose.[57]

In Boston, the *Herald* underwent a similar change after the paper was sold to a group of employees in 1869.[58] And the New York *Sun* did so also when Charles Dana took over as editor in 1868. Dana advised aspiring reporters to obtain a literary education. Latin and Greek he thought helpful, as well as Shakespeare and Milton. "I had rather take a young fellow who knows the 'Ajax' of Sophocles, and had read Tacitus, and can scan every ode of Horace—I would rather take him to report a prize fight or spelling match, for instance, than to take one who has never had these advantages."[59]

As the 1870s progressed, the popular papers read more like the refined papers. Yet there were differences. At the same time that the New York *Sun* was encouraging readers to learn the secrets of refined deportment to raise themselves in the world, the New York *Evening Post* was running editorials about the problem of finding servants. One spoke to the aspiring, the other to the secure.[60] It should not be surprising that large discrepancies in circulation persisted.[61]

I do not want to overestimate the shift in tone. To be sure, there were editors, Joseph Pulitzer to name just the most famous, who resisted the trend. And even those popular papers that edged away from more raucous styles were not uniformly refined. In 1887, the nation's first magazine for professional writers contrasted papers like the *Chicago Inter-Ocean*, *Baltimore Sun*, and Philadelphia *Public Ledger* with the *Chicago Times*, *St. Louis Globe-Democrat*, and *New York Herald*. Unlike the first three, the latter papers did "not pretend to be moral educators of the community." For the popular papers a writer had to have "a vivid way of using words." Indeed, in the New York *Sun*, Dana in the 1880s could still launch into vicious billingsgate and condemn the uniform civility of the refined papers as "mealy-mouthed." Dana justifiably earned the scorn of editors like E. L. Godkin.[62]

In general, though, such outbursts were less frequent than before. In the 1870s and 1880s, it took a fine ear to detect most middling vulgarity. In an 1874 editorial on the *Herald*'s Personal column, *The New York Times* discussed the shift in middling style. The Personal column, begun in the late 1860s, was a sort of dating service. Men wrote in asking women they had met (but to whom they had not been formally introduced) to communicate by post. In the course of condemning this illegitimate thrust of the intimate into public, the *Times* briefly discoursed on the history of the *Herald*: "From the day of its first publication to the present time, as all the world knows, the *Herald* has been an indecent newspaper. By its indecency it gained no small part of both its notoriety and pecuniary success." The *Times* remembered when "no respectable woman of the educated classes would be seen reading that paper. Its contents were such that an avowed taste for them would have justly tarnished such a woman's reputation." But in recent years, it continued, the *Herald* had varied its indecency. "For the 'spicy' picturesqueness of its earlier years, it has substituted the shallow stupidity of its later 'intellectual department,' but with a steady eye upon the profits to be made by pandering to the tastes of the class before mentioned [the half-educated], it has transferred much of its indecency to its advertising columns." The advertising for mates in the Personal column made the *Herald* "more offensive to moral sense and good taste than ever before. . . ."[63]

Still, the popular papers moved closer in tone to the refined papers. They began to encourage the return of educated men to public affairs.

When running an article on the subject in 1882, the *Boston Herald*'s headline was CULTURE IN POLITICS: WHY THE AMERICAN SCHOLAR IS NOT IN POLITICS. The word *scholar* in this sense evoked not expertise but a sense of history and literature, an acquaintance with the accumulated experience of the West instead of some arcane specialism. That was how Whitelaw Reid understood the word in "The Scholar in Politics," his favorite oration. That is how the mugwump William Curtis used the word in an address on education in politics that the *Chicago Tribune* reprinted in 1882. Middle-class spokesmen like John Bright and Henry Ward Beecher lectured on the importance of having a collection of good books: The iconic value of a shelf of fine literature had not yet disappeared. In 1882, the *Chicago Tribune* noted in an editorial that books were "a personal introduction to the great and good men of all past times."[64]

The papers not only hired college men and portrayed refined men as appropriate leaders, they also actively encouraged the refinement of their readers. And there is good evidence that is what readers wanted. By the early 1880s, the editors of the New York *Sun* regularly discussed basic questions of etiquette on the front page of the paper. They were responses to hundreds of reader queries. In one instance, a reader living in a boardinghouse reported a dinner discussion about the fork and wondered, couldn't a knife just as easily pick up peas? The editor assured readers that the fork was an essential part of urban life, thus continuing the diffusion of a civilized form introduced to the West more than two hundred years before. On other occasions readers wrote asking about how to improve themselves intellectually, or how to become a minister or doctor. The *Sun* did not automatically advise college; skills were more important than degrees. But "skills" also included cultural refinement.[65]

The changed tone in the popular papers meant an increased respect for literary language and verbal criticism. In 1871, none of the popular papers I surveyed made any mention of verbal criticism while all of the refined papers had. By the early eighties, the popular papers were also spreading the message of the critics and rhetoricians. One reader wrote into the *Sun* asking how to form a good English prose style. The editor suggested reading Goldsmith, Thackeray, Dickens, Shakespeare, Milton, Bacon, Scott, and Irving. Through the seventies the *New York Tribune* regularly ran favorable reviews of new rhetorics. In 1883 the paper editorially praised Britain's Lord Grenville for disparaging the "grotesque words and slovenly phrases" of British foreign service officers. To avoid the impression that the consuls were "barely more than half-educated," it said, they must use "English pure and undefiled." The *Chicago Tribune* editorialized against the bombast of inflated titles and the obscenity of Walt Whitman. And the *Boston Herald* urged its readers to study Alfred Ayres's *The Verbalist*, calling it "the best book of this kind ever printed."[66]

# IV

Who read all this popular literature? Who picked up the handbooks of verbal criticism? Who read the popular urban newspaper? There was no survey research in the late nineteenth century, so we have no firm evidence. We can, however, tease out reasonable answers from more indirect sources. William Dean Howells again deserves mention as a superb ethnographer of middling and refined life. The novels that were discussed in chapter 5 suggest that the drive for improvement was dominated by ruralites recently moved to the city. Certainly with some money, at times with much money, these characters in the Howells novels worry about their speech and manners. That impression is lent support by some of the letters asking for advice that were written to the New York *Sun*. The writers occasionally identify themselves as either country people trying to improve themselves or as recent arrivals to the city trying to fit in.

The tensions between the refined and the aspiring are similar to those discussed in Altina Waller's fine monograph on Henry Ward Beecher's 1870s sex scandal. Waller has delved into the local tensions underlying the scandal and has found the same divisions between refined and middling that I have been discussing. On one side was Beecher, who knew his Wordsworth, Burns, and Milton, who had studied his rhetoric assiduously, but who also spoke extemporaneously and in a highly emotional manner. On the other side was Richard Storrs, a refined Congregationalist minister, a dignified gentleman of the old school. Beecher's flock was larger; Storrs's was better educated. Beecher's parishioners had a wider economic range, reaching from modest office clerks to very rich doctors, lawyers, and merchants. Storrs's parish was dominated by wealthy professional men. The most important and clear dividing lines between the two groups were not economic but cultural. Most families in Storrs' parish had roots in Brooklyn reaching back to the 1840s. Most of Beecher's flock had only recently migrated to Brooklyn from rural New England or upstate new York. And even the wealthy doctors and lawyers in Beecher's parish were almost all self-made men, that is, without any college education. Almost all the doctors and lawyers in Storrs's parish, on the other hand, had attended college. Beecher's disdain for theology, his emotionalism, and physical closeness to his flock almost literally sickened Storrs, who, like E. L. Godkin in "The Chromo-Civilization," argued that Beecher was eroding the traditions of Western Civilization. Finally, Waller notes the Beecher flock becoming "more conservative" in the seventies and early eighties, and in the process moving closer in outlook to Storrs's parish. This parallels the increase in the popular literature of refinement that I have been discussing.[67]

The popular drive for refinement was probably led by the recent arrivals from the countryside. But it would be wrong to slip the self-help literature into any easy class or ethnic slot. In the last decades of the century, middling women of Irish descent were beginning to adopt genteel forms. Certainly Catholic educators tried to teach their students literary English. In the years after the Civil War, thousands of blacks attempted to learn refined English; indeed as Lawrence Levine has pointed out, more educated blacks became bidialectal, able to use both refined and Black English.[68] Moreover, "court Jews" like Bernard Berenson were able to fit into Harvard in the late nineteenth century by learning the refined English their parents could not command. Publishers shrewdly advertised relevant books to the aspiring young and insecure middling. As it was put in an ad for *Live and Learn: A Guide for all who wish to speak and write correctly*:

> There are hundreds of persons engaged in professional and commercial pursuits, who are sensible of their deficiencies on many points connected with the grammar of their own tongue, and who by self-tuition, are anxious to correct such deficiencies, and to acquire the means of speaking and writing, if not with elegance at least with a due regard for grammatical accuracy, to whom this little work is "indispensable." . . . It should be in the hands of every man, woman and child in the country, and is alike invaluable to the Scholar, the Merchant, the Farmer and the Artizan.[69]

Simply calling the advice literature "middle-class" also ignores the problems central to this study, that various long-trend forces succeeded in confusing economic and cultural lines in the nineteenth century. Mass education, democratic populism, technological innovation, and economic mobility all blurred lines by which earlier generations had mapped the world.

Finally, fitting this literature into neat socioeconomic slots assumes a conceptual idiom based on class instead of civil refinement. Class categories— those based on occupational or economic stratification—make sense to us but violate other assumptions that were still remarkably important in the late nineteenth century. To those schooled in humanistic canons, culture created the social order. One did not speak in a certain way because one belonged to a particular socioeconomic class. One found a place in the social order by one's cultural attainments. (Remember John Adams saying that a liberal education was a far more important social marker than either wealth or birth.[70]) Language was not a reflex of class but a determinant of class. To speak of *those hoping to improve themselves* appears hopelessly fuzzy sociology to our ears, to speak of *the vulgar* impossibly vague. But such terms were neither odd nor vague to those schooled in assumptions different from ours—assumptions that did not reduce culture (implicitly or explicitly) to an epiphenomenon of the social order. Such thinking was still quite important in the nineteenth century. As Robert Darnton has pointed out, the nineteenth century was the age of Balzac as much as Marx. In America, it was the age of Howells before it was the age of Veblen.[71]

For the well-educated, the terms *lady* and *gentleman* were still important, resonant social markers in the years after the Civil War. The social types were still invested with meaning; people continued to code their experience with the ordering vocabulary of civility. *The New York Times* editorialized in 1879: "The only social distinction that can be made in a Republic" was that between "the vulgar and the genteel." Americans suffered no hereditary ranks, *Peterson's Ladies' National Magazine* had noted four years before, but there were still useful distinctions: "Of course, the true test of social superiority ought to be culture." Even in the untamed West civil culture's keywords still ordered society. Army officers on the frontier continued to think of themselves as "educated gentlemen." Most had gone through West Point. One officer noted that the "black sheep" promoted through the ranks "generally try to refine themselves, but if they don't they are treated as intruders." Officers out west searched for refined "ladies" to wed, and the officer who married the "unpolished beauty" of the local village met with his peers' disdain.[72]

For the highly educated, words like *culture, gentility*, and *civility* implied more than surface grace, more than a passing knowledge of polite literature. They implied a whole way of life. Such terms had deep cultural echoes. When distinguishing between the vulgar and the refined, *The New York Times* casually quoted Horace. When mugwumps spoke of the "best men" they followed Aristotle, Machiavelli, Harrington, and others who had invoked the term. According to *The New York Times*, culture meant "not only education, not merely intellectual preeminence, but refinement of manners and purity of morals." Echoing an argument first presented in Aristotle's *Ethics*, the *Times* called vulgarity a commitment to "sensuality" and "selfishness." The "gentle life" accorded "education and character the chief honor."[73]

Such sentiments, moreover, were tied to long-standing suspicions about professionalism. In Johnson's 1755 dictionary the only illustrative quotation of *professional* is slightly negative. And as Robert DeMaria, Jr., has shown, Johnson's whole treatment of the learned professions was sarcastic.[74] *Professional* often connoted something crude, narrow, and pursued for grubby selfish ends, and in the United States it was commonly used this way.[75] Newspapers like *The New York Times* and Boston *Daily Advertiser* explicitly contrasted narrow or shoddy "professional" behavior with more refined, "gentlemanly" deportment.[76] In 1871, Henry Ward Beecher told ministers to "avoid a professional manner." "There is no reason why a clergyman should be anything but an earnest Christian gentleman," he added. Even Johns Hopkins University, the epitome of the new research institution, announced in 1877 to prospective graduate students that it provided "advanced instruction, *not professional*. . . ."[77] Indeed, the first positive citation of the word *professional* in the *Oxford English Dictionary* dates only from 1890.

The point here concerns identity. *Profession* and *learned profession* date from the sixteenth century and could be used without any taint. *Professional*, as a noun, is only from the middle of the eighteenth century and often had negative implications.[78] It appears that *professional* began to be widely used in a positive sense only in the late nineteenth century, although a more thorough study of the matter is certainly warranted. And it appears that the word gained currency when associated with specialized training and expertise. The term "professional school" dates from 1881. Still, even in the 1880s, "professional" impulses could be combined with or subsumed under other identities, as in an 1883 letter of William James: "Hodgson is . . . a *gentleman* to his fingertips and a professional philosopher as well."[79]

Yet if the iconic power of civil culture remained strong, there were problems. It was not only that the new experts were unduly narrow. More troubling to many ladies and gentlemen was how the spread of genteel forms was blurring social lines. All the problems were invoked—the diffusion of basic civilities, the inability to police cultural borders, the confusion of cultural and economic ranks, the draining of substantive meaning from refined cultural forms—to suggest that inherited terminology might no longer serve. In 1870, an educated gentleman told a Chicago audience that he never used *lady* and *gentleman* "with any degree of satisfaction." Refined forms, he went on, were now free of any ethical correlates: "Every one who wears a female garb is a lady, whether a lady's heart beats beneath that breast or no. Every man is reputed to be a gentleman whether he is gentle or no." *Lady* and *gentleman* were now "cheap terms" used by "Bridget, the lady-like scullion" and "Morrisy, the gentlemanly prize-fighter, gambler, and Congressman." At the same time *Harper's Bazar* found the words *gentility* and *respectable* void of meaning. In various editorials in the 1870s, *The New York Times* also worried about the problem. In 1875 it noted that each passing year made it more difficult to define *gentleman*. Four years later the paper called attention to the violent gentlemen of the South. What a strange use of the word this was, the paper mused. Three months later the paper unhappily reported that no longer could one be removed from a men's club for "conduct unbecoming a gentleman." The term *gentleman* was now "virtually meaningless." Elsewhere the *Times* defended "true" gentlemen, but it also stressed how easy it was to affect the outward show of the type.[80]

Nor were these critics entirely wrong. Others, usually from less refined circumstances, actively resisted the hierarchy implied by civil language. When an editor of *Appleton's Journal* argued for precision in the use of *lady* and *gentleman*, a disturbed reader wrote in complaining of the use of the word *rank* in the discussion. *Lady* and *gentleman* referred to a "quality," not a "rank." In other words, they invoked a way of life but not a class hierarchy. In 1873, as the verbal critics worked to contract the meaning of *lady* and *gentleman*, Henry Ward Beecher told his congregation of clerks, shopkeepers, and self-trained doctors and lawyers that those words should be available to *everyone* who earned a modest income. The words were used to define an appropriate way of life but resisted when solidified into any but the vaguest corporate identity. Elsewhere, when a woman was casually described as "not a lady, but of the middle class," an observer took great offense. Distinctions in America were individual, she argued, not social. There is "no such thing recognized as 'Middle Class' or any other 'class.' "[81]

The same distinction was evident in one of the more fascinating letters to the editor in the New York *Sun* in 1882. It was from a woman studying one of the linguistic self-help books, Alfred Ayres's *The Verbalist*. Having read Ayres's discussion of *lady* and *gentleman*, the woman wanted to know why the *Sun* did not use those terms. Her tone was not contentious. She simply wanted guidance on appropriate usage.

The paper responded that calling a man "a man" and a woman "a woman" was "dictated by good taste wherever the English tongue is spoken." The *Sun*, even while it encouraged its readers to adopt the way of life of the gentleman and the lady, staunchly opposed using the terms as social markers: "The *Evening Post* used to talk about gentlewomen [it still did], though the term does not belong here, and presupposes an aristocracy like that of England, where it is applied to a woman who is of the gentry, a class unknown in this republic. People here are well-bred or ill-bred, refined or unrefined, rich or poor; but we have no gentry to whom, as a class, the quality of good breeding specially belongs." This discussion runs in direct contrast to the verbal critics (two of whom worked at the *Evening Post*), who hoped to renew the power of those words to define a social order.[82]

Clearly, the traditional idiom of civil authority was leading a precarious life. But to dismiss the above as the outpourings of a fading genteel tradition misses all that is crucial about the sentiments. First, the fears that civil decorum could no longer order the world appeared when emulation of refined ladies and gentlemen was on the rise. It was not simply that the tradition thinned out and died. Rather, aspects of the tradition spread so far into the middling classes that it ceased to be a firm social marker. The widespread diffusion of civil behavior was undermining civil social thought.

Second, dismissing late-nineteenth-century worries about refinement as the fading of the genteel tradition ignores the subtle anthropology involved. Late-nineteenth-century defenders of civility were not simply consumed by the trivia of manners or unable to come to terms with the emerging industrial order, as their critics so often charge.[83] They were, rather, defending a certain way of life that had long had serious ethical status. Late-nineteenth-century publicists, most with a deeper historical sense than contemporary professionals, were trying to reinvest meaning in time-honored conventions. Making distinctions between the refined and crude is perhaps a human universal. It was commonplace in ancient Rome and the eighteenth-century West. Max Weber found the categories in ancient China; Clifford Geertz in contemporary Java.[84] But even if "refined/crude" may be one of those fundamental binary oppositions that Lévi-Strauss has spoken of, that does not mean that the terms have the same sociological resonance in different settings. In the Roman Empire, being refined marked you as a member of the ruling social class, but it doesn't in contemporary America, where we expect almost all of the population to be polite. Since all our children are supposed to be little "ladies" or "gentlemen," the words no longer denote significant social prestige. We are now comfortable with this, but in the late nineteenth century it was not so clear that a "civilized" social order could be built without those categories. After Rome came barbarism. When refinement was defended in the late nineteenth century, it was not simply because defenders of gentility had become preoccupied with manners. They were defending a way of life long-invested with moral authority. They were using categories of thought used by Horace and Cicero, Addison and Burke.

Finally, dismissing the debate over refinement as part of a fading genteel tradition ignores its connection with the nineteenth-century debate over education and educational authority. Civility was an educational program. Should the refined or the half-refined be in control of American institutions? Should Dana or Godkin shape public opinion? Should the college-bred man or the self-made man set the linguistic tone of the nation?[85] These were but different ways of asking the same question.

But even as we stress the differences between the two groups, we must quickly add that that was not the whole story. The new leadership was not uneducated, it was half-educated. What so maddened Godkin was the middle's appropriation of the trappings of high culture. There was significant overlap between the two cultures. I have traced the effort of the refined to redraw sharp boundaries between high and popular language after the Civil War. By the early 1880s, some gentlemen were realizing it would not work. Verbal criticism was becoming a popular activity; it was turning into a cheap substitute for humane learning. And by the 1880s, a few refined newspapers were looking in new directions.

The New York *Evening Post* was long a bastion of verbal criticism. Edward Gould and Richard Grant White worked there. Its editor was William Cullen Bryant, compiler of the famous *Index Expurgatorius*, until the paper was sold in 1882, when E. L. Godkin became the new editor. Godkin, of course, was the longtime friend of the Yale philologists. As late as 1881, Fitzedward Hall was pilloried in an extensive front-page article in the *Post*, but by early the next year, with Godkin in control, the paper reprinted (on the front page) an article by Thomas Lounsbury condemning Alfred Ayres's *The Verbalist* as a quintessential example of middling vulgarity. It was just eight days later that the more popular *Boston Herald* enthusiastically described Ayres's book as "the best" of its kind ever printed.[86]

The *Chicago Tribune*, by the early 1880s, also paid no lip service to verbal criticism. After a woman wrote to the editor complaining about *illy*, a word often condemned by verbal critics, the editor responded that usage defined the language, not the critic.[87] The editor of the *Tribune*, Joseph Medill, having grown prosperous by the 1880s, was an establishment figure, retaining little of the folksiness that he carried with him to Chicago in the 1850s as a young rural editor whose hero was Horace Greeley. Like so many middling figures, he had refined himself over the years. Yet the rise of the scholarly experts allowed Medill to voice some of his old ideas with a new "scientific" authority. Medill continued to distrust the literary elite, but by the 1880s he had the "scientific" doctrine of "usage" to buttress his opinions. In the 1860s, he had advocated simplified spelling as part of his populist hostility to the entrenched conservatism of the intellectual tradition. Spelling reform was, to Medill, simply the common sense of one who thought about it. By the 1880s, the same ideas were espoused with the authority of the nation's leading philologists. Certain ideas about language that in the middle of the century were part of the anti-intellectual populist tradition were by the end of the century justified with the arguments of linguistic experts.[88]

These few changes in the early 1880s cannot be pushed too far. Most literary monthlies and refined newspapers still defended the verbal critics. The changes marked no major shift in public opinion; rather, they were small hints of what was to come. The high/popular tensions were being pressed by the popularization of refinement and the emergence of academic expertise. The old cultural polarities were to soon fade away with new tensions to replace them.

# CHAPTER SEVEN

# The Dictionary and Bible
# in an Age of Science

I fear we are not getting rid of God because
we still believe in grammar.

NIETZSCHE

The dictionary becomes an encyclopedia because in fact it was *a disguised encyclopedia*.

UMBERTO ECO

Through the seventies and the eighties, the philological scholars failed to
win much favor in either schools or the press; rhetoric and verbal criticism
weathered blows but seemed resilient. But in those same years, philologists
were at work on other projects—projects just as important but much less
public. In small rooms in Cambridge, New Haven, New York, and a few
other cities, scholars worked, day after day, year after year, remaking the
English Bible and dictionary. Periodically through the eighties and nineties
the transformed texts were delivered to the public. The new dictionaries
displayed all the ideas of the scholarly philologists. They absolutely re-
vered technical language—jargon—and also championed informal spoken
dialect. Bible revisers suggested that rhetorical impact must stand aside
for pinpoint accuracy. Scientific philology could reveal the Word with a
purity unknown to poetry. And by the end of the century, this was
connected to calls for a more colloquial English Bible.

The new texts met with a public response impossible to imagine earlier
in the century. In the 1890s, the new dictionaries slid into the nation's
schools and offices with only scattered and weak protests. The bitter
dictionary wars of the 1840s through 1860s had disappeared, along with

their troubling implications about cultural authority and the literary language. Gone too was the rampant opposition to Bible revision. The ballyhoo over the publication of the new English Bible was, as we shall see, nothing short of remarkable. Yet despite the public's initial interest, the revised Bible ultimately failed to replace the King James Version as the "popular" Bible of the English-speaking people. The lessons left about the cultural authority of biblical experts were not simple. The public, by the 1880s, granted the religious philologist the right to attempt a new Bible, which in itself was far different than the attitude of the 1850s. That same public, however, would not blindly accept revised Scripture; they asserted their right to judge the scholars' work. As before, the Bible remained a special and complicated case.

Today, Americans look at dictionaries more than they do at Bibles, a rather recent phenomenon in our cultural history. The balance was shifting only in the last third of the nineteenth century. While the following pages here are preoccupied with the ways that linguistic arbiters reshaped these books, the actual histories of such vertebral texts are about more than scholars and publishers. They are intimately bound up in the ways whole civilizations organize themselves. The turn to the colloquial and the celebration of the technical by both biblical scholars and lexicographers reflected complicated reactions to changing patterns of everyday life.

# I

Scholars interested in popular Bible reform were not discouraged by the setbacks of the 1850s. Instead, they took the advice Richard Chenevix Trench offered in his influential 1857 book on revision—proceed with textual criticism and tentative scholarly translation, and public opinion would shift in due time. In the 1860s, biblical scholarship, especially New Testament scholarship, flourished on both sides of the Atlantic. Slowly interest in revision built. The real breakthrough occurred in 1870, when Bishop Samuel Wilberforce introduced a resolution at the Convocation of Canterbury calling for a revision of the King James Bible. The motion carried, and the work, now sponsored by the Church of England, began in earnest.

The British revisers knew that success depended on winning more than the Anglican public. The British scholars added British dissenters to their company and asked Phillip Schaff to form an American committee. Schaff, a famed Church historian and prolific scholar, had migrated to America from Germany in the 1840s. He created a committee of thirty-four American scholars, nineteen of whom worked on the New Testament and fifteen on the Old. (The British Committee consisted of sixty-seven scholars, thirty in the New Testament company, thirty-seven in the Old.) Episcopalians dominated the British group, but the Americans were rather more evenly distributed among nine different denominations. Prominent Americans other than Schaff included Theodore Woolsey, the former president of Yale; Ezra Abbot, professor of New Testament Exegesis at Harvard; William Henry Green, professor of Hebrew at Princeton; Howard Osgood, professor of Hebrew at the Rochester Theological Seminary; and Henry Thayer, professor of the New Testament at Andover. James Hadley, until his untimely death in 1872, was also a member of the New Testament Revision Committee. Hadley was a professor of Greek at the Yale Sheffield School and a close friend of William Dwight Whitney.[1]

The British and American groups each checked the other's work. The British made the first draft of revision, which they then sent to the American committee, who offered its own changes and challenged certain of the British readings. The draft was then sent back to Britain, where the British then responded to the Americans. Each book of the Bible went through three rough drafts. Every month the Americans met in New York City at what was known as the "Bible House," the headquarters of the American Bible Society. For nearly fifteen years the process continued. The New Testament was finished in 1880 and published in May of the next year. The Old Testament appeared in 1885.[2]

Some revisers, like Brooke Westcott, were connected with Christian socialist movements. Others, like Ezra Abbot and Henry Boynton Smith, were theological liberals. But it would be wrong to associate the Bible reform with any of the "advanced" doctrines of the nineteenth century. Theodore Woolsey of Yale was a noted political conservative; Howard Crosby was a vocal anti-Darwinist. Princeton, the stronghold of theological conservatism, contributed three scholars to the American committee. There was not one single theological or political dogma dominating the revision.

Outsiders, however, still viewed the new Bible as vaguely contributing to Christianity's modernization. Opinion about the Revised Version usually was connected to diffuse opinion about the grand question of "religion in the modern age." Should Christianity resist the utilitarian rationalization of the nineteenth century? If so, then King James English must be guarded. Or should religion adapt itself to modernity? If so, then proceed with revision. Should ritualistic language be separated from the colloquial or should religious language be in tune with everyday life? Modernizing the Bible might undermine an ancient and sacred diction, but it also expressed faith in the ability of modern "scientific" scholarship to reorient religion to the modern age.

Although rarely discussed in public, there were many disagreements among the revisers. One disagreement was over how far to carry their mandate. In part this reflected differences in age: The younger the reviser the more daring the revision.[3] But it was also a dispute over purpose. The Convocation of Canterbury set down as the first principle of revision that there should be "as few alterations as possible in the text of the Authorized Version, consistently with faithfulness." Yet it was unclear to the revisers what this exactly meant, and it became a subject of debate early on. The winning side, led by Brooke Westcott, Joseph Lightfoot, and Fenton John Hort, argued that the revision must be a thorough one. There would not be another opportunity for a long time, they claimed; the moment must not be squandered. Prominent on the losing side were Charles Ellicott, Richard Chenevix Trench, and Henry Alford, all of whom wanted a more modest revision of the Scriptures.[4]

The debate over the scope was settled in the early 1870s, but the debate over the Greek text continued for the next decade. The discovery of the Sinaitic and Vatican manuscripts in the nineteenth century raised important questions about the Greek text used in 1611. The further removed the revisers' Greek was from the *textus receptus* of the seventeenth century, the further removed would be the Revised Version from the King James. Lightfoot, Westcott, and Hort were the textual scholars leading the battle for a radically reformed Greek text; the Reverend Frederick Scrivener was the conservative textual scholar on the committee. For years the two sides debated, sometimes violently, and although the modernists did not win every battle, the 1881 revision of the New Testament owed far more to Wescott and Hort than it did to Scrivener.[5]

The revisers also disagreed about how far to modernize the diction. There were conservatives and liberals on both sides of the Atlantic, but the Americans, in general, wanted more reform than the British. American conservatives were less conservative and American liberals were more liberal. Americans saw much of the Elizabethan diction not as noble but as quaint, at best cloying, at worst confusing. A few revisers dreamed of a modern, nineteenth-century diction. Howard Crosby of the American New Testament committee was one, asserting that "we need not go to antiquity to borrow the vestments of grandeur and sublimity for our thought."[6]

Yet revisers like Crosby were the exception. Overwhelmingly, the revisers portrayed their project as a conservative one. Both liberals and conservatives differed within a broad consensus about the ends to be realized. And the scholars who remade the English Bible in the late nineteenth century constantly pointed out that theirs was a work only of *revision*, not a complete retranslation. They portrayed their endeavor as a modest one, as in the Preface to the Revised Old Testament:

> In regard to the language of the Authorized Version, the Revisers have thought it no part of their duty to reduce it to conformity with modern usage, and have therefore left untouched all archaisms, whether of language or construction, which though not in familiar use cause a reader no embarrassment and lead to no misunderstanding.

Similarly, Phillip Schaff claimed that the Revised New Testament "has the familiar ring and flavor of the old version, and whole chapters may be read without perceiving the differences between the two."[7]

The revisers also agreed, again with a few exceptions, on a theory of translation. Almost all understood the injunction to faithfulness as a call for literal accuracy: Wherever possible, they would effect a word-for-word transfer from one language to the other. The revisers cared far more about a minutely accurate rendering of the Greek or Hebrew than they did about the literary sense of the English. Like Whitney, March, and Hall, the Bible revisers thought that scientific philology was antiliterary, simply committed to "truth."

Throughout the revising process, then, there was a collision between the Elizabethan literary language and textual research. But, it is important to note, the revisers believed in the research, whereas they accepted the diction as a pragmatic burden. They feared their public and sensed that the Protestant world wanted no massive overhaul of the Authorized Version. Hoping to create a popular Bible, hoping somehow to integrate the Elizabethan diction with the insights of modern scholarship, the revisers did not want to tread too far.

But the revisers also left no doubt about which was more important. "The literary claims of the Bible are and must be subordinate to its character as a record of revelation," wrote one American. "Taste must yield to conscience." According to Phillip Schaff, the new revision was "far more accurate and consistent," although the rhythm of the older version was at times sacrificed. As another of the Americans said of the Revised New Testament:

A new element asserts itself throughout; the savor of a modern time breathes through the book; the impress of a riper, broader, richer, more accurate scholarship is upon it. . . . Its lines are sharpened and their mellowed blendings often dissipated, rudely it may sometimes seem, by the firm touch of an incisive criticism. We have the New Testament in plain if not classic English, an immeasurable *practical* gain, if not an *artistic* gain.

Howard Crosby put it most bluntly: "The truth—the truth is what we desire."[8]

Yet, this said, how could the revisers also say they maintained the Elizabethan language? The simplest answer is that they were convinced they had done their job well, that they had successfully integrated modern scholarship with ancient diction. Timothy Dwight found no contradiction in saying that the reader "will find improvements on every page, almost in every verse, and yet, as he reads aloud, the same sound and music will come to his ear."[9]

Given the antiliterary sentiments of the revisers, it should not be surprising that the pre–Civil War defenders of the King James Bible were skeptical. Even before publication of the revised text, writers like George Perkins Marsh and A. Cleveland Coxe expressed doubts. Coxe feared a "mechanical" approach that would produce a Bible "without dignity or grace." Marsh thought philologists not well suited to undertake revision. Linguistic scholars, he contended, might have faultless historical information, but they were just not good prose stylists. He suggested two committees, one philological and one literary, each to check the other.[10]

Coxe's and Marsh's interest in literature is crucial, reflecting key differences in translation theory. Postwar revisers pushed "literary" concerns to the side. Style got in the way of accurate translation; it was something a "lazy" reading public would not give up. The older defenders of the King James Bible, on the other hand, understood translation as a complicated exchange of complete cultural idioms, an exchange in which literary style conveyed cultural identity. To the revisers such arguments had no bearing on the key issue—a literal rendering of the Hebrew and Greek into English. The literary arguments of a Marsh or Coxe were dismissed as—well, as just literary. And that is the key point. The revisers did not understand arguments in favor of the King James Bible as about translating cultural idioms or preserving the specialness of the sacred's diction. The larger implications of the literary arguments were ignored by revisers who did not comprehend them. The revisers turned discussion of translation into a rather prosaic debate over the merits of thousands of discrete bits of prose. This word, that phrase, those idioms—that was the debate over revision in the 1870s and 1880s, as true of conservatives as of liberals. By focusing on small units, philological revisers could convince themselves that they were not changing the essential character of the Authorized Version while correcting many of its errors.

# II

Given the number of changes in the Revised Version, any simple judgment on the revision will be problematic; counterexamples will always be found. Moreover, the revisers left much untouched. Many familiar passages read exactly as they did in the King James Bible. Many other changes did no harm. In the Twenty-third Psalm, for example, the Revised Version altered but one word, removing *leadeth* and inserting *guideth*, a change that violated neither cadence nor tone. And unless readers had the psalm memorized or were hunting for changes, no notice would likely be taken.

At times the revisers clearly improved on the Authorized Version. They made comprehensible the opening eleven verses of Job 28 which were notoriously muddy. Too, their removal of many archaisms also cleared up meaning. Some words become archaic because they drop out of use, but other words become archaic because their sense has changed. In the latter case it is the meaning rather than the form that has become obsolete. Such archaisms can easily mislead. Here the revisers were particularly successful. In the early seventeenth century *cunning* meant "skillful," but by the late nineteenth century the word had more nefarious connotations. The revisers removed *cunning* and used *skillful*, a change that did no harm to meaning. In the Authorized Version *thought* meant "anxious." Shakespeare, Bacon, and other authors of the time also used the word in that way. By the mid-nineteenth century, however, the Common Version's Matthew 6:25—"Take no thought for your life"—read as an exhortation to recklessness. The 1881 revision rendered the passage "Be not anxious for your life," a subtle change that, in context, suggested that we not fret unduly over worldly matters. *Meat*, to seventeenth-century readers, simply meant "food," but by the nineteenth century the word was strongly associated with "flesh." To speak, as the King James Bible did, of a "meat-offering" consisting entirely of cereal just seemed ridiculous, so the revisers altered it to "meal-offering."

A more controversial instance of a passage superior in the Revised Version is the thirteenth chapter of Paul's First Epistle to the Corinthians, one of the most famous chapters in the Bible. From this chapter in the King James Bible comes the phrase "through a glass, darkly." Verse 11 of the chapter has also become part of our cultural heritage: "When I was a child, I spake as a child, I understood as a child, I thought as a child: but when I became a man, I put away childish things." Verse 13 has left us: "And now abideth faith, hope, charity, these three; but the greatest of these is charity." Just thirteen verses long, one of the shortest chapters in the New Testament, Corinthians 13 is one of the most moving pieces of literature in the English language.

At nine places in this chapter, revisers removed the word *charity* and inserted *love*, a change that was immediately and widely assailed. There was, however, a logic both literary and linguistic to the change. The word *charity* did mean "love" in the early seventeenth century, but over the years its meaning had contracted. The associations it raised by the mid-nineteenth century were false, and verse 3 had become a flat contradiction: "And though I bestow all my goods to feed the poor, and though I give my body to be burned, and have not charity, it profiteth me nothing." By the nineteenth century, *love* was the correct rendition. It was also, as Phillip Schaff argued, "a strong Saxon monosyllable." Schaff rightly observed that those who held fast to "faith, hope, charity" did so out of stubborn, uninformed habit, but he was on less firm ground when asserting that "good rhetorical taste will ultimately decide in favor of the strong monosyllabic trio."[11]

Despite the improvements, there were changes, hundreds of them, that did not serve English prose. Basing their decision on textual evidence, the revisers eliminated some of the most time-honored words of the Scriptures. "Blessed art thou among women" (Luke 1:28), Angel Gabriel's words to Mary, were removed because they did not appear in the most ancient texts. Luke 17:36 was also dropped: "Two men shall be in the field; the one shall be taken, and the other left." Acts 8:37 disappeared: "And Philip said, If thou believest with all thine heart, thou mayest. And he answered and said, I believe that Jesus Christ is the Son of God." Also gone was Luke 9:56—"For the Son of man is not come to destroy men's lives, but to save them." Of the several hundred elisions none raised more of an outcry than the doxology of the Lord's Prayer: "For thine is the kingdom, and the power, and the glory, forever. Amen." (Matthew 6:13) The revisers claimed that the commentaries of Origen, Tertullian, and Cyprian did not mention the doxology, and that the first manuscripts to include it dated from the sixth century. Yet the case was not so clear, and within the New Testament revision committee there were fights over which ancient texts were the best. Critics argued that until a definitive text could be agreed upon traditional prose should not casually disappear. The revisers, despite their internal disagreements, did not want to appear tentative. To Schaff, even including the doxology in a marginal footnote was the unfortunate triumph of "prudence" over "honesty."[12]

The revisers committed other sins. Oddly enough, their faith in word-for-word accuracy at times led to confusion. Dissatisfied with *offend* in the famous "And if thy right eye offend thee, pluck it out. . . . And if thy right hand offend thee, cut it off" (Matthew 5:29–30), the revisers substituted *stumble* ("If thy right eye causeth thee to stumble . . ."). This, according to the committee, more accurately reflected the Greek. That may have been true, but it also made the English less clear. Matthew, of course, was trying to say that if your right eye leads you into sin, it should be removed. In ordinary usage, however, *stumble*, unlike *offend*, conveys no opprobrium. The concept of sin was lost in the more "literal" rendition in the Revised Bible. Moreover, readers were left with the ludicrous image of someone stumbling over his own hand. Perhaps *offend* was not a perfect choice, but it served better than the alternative.

The press for a literal rendering also led to confusion in James 3:3. The Common Version reads: "Behold, we put bits in the horses' mouths, that they may obey us." The Revised Version, however, reads: "If we put the horses' bridles into their mouths, that they may obey us, we turn about their whole body also." The revision is not only wordy; it is also confusing. As one reviewer wrote: "To put a bridle into a horse's mouth would be an unusual operation, and its results are not easily calculable."[13]

The largest problem was that too much of the revision was wooden and flat. In the Authorized Version, Galatians 5:1 sings: "Stand fast therefore in the liberty wherewith Christ hath made us free." The Revised Version, however, lacks all music: "With freedom did Christ set us free: stand fast therefore." The sense has become banal; the prose redundant and clumsy. The lilt of the Common Version—"Thy will be done in earth, as it is in heaven"—in the revised text turns choppy and uninspired: "Thy will be done, as in heaven, so on earth" (Matthew 6:10). The revisers argued that they were accurately following the best ancient texts, and that literalness had to reign over literature, truth over sound. This resulted in dozens of passages that appeared to be of no idiom at all, except perhaps a flaccid "translatorese."

At many places, the prosaic replaced the grand. The Common Version's "tabernacle of the congregation" became the Revised Version's "tent of meeting" (Exodus 29:42). Matthew Arnold hoped that Isaiah 9:5 would not be altered, for the words "have a magnificent glow and movement." Replied the American reviser Talbot Chambers, "Could there be a more conspicuous instance of dilletantism?" Arnold, in turn, feared the "charm has vanished, never to return."[14]

The press to reproduce the very order and turn of words, to use just one English word for each particular Greek or Hebrew word, to find the literal force of each tense and mood, all led to thousands of changes in the English that had little or nothing to do with clarifying meaning or improving the literary sense. Over and over, these changes were small, just changing one word, just twisting one phrase. Yet there was usually no idiomatic English reasoning for them. What was the use of turning Revelations 19:5 from "Praise our God, all ye his servants" to "Give praise to our God, all ye his servants?" The revisers simply argued that the Greek and Hebrew texts demanded these changes. According to the revisers, changing Luke 5:5 from "we have toiled all the night, and have taken nothing" to the more prosaic "we have toiled all night and took nothing" was justified because the Greek aorist tense was used in the original. Such references to the niceties of Greek grammar combined with a disregard for idiomatic English could only lead critics to ominous conclusions. The whole revision smacked of pedantry.

Despite their disregard for idiomatic English, the revisers took seriously their commitment to Elizabethan diction. To counterbalance the effect of their more prosaic changes, the revisers added several hundred *untos*, *soevers*, *aforetimes*, and other archaic connecting words. In many places where *but* appeared in the Common Version, the Revised Version inserted *howbeit*. Often clumsily done, there seemed to be no method to this madness. The revisers tried to accomplish *deus ex machina* what the revision could not do on its own—maintain the tone of the Authorized Version. They succeeded with their archaisms only in raising questions about their purpose, consistency, and competence. The modern archaisms reminded one critic of art dealers who added wormholes to modern Chippendale.[15]

The revisers thought in terms of the Greek and Hebrew texts, the Elizabethan diction, and idiomatic English. In that order. It should not be surprising that the English rendition seemed aimless and contradictory—they gave that aspect of the translation little of their attention. Of course, the King James Bible was not idiomatic English either. But it was not meant to be. King James English was meant to be special, sacred, removed from the commonplace, and spiritually ennobling.[16] The Authorized Version strides with dignity; the Revised Bible stumbles in confusion.

# III

The revisers considered enlightening public opinion part of their job. Through the seventies they proceeded on a number of fronts, doing work that today would be done either by a marketing division or a public relations firm. They published dozens of books and pamphlets explaining the history of the English Bible and why the revision was necessary. They toured the country explaining the revision to various congregations. They also successfully made their work a topic of Sunday school discussion. In December 1880, the *Sunday School Times*, the most important journal of its kind in the nation, devoted sixteen pages to the need for revision. Two years earlier, *The World*, the organ of the American Sunday-School Union, had devoted an issue to criticisms of the 1611 Bible. That magazine was "sent to all the cities, towns, villages, from the center to the frontier, to which this vast national agency is accustomed to reach out its hand."[17] Anticipation gradually built. The Protestant ministry was less rustic than before the Civil War; the Protestant public more sophisticated. By the late 1870s, even the average newspaper reader was aware of the issues involved in the revision. (The importance of the revision to American religious history cannot be underestimated. The revision discussions first acquainted the general public with the issues of higher criticism.[18]) After a decade of promotional activity, revisers carefully kept the completed text a secret before publication, despite bribe offers from newspapermen—the general climate of anticipation was seasoned with a touch of suspense.

In the middle of May 1881, after eleven years' work, the Revised New Testament was published. To call the publication an event in literary history would be misleading. It was, more accurately, an event of social history. The tome exploded on an eager public. In Great Britain, prior to publication more than one million copies were ordered from Cambridge University Press, and nearly one million additional copies were sold in England within a week. In America, the revised text raised just as much interest. On the streets of New York, newsboys hawked the Bible with their papers. Up and down Wall Street you could hear them yelling, "Here's yer New Testament, jest out!" Printed on the East Coast, thousands of copies were immediately shipped out west. Rural ministers rode into New York, Chicago, Denver, and other cities to purchase Revised Versions for themselves and their flocks. In Chicago, both the *Times* and the *Tribune* had the complete text telegraphed from New York so they could publish the text (in its entirety!) in their Sunday editions, just two days after publication. The *Tribune* worked ninety-two compositers around the clock to set the type. In the next few weeks ministers all over the nation discussed the merits and demerits of the text from their pulpits. It was a regular topic of Sunday school conversation. It was a topic on the streets. Six days after publication, the *New York Independent* observed:

> Everywhere—on the cars, on the ferry-boats, and in other public convey-ances and places—attentive readers of the revised book are to be seen; and the most frequent question, when two friends meet, is "Have you seen the New Testament? How do you like it?"[19]

The critical response of the American scholarly community was over-whelmingly favorable, and the revision was given some support by most major urban newspapers. In the cities, at least, the Protestant clergy also was initially enthusiastic. But in spite of the media support and enormous public interest, it became clear in the next few months that something was going wrong. Immediately on publication of the Revised New Tes-tament, *The New York Times* complained about the widespread hesitancy of the New England clergy. In August, *Scribner's Monthly* reported that the new text was making little headway in the New England countryside. In November, the *Times* editorialized that "up to the present time the attitude of the educated public toward the revised version of the New Testament, whether in England or America, has been anything but friendly." One week later the paper reported that the "enthusiasm with which the Protestant clergymen of this city approved the revision seems to have abated." It became clear that regardless of the favorable first impression, the clergy disliked the revision. And despite the willingness of the Protestant public to try the new Bible, the old chasm between scholars and the public remained. There is no better indication of this than the response in New Haven, Connecticut. In September 1881, Yale University adopted the revision as its standard in campus devotional ser-vices. Two months later, however, the ministry of the town met at Centre Church and roundly denounced the revision, with the town ministers resolving to keep the King James Bible. Commented *The New York Times* on the meeting: "The great burden of the criticism upon the revision was in relation to its bad English."[20]

In the years after the New Testament was published, and again after the Old Testament appeared in 1885, hostile critics most often cited the "excessive literalness" of the Revised Version. According to John Fulton, one critic of the new Bible, the revisers had made a "photograph" of the Greek. This "almost finical refinement," he continued, so characteristic of the nineteenth century, was "wholly foreign to the genius of the sacred writings." According to many of the critics, the revisers' preoccupation with the accurate rendering of the Greek aorist tense was a good example of how a minor consideration was propelled into a major issue. That the revisers had also strongly condemned the King James translators for not rendering each Greek word in a single English equivalent, critics saw as ignoring the flexible nature of good translation and the literary demands of the Bible. As verbal critic George Washington Moon put it, the revisers had succeeded in rendering the Greek but had failed to produce a Bible "worthy" of the "noble native tongue." In an oblique criticism of the revisers, the Princeton rhetorician Theodore Hunt claimed that "no English philologist studying the language from the scientific side only" could possibly account for the "marvelous" simplicity and strength of the King James Bible.[21]

The literary dimension was important because the Bible mediated learned and popular culture. To ignore style was to ignore the religious needs of the Protestant public. "Translations are not made for the special accommodation of comparative critics," wrote one hostile to the revision. Most readers look for the moral of any particular passage, not its "exact phraseology," noted the editor of *Appleton's Journal*. The microscopic changes of the Revised Version would only bring into question the sacredness of the Scriptures and destroy old associations. (Even E. L. Godkin, who approved of the revision, admitted that the debates over it would hurt Protestantism.) Theodore Hunt, citing Max Müller, noted that language had a spiritual dimension and that a strictly "physiological" view of biblical English would coarsen Protestant morality. John Fulton observed that what the Protestant world needed was not a photograph of the Greek or Hebrew but a "broad-brush picture" capable of reaching people's souls. And Matthew Arnold, in his earlier essays on the revision, made a similar point. Only by connecting religion with the literary—that sphere that *moved* people—could the Anglo-Saxon world be saved from encroaching secularism.[22]

Much less frequently, at least in the 1880s, other critics focused on how the revision had not gone far enough in modernizing the diction. Within the revision committees, there were many Americans who held this view. Like the defenders of the King James Bible, the modernizing critics complained about the pedantic and mincing work of the revisers, but they argued that a comprehensive modern diction was what was needed. This group, in the 1880s, was small and inconsequential. Most recognized that a modern-language revision could not succeed with the public at that time.[23]

Over the years, it became clear that despite the initial positive reaction, the Revised Version would not become the new popular Bible of the English Protestant world. In fact, even as the Revised Old Testament appeared in 1885, its fate was sealed. Protestant churches simply refused to accept the new Bible. Although all Protestant sects discussed officially adopting the new Bible, none did so. Northern Baptists were sharply divided among defenders of the King James Bible, the sectarian immersionist Bible, and the Revised Version. The Southern Presbyterian Church curtly dismissed the Revised New Testament in 1882; the Revised Old Testament was not even debated. The General Assembly of the Northern Presbyterian Church in 1887, 1888, and 1889 refused to approve the Revised Bible because it was "still on trial among the English-speaking people." How the new Bible could win a following when it could not be used in church was never discussed. Only in 1892, when it was clear that the Revised Version would not gain wide acceptance, did the Presbyterian assembly announce that it was not forbidden. The American Episcopalian Church, on the other hand, adamantly opposed the new Bible and never authorized its usage.[24]

By the 1890s, the Revised Version was most often used by ministers in their studies, as a check on the King James Bible. The public had rejected it and the disposition of the ministry to use it in the pulpit was, as one observer put it, "extremely slight." In 1895, a speaker at the General Convention of the Episcopal Church observed that the "popular verdict" on the Revised Version was negative. For the "general purposes of edification, the older is better. The revisers were, no doubt, famous Grecians, but there seems to have been lacking among them that quick ear for melodious English. . . ." This judgment was shared across the Protestant spectrum. Sales of the Revised Bible were estimated in the late 1890s as between 5 and 10 percent of total Bible sales. Those sold, moreover, were generally used as reference texts. As one commentator summed up in 1897, the Revised Version had been "adopted by very few of our churches and ministers as the pulpit Bible."[25]

The Revised Version failed for several reasons. First, it lacked integrity as an English text. It was a tortuous net of compromises—compromises not only among the various revisers, but between philology and literature, between the revisers and the reading public, between ancient manuscripts and modern English, between King James English and the nineteenth century. The revisers hoped their compromises would satisfy everyone. In the end, they only robbed their project of any controlling vision. We may no longer like Pope's translation of Homer, we may find Florio's Montaigne quaint, and certainly Longfellow's Dante now sits dustily on library shelves, but we also know that those translations were sharply focused. Pope, Florio, and Longfellow sat down with a defined aim, and they succeeded with a literary public because of it. But the various compromises of the Revised Version intruded on one another. The whole project seemed patchwork. To borrow a phrase from George Steiner, the Revised Version fell into "a no man's land of psychological and linguistic space."[26]

The failure in prose had larger repercussions. The Revised Bible could not tie itself to any of the major cultural trends of late-nineteenth-century Protestantism. Maintaining the diction of the King James Bible, the Revised Version did not move those committed to liberal Protestantism or the social Gospel, and despite the revision of the 1880s, in 1894 Washington Gladden was still asking for a new Bible. Nor did the revision speak to conservative sentiment. Several historians have noted the growth of Protestant ritualism in the closing decades of the nineteenth century. The love of Gothic architecture and elaborate ritual was, they have pointed out, not merely a search for status but a way for middle- and upper-class Protestants to ease their participation in the modern commercial world. Meaningful ritual and medieval ceremony were psychological buffers against the acids of modernity. The Bible revision, with its "scientific" philology, its antiliterary bias, ran counter to the move toward symbolically resonant aesthetics. The Elizabethan diction of the King James Version touched Protestants in the same way that Gothic spires did. It should not be surprising that the 1881 Church Congress, an annual meeting of Protestant clergy, spent nearly two days castigating the Revised New Testament as "a child of the nineteenth century—scientific, but not poetic; accurate, but not spiritual," *and* calling for increased ritualism in worship.[27]

Finally, the project failed because the revisers misjudged their role as biblical experts. They assumed that because they were experts, the public should simply accept what they had to say. But despite their gestures toward recognizing the public's desire for modest revision, the revisers had little true sympathy for their readers. Nothing is more revealing than the frequency with which the revisers referred to opponents of revision as "lazy," or "simpleminded," or even "stupid." This happened before, in the course of, and after publication.[28] The revisers treated their public with contempt—in their own minds, the revisers were the experts and that solved all the problems.

Yet it did not solve all the problems. The biblical expert had to contend with the Protestant public. He had to create a text that not only had scholarly precision but also moved the soul. Far different from the public suspicion of revision in the 1850s, the public, by the 1880s, granted the experts the right to try a revision; the stunning public response in the summer of 1881 is clear evidence of that. Yet the public, even after the Civil War, retained the right to judge the scholars' product. Bible revisers had to run the gauntlet of public opinion. They needed to be sympathetic to their audience as well as faithful to their texts. The Bible revisers thought of themselves as specialists who should be listened to. They would have done better to choose a different model of the biblical scholar—the moral steward with a deep and humbling responsibility to the religious public.

# IV

Popular Bible reform was a failure. But just as in the 1850s, the failure did not kill enthusiasm for revision. Instead, in the 1890s, the modern-language Bible movement was born.

The modern-language movement, which continues to thrive in the 1980s, has tried to create an English Bible in modern, colloquial speech. Unlike the King James translators, who sought a dignified sacred diction, the modern-language translators have struggled to create a comfortable, idiomatic English Bible. Unlike the nineteenth-century defenders of the King James Bible, who wanted to save the folk quality of the English Bible as a buffer against middling vulgarity, the modern-language translators have tried to put the Bible into the idiomatic middle-class speech of twentieth-century America (or Britain).

Many of those who worked on the Revised Version, particularly the Americans, were not committed to the ancient diction. The British revisers, however, did retain the Elizabethan cadences. After an agreed lapse of fourteen years, the Americans published their own version of the revision. Appearing in 1901, the American Standard Version (or American Revised Version) showed the influence of the modern-language enthusiasts. The *howbeits* were gone. The subjunctive *be* was replaced with *is*. People were no longer referred to as *which*—the Americans changed "Our

Father, which art in heaven," to "Our Father, who art in heaven." *Know* and *knew* replaced *wot* and *wist*. Various other changes show a tendency toward informality. *Teacher* replaced *master*. *Treated* was substituted for *entreated*. *Ghost* replaced *apparition*. The definite article was also dropped in various places to create a more informal tone ("the Christ" of the King James Bible often becomes simply "Christ" in the American Revised Version).

In spite of the steps toward modernism, the American revision was not a modern-language translation. Only a handful of the original revisers remained alive in the late 1890s, and they had not the manpower, energy, or desire to thoroughly rework the revision. Indeed, the American Bible of 1901 was very close in tone to the 1885 Revised Version, and it suffered from the same lack of focus. The American Revised Version shows the direction translators were heading, but little else.[29]

Beginning in the late 1880s, a number of projects got under way to create an unabashedly modern Bible. The best known was a team effort led by Paul Haupt of Johns Hopkins. Many leading British and American scholars lent their support to this effort, the results of which appeared serially in the next few years. *The Sacred Books of the Old and New Testaments*, as it was called (commonly known, though, as *The Polychrome Bible*), never came close to completion, but it was the one project of the 1890s to have widespread scholarly support.[30]

Bible reform in the 1890s was not successful. But most scholars did not expect it to be. The Bible reform movement of the 1890s was quite similar to the movement of the 1850s: Idiosyncratic reformers and scattered scholars worked on revision while the public remained indifferent. There is no better indication of the decline of public interest than the coverage of the movement in *The New York Times*. Between May and December of 1881, the *Times* ran eight editorials and seventeen news articles about the Revised New Testament. In 1885, the *Times* published five editorials and seven news stories about the Revised Old Testament. But in 1901, when the American Revised Version appeared, the *Times* gave it but one short review; the paper had lost interest in covering Bible revision.[31]

Of course, in the twentieth century there have been modern-language Bibles to win favor. Moffatt's Bible completed in 1928, Goodspeed's in 1931—these Bibles became well known to the public. Yet none of them could generate the mass enthusiasm that the Revised New Testament had generated in 1881.[32] With this in mind, the historical moment in which the Revised Version appeared becomes even more unique. It was a time when the Protestant public would test a new version and a time when the Protestant public cared deeply about the quality of the version.

Even in the 1880s, there were those who saw that this was changing. "The fact that the Bible occupies a somewhat different place in the thoughts of well-instructed Christians from that which it held twenty-five or fifty years ago is a fact that cannot be denied," one minister noted in 1884. "The home study of the Bible has largely fallen out of use," wrote another in 1886.[33] The sociolinguistic power of the King James Bible had always been based on its mass audience. But by the early twentieth century, the Bible was no longer read by enough people with enough regularity to be considered a text that shaped the language. The 1890s modern-language Bible movement was a response to this decline. There was nothing unique, as we shall see, in the fascination with the colloquial. It could also be found in contemporary lexicography, philological theory, school English programs, magazine literature, and public address. Yet the turn toward the colloquial by Bible translators was defensive, a somewhat desperate effort to counteract the disappearance of a mass audience. The modern-language Bible movement was a clear sign that the Bible no longer held the nation's attention, that the Scriptures were no longer a linguistic standard.

# V

Unlike Bible reform in the 1880s, in the next decade a set of major new dictionaries made by philologists had no trouble being accepted by the American public. This was partly because the dictionary was a less emotionally charged text than the Bible. But there was also a more accepting attitude toward specialists in the 1890s. Ten years made a big difference. The public passively accepted what the philologists told them was "good" English.

After the dictionary battles between *Webster's* and *Worcester's* faded in the 1860s, lexicographical élan passed to England. In the 1870s, work began on *The New English Dictionary on Historical Principles* (the *Oxford English Dictionary*), and in 1879 James Murray took over as editor of the project. Many Americans—including George P. Marsh, James Russell Lowell, and Fitzedward Hall—contributed to that great dictionary. In the United States, however, lexicography stagnated—through the 1870s, no major work was done.

That changed in the next decade. In 1880, when Orlando Baker took effective control of the G&C Merriam Company, he asked Loomis Campbell to start on a new *Webster's*. Two years later, Roswell Smith, president of the Century Publishing Company, contracted William Dwight Whitney to oversee a major new dictionary. Concurrently Isaac Funk—minister, editor, writer, and publisher—began work on an important lexicon. At the decade's close, the American Publishing Company turned to doing an American edition of Robert Hunter's *Encyclopaedic Dictionary*, which was first published in England in 1883. *The Century Dictionary* appeared in installments between 1889 and 1895. Both *Webster's International* and Funk and Wagnall's *Standard Dictionary of the English Language* were published in 1890. And *The American Encyclopaedic Dictionary* was published in 1894.[34]

The new dictionaries were huge. The 1860s' *Worcester's* and *Webster's* had contained 104,000 and 114,000 entries respectively. The smallest of the 1890s dictionaries, *Webster's International*, included 175,000 words. The others were even larger, no longer able to squeeze into one volume. The *Standard* had 304,000 entries. The *Century* told the history of each of the 200,000 covered words (annoying *OED* editor James Murray, who thought Whitney's dictionary would steal public interest from the Oxford project).[35] *The Century Dictionary* filled six volumes; the *American Encyclopaedic*, four.

These dictionaries were awash in scholarly philology, especially the *Century*, the *Standard*, and the *American Encyclopaedic*. Whitney edited the first and was liberally quoted in the third. Francis March was the consulting editor of the second. Just as the philologists denied the verbal critics' right to judge the language, so too they denied the dictionary's authority as a critical standard of the language. Usage was king, they maintained, and the new wordbooks were simply to record that usage. According to the *Standard*: "The question that should control the lexicographer is not, should the word be in the English language? but *is* it?" The *American* agreed, adding that the dictionary was "no longer to be devoutly worshipped by the student of language" or a "supreme court of reference." In this the new dictionaries followed Trench, who in his famous 1857 pamphlet on lexicography (chapter 3) argued that the dictionary should inventory the language, not arbitrate it. Thus as the new dictionaries ballooned in size, their purpose became much more modest.[36]

There was also much of the new science in *Webster's International*, which, according to its publishers, embodied "the ripest results of modern philology." The etymologies were done by the Harvard linguist Edward Sheldon and the introduction included a history of the English language written by James Hadley, who was a Bible reviser and a colleague of Whitney's. (This history was used at the Yale Sheffield School before Thomas Lounsbury's history was published in 1879.) For the 1890 *Webster's*, Hadley's history was updated by Harvard philologist George Lyman Kittredge.[37]

The new philology, however, did not reign unchecked in *Webster's*. The Merriams may have claimed the book included the "ripest results" of the new science, but they also added an important qualifier: ". . . in the degree and form appropriate to its class." They had bought the rights to Webster's dictionary in the 1840s and approached the science of lexicography with a temperamentally cautious spirit which persisted into the 1880s. Modernizers like Loomis Campbell were held in check. The nominal editor of the 1890 edition was the aging Noah Porter, who in the early 1860s was hand-picked by Chauncey Goodrich to take control of the dictionary. Porter championed romantic philology but showed little enthusiasm for Whitney's linguistics. (As president of Yale, Porter reportedly *never* visited the Sheffield School. His interest was in the fate of the college.) Thus the 1890 *Webster's* included many of the ideas of the new philology, but it was also more conservative than the other dictionaries. At times the book seems schizophrenic. It included both a preface written by Porter *and* a publisher's statement, probably written by Loomis, each covering the same ground with strikingly different emphases. Porter's comments were elegaic in tone, regretting some of the new innovations, praising first the large staff devoted to "literary research" and "verbal criticism" and only then the many "experts" who worked on the dictionary. The publisher's statement, however, touted the "scientific methods" and "scholarly conscientiousness" of the new dictionary and argued that the dictionary should no longer be an arbiter of usage.[38]

The Victorian philologists not only produced a striking theory of language, they were also part of an educational movement stressing expertise over broad, humane learning. The new dictionaries, in turn, reflected educational theory as much as linguistic theory. While philologists were in charge, experts from all fields were drafted into service—geologists, lawyers, engineers, economists, musicians, historians, and metallurgists were just a few of those who contributed. Hiring expert consultants actually began on a small scale in the 1840s, one outgrowth of the Webster-Worcester dispute. Yet prior to the 1870s, this was done for entrepreneurial reasons. No one had any intention of creating a "new" kind of dictionary; dictionary making was still described as a "literary" activity. For example, *The Springfield Union*, commenting in the early 1860s on the expanded staff of

*Webster's*, noted that the "whole guild of literary men was put under requisition."[39] At the close of the century, however, the dictionaries radiated different sentiments. In 1887, Thomas Lounsbury noted that the *Oxford English Dictionary* was not at all like Samuel Johnson's: "It is with no thought of expressing the slightest disrespect for those engaged in its preparation [the *OED*] that we say it is in the hands of scholars rather than men of letters. The interests of literature will therefore always meet with scant courtesy as contrasted with the interests of philology." The *American Encylopaedic* announced that it was "prepared and arranged by an editorial staff of American scholars, assisted by a core of specialists eminent in art, science, and literature." Funk and Wagnall's title page displayed no false modesty: "Prepared by MORE THAN TWO HUNDRED SPECIAL-ISTS AND OTHER SCHOLARS."[40]

The conjunction of the fascination with expertise and the new philological theory resulted in the inclusion of thousands of new technical terms, which was one of the major innovations of the dictionaries of the 1890s. Scientific terms like *rachiotome*, *radiophony*, *catadromous*, and *crotalidae* found their way into the new lexicons. So did technical terms like *stereotype*, *stereoscope*, *stereopticon*, *stereography*, *stereoblastula*, *stereo-electric*, *stereogram*, and *stereotypography*. *The Standard Dictionary* boasted of nearly four thousand electrical terms on its pages, terms coined only in the ten years before publication. *The Century Dictionary* also noted that it included thousands of scientific, technical, and commercial words new to the past twenty years. "The progress of invention has brought nearly as great a flood of new words and senses as has the progress of science," wrote Whitney in the introduction. Excluding them would exclude what was most "vital" in contemporary life.[41]

Part of the success of Samuel Johnson's dictionary rested on his elision of many technical words that were in Bailey's *Universal Etymological English Dictionary* (1721). Johnson's practice was mirrored in the eighteenth-century rhetorical theory of George Campbell, who argued that technical words were not part of the language. But as with the use of outside experts, the Webster-Worcester dictionary wars had spurred the inclusion of more and more technical language. Lexicographers before the Civil War had not thought they were changing the essential character of the dictionary, although some commentators were not so sure. The constant drive of each lexicographer to outdo the other might have bad consequences, one reviewer thought in 1860. The "old stock of English undefiled" was "in danger of being overwhelmed and crushed out by a multitudinous eruption of barbarous and unsightly terms which not a soul can take the least interest in except the student of special science." Only scientific words in general use, he added, should be included.[42]

Late-nineteenth-century critics and rhetoricians repeated the arguments against jargon, but lexicographers were unimpressed, maintaining that jargon revealed the "vital" in modern life. Whitney implicitly disputed the rhetoricians' claims by arguing that no longer was there any sharp division between technical language and common speech; the two were now "interwoven." The notion of a common, refined language had disappeared, he went on. Instead, popular and technical words would melt into each other.[43]

No late-nineteenth-century dictionary could avoid the rush to jargon. Even *Webster's International* joined in. Noah Porter, with a sadness that matched Whitney's hubris, explained the policy:

> The prominence given to the definitions and illustrations of scientific, technological and zoological terms will attract the attention of every reader and perhaps elicit the displeasure of many critics. While we sympathize with their regret that so much space is given to explanations and illustrations that are purely technical rather than literary, we find ourselves compelled to yield to the necessity which in these days requires that the dictionary which is ever at hand should carefully define the terms that record the discoveries of Science, the triumphs of Invention, and the revelations of Life.[44]

The dictionary must capitulate to the onslaught of modernity.

The new dictionaries reflected philological thinking in more than their commitment to expert vocabulary. Funk and Wagnall's *Standard Dictionary* used a modified form of simplified spelling, reflecting Francis March's contention that the written must follow the spoken. Respect for the spoken language was also shown by the inclusion of Americanisms. No longer was it feared that British and American English would drift into mutual incomprehension if one unitary Anglo-American literary language was not maintained. The English language was now international, lexical idiosyncrasies were to be made known, not hidden. The 1890 *Webster's* reflected the easy cosmopolitanism in its title. For the first time the dictionary was called *Webster's International*.

All the dictionaries also included slang. According to *Webster's*, modern life dictated the policy: "The Londoner, reading a story of Bret Harte, will turn to such a dictionary for the slang of a California mining camp, and the Melbourne merchant will consult it for the usage of the New York Stock Exchange." Editors also cited philological theory. The speech of the "common people" often enriched languages, Funk and Wagnall's

claimed; the "slang words of one age are often the accepted literary words
of a succeeding age." William Dwight Whitney wrote in *The Century
Dictionary* that "colloquialism and even slang must be noticed by the lexicographer who desires to portray the language in its natural and full
outlines." In 1890, *Webster's International* observed that slang, "scouted by
purists not many years since," was now "felt to be indispensable."[45]

Accepting slang was a sign of the philologists' ease with middling or
popular customs. One more sign of this new attitude was using the daily
newspaper to illustrate a word. This had been unthinkable for eighteenth-
century lexicographers, who had felt that newspapers were the "insects
of a season," not part of the nation's literature. With the rise of newspaper
culture in the early nineteenth century, it became even more important
to maintain standards. Both Goodrich and Worcester looked for citations
from the great authors. Worcester told readers he combed "the gems of
English literature" to illustrate his definitions,[46] considering the dictionary
a buffer against the ephemeral and rank democratic culture of the newspaper. Late-nineteenth-century lexicographers, however, had other ideas.
According to the *Standard*, "the newspaper is near the people and indicates
the common or current usage. . . ." According to the *American Encyclopaedic*, "no other source affords so many instances of words in every day
use." The nineteenth-century newspaper had reshaped the way a nation's
language survives: "It is the growth of the newspaper press which has
given importance to the English oral language." Mass newspaper reading
not only made newspaper quotation important, it made it imperative.[47]

Late-nineteenth-century American dictionaries were made through an
alliance of scholarly philologists and private entrepreneurs, with neither
having any qualms about using newspapers for source material. For at
least one British dictionary, however, there was a different arrangement.
The *Oxford English Dictionary* was funded by Oxford University Press and
Oxford faculty sat on the governing board. In the early 1880s, various
professors, notably Benjamin Jowett, objected to some of the dictionary's
methods. In particular, they did not want slang included, wanted only a
minimum of scientific words, and argued that newspapers should not be
used to illustrate words. The differences could not be clearer. Jowett, a
classical scholar, indifferent to the new efforts to make education professional, wanted the dictionary to be a literary endeavor. Murray, not a
faculty member but clearly a proponent of the new scientific research,
had other ideas about what a dictionary should be.[48]

We must here underscore the conjunction of new attitudes toward
technical words and new attitudes toward slang. As philologists began to

associate education with expertise instead of cultivated sensibilities, they also began to worry less about popular vulgarity. Slang used to be considered crude; now it was picturesque. Slang lost its incivil edge. The highly educated perhaps did not use slang themselves, the philologists noted, but slang did not threaten the nation. So long as specialized, technical vocabularies flourished, educated culture would survive.

The new dictionaries were quite liberal in theory, but were they in practice? When compared to the verbal critics, the lexicographers were distinctly latitudinarian. Almost every bête noir of the critics was ignored or singled out for ridicule. The 1890s dictionaries also upgraded many words earlier lexicons either ignored or condemned. Previously meaning "pertaining to an editor," *editorial*, in the sense of an essay of opinion, was a neologism of the 1860s. Verbal critics strongly condemned this new usage and it was not in any dictionary prior to the 1890s. The lexicons of the 1890s, however, included the new meaning with no opprobrium.

Three of the dictionaries, the *Century*, the *Standard*, and the *American Encyclopaedic*, also included thousands of words neither obviously crude nor obviously formal. Words like *quiz, rampageous, jolly* (for *surprising*), *awfully* (for *exceedingly*), *boss*, and *bub* (a small boy) reflected a profound ease about colloquial speech. And this introduction of informal, casual speech marked a shift as important as the new ideas concerning slang and jargon. It reflected the acceptance of the kind of colloquial oratory used by Henry Ward Beecher. This is something earlier lexicographers would have been loath to do.

Many colloquial terms ignored or condemned in earlier dictionaries were accepted in the 1890s. Previous lexicons had excluded *hard up*, but the *Century, Standard*, and *American Encyclopaedic* all viewed it as standard English. *Ad*, for *advertisement*, was first included in Funk and Wagnall's *Standard*. Bartlett's *Dictionary of Americanisms* (1877 edition) labeled *by and large* "slang," but to the *Century* and *Standard* it was fine English. Bartlett also had called *catch on* "vulgar slang," but the *Standard* upgraded it to "colloquial." The *American Encyclopaedic* called *catch on* a legitimate Americanism. *Goner* ("That guy is a goner.") was another piece of informal speech first sanctioned in the 1890s dictionaries. Coined in the 1830s, *goner* was included in no English dictionary until the close of the century, being labeled "colloquial" by the *Century* and the *Standard*. *Chucklehead* was called "vulgar" in Worcester; "low" in the 1880s Webster. In the 1890s, the *Century, Standard*, and *American Encyclopaedic* all accepted the word. Other words that became either literary or colloquial speech in the 1890s dictionaries included *pesky*, *right away*, *shut up* (be quiet), *shoddy*, *to let slide*, *to let on*, and *to peach* (to inform against someone).

*Webster's International* was far more conservative than the other three. It still labeled *pesky*, *to peach*, and *chucklehead* "low"; it still called *hard up* "slang." Although it did not yet recognize *goner*, *by and large*, *to let on*, and *shut up*, even *Webster's* did not completely avoid the trend toward informality. Many words not part of the 1873 *Webster's* became standard or colloquial in the 1890 edition, for example, *goober*, *to let slide*, *right away*, *shoddy*, *bang* (the woman's hair style), and *jab*. The status of other words was upgraded in the new dictionary. *Squatter*, an Americanism in the 1873 *Webster's*, became standard English in 1890. *Reckon* ("I reckon he's at the store.") was provincial and vulgar in 1873; it was colloquial in 1890. *Quit* in the sense of to stop or desist from doing something ("I quit my job.") as opposed to leaving someplace ("He quitted the parish.") was a troubling usage in the mid-nineteenth century. The *OED* called it an Americanism and many verbal critics condemned it. The 1873 *Webster's* did not accept the new meaning; the 1890 edition did. Still another example was *Uncle Sam*, coined during the War of 1812. It was "vulgar cant" to the mugwumpish *Webster's Dictionary* (1873), but good colloquial English to the philological *Webster's International* (1890). Although the 1890 *Webster's* was the most conservative of the four new dictionaries, it was still far more informal than any earlier lexicon.

If the new dictionaries were full of slang and colloquialisms, there were still firm and impassible barriers. The ultimate vulgarities—*fuck*, *suck*, and *cunt*—were not printed on any page. (Although *shit*, after a 170-year hiatus, reentered the standard English dictionary via the *American Encyclopaedic*. Shockingly, it had no cautionary marker attached, a testament not to the status of the word but to the editorial sloppiness of the dictionary.) But other dirty words were carefully marked. *Poop* (meaning, in the nineteenth century, "to fart") was called "vulgar" when included.[49] *Whore* was alternatively labeled "low" or "excluded from polite speech."[50] All called *damn* a profane oath and none included *goddam* in any way.

Moreover, although the new lexicographers dismissed much of the verbal criticism, there were striking exceptions. The *Century* and *Standard* both agreed that using *limb* for *leg* was affected or prudish. Only *Webster's International* accepted *proven* for *proved*. The *Century* thought *pants* colloquial and vulgar. *Varmint* was vulgar or dialect in the three dictionaries mentioning it.[51] Each dictionary as well devoted several paragraphs of minute type to explicating the byzantine subtleties of *shall* and *will*.

Although some slang words were added, others were not. Slang synonyms for hard liquor like *red-eye, eye-opener*, and *moonshine* all entered one or more the new wordbooks, but *bald-face, corpse-reviver*, and *phlegm-cutter* did not.[52] Slang was part of the dictionary, but it was unclear with what system.

But even more important, it was unclear as to what purpose. The dignified vocabulary of the old dictionaries was meant to be formal and that formality was designed to establish civil respect. In quite a departure from this, some of the new informality was simply insulting. The new dictionaries included a number of ethnic and racial slurs. *Darky* had not appeared in the literary dictionaries except to be called "low." Three of the 1890s dictionaries, however, called it "colloquial" and *Webster's* termed it "slang." *Coon* did not exist in any English dictionary prior to the 1890s; when it was included in both the *Standard* and the *American Encyclopaedic* it was labeled "slang." For the first time in the 1890s, too, two major dictionaries sanctioned *woolly-head*.[53] Earlier dictionaries had labeled *piccaninny* a Southern regionalism, and therefore not literary speech. The dictionaries of the 1890s accepted it as standard usage. And although three of the dictionaries labeled *nigger* "vulgar" and "opprobrious," the *American Encyclopaedic* included no usage marker next to the word.

Other ethnic groups were also affected by the new informality. *Dago* was widely used beginning in the 1830s, referring in the nineteenth century to someone from any Southern European nation. It was first included in the 1890s lexicons. Similarly, *greaser* (for *Mexican*) dated from the 1830s but did not enter any English dictionary until the 1890s. *Webster's* called it "low," but the *American Encyclopaedic* and the *Century* thought it standard English. *Sheeny* (for *Jew*) also appeared in English dictionaries for the first time.[54]

Slang was the daring new innovation of the turn-of-the-century dictionaries, but that did not necessarily mean it was acceptable usage. Clearly, the dictionaries offered more damning markers—"provincial," "vulgar," "low." But the dictionary makers also saw slang as something different from colloquialisms. Would not readers who saw the label "slang" still consider the words substandard? In fact, with one exception, the scholars saw it that way. They agreed that one generation's slang often became the next generation's standard speech, that slang must be included in dictionaries. But they felt that did not mean that the educated should actually use slang—barriers should remain, although the scholars assumed they would be scaled. What seemed such a bold theory in the 1890s now appears quite tame to us.[55]

The one dictionary that did not hesitate was the *Century*—Whitney's dictionary. Slang was "regarded" as "vulgar," according to the *Century*, but it entered "more or less" into "all colloquial speech." Did that mean slang crossed all social boundaries? That ladies and gentlemen used slang? Indeed it did. There was slang "of the vagabond or unlettered classes" and the slang of "standard speech." Slang appeared not only in "inferior popular literature, as novels, newspapers, political addresses"; it was also found in "more serious writings." Slang, the *Century* concluded, was "not necessarily vulgar or ungrammatical," it was often "correct in idiomatic form." It was one form of colloquial speech, that of "extravagant meta-phorical meanings." Going much further than the other dictionaries of the time, only the *Century* accepted the idea that everyone used slang. Slang was a cultural style that was truly "popular," stretching across class boundaries. Even the highly educated indulged.[56]

Despite their limitations, the lexicographers viewed their linguistics as democratic. There was nothing disingenuous about this. Whitney did not think that jargon would become a source of exclusion but that it would melt into daily usage. Science and democracy were joined in contrast to more "elitist" theories of language, theories that owed more to those rhe-torical traditions that moralized about style. Nor were the linguists alone in such beliefs. William Dean Howells defended the slang and provin-cialisms of realistic fiction in the same way he did the scientific temper of the age. They were democratic. Just as Whitney had little patience with the verbal critics, Howells condemned mid-century Romantics as aris-tocrats.[57]

The new dictionaries reflected the philologists' rapprochement with popular culture, the culture of the daily newspaper. The inclusion of slang and the massive influx of colloquial speech indicated attitudes about lan-guage quite different from those embodied in the literary dictionaries. But at the same time, the hesitations about slang; the dark, insulting side of popular language; and the riot of technical terms all revealed how the reconciliation with mass culture was connected to new forms of authority. The colloquial would be channeled and expertise championed. Just as with the modern-language Bibles, embedded in the new wordbooks were attitudes about the organization of everyday life.

# VI

What is most striking about the 1890s debate over the new dictionaries is that it never took place. There were reviews of the new wordbooks, some good, some bad, but the fundamental reorientation of lexicography occasioned no sustained debate over the nature of the dictionary. Overwhelmingly, the work of the philologists was simply accepted. In 1890, *The New York Times* reported that both Webster's and Worcester's dictionaries were out of date. Every periodical and book "bristles with new words," noted the *Times*, and the public wanted "the latest results of linguistic research." They wanted, "in short, the complete encyclopaedic dictionary."[58] Contrast this with the dictionary wars of the 1840s through 1860s, when the passionate discussion of what made up a good dictionary sucked in educators, politicians, lawyers, doctors, and literary people on both sides of the Atlantic. Contrast this also with the heated debates over the Revised Bible that took place just a few years earlier. By the 1890s, the scholarly experts were clearly in charge; the public readier to accept the expert's authority. The new dictionaries were quietly distributed across the nation. No one of consequence objected.

The reviews of the new dictionaries were almost all favorable, with many praising the new scientific spirit. "The secret of this triumph of execution," *The New York Times* said of Whitney's *Century Dictionary*, was "the division of labor specialization under intelligent leadership." The new scientific and technical vocabulary was as attractive as were the new philological methods. Melville Anderson praised the huge number of "special terms in science and specific names of animals and plants" that he found in *Webster's International*. The *Times* marveled that the *Century* included twenty-four columns of words prefixed with *meta-*, ten columns of *meso-*, nineteen of *micro-*, twenty-nine of *mono-*, and thirty-eight of *poly-*.[59]

Just as often the new slang words were celebrated. W. A. Mowry praised the *Century* for including not only *peritonitis* but also *cussedness*. Another reviewer observed that Funk and Wagnall's *Standard Dictionary* included *to be in it* and *get a move on*. "Martinets and precisions [*sic*] of language will grumble at such license, but the principle of keeping abreast of the colloquial is entirely a right one. . . ." Indeed, the new dictionaries were seen as part of the war against verbal critics. Lounsbury hoped the *OED* would "form an impregnable defense against the noisy pests of the period, the smatterers in language, who, through the medium of newspapers and widely-circulated manuals, persistently inflict upon the half-educated their own crude conceits about the forms and use of words." Although some gave a "little shudder" to see *catch on, conniption, cockolorum, out of sight*, and *in it* actually in print, they also realized that such words were in "the talk of millions" as well as in "the newspapers abundantly" and that they should be part of the English dictionary.[60]

A few did criticize the new dictionaries. As early as 1883, W. H. Wells criticized the British precursor of the *American Encyclopaedic*. The "encyclopaedic dictionaries," he argued, have not matched the "defining dictionaries" in what the latter did best, "the discrimination of nice and exact shades of meaning." Similarly, in 1895 another commentator complained that by ransacking newspaper columns, hunting through the "by-ways of literature," and "zealously" noting the "oddities of colloquial speech," the new lexicographers have set down "thousands of 'words' which have no place or value in the language, and which disfigure rather than adorn the dictionaries."[61]

The critique of the encyclopedic dictionary changed over the decades. Richard Grant White in 1870 condemned the new swollen wordbooks for undermining the taut clarity of literary English. Including fifty-six meanings for *run*, as *Webster's* did, only confused most readers. White argued that provincial words should be excluded, and while scientific terms like *zenith* and *nadir* were fine, *zeolitiform*, *zinkiferous*, *zinky*, *zumosimeter*, and *zoophytological* had no place in an English dictionary. He repeated the old argument that such words were not part of the English language since they did not "represent the English of literature or of common life." White saw the bloated new dictionaries as resulting from the entrepreneurial ethos. In 1870, it was not science that dictated the new dictionary, but the marketplace. White clearly associated the new encyclopedic dictionaries with the entrepreneurial desire to cater to a mass audience, the "half-educated." Moreover, he felt that the dictionaries themselves exemplified that culture: The mindless garnering of facts, the absence of taste, the hodgepodge arrangement all were part of what White saw going wrong with America. Indeed, the salesmanship of the publishers, the competing claims that "this dictionary has ten thousand words more than the other," White viewed as a sign of unconcern for literary standards. We "might well believe that our language spawns words as herrings spawn eggs," wrote White.[62]

By the 1890s, the villain had changed. In 1891, the Princeton rhetorician Theodore Hunt wrote in the *New Englander* about contemporary lexicography, citing all the same problems that White had: the tendency toward all-inclusiveness, the proliferation of technical words, the new attitude toward slang and provincialisms. Yet the culprit no longer was the entrepreneur and his half-educated audience. Instead, Hunt worried about the new linguistic experts. Whose assumptions were right, Hunt asked, the editors of the seventeenth and eighteenth century or those of the present age? The new "encyclopedic theory," thought Hunt, with its "wide inclusion of all forms of technical language," lessened the literary spirit of the dictionary. "There is imminent danger here," he claimed, "and the pressing need on the part of English and all literary students of counteracting it." It must be asserted, Hunt argued, that "the final end of language is literature." By the 1890s, the new mass audience no longer directly threatened the literary dictionary, scientific experts did.[63]

In the last decade of the century, however, such critiques were rare. Only a few philologists, like the contumacious Fitzedward Hall, even bothered to respond.[64] Given the massive changes in the conditions of life in the later nineteenth century, it was absurd to constrict the dictionary to the literary language. Given the new vocabularies of sport, technology, and science that floated through the culture, it was only natural that the dictionary should expand. How else was one to learn about electricity, Darwin, or baseball? Even literary elites offered no real opposition. The new dictionaries became a part of American life, finding their way into schools, offices, and homes. In 1898, The Merriam Company published *Webster's Collegiate Dictionary*, which, based on scientific research into everyday usage, became the most popular lexicon of the twentieth century. The literary dictionary disappeared.

# CHAPTER EIGHT

# Refined and Colloquial, 1885–1900

The hallmark of modern consciousness, as I
have been insisting to the point of obsession,
is its enormous multiplicity.

CLIFFORD GEERTZ

The new dictionaries reflected the rise of an official alternative to refined language during the 1890s. So, too, did the modern-language Bible movement. Also by that time, literary language was losing its home in the nation's schools. The birth of the modern university created a variety of forums for scholars to think about language. In the lower schools, progressive reformers were suggesting new ways to transmit English to the nation's youth. These reformers did not so much attack literary language as they carefully segregated it. As in the new dictionaries, the reformers treated literary language as one idiom among several.

These school debates, moreover, had clear echoes in contemporary discussions of how public figures should speak. The stylistic debates appeared in various forms with various buzzwords: the colloquial versus the refined, the nervous versus the leisurely, the natural against the literary, the spellbinder versus the orator. Less and less did the educated worry about presenting themselves as refined gentlemen, articulate in the old rhetorical sense. Colloquial informality became more acceptable.

But buried in the debate was more. As always, discussion about language was also about ways of life. Fights over refined versus colloquial speech implied different ways of organizing the self. Competing attitudes about usage reflected conflicting opinion about the new culture of expertise.

# I

In the 1880s and 1890s, the modern American university was born, and with it was born the departmental system. In school after school across the nation, the faculty divided itself up along disciplinary lines. For those interested in the native tongue, this merely institutionalized the drift of previous decades. The study of language became distinct from the study of literature. Rhetoric drifted from philology.

The new language departments secured the place of philology. If in the mid-1870s only a handful of colleges taught the subject, by the mid-1890s no respectable English department was without some philological courses. In the 1870s, there was but a tiny number of linguists who were working on the English language, but by the late 1880s, a new generation of scholars had entered the field. Men like James Bright, Albert Cook, R. O. Williams, C. V. Von Jagemann, Oliver Emerson, and George Kittredge were just a few. Armed with Ph.D.s, often schooled in Germany, these men became the first full-fledged professional students of the English language. Their forums were the monograph and scholarly journal. They wrote and edited *The American Journal of Philology*, *Dialect Notes*, *Publications of the Modern Language Association*, and *Modern Language Notes*, all of which began publishing in the 1880s.

The scholars' research was decked out in all the philological theory. Language, the most assertive argued, was essentially the spoken tongue. "Writing is of course nothing but a set of signs for the spoken words," it was reported in one of the better-known histories of the 1890s, "and the language of books follows the language as spoken, though slowly."[1] By 1909, Columbia University professor George Krapp wrote in *Modern English: Its Growth and Present Use*: "In all study of language as expression, it is now generally conceded . . . that the spoken, as compared with the written or literary language, is of far greater importance. . . ."[2] Not all philologists had yet discarded the literary language; many continued to define language as a mix of the spoken and written. When they sat down to write their histories, however, they implicitly made the division, sharply dividing language from literature.[3]

By the 1890s, the separation was also apparent in the way English departments organized their course work. In virtually every major department in the nation, classes in English literature were rigidly segregated from those on the English language.[4] Not only was philological study distinct from literary study, philology now had no bearing on the practical use of the language. The hundreds of articles and monographs on the history of language were entirely descriptive, written by specialists for specialists. Occasionally, a few linguists (usually European-born) raised their voices to argue that philologists *should* influence the language, but they were largely ignored.[5] Usage was king, and good philologists simply recorded usage.

The rise of philology within the university, then, was accompanied by an increasingly passive attitude toward public usage by the philologists themselves. In the 1850s, writers like George Perkins Marsh and Richard Chenevix Trench advocated the study of Anglo-Saxon for entirely practical reasons. Romantic philologists hoped that widespread study of Anglo-Saxon could ameliorate the troubling vulgarity of democratic speech. Their audience was the literate public. In the 1870s, Fitzedward Hall began his exploration of the history of English words to attack the bad ideas about usage perpetrated by Richard Grant White. Hall wanted to affect public opinion.

Whitney in the 1870s and 1880s articulated a more reserved point. He contended that philology could not aid in teaching "good" speech but was useful for the mental discipline it offered. The new generation of scholars went further. Philological research, they said simply, advanced knowledge. That was sufficient in itself.[6] Between 1870 and 1900, philological conversation ceased to be civic in intent and became professional. Knowing rhetoric had been considered essential to one's character; knowing philology was a way to make a career.

Divorcing philology from practical linguistics left a gaping hole in the college curriculum. With the inauguration of the elective system came widespread complaints that college students could not write. The increasing number of philological courses by no means meant that the student body was learning more about language. Indeed, since philology was an elective, most students probably spent less time learning about language than in the old collegiate system where rhetoric was studied for several years.[7] By the 1890s, the absence of practical language skills in the nation's colleges had become a national scandal. "The Growing Illiteracy of American Boys" was one of Godkin's essays on the subject.[8] Businessmen like Andrew Carnegie and Charles Francis Adams berated the universities for their failure in this and college administrators all over the nation pondered the problem. In 1891, the Harvard overseers created a committee, including Godkin and Adams, to gauge the linguistic skills of students. In a series of reports issued throughout the decade and influential throughout the nation, the committee blamed the preparatory schools for students' defects. Preparatory teachers, in turn, blamed the general indifference to literature in the culture at large.[9] There was no shortage of other suspected villains: Various educators blamed the new linguistics, academic specialization, the new immigration and the popularity of dialect and slang literature.[10] Whatever the cause, it was clear that college students could not write. (In 1891, Herbert Hoover was forced to do remedial English work as a condition of admission to Stanford.[11]) By that year, rhetorician James Morgan Hart could write that "the cry all over the country is: Give us more English! Do not let our young men and women grow up in ignorance of their mother tongue."[12]

The response was Freshman English. The basic model for the college composition class was Harvard's English A, created in 1885 by Adams Sherman Hill and Barrett Wendell. Within fifteen years, the freshman composition course was a standard part of university curriculums across the nation. Most of these classes had students write short daily themes, an innovation of Wendell's. By the 1890s, small staffs handled hundreds of students and corrected thousands of daily themes on each campus.[13]

With but a few exceptions,[14] freshman English classes were the same throughout the country, sharing a very conservative approach to the language. One of the best-known texts of the 1890s, Arlo Bates's *Talks on Writing English*, told students that all barbarisms, improprieties, and solecisms should be avoided despite their ubiquity in daily newspapers. Similarly, Edwin Woolley of the University of Wisconsin argued that it was wrong to suppose that newspaper English was good English: "Our newspapers are almost universally characterized by provincial and vulgar diction."[15] A few teachers also noted that inclusion in a dictionary was no longer proof of a word's legitimacy—students were to carefully look at markers like "slang" or "colloquial."[16] The textbooks were quite frank that written English was their model.

The new composition teachers held attitudes about language far closer to the old rhetoricians than the new philologists. Yet there were also crucial differences. The new composition texts, for example, made no effort to define their subject in relation to other disciplines. Rhetoricians, having always explicitly thought about their place in the panoply of humane learning, directly confronted the issue of rhetoric's contribution to the formation of a gentleman or lady of character. This was as true of Aristotle,

Quintilian, and Cicero as it was of John Bascom (*Philosophy of Rhetoric*, 1879) and James De Mille (*Elements of Rhetoric*, 1878). But with the flexible new curriculum, it was no longer necessary to place rhetoric in relation to other subjects. The textbooks of Genung, Hill, and Brainerd Kellogg in the 1870s began the process, and by the time of Wendell's *English Composition* in 1891, the break was complete. Writing had become an introductory, utilitarian subject for freshmen. The old tradition was gone. Composition, unlike rhetoric, taught basic skills; it was not part of a larger formation of character.[17]

The new freshman English classes also hid any close ties with English literature. Most composition teachers emphasized daily writing drills over cultivating a literary sensibility, the tone that had been set by Barrett Wendell when he developed the idea of the "daily theme" in 1885. Students learned to write by writing, Wendell claimed; they were to be drilled in the simple utilitarian art of putting words on paper. Others agreed. "A student learns to write as a boy learns to swim," wrote MIT composition teacher Henry Pearson, "—by doing it." As Arlo Bates, another Harvard composition teacher, put it: "Just as one acquires skill in the use of the piano by innumerable exercises and continual practice, so one attains to mastery in written language only by writing and writing and writing."[18] Rhetoricians like John Genung and Theodore Hunt did not disagree that writing practice was important, but they argued that modern composition classes underemphasized literary appreciation and that appreciation was a vital part of learning to write.[19]

It was the daily theme group, however, led by the composition teachers at Harvard, who set the style for the whole nation through the 1930s.[20] Their textbooks deemphasized literature in striking ways. Discussion of style disappeared, replaced by detailed attention to "correctness." Fine distinctions between *like* or *as*, or discussion of the split infinitive, took space formerly occupied by the different genres of literature—oratory included. Plain speech became the preferred style. Simple, clear exposition, totally unornamented and without any author's presence, was the ideal. This was the classical plain style, although the textbook writers did not name it such. The style that the ancients had thought most suitable for teaching ignorant children became the model for all of the culture's written discourse.

The very term *composition* also reflected the new approach to the subject. By the 1890s, the word was often used in opposition to *rhetoric*. Composition was practical while rhetoric was theoretical. Although it dated back to the 1870s, only in the 1890s was this distinction widely taken for granted. The titles of the new books reflected this: Barrett Wendell's *English Composition* (1891), Henry Pearson's *The Principles of Composition* (1897), Edwin Woolley's *Handbook of Composition* (1907). While there were still books called "rhetorics," they too often reflected the drift toward a narrow utilitarianism. John Genung in his *Practical Elements of Rhetoric* (1886) noted that "literature is of course infinitely more than mechanism," but it was "as mechanism that it must be taught; the rest must be left to the student." In his 1898 text *Elements of Rhetoric*, subtitled *A Course in Plain Prose Composition*, Alphonso G. Newcomer asserted that the "bulk of matter in our rhetorics is traditionally and, except for higher critical purposes, useless." The drift was clear. By the early twentieth century, rhetoric (the word) was out of date and rhetoric (the subject) was old-fashioned. The most authoritative student of late-nineteenth-century rhetoric has written: "To the present day, rhetoric has never fully recovered the ground then lost."[21]

By 1900, civic rhetoric was on the way to becoming an anachronism. And the new composition classes meant that university English programs were split into *three* separate fields—language, literature, and composition. Each treated linguistic questions in its own fashion. The language courses focused on everyday usage, the literature courses on style, and composition classes on basic correctness. There was little sense that each should be related to the other. Brander Matthews of Columbia wrote: "Perhaps these three divisions, rhetoric, English language, and English literature, include all the courses which can fairly be called English." At the University of Illinois it was noted: "The English courses fall into three distinct natural groups—language, composition, and literature." Professor L. A. Sherman observed: "The study of English as rhetoric and composition, and as literature and philology, is completely differentiated in the University of Nebraska." William Morton Payne, summing up an 1894 survey of twenty university English programs, wrote of "a well-marked differentiation of literature from linguistics," adding that composition was "an equally distinct" field.[22]

Older traditions of civic rhetoric thought in terms of a coherent "refined" language that was nurtured and preserved through literature. This was the language of the public sphere—the idiom of civil society. The very institutional complexity of the modern university militated against the preservation of that idiom. Literary language, the spoken word, and basic written communication were parceled out to separate experts. Language theories might come and go but the university's intense specialization virtually guaranteed the marginalization of civic rhetoric.

The modern composition class was a residue of older traditions. It at least taught public communication. But it also severely constricted the stylistic possibilities of approved language; and it created the illusion that language could be divorced from the *ethos* (or even *persona*) of the speaker, that plain language was somehow free from the subjectivity of literary prose or political opinion.

# II

As the teaching of English fragmented in the higher schools, the lower schools searched for systematization. One New York writer summed up the dilemma in 1902: "There is a bewildering output of educational textbooks—Language Lessons, Readers, and Spellers; Grammars and Rhetorics; special school editions without end of the classics, old and new. Our educational journals are full of reports of new methods and experiments."[23] Beginning in the 1890s, educational reformers struggled to bring some order to the chaos. Between 1896 and 1903, for example, three book-length efforts to systematize the English program were published, hoping to create a comprehensive English program that would progress in an orderly fashion from kindergarten through the senior year of high school.[24] The paradoxical result of their reforms, however, was to break up the English program just as it was being broken up in the universities. Important to these early progressive English reformers was to have every element of the English program in its place, which entailed segregating each aspect of the English program. And this meant deemphasizing literary English.

A few reformers continued to restate the ideas of civil, literary English. Notable among them was Percival Chubb, a principal of a New York high school who in 1902 published *The Teaching of English in the Elementary and the Secondary School*. Chubb wanted the literary spirit to suffuse the whole English program. Even elementary composition Chubb thought should be seen as a form of literary effort. He also emphasized that "the supreme aim of literary and linguistic training was the formation of character," repeating "the quiet assumption that refined speech is an indispensable part of good manners and gentle breeding. . . ." And literature was at the core. The corrective to "pedantic English," wrote Nicholas Murray Butler in the editor's introduction to Chubb's book, was to bring "the child early and late into contact with literature that has character and distinction.

Teach him to love this, to return to it often, and his own spoken and written English will be worthy."[25]

Chubb attempted to restate the principles of civil English with some of the new psychological terminology of the Progressive Era.[26] His position was a minority one, as most of the 1890s reformers stressed a multidimensional approach to the English program. The language had many things to teach—conversational agility, reasoning ability, written skills, literary appreciation. A good elementary and secondary program must cultivate all and neglect none. There was no core value that defined the whole program, rather there were numerous skills that needed to be transmitted. Probably the most quoted author on English reform in the 1890s was S. S. Laurie, whose *Lectures on Language and Linguistic Method* was first published in 1890. Laurie divided the subject into three fields, "language as substance of thought," or written and oral communication; "language as a formal discipline," or grammar; and "language as literature." The first taught practical skills, the second mental discipline, and the third truth and beauty.[27] Laurie's division of the English program was remarkably attractive to scholars and reformers during the 1890s.

It was not that the proponents of the pluralistic English program dismissed literature. They held it in high esteem. "Literature has a grand teaching function," wrote B. A. Hinsdale in *Teaching the Language Arts* (1896), "instructing men in politics, in morals and manners, in taste, in religion, expanding their minds, filling them with high ideals and in all ways refining their life." Literature was important, but by separating the English program into separate categories the reformers in effect segregated literature. Literature was vital, to be sure, offering the most elevating thoughts and dazzling beauty the language had to offer. Yet the reformers turned literature into something special, something distinct from daily speech. They denied the interplay between literary and quotidian language that reformers like Chubb continued to maintain. Laurie argued that literature could not teach everything: "A young child may receive and enjoy the sentiment of Tennyson's *May Queen* or Wordsworth's *We Are Seven*, and yet find the formal analysis of language to present insuperable difficulties." According to Laurie, "it is the formal and abstract exercise in the mere vehicle of expression that we must give, if we are to give power to the mind."[28]

The schools themselves had no uniform reaction to the agitation of the 1890s. Some resisted reform while others grasped at it. Most schools around the nation, however, responded to the call for systematization with piecemeal change, with entrenched interests and bureaucratic inertia allowing much of the old to remain. The countless minor changes that there were fell into no clear pattern.[29]

In 1900, the nation's schools were not ready for major curricular reform. That would come later, in the twenties and thirties. And by that time, the reformers of the 1890s would seem terribly old-fashioned, indeed, not as reformers at all. To post–World War I progressive educators, the efforts of a Percival Chubb or a B. A. Hinsdale to use language study to build character were hopelessly out of date. To them, language studies were to "socialize" children, the term expressly used to contrast with "character building." Moreover, progressive educators drifted further away from a literary emphasis. Even the limited appeal to literature among the pluralist reformers of the 1890s seemed dangerously aristocratic. Students after World War I were taught daily speech skills and introduced to contemporary "literature" that included popular magazines, newspapers, and even radio speech.[30]

Hints of the new agenda appeared at the turn of the century. In 1903, just one year after Percival Chubb defended literary language in *The Teaching of English*, three university professors, George Carpenter and Franklin Baker of Columbia University and Fred Scott of the University of Michigan, published a three-hundred-page study entitled *The Teaching of English in the Elementary and Secondary Schools*. In some ways their book looked like the pluralist approach to the subject favored by B. A. Hinsdale and S. S. Laurie. In other ways, however, the book was far different. The split between language and literature, often only dimly perceived by the pluralists, was firmly in the minds of Carpenter, Baker, and Scott. To those acquainted with the academic philologists, the sentiments were not unusual: "The living language is the spoken language. The written language is merely a conventional form of the spoken language." This had important pedagogical consequences: "The most important aim of education in the mother tongue must, therefore, always be the development of power over the spoken language rather than over the written language." Much emphasis was placed on what was called "oral composition." To these authors, however, this meant not formal rhetoric but colloquial conversation. They also distrusted teaching writing by holding up the best models. This practice, advocated by Quintilian, Ascham, Johnson, and Blair, would only bore young boys, the progressives argued. Carpenter, Baker, and Scott also denied that composition was necessarily literary. Carpenter argued that it was possible to teach a youngster to write without any study of English literature—"perhaps, in an extreme case, without reading books at all." Too early an emphasis on style would only confuse the young, Carpenter asserted. These authors did not dismiss literature, but they firmly made it a subordinate part of the English program.[31]

In one other important way Carpenter, Baker, and Scott differed from the other reformers. They completely ignored the question of character and language. The study of English, they argued, should develop functional and aesthetic skills; in this they included no discussion of morals. This turn was connected, in part, to their own devaluation of literature, for they conceived of literature as purely aesthetic. For Carpenter, as opposed to writers like Hinsdale, Laurie, or Chubb, literature was not about morality. There was surely no conception of the morality of style in Carpenter's book. Beauty was severed from the good. In "modern civilization," the three argued, basic world views came *not* from literature but from "history, economics, and social science. . . ." Not only did this reveal how far these authors were from older ideas about language and *ethos*, it also reflected the new definition of literature which restricted it to imaginative prose.[32]

Like the pluralists, these authors carefully split up the English program into constituent parts and segregated literary language, which had a pronounced effect on later reformers. Literature was never pushed out of the lower school English program, but the emphasis during the 1920s and 1930s on "functional skills" and "life adjustment" shifted priorities—literature had to find a niche among several distinct branches of the subject.[33] To be sure, in 1900 many still resisted the change, like Samuel Thurber, who argued that in secondary schools English should not be separated into "language, composition, and literature. . . . The course in English should be concentric," Thurber claimed, "and all its elements should center about literature." Or there was the high school teacher Mary A. Dean, who in 1906 wrote in the *School Review*: "The moment the separation in the English work begins, the pigeon-holing of composition from literature, and again from rhetoric, that moment begins the deadening of impulse."[34] But at the same time reformers were arguing that English teaching must become "scientific" or "practical" and that entailed neatly categorizing language, literature, and composition. It was the latter group that set the tone of much twentieth-century English teaching.

# III

In both the colleges and the lower schools, institutional and theoretical complexity subtly corroded the overarching faith in literary models. There was a growing respect for the ordinary and technical which we have seen in the major dictionaries of the 1890s and in the new colloquial Bible movement. Everywhere after 1885, the status of literature and literary language was uncertain. In previous chapters I have discussed the challenges to civic, literary culture from middling sources. What made the challenge of the 1890s different was that it came from the highly educated.

To be sure, many continued to praise literary English. In *The Atlantic Monthly* of 1900 Benjamin Ide Wheeler complained about the "ultramodern idea" that "art and language have no proper dealings with each other," an idea he traced to "the modern scientific study of language." Woodrow Wilson similarly raised his voice in defense of rhetoric and "mere literature." And in the years surrounding 1900 it was not difficult to find celebrants of literature who asserted its importance in shaping everyday usage.[35]

At the same time, however, other voices were raised, voices that *did* deny the defining importance of literature. Some philologists and educators were claiming that the language was essentially the spoken dialect, and no one was more important in presenting this idea to a wide audience than Brander Matthews, a professor of dramatic literature at Columbia University. Beginning in the late eighties, Matthews wrote on the English language for magazines like *Harper's Monthly*, *Scribner's*, and *Munsey's*. He attacked verbal criticism, praised the new philologists, and defended slang and provincialisms. He thought the old rhetorics musty, and urged readers to discard received wisdom: "The real language of a people is the spoken word, not the written. Language lives on in the tongue and in the ear; there it was born, and there it grows." Words were made by "the man in the street," wrote another of this school: "There is absolutely no referee upon the subject to whom the people look even in theory for guidance, or who can control usage in any degree whatever. No university, no corporation of critics, no maker of dictionaries, possesses on this subject any authority, nor has any poet or author or orator any power, recognized or informal, of exercising a veto." Such writers were usually men of letters themselves, but their message was one of cheerful impotence: The literate had no control over the language.[36]

And while some continued to defend the ethical import of the refined literary tradition,[37] literary naturalists argued that the dead weight of tradition must be cast aside for "life." Novelists like Stephen Crane, Theodore Dreiser, and Frank Norris all apprenticed at newspapers and popular magazines. So did Rudyard Kipling, who was also widely read in the United States in the 1890s. All developed an aggressively antirefined style. Norris, for example, despised any talk of style: "It is precisely what I try most to avoid. I detest 'fine writing,' 'rhetoric,' 'elegant English'—tommyrot. Who cares for fine style! Tell your yarn and let your style go to the devil. We don't want literature, we want life."[38]

The same debate reappeared over magazine prose. After 1885, a whole set of magazines appeared that suddenly became far more popular than the refined literary monthlies of the nineteenth century ever were. The writing of the new magazines—*Munsey's*, *McClure's*, and *The World's Work*—was more direct and colloquial than the measured cadences of magazines like *The Atlantic Monthly*, *Harper's Monthly*, or *Scribner's*. The new women's magazines, *Ladies' Home Journal*, *Cosmopolitan*, and *The Saturday Evening Post*, were more complicated, but they were also less thoroughly refined than *Godey's Lady's Book*. To us, the prose of the new magazines does not seem especially vivid; the gossip and adventure tales tame. The penchant for narrative instead of analysis and for bits of colloquial prose is different from the refined literature of the same era, but it no longer appears shocking. The more aggressive slang of *Time* and more relentless gossip of *People* have dulled our appreciation for these earlier efforts.[39]

At the time, however, the differences appeared sharp. Like the literary realist, the new editors, men like Edward Bok, S. S. McClure, Walter Hines Page, Frank Munsey, and George Horace Lorimer, attacked refined prose. Edward Bok of the *Ladies' Home Journal* argued that a "readable, lucid style is far preferable to what is called a 'literary style'—a foolish phrase since it often means nothing except a complicated method of expression." Walter Hines Page of *The World's Work* called for a "homely realism," arguing that modern life demanded writing with "more directness, more clearness, with greater nervous force." On the other side, Robert Underwood Johnson of the *Independent* argued that magazines had to continue to set a high tone for American life. He maintained that they were not to ignore literary tradition and had to guard against slang and vulgarity. Similarly, *The Nation* defended the "leisurely style" of Carlyle, Thackeray, Bagehot, and Arnold: "It is the public that needs to be converted to intellectual leisureliness; not the writer who needs to catch the fever of modern life."[40]

This turn-of-the-century debate between the refined and the colloquial also appeared as a controversy between the orator and the spellbinder. The last years of the nineteenth century witnessed the revival of the former and the birth of the latter. The orator was refined and well-read. His language was civil and well-wrought. Suddenly, at the close of the century, dozens of article appeared on contemporary and historical rhetoric. Two full-length histories of the subject were published in 1896.[41] In the following decade, six multi-volume collections of oratorical literature were published.[42] Among the editors were David Brewer of the U.S. Supreme Court, Chauncey Depew of the U.S. Senate, and William Jennings Bryan. It was all interpreted as part of the returning influence of educated men to public life. The tone of the collected orations was high (higher at times than the editors' own speech). T.B. Reed, Speaker of the House of Representatives, edited *Modern Eloquence*, a ten-volume set published in 1900. Reed noted that all speeches "delivered in the heat of debate" were excluded. Only included were those considered "oratorical literature."[43]

But at the same time that some were celebrating the orator's return, others were mourning his death. "Formal addresses in the large towns yielded chief place to the new spellbinding," wrote Cleveland Frederick Brown of the 1900 campaign. The orator was gone, argued Curtis Guild, Jr., replaced by the "spellbinder," who, like the modern business man, "concerns himself more with results than conventional methods, with matter rather than form."[44] The word *spellbinder* was coined in 1888, when two hundred Republican campaign orators attended a dinner in Delmonico's in New York and the city's press termed it the Spellbinder's Dinner. By the 1890s, the word was associated with modern stump speaking. The spellbinder was colloquial. He used slang. He flattered his audience. He habitually exaggerated. Yet *spellbinder* was not simply the late-nineteenth-century name for the vulgar rustic. Spellbinders were more relaxed, emphatic at times, but rarely vituperative. Moreover, the speeches were short. Speaking from the back of a train was a particularly important innovation and one that did not become standard campaign practice until 1900. Instead of candidates giving one or two very long speeches each day in the center of town, they now gave dozens of short speeches in dozens of towns, each speech often only five to ten minutes in length. Generally extemporaneous, the speeches were, as one commentator wrote, "frank and personal. . . ."[45]

One of the best spellbinders was Teddy Roosevelt. He had studied rhetoric at Harvard in the 1870s under Adams Sherman Hill and had, in fact, gotten extremely high grades in the subject. Yet his style owed very

little to the training. He was much too informal. His language was de-
cidedly colloquial; his gestures jerky. "If one were to judge by some
academic checklists of technical speech standards," a student of his rhetoric
has noted, "Roosevelt would rank low."[46] It was a judgment shared by
Roosevelt's contemporaries. "He had a style that did not lend itself to
moving oratory," Oscar Davis wrote. "As an orator," said Edgar Lee
Masters, "Mr. Roosevelt has nothing to say and says it as poorly as possible."[47]

Roosevelt never denied his lack of formal oratorical skills, yet he also
held such skills in low esteem. Like the literary naturalists, for T.R. the
very term *rhetoric* was one of abuse. He regularly attacked Woodrow
Wilson for his "empty elocution," his "veil of rhetorical phrases."[48] Nevertheless, Roosevelt was an extremely popular speaker, one of the "most
effective" in the nation.[49] His oratory was generally short, vigorous, and
direct. "Make your point as clear as possible," he once wrote, "and thrust
the steel well home."[50] Nothing was more important to Roosevelt than
dramatizing main points, something that explains both the disjointed,
shapeless character of his speeches and his penchant for striking phrases.

On the one hand, as Richard Murphy has pointed out, Roosevelt's
speeches are episodic, "excursionish," leaping from point to point. Even
T.R. himself admitted to "a certain lack of sequitur that I do not seem
able to get rid of." As Murphy writes:

> But one does not discover in the marked-up manuscripts of Roosevelt's
> speeches much experimenting in rhetorical architecture. Nor does one dis-
> cover in the final versions much consistent drift of thought, nor clearly
> marked progression to climaxes.

But if Roosevelt had little interest in crafting extended speeches he did
care about dramatically highlighting key points (and, one must add, dramatically highlighting himself). At this he was particularly good. "Speak
softly and carry a big stick," "the strenuous life," "the Square Deal"—all
are Roosevelt creations that have entered the public domain. He spoke of
"roughriders" years before the Spanish-American War, and he was one
of the first to talk about "throwing his hat in the ring." In 1898 he described
himself "as strong as a bull moose." He had the knack for finding just the
right word—"bully!"[51]

There was nothing unconscious about this. "I try to put the whole
truth in each sentence," he once claimed. And he argued that this was
necessary because of modern mass communication. "I've found how one

sentence quoted without context can be made to stab back and hurt me."
Find the phrase that newspapers will quote, Roosevelt thought, and you
can make sure *your* message gets across.[52]

Roosevelt's search for pithy sayings that would catch an audience's
attention also explains one of the most tedious elements of his rhetoric—
it is hopelessly cliché-ridden. Mom, pie, and the flag figure prominently.
Henry Steele Commager once explained this by saying that Roosevelt was
not really a political philosopher, but that misses the point.[53] Neither was
Lincoln a political philosopher, nor Churchill, Pericles, or Susan B. Anthony. Yet their speeches do not sound as tinny as T.R.'s. In large measure
this was because they reasoned with their audiences while Roosevelt ex-
horted his. Theirs was not a dry, formal, abstract reason, not a reason
divorced from humor, phrasemaking, or even insult. It was that discursive,
practical reasoning associated with classical public debate. For Roosevelt,
however, striking turns of phrase no longer complemented his rhetoric,
they *were* his rhetoric. They were what mass communication was all about.
With Roosevelt, we stand at the edge of the advertised politics of the late
twentieth century.

With Roosevelt, we can also see the casual and informal becoming an
aggressively masculine style. Kathleen Hall Jamieson has observed that
for centuries colloquial narrative was considered "feminine" and unsuited
for public discourse.[54] In fact, mid-nineteenth-century pioneers of the
colloquial like Henry Ward Beecher were sometimes labeled "effeminate."
But the informality of the spellbinders, literary naturalists, and the new
magazines was put in the service of a tough, postgenteel masculinity.
Indeed, T.R.'s speeches are full of militaristic and pugilistic metaphors.
Use "all the most bitingly severe language you can muster," he told an
ally, "it is useless to show mercy." What refined verbal critics thought
was *maybe* acceptable for men in private, the spellbinders treated as normal
public speech. As one commentator said of spellbinding: "Every-day man-
to-man talk was the rule."[55]

Yet this should not be taken to mean that the colloquial had the field
to itself. In 1900, there was open war between orators and spellbinders,
between "refined" and "modern" editors, between men of letters and
naturalists. And while the colloquial would become increasingly important
in twentieth-century political speech, it would never be the only style.
At the same time *spellbinding* was becoming a popular term, editors like
William Randolph Hearst and Joseph Pulitzer were reviving more raucous
styles, and papers like *The New York Times* were adopting those stylistic
principles taught in college composition classes—the plain style.[56] Just as

the new dictionaries and school English programs implied, there would always be a variety of idioms.

# IV

The debate was also about the self. The informality in magazines and public oratory had distinct nineteenth-century popular precedents, but until this period, such styles had never been so attractive to so many of the highly educated. That the colloquial entered the modern dictionary, school English program, and modern-language Bible movement indicated something very new. The debate between the formal and informal was in part about ways of life, about the identity of educated adults.

A number of historians have traced the rise of a more informal culture within the upper-middle class between 1890 and 1930. The 1890s saw the new celebration of the strenuous life, with men like Theodore Roosevelt and Alfred Mahan urging vigor over gentility. Shortly after the turn of the century, historian Beth Bailey has noted, the middle class began dating, a social custom previously thought vulgar and only for the lower classes. At the same time architects designing middle-class houses began doing away with the sitting room, the former locus of courtship. Previously a symbol of refined life, after 1900 it came to be seen as stuffy and formal. Lewis Erenberg has analyzed the rise of the cabaret in the teens and twenties; the middle class now had informal jazz emporiums to visit at night. And Lary May has analyzed the new popularity of movies in similar terms. Movies encouraged an easy informal, anti-Victorian approach to leisure culture, emphasizing consumption and expressiveness over thrift and restraint. Even etiquette books became more relaxed in the 1920s. Although they were still repositories of complicated rituals of interaction, a new toleration for smoking, slang, and other informalities previously forbidden crept into them after the First World War.[57]

The new interest in colloquial language should be seen as part of this larger drift to a more informal style of leisure life. Again, this was not an attack from below, as in the early nineteenth century. It was erosion from within. The currents of informality were not disconnected from the new preoccupation with expertise, rather they were part of a common assault on "gentlemanly" culture. Roosevelt's breezy public speaking was only the flip side of his well-known fascination with expert commissions and scientific research. While he owed little to rhetoricians, Roosevelt was a friend of Brander Matthews, the Columbia professor so important in popularizing the new philology. In 1906, after advice from Matthews, Roosevelt tried to convert the Government Printing Office to simplified spelling, one of the pet projects of late-nineteenth-century linguists.[58]

The new magazines reflected the same. Their breezy colloquial style was the flip side of their accent on specialization, a fact shrewdly observed in 1906 by Henry Mills Alden.[59] Edward Bok of the *Ladies' Home Journal* told women not to worry so much about refining themselves but to become "expert" homemakers. Walter Hines Page of *The World's Work* thought that one advantage of the "new" cultivated man over the old was his present-mindedness. Freed from the dust of the past (that is, the refined cultural heritage), the new educated man could keep up with the latest timely research.[60] In the original announcement of *McClure's* in 1893, it was said the magazine would be flashy *and* informative, promising adventure stories, truth "stranger than fiction," and the inside stories of personalities alongside the "newest knowledge"—"A popular and comprehensive report as gleaned in universities and elsewhere in all departments of knowledge."[61] In the next years *McClure's* contained reports on everything from new biblical anthropological research to the work of Harvard's new psychological laboratory. Also included was Brander Matthews explaining the linguists' new theories of language. Indeed, Matthews celebrated the new informality by citing the latest research. In this way, slang, the democratic idiom, was justified by the authority of experts.[62]

Educators favoring professionalism argued that modern life dictated the new accent.[63] But defenders of the gentleman saw only fractured human beings. Defenders of refined life bemoaned the loss of the "four-square man," the "Aristotelian man," the "well-rounded man." The gentleman's "hunger for wholeness" surfaced once more. "His dress, his gait, his bearing all combined to give the impression of careful dignity which yet had no suggestion of effort," wrote Ephraim Emerton of the gentleman. You didn't ask the gentleman what he had done, Emerton asserted. The gentleman simply *was*. Emerton implicitly noted the point being made at roughly the same time by the German sociologist Max Weber. Status was accorded to being instead of function. But that was changing. By 1900, Emerton wrote, "training" rather than "culture" was the educational ideal. Intellectual refinement fell to a "semi-civilized demand for a certifiable kind of expert." We were creating "mere specialists."[64]

The lopsided education of the specialist left everything save one area untrained. One by-product of "our modern system of specialists," wrote Rollo Ogden in 1892, was that "a man out of his speciality is no better than any other person."[65] The new experts, gentlemen argued, defined their authority through their special knowledge or skill and did not feel it necessary to distance themselves from popular customs.[66] From the late 1860s, Charles Eliot had hoped that the new education would mold young men who combined some special talent with "literary and linguistic culture," but the coming of football to campus raised some doubts. Eliot likened football to cockfighting and bullfighting, finding players and students "swayed by a tyrannical public opinion—partly ignorant and partly barbarous." In several editorials, *The Nation* and the New York *Evening Post* agreed.[67] Charles Eliot Norton also spoke of "vulgarity" replacing "refinement" among "the upper classes." Considering the "new" Harvard without civil cultivation, he wrote in 1900: "Our scholars are men of learning in the modern sense, and of very little literature. . . . No, the Cambridge of today is a town of prose, and the College is given over to science and athletics." Science and athletics—expertise and popular culture.[68]

Similarly, Arthur Reed Kimball was appalled to hear a Johns Hopkins Ph.D. lapse into slang when lecturing on Ruskin. "Young man," the lecturer enthused, "tie up to John! Tie up to John!" Kimball thought this "extreme" example did not "stand alone"; he found university lecturers of all kinds "dropping into slang."

> They are so much afraid of being thought conventional and formal, they seek so far afield to find the smart or clever thing to say, they are so well aware that the strong or clever phrase will "stick," that they resort to the same tricks of slang used in the newspaper.[69]

People like Norton and Kimball understood the alternation of learned and popular speech as a capitulation to nineteenth-century middling customs. It was a reasonable position. Indeed, machine politicians in the 1890s continued to defend sharp shifts in linguistic register as necessary to popular politics.[70] But now they were joined by academic linguists who argued that this was the normal way of talking. One of the best known works of the new philology was *Words and Their Ways in English Speech* (1901), written by two Harvard philologists, James Greenough and George Kittredge. "Popular" language, they argued, was not "the exclusive possession of a limited class"; it belonged to "the people at large." What made the educated unique was *not* their distance from popular language but their ability to roam through *both* learned and popular speech. "Every educated person," they wrote, "has at least two ways of speaking his mother tongue." A few years later, H. L. Mencken put it this way: "The exigencies of my vocation make me almost completely bilingual; I can write English, as in this clause, quite as readily as American, as in this here one."[71]

Writers on civic rhetoric believed that all approved behavior occurred within the frame of a "high" culture. Styles varied, of course. Learning to handle the varied idioms of refined culture was one key part of a liberal education. But even the informal speech of the gentleman or lady was a *refined* informality. One did not drop below the line separating the educated from the uneducated. The new linguists, however, had fewer scruples. Matthews claimed the "man in the street" was the only legitimate standard of usage. Greenough and Kittredge noted that the educated jumped back and forth from the "learned" to the "popular." Mencken claimed the same.

We should not ignore the limits of their populism. What seemed so "democratic" at the time was in fact part of a shift in the self-definition of the educated. "Popular" was no longer threatening because "learned" meant something new. Still, in 1900, the new linguistic informality seemed so daring, the idea of popular slang so shocking, that it appeared to *all* participants in the debate as a justification of common speech. The idea that immigrants might add to the language, as argued by Lounsbury and Matthews, appeared, and indeed was, quite progressive. No one explored the possibility that there might be various kinds of informality, each of them class-bound. No one pondered the implications of gender. No Gramsci appeared to explain linguistic status as an element of capitalism's hegemony.

Most of the debates at the turn of the century revolved around the simple poles of refined/colloquial, written/spoken, rhetoric/journalism. Yet a few saw deeper, suggesting that there were actually a number of distinct idioms, each with its own purpose. In *Words and Their Ways in English Speech*, Greenough and Kittredge argued that there were a plurality of acceptable usages. They included separate chapters on technical dialects, slang, learned and popular words, and literary language, as well as abundant material on various sorts of regional dialects, including Americanisms. With the exception of crude vulgarity, they contended, none was without a place in the language. Indeed, *Words and Their Ways* was without any "core" idiom around which the others floated. Instead, there were various dialects, each with its own logic, each with its own purpose. No simple test determined good or bad English: "The sole criterion of choice consists in the appropriateness of one's language to the subject or occasion."[72]

Seven years after *Words and Their Ways in English Speech* was published, the first attempt was made to develop the notion of "appropriateness" into a scientific linguistic theory. In 1909, George Phillip Krapp, an English professor at Columbia and friend of Brander Matthews, published *Modern English: Its Growth and Present Use* which contained the first tentative formation of what later would be called the theory of functional variation in speech. Krapp's theory was more subtle than can be described here,[73] but his basic idea that we varied speech styles to fit different situations proved enormously attractive to future linguists and became one of the guiding theories of much twentieth-century discussion of usage.[74] There was no absolute standard of correctness, Krapp argued, we shifted from one idiom to another to suit our needs. No words were intrinsically better or worse, they were only more or less appropriate to a particular situation. Krapp claimed that "popular" speech was equal to any other, the odor surrounding it was in reality sociological, not linguistic. It was considered "vulgar" only because of its class position. Thus, for Krapp, a black man speaking Black English or a factory worker speaking a vulgar dialect was using language appropriate to his situation, and therefore "correct." The message William Dwight Whitney had waffled over, Krapp spelled out boldly:

> One learns the lesson of the complete relativity of the value of language, that there is no such thing as an absolute English, but that language is valuable only as it effects the purpose one wishes to attain, that what is good at one time may be bad at another, and what is bad at one time may be good at another.[75]

Linguistic theories about the functional variation of speech reflected the growing trend among social scientists to refuse to define a core self, to think of human beings in terms of their roles.[76] Since the eighteenth century, social theorists have worried about the splintering of the self, but twentieth-century academics have taken it for granted, raised it to the level of theory. George Herbert Mead: "We divide ourselves up in all sorts of different selves with reference to our acquaintances. . . . There are all sorts of different selves answering to all sorts of different social relations. . . . A multiple personality is in a certain sense normal. . . ."[77] Already in 1890 in his *Principles of Psychology*, William James was spending a hundred tortured pages discussing the many different selves that each of us has.[78] Similar thoughts can be found in Weber, Parsons, Geertz, Berger and Luckmann, and a host of others. In much contemporary social science, man is pictured with roles to play instead of a character to preserve. One thinks of Erving Goffman's sociology, where the self disappears into an endless series of role-playing scenes. To Goffman, as one critic notes, "the central error is to suppose there *is* a substantial self over and beyond the complex presentations of role-playing, a mistake committed by those who wish to keep part of the human world 'safe from sociology.' "[79] *Ethos* dissolves into *persona*.

Yet where did all this leave the notion of character? Most philologists did not worry about it, they simply ignored the implications of their theory.[80] And progressive social thinkers like David Starr Jordan and Herbert Croly could still talk about character, although now often emphasizing doing one's job well instead of "personal culture."[81] But if the new academics were right and the self was simply an amalgam of roles, what happened to the very idea of principled behavior? The new theory solved nineteenth-century problems, undermining the aesthetic elitism of rhetoric and reconciling educated and popular culture. But it created new problems in the process. The most advanced linguistics, as a form of role theory, also destroyed the old rhetoric's capacity for criticism. The new linguistics became a theory of the actual, a *descriptive* theory of language that sanctioned all forms of popular speech simply because they were there.

Not only did new social theory have to be created; old theory had to be discredited, and in 1899, a book appeared that did just that. Only the last three pages of the book were on what was termed "classic English," but those three pages were important because they were embedded in a powerful social critique. The book became one of the most widely read pieces of social theory of the twentieth century. The author was Thorstein Veblen and the book was *The Theory of the Leisure Class*.

Veblen saw "elegant English" as conferring dignity and status. However, he also saw it as archaic and wasteful. He theorized that the upper classes expressed their status by their very leisure, by demonstrating their freedom from the constraints of productive labor. "Great purity of speech" revealed time "wasted in acquiring the obsolescent habit of speech," a life spent "in other than vulgarly useful occupations." Defenders of literary English had long associated refinement with civilization. Veblen turned that assumption upside down. Classic English, like all leisure-class culture, was "archaic," a sign not of civilization but of the residual leisure class attitudes of barbarians.

By interpreting "classic English" as an expression of the pecuniary culture, Veblen reinterpreted the social place of refined language. The verbal critics of the 1870s and 1880s defended their refinement in opposition to the moneymaking culture of America. They wanted to carve out a social space distinct from both the vulgar middling and the vulgar rich. Veblen, however, collapsed interest in refined speech into upper-class culture. People like the verbal critics were the educational arm of that culture.

Finally, Veblen denied that refined English actually contributed to easy communication. To Veblen, refined English was simply a status marker. A simple idea in itself, readers should understand what a monstrous challenge this was to the fundamental assumptions of civic eloquence. Defenders of rhetorical English argued that a reputation was secured for the effort in mastering the civil idiom. Effort and talent gave one a social reputation. Veblen, however, turned this around. Culture was an epiphenomenon of class. There was no intrinsic merit to learning classic English: "It is contended . . . that a punctilious use of ancient and accredited locutions will serve to convey thought more adequately and more precisely than would the straightforward use of the latest form of spoken English; whereas it is notorious that the ideas of to-day are effectively expressed in the slang of to-day." Refined English was no better than popular speech. It was an aesthetic tool of the ruling class.[82]

With Veblen we turn a corner. The defense of popular speech is connected to a distinctly postgentlemanly sense of self. The cool neutrality of science replaces the aesthetic elitism of rhetoric. The expert displaces the gentleman. The mystifications of the twentieth century appear in full dress. A new emperor is wearing all new clothes.

# Epilogue:
# The Post-Rhetorical Age

> . . . and human speech is like a cracked kettle
> on which we beat out tunes for bears to
> dance to, while all the while we long to move
> the stars to pity.

GUSTAVE FLAUBERT

It is a deep theme of literary modernism that language is exhausted. Mallarmé, Rimbaud, the early Wittgenstein, and others have all told us that language is dead, either false from the start or ruined by the modern world. Characteristically, American modernism entered more optimistically. Writers from Emerson to Mencken reveled in the American indifference to conventional speech. It harbored liberation, a new beginning. But pessimism could sink in here as well. Faulkner's Addie Bundren: "That was when I learned that words are no good; that words don't ever fit even what they are trying to say at." A word was "just a shape to fill a lack."[1]

Flaubert, however, suggests something else: Language is not exactly decrepit so much as hostage to the commonplace. The terror is more subtle. Language cannot call us to the high power that the old rhetoric wanted it to. It has no splendor. It is trapped in the mundane.[2]

Indeed, some of the most pervasive forms of mass communication suggest that Flaubert is on the mark. Informal, colloquial language now intrudes on all our public discussion. It is the idiom of the most effective popular oratory. Long infecting mass advertising, it is now critical to American politics.[3]

This was *not* simply the result of electronic media. The colloquial style's roots lie in Henry Ward Beecher's theology of feeling, a style implicitly blessed by academic linguists at the turn of the century. Politically, as Michael McGerr has noted, politics as advertising became important as early as 1916. And Robert Westbrook has observed that public relations entered American politics roughly the same time.[4] Nobody summed up the shift better than Dale Carnegie, the author of the phenomenally popular *How to Win Friends and Influence People*. Beginning in 1912, Carnegie taught businessmen the post-rhetorical sensibility, over the years reaching thousands and making a fortune. In 1926, Carnegie described the new idiom:

> An entirely new school of speaking has sprung up since the Civil War. In keeping with the spirit of the times, it is direct as a telegram. The verbal fireworks that were once the vogue would no longer be tolerated by an audience in this year of grace.
>
> A modern audience, regardless of whether it is fifteen people at a business conference or a thousand people under a tent, wants the speaker to talk as directly as he would in a chat, and in the same general manner that he would employ in speaking to one of them in conversation.[5]

The colloquial was connected to new forms of ritual interaction stressing friendliness over formality as a source of politeness. This is eminently democratic decorum, one that I love. Nothing is more ridiculous than those periodic efforts to undermine the egalitarian force of the colloquial by evoking more formal deportment. Slang (or blue jeans) will not destroy civilization and arguments that they will rest at least implicitly on misguided, and offensive, assumptions that a certain sort of taste is connected to principled behavior.[6]

But what is so comfortable in face-to-face behavior is problematic when extended to civic forms of public speech. Since Beecher, and into the television age, the public colloquial has valued feeling over information, personality over character. Far from trying to contribute to civic discussion, it has characteristically tried to evade it by placing undue emphasis on soothing conciliation. Thus Beecher's claim that speakers should evoke sympathy instead of argue theology. Soothing conciliation was also the goal of Franklin Roosevelt's fireside chats and Ronald Reagan's homiletics. The colloquial in public oratory has dulled critical faculties instead of exercising them.

The style also teaches disrespect for language. Words are undermined by being treated loosely. Here the sloganeering of mass advertising is crucial. Does "Wonder build strong bodies twelve ways?" What does it mean to say "Coke is it"? On a page like this such words seem trite and even silly. Analysis of their "truth claims" would be absurd. But that is the point. The characteristic half-truths and inflated claims are so common that they are taken for granted ("a lot more Chevette for a lot less money"). We accept them without having to believe them (". . . the first roast beef sandwich big and tasty enough for Burger King"). And we accept them in part precisely because they are so casually presented. The anthropologist Jules Henry once called this "pecuniary pseudo-truth" and saw it as characteristic of our time. After hearing so many puffed claims, so many slogans, people begin assuming that is what language is. "Pseudo-truth" is presumed normal.[7] And when this style is applied to political discourse ("Nixon's the One"), the problem only magnifies. In the United States (and the West), the distrust of language expressed in the phrase "that's just rhetoric" owes far more to colloquial inflation than to the kind of totalitarian big lie analyzed by Orwell. The sanctity of words slowly erodes like rock battered by the sea.

Another contemporary form of the commonplace is the plain style. The impulse for simple, declarative sentences is strong in twentieth-century culture. It is found in many of the best newspapers, and in one college composition text after another. By the 1930s, the College Entrance Examination Board had stopped asking prospective college students about literature and began asking about vocabulary and syntax. Interest in the mechanics of language took the place of literary English. The preference was codified in perhaps the most influential writing manual of our time, Strunk and White's *Elements of Style*. "The approach to style," they write, "is by way of plainness, simplicity, orderliness, sincerity."[8]

The idiom has its virtues. It is clear and informative. It treats its audience with respect. Unlike the colloquial, it is supposed to contribute to discussion and not evoke feeling. Yet the plain style also has drawbacks. There is an unhealthy preoccupation with *like/as* distinctions or avoiding split infinitives. What is "correct" is studied at the expense of what is appropriate to the setting. The plain style also creates the illusion that language can be like glass, a medium without the infusion of a self. It pretends the facts can speak for themselves in ways that the old rhetoric never did. The very style has helped perpetuate the belief that there are technical, apolitical solutions to political problems. It is perhaps the most deceptive style of them all.

The plain style and the colloquial were devised to address a large and diverse public.[9] Both helped submerge civic contention. So too did technical talk, another form of speech newly prominent at the close of the nineteenth century. Long opposed as anticivic, and condemned as a speech with a touch of vulgarity about it, specialized languages became celebrated as critical to the culture's health.

It is often said that jargon undermines civic discussion. But it does this variously. In some places it might contribute to elite control of public policy. Without understanding economics, how can I talk seriously about interest rates or unemployment? How many today understand nuclear physics with enough depth to argue cogently about safe levels of nuclear waste?

In other fields, however, professional vocabularies might breed irrelevance. Already in 1885, *The New York Times* demonstrated the possibilities. In an article entitled "The Philologists," the *Times* discussed a paper Francis March read at a professional convention. March had attacked another linguist for "recklessly" asserting that "glottogonic problems are insoluble" and that "inflections did not originate through agglutination." The paper took up mock outrage: "The shameless and brutal theories have been published, not in some obscure and disreputable newspaper, but in the great encyclopedia of the English-speaking race . . . No wonder Professor March's blood boiled."[10]

By the 1880s, making a career could mean moving *away* from civic concerns. One became a star by writing for one's peers in professional journals, not by addressing the public in the newspapers. At the same time the culture began awarding status to experts, professional conversation too easily became opaque and irrelevant to the uninitiated. And the 1885 editorial indicates that the *Times* was already capable of using what has become a stock gesture against professional pretensions. When the American Philological Association was created in 1869, it was worth three front-page articles in the *Times*.[11] The editors hoped the new organization would contribute to the fight against the shoddy standards of the half-educated. By 1885, the philological dispute occasioned only gentle ridicule, and the intramural debates of the experts were seen as pedantic, silly, and culturally insignificant. Philological jargon helped make philology irrelevant to civic discussion.[12]

The professional, the colloquial, and the plain styles all corrode civic discussion. The sanctioning of these styles in elite culture at the turn of the century is worth note, for the need to reconstruct a spirited public was a central concern of progressive social thought.[13] Yet it was not to be. Voting rates began to decline at the turn of the twentieth century, at roughly the same time that the new antipolitical styles were celebrated by the highly educated.[14] Of course, much was involved in the gradual decline of political partisanship, but certainly anticivic theories of language played their small part in the change.

Rhetoric's moralizing about style, still so common in the eighteenth century, fell into disrepute for good reason. It conflated refined words with refined morals. And whatever the problems with the culture of expertise, it has distinct benefits, helping generate, among other things, a standard of living not matched in human history. Still, the changes have not all been for the good. The same strains of thought that sanctioned popular speech also helped create one of our most potent forms of social power—the expert. The culture will continue to need and want such people, and for good reason. But while we should expect civic and technical discourse to mingle, we should also distrust either when it becomes imperious.

The new thinking about language has also, in small and subtle ways, helped sap the will for informed public debate. The blanket acceptance of popular speech paved the way for twentieth-century politics-as-advertising. And the plain style helped support the illusion of civic discussion void of civic debate. Of course, many kinds of rhetoric were used in the twentieth century. Martin Luther King's essentially romantic eloquence should by itself dispel any idea that I have surveyed all contemporary idioms. Still, the weight has shifted. We think about language differently, and this is connected to changed ways of life. Today, highly trained technocrats rule instead of aristocratic gentlemen. In such a culture we have less need to fear rhetoric's moralizing about style and more need of its civic lessons. In our public oratory, at any rate, we would be well served to relearn how to distrust the colloquial and manage the technical.

# APPENDIX

## Editions of Verbal Criticism and Scientific Philology Listed in the National Union Catalogue

| VERBAL CRITICISM | pre–1860 | 1860–70 | 1871–75 | 1876–80 | 1881–85 | 1886–90 | 1891–95 | 1896–1900 | 1901–05 | 1906–10 | Total |
|---|---|---|---|---|---|---|---|---|---|---|---|
| H. Alford, *Plea for the Queen's English* (1864) | — | 2 | 2 | 1 | 3 | 0 | 1 | 0 | 0 | 0 | 9 |
| G. W. Moon, *The Dean's English* (1864) | — | 4 | 2 | 0 | 2 | 0 | 0 | 0 | 0 | 0 | 8 |
| Edward Gould, *Good English* (1867) | — | 2 | 2 | 1 | 0 | 0 | 0 | 0 | 0 | 0 | 5 |
| G. W. Moon, *Bad English Exposed* (1868) | — | 1 | 0 | 0 | 0 | 0 | 0 | 0 | 0 | 0 | 1 |
| R. M. Bache, *Vulgarisms and Other Errors* (1869) | — | 2 | 0 | 0 | 1 | 0 | 0 | 0 | 0 | 0 | 3 |
| R. G. White, *Words and Their Uses* (1870) | — | 7 | 2 | 0 | 8 | 3 | 2 | 2 | 0 | 0 | 24 |
| W. Mathews, *Words: Their Use and Abuse* (1876) | — | — | — | 6 | 4 | 1 | 1 | 2 | 0 | 1 | 15 |
| R. W. White, *Everyday English* (1880) | — | — | — | 1 | 3 | 1 | 2 | 1 | 0 | 1 | 9 |
| L. T. Townsend, *The Art of Speech* (1882) | — | — | — | — | 5 | 0 | 1 | 0 | 0 | 0 | 6 |
| A. S. Hill, *Our English* (1890) | — | — | — | — | — | 2 | 1 | 1 | 0 | 0 | 4 |
| Total | 0 | 18 | 8 | 9 | 26 | 7 | 8 | 6 | 0 | 2 | 84 |

## MANUALS OF GOOD USAGE

| MANUALS OF GOOD USAGE | pre–1860 | 1860–70 | 1871–75 | 1876–80 | 1881–85 | 1886–90 | 1891–95 | 1896–1900 | 1901–05 | 1906–10 | Total |
|---|---|---|---|---|---|---|---|---|---|---|---|
| S. Hurd, *A Grammatical Corrector* (1847) | 1 | 0 | 0 | 0 | 0 | 0 | 0 | 0 | 0 | 0 | 1 |
| A. Peabody, *Conversation: Its Faults* (1852) | 3 | 1 | 0 | 0 | 1 | 0 | 0 | 0 | 0 | 0 | 5 |
| Anon., *Over 1000 Mistakes Corrected* (1856) | 2 | 0 | 0 | 0 | 0 | 0 | 0 | 0 | 0 | 0 | 2 |
| W. G. Farrington, *3000 Mistakes in English* (1860) | – | 1 | 0 | 0 | 0 | 0 | 0 | 0 | 0 | 0 | 1 |
| L. P. Meredith, *Everyday Errors of Speech* (1872) | – | – | 3 | 4 | 1 | 1 | 0 | 0 | 0 | 0 | 9 |
| W. Larrabee, *Helps to Speak and Write* (1873) | – | – | 1 | 0 | 0 | 0 | 0 | 0 | 0 | 0 | 1 |
| Anon., *Live and Learn* (187?) | – | – | 1 | 1 | 0 | 0 | 0 | 0 | 0 | 0 | 2 |
| H. Ballard, *Handbook of Blunders* (1881) | – | – | – | – | 1 | 2 | 0 | 0 | 0 | 0 | 3 |
| A. Ayres, *The Verbalist* (1882) | – | – | – | – | 5 | 5 | 4 | 4 | 2 | 2 | 22 |
| W. Hodgson, *Errors in the Use of English* (1882) | – | – | – | – | 3 | 4 | 1 | 0 | 1 | 0 | 9 |
| W. Griswold, *A Manual of Misused Words* (1882) | – | – | – | – | 1 | 0 | 0 | 0 | 0 | 0 | 1 |
| C. W. Bardeen, *Verbal Pitfalls* (1883) | – | – | – | – | 1 | 0 | 0 | 1 | 0 | 0 | 2 |
| O. Bunce, *Don't* (1884) | – | – | – | – | 2 | 3 | 0 | 2 | 1 | 0 | 8 |
| M. Bigelow, *Mistakes in Writing English* (1886) | – | – | – | – | – | 2 | 1 | 0 | 0 | 0 | 3 |
| S. Fallows, *Discriminate* (1886) | – | – | – | – | – | 1 | 0 | 1 | 1 | 0 | 3 |
| E. Avery, *Words Spoken Correctly* (1887) | – | – | – | – | – | 2 | 0 | 0 | 0 | 0 | 2 |
| J. H. Long, *Slips of the Tongue and Pen* (1888) | – | – | – | – | – | 2 | 0 | 1 | 0 | 0 | 3 |
| J. Bechtel, *Practical Synonyms* (1893) | – | – | – | – | – | – | 0 | 2 | 1 | 0 | 3 |
| J. Bechtel, *Slips of Speech* (1895) | – | – | – | – | – | – | 2 | 0 | 1 | 0 | 3 |
| J. Fitzgerald, *Pitfalls in English* (1895) | – | – | – | – | – | – | 2 | 3 | 3 | 1 | 9 |
| L. Bugg, *Correct English* (1895) | – | – | – | – | – | – | 1 | 1 | 0 | 0 | 2 |

## MANUALS OF GOOD USAGE

| | pre–1860 | 1860 –70 | 1871 –75 | 1876 –80 | 1881 –85 | 1886 –90 | 1891 –95 | 1896– 1900 | 1901 –05 | 1906 –10 | Total |
|---|---|---|---|---|---|---|---|---|---|---|---|
| A. Compton, *Some Common Errors of Speech* (1898) | – | – | – | – | – | – | – | 1 | 1 | 0 | 2 |
| J. Fitzgerald, *Word and Phrase* (1901) | – | – | – | – | – | – | – | – | 1 | 0 | 1 |
| R. H. Bell, *The Worth of Words* (1902) | – | – | – | – | – | – | – | – | 3 | 0 | 3 |
| Total | 6 | 2 | 5 | 5 | 15 | 22 | 12 | 14 | 14 | 3 | 98 |
| | | | | | | | | | | | |
| Total of Criticism and Handbooks | 6 | 20 | 13 | 14 | 41 | 29 | 20 | 20 | 14 | 5 | 182 |

## SCIENTIFIC PHILOLOGY

| | pre–1860 | 1860 –70 | 1871 –75 | 1876 –80 | 1881 –85 | 1886 –90 | 1891 –95 | 1896– 1900 | 1901 –05 | 1906 –10 | Total |
|---|---|---|---|---|---|---|---|---|---|---|---|
| F. March, *Method of Philological Study* (1865) | – | 4 | 3 | 3 | 1 | 0 | 1 | 0 | 0 | 0 | 12 |
| W. D. Whitney, *Language and Study of Language* (1867) | – | 4 | 4 | 0 | 2 | 2 | 4 | 1 | 2 | 0 | 19 |
| F. March, *Comparative Grammar of Anglo-Saxon* (1869) | – | 2 | 2 | 2 | 1 | 1 | 0 | 1 | 0 | 0 | 9 |
| F. March, *Introduction to Anglo-Saxon* (1870) | – | 2 | 3 | 2 | 2 | 1 | 1 | 1 | 0 | 0 | 12 |
| H. Corson, *Handbook of Anglo-Saxon* (1871) | – | – | 2 | 2 | 2 | 2 | 0 | 0 | 0 | 0 | 8 |
| F. Hall, *Recent Exemplifications of False Philology* (1872) | – | – | 1 | 0 | 0 | 0 | 0 | 0 | 0 | 0 | 1 |
| F. Hall, *Modern English* (1873) | – | – | 1 | 1 | 0 | 0 | 0 | 0 | 0 | 0 | 2 |
| W. D. Whitney, *Oriental and Linguistic Studies* (1874) | – | – | 3 | 2 | 0 | 0 | 1 | 0 | 0 | 0 | 6 |
| W. D. Whitney, *Life and Growth of Language* (1875) | – | – | 1 | 3 | 2 | 4 | 0 | 4 | 3 | 1 | 18 |
| T. Lounsbury, *History of the English Language* (1879) | – | – | – | 1 | 2 | 3 | 2 | 1 | 2 | 2 | 13 |

| SCIENTIFIC PHILOLOGY | pre–1860 | 1860–70 | 1871–75 | 1876–80 | 1881–85 | 1886–90 | 1891–95 | 1896–1900 | 1901–05 | 1906–10 | Total |
|---|---|---|---|---|---|---|---|---|---|---|---|
| F. Hall, *Doctor Indoctus* (1880) | – | – | – | 1 | 0 | 0 | 0 | 0 | 0 | 0 | 1 |
| G. Tucker, *American English* (1883) | – | – | – | – | 1 | 0 | 0 | 0 | 0 | 0 | 1 |
| R. O. Williams, *Our Dictionaries* (1890) | – | – | – | – | – | 1 | 0 | 0 | 0 | 0 | 1 |
| O. F. Emerson, *The Ithaca Dialect* (1891) | – | – | – | – | – | – | 1 | 0 | 0 | 0 | 1 |
| W. D. Whitney, *M. Müller and the Science of Language* (1892) | – | – | – | – | – | – | 1 | 0 | 0 | 0 | 1 |
| O. F. Emerson, *History of the English Language* (1894) | – | – | – | – | – | – | 1 | 0 | 0 | 0 | 1 |
| G. Tucker, *Our Common Speech* (1896) | – | – | – | – | – | – | – | 2 | 2 | 2 | 6 |
| O. F. Emerson, *Brief History of the English Language* (1896) | – | – | – | – | – | – | – | 1 | 0 | 0 | 1 |
| R. O. Williams, *Some Questions of English* (1897) | – | – | – | – | – | – | – | 3 | 0 | 2 | 5 |
| J. B. Greenough & G. L. Kittredge, *Words and Their Ways* (1901) | – | – | – | – | – | – | – | – | 3 | 4 | 7 |
| Total | 0 | 12 | 20 | 17 | 13 | 14 | 13 | 13 | 12 | 11 | 125 |

# Notes

## Introduction

1. Scholars writing about rhetoric often treat their subject as a history of ideas. The story then becomes the battle between philosophy and rhetoric, or science and rhetoric, or Romanticism and rhetoric. See, for example, Bruce Kimball, *Orators and Philosophers: A History of the Idea of Liberal Education* (New York: Teachers College Press, 1986); Samuel IJsseling, *Rhetoric and Philosophy in Conflict* (Netherlands: Martinus Nijhoff, 1976). Such works are extremely valuable, but they lose sight of the cultural dimension of their subject. The nineteenth-century attack on rhetoric, I want to stress, was rooted in popular culture as much as in any philosophical ideas. It became more difficult to live a rhetorical life.

Two notable books that take rhetoric seriously as cultural practice are Michael Mooney's *Vico in the Tradition of Rhetoric* (Princeton: Princeton University Press, 1975) and Kathleen Hall Jamieson's *Eloquence in an Electronic Age: The Transformation of Political Speechmaking* (New York: Oxford University Press, 1988). Even Brian Vickers's monumental *In Defense of Rhetoric* (Oxford: Oxford University Press, 1988), while calling for more attention to the culture of rhetoric, is basically a history of ideas.

2. J.G.A. Pocock, *The Machiavellian Moment: Florentine Political Thought and the Atlantic Republican Tradition* (Princeton: Princeton University Press, 1975), p. 501.

3. Jamieson, *Eloquence in an Electronic Age*, pp. 50–51. Jamieson's book appeared just as I was finishing my own. Her emphasis on the conversational style of contemporary discourse fits very well with my discussion of the new respect for the colloquial at the end of the nineteenth century.

4. C. S. Lewis, *European Literature in the Sixteenth Century* (Oxford: Clarendon Press, 1954), p. 61.

5. Jamieson, *Eloquence in an Electronic Age*, pp. 44–45.

6. For similar comments about the vagueness of the word *bourgeoisie*, see Simon Schama, *The Embarrassment of Riches: An Interpretation of Dutch Culture in the Golden Age* (Berkeley: University of California Press, 1988), p. 6; and Michel Foucault, *Power/Knowledge: Selected Interviews & Other Writings 1972–1977* (New York: Pantheon Books, 1980), p. 100.

Stuart Blumin's brilliant *The Emergence of the Middle Class: Social Experience in the American City, 1760–1900* (Cambridge: Cambridge University Press, 1989) appeared too late for me to incorporate his findings into my study. Blumin's social history goes far in making the term "middle class" a concrete social category. Let me point out that Blumin stresses the vagueness of language about the middle class prior to the Civil War (pp. 240–49), a theme compatible with what I say in chapter 2. I agree with Blumin that awareness of social differences was rising after the Civil War (pp. 285–90). I argue this in chapters 4, 5, and 6. I would add, however, that in those same postbellum years the denial of any sort of class structure had become a potent hermeneutic strategy, particularly in the middle of the social order (see chapter 6).

7. Roger Chartier, "Texts, Printing, Readings," in Lynn Hunt, ed., *The New Cultural History* (Berkeley: University of California Press, 1989), p. 169.

8. John Fiske, "Television: Polysemy and Popularity," *Critical Studies in Mass Communications* 3 (December 1986): 391–408.

9. Jeffrey Stout, *Ethics After Babel: The Languages of Morals and Their Discontents* (Boston: Beacon Press, 1988), p. 266; Alasdair MacIntyre, *After Virtue: A Study in Moral Philosophy* (Notre Dame: University of Notre Dame Press, 1981); on Adorno, see Martin Jay, "Hierarchy and the Humanities: The Radical Implications of a Conservative Idea," *Fin De Siècle Socialism* (New York: Routledge, 1988), pp. 37–51.

10. David Hollinger, "American Intellectual History: Issues for the 1980s," *Reviews in American History* 10 (1982): 306–17; Martin Jay, "Should Intellectual History Take a Linguistic Turn? Reflections on the Habermas-Gadamer Debate," *Fin De Siècle Socialism*, pp. 17–36. See also John Diggins, *The Lost Soul of American Politics* (New York: Basic Books, 1984), pp. 359–65.

11. Roland Barthes, *A Barthes Reader* (New York: Hill & Wang, 1982), p. 461.

12. For a critique of Gadamer, see Jay, "Intellectual History," esp. pp. 33–36. For criticisms of Geertz, see Ronald Walters, "Signs of the Times: Clifford Geertz and Historians," *Social Research* 47 (Autumn 1978): 537–51.

13. Hans Blumenberg, "An Anthropological Approach to the Contemporary

Significance of Rhetoric," in *After Philosophy: End or Transformation?*, ed. Kenneth Baynes, James Bohman, and Thomas McCarthy (Cambridge: MIT Press, 1987), p. 448.

# Chapter 1

1. *The Odyssey of Homer*, trans. Richmond Lattimore (New York: Harper & Row, 1967), p. 125; Cicero, *De Oratore*, 2 vols. (Cambridge: Harvard University Press, 1942), vol. 1, p. 25; the quotation on Webster is from Kathleen Hall Jamieson, *Eloquence in an Electronic Age: The Transformation of Political Speechmaking* (New York: Oxford University Press, 1988), p. 53.

2. Henry Peachum, *The Compleat Gentleman* (1622; reprint, Oxford: Oxford University Press, 1897), p. 8.

3. Hamilton Mabie, ed., *Plutarch's Lives*, 4 vols. (Philadelphia: John C. Winston Co., n.d.), vol. 4, p. 1709. For the best discussion of the civic character of rhetoric, see Michael Mooney, *Vico in the Tradition of Rhetoric* (Princeton: Princeton University Press, 1975), *passim*.

4. John Pocock, *The Machiavellian Moment: Florentine Political Thought and the Atlantic Republican Tradition* (Princeton: Princeton University Press, 1975), pp. 58–59; Elizabeth Eisenstein, *The Printing Press As an Agent of Change* (Cambridge: Cambridge University Press, 1979), p. 296; Hanna Gray, "Renaissance Humanism: The Pursuit of Eloquence," *Journal of the History of Ideas* 24 (1963): 497–514; Jerrold Seigal, *Rhetoric and Philosophy in Renaissance Humanism: The Union of Eloquence and Wisdom, Petrarch to Villa* (Princeton: Princeton University Press, 1968); Natalie Davis, "Poor Relief, Humanism and Heresy," *Society and Culture in Early Modern Europe* (Stanford: Stanford University Press, 1975), pp. 31–32.

5. Mooney, *Vico in the Tradition of Rhetoric*, p. 85.

6. J.A.W. Gunn, *Beyond Liberty and Property: The Process of Self-Recognition in Eighteenth-Century Political Thought* (Kingston: McGill-Queens University Press, 1983), pp. 260–315. The quote is from p. 281.

For a classic statement on the expanded reading public in the eighteenth century, see Ian Watt, *The Rise of the Novel* (Berkeley: University of California Press, 1967).

The work of Jürgen Habermas and Hannah Arendt on the "public sphere" has helped enormously in shaping my ideas about rhetoric. See Jürgen Habermas, *The Structural Transformation of the Public Sphere: An Inquiry into a Category of Bourgeois Society* (Cambridge: MIT Press, 1989); and Hannah Arendt, *The Human Condition* (Garden City, N.Y.: Anchor Books, 1959), esp. pp. 25–27, 82–83, 155–78. Also helpful on Habermas, Arendt, and the public sphere were Peter Uwe Hohendahl, *The Institution of Criticism* (Ithaca: Cornell University Press, 1982), pp. 242–80; and Claude Lefort, *Democracy and Political Theory* (Minneapolis: University of Minnesota Press, 1988), pp. 45–55. For a good discussion of the creation of the public sphere in eighteenth-century England, see Terry Eagleton, *The Function of Criticism* (London: Verso, 1984), pp. 9–20.

7. Erich Auerbach, *Literary Language and Its Public in Late Latin Antiquity and the Middle Ages* (New York: Pantheon, 1965), pp. 274–77.

8. Cicero, *De Oratore*, vol. 1, p. 101; vol. 2, pp. 31–33; Quintilian, *Institutes of Oratory*, 2 vols. (London: George Bell & Sons, 1891), vol. 1, pp. 37–39. On the Christian willingness to include vulgar language, see chapter 3.

9. Aristotle is quoted in James May, *Trials of Character: The Eloquence of Ciceronian Ethos* (Chapel Hill: University of North Carolina Press, 1988), p. 1; Thomas Elyot, *The Boke Named the Governour* (London: Everyman's Edition, 1907), p. 153; Hugh Blair, *Lectures on Rhetoric and Belles Lettres*, 3 vols. (London: W. Strahan, 1785), vol. 2, p. 460; and Ralph Waldo Emerson, "Eloquence," *Society and Solitude* (Boston: Houghton Mifflin & Co., 1885), p. 97.

10. See the important comments on the different possible ends of education in Hans Gerth and C. Wright Mills, eds., *From Max Weber: Essays in Sociology* (New York: Oxford University Press, 1946), pp. 426–38. Weber's distinction between education that cultivates a way of life and habits of thought (the gentlemanly ideal) and that which attempts to "train the pupil for practical usefulness for administrative purpose" (p. 426) will be very important throughout this work. So too will Weber's contention that education is more than schooling, that its purpose is to reproduce the social personality wanted by the culture at large.

Some of the last work of Michel Foucault has also been helpful in shaping my ideas about the self. Foucault was especially impressed with the classical effort to establish a "morality of style," an aesthetic of the self that embodied moral standards. This style, Foucault noted, embraced a whole self. An *ethos*, or character, was embodied in one's deportment. See Michel Foucault, "The Ethic of Care for the Self As a Practice of Freedom: An Interview," in *The Final Foucault*, ed. James Bernauer and David Rasmussen (Cambridge: MIT Press, 1988), pp. 1–20; and Michel Foucault, *The Use of Pleasure* (New York: Vintage Books, 1986), pp. 25–32.

11. Jonathan Lear, *Aristotle: The Desire to Understand* (Cambridge: Cambridge University Press, 1988), p. 168; on Foucault see Hayden White, "Foucault's Discourse: The Historiography of Anti-Humanism," in *The Content of the Form* (Baltimore: Johns Hopkins University Press, 1987), pp. 135–36; Foucault, "The Ethic of Care," p. 6; Cicero is quoted in Neal Wood, *Cicero's Social and Political Thought* (Berkeley: University of California Press, 1988), p. 102.

12. John Henley, *A Course of Academical Lectures* (London: J. Mac-Euen, 1731), p. 81; Sir Joshua Reynolds, *Discourses on Art* (New York: Collier Books, 1961), p. 151; L. H. Butterfield, ed., *The Book of Abigail and John: Selected Letters of the Adams Family, 1762–1784* (Cambridge: Harvard University Press, 1975), p. 284; David Hume, *Essays and Treatises on Several Subjects*, 3 vols. (London: A. Millar, 1764), vol. 1, p. 5; Richard Hurd, ed., *The Works of the Right Honourable Joseph Addison*, 8 vols. (London: T. Cardwell, 1811), vol. 2, p. 266. For the most comprehensive survey of humanistic educational theory from the Renaissance to the twentieth century, see R. S. Crane, *The Idea of the Humanities and Other Essays Critical and Historical* (Chicago: University of Chicago Press, 1967).

13. On the ancients, see Lear, *Aristotle*, pp. 164–91; and Wood, *Cicero's Social and Political Thought*, pp. 100–104. As Michel Foucault put it: "Care for the self is ethical in itself, but it implies complex relations with others, in the measure where this *ethos* of freedom is also a way of caring for others."

On modern decorum, the restraint of instincts, and civil respect for others, see Nobert Elias, *The Civilizing Process* (New York: Urizen Books, 1979).

14. On the Scottish philosophers, see Pocock, *Machiavellian Moment*, pp. 501–05; on Rousseau, see Karl Lowith, *From Hegel to Nietzsche* (Garden City, N.Y.: Anchor Books, 1967), p. 232; on Franklin, see Stephen J. Whitfield, "The Masters of Impression Management: Benjamin Franklin, Booker T. Washington, and Malcolm X As Autobiographers," *South Atlantic Quarterly* 77 (1978): 399–417; and Robert Sayre, *The Examined Self: Benjamin Franklin, Henry Adams, Henry James* (Princeton: Princeton University Press, 1964). Also see J. E. Crosley, *This Sheba, Self: The Conceptualization of Economic Life in Eighteenth-Century America* (Baltimore: Johns Hopkins University Press, 1974), *passim*.

15. Work that helped formulate my thoughts on the distinction between character and role playing include Vytautas Kavolis, "Logics of Selfhood and Modes of Order: Civilizational Structures for Individual Identities," in *Identity and Authority: Explorations in the Theory of Society*, ed. Roland Robertson and Burkart Holzner (New York: St. Martin's Press, 1979), pp. 40–60; George Arditi, "Role As a Cultural Concept," *Theory and Society* 16 (1987): 565–91; and Alasdair MacIntyre, *After Virtue: A Study in Moral Philosophy* (Notre Dame: University of Notre Dame Press, 1981), *passim*.

16. Diderot, *Rameau's Nephew and Other Works*, trans. Jacques Barzun and Ralph H. Bowen (Indianapolis: Bobbs-Merrill Co., 1956), p. 60. I have altered the translation somewhat.

17. John Strachey, ed., *The Letters of the Earl of Chesterfield to His Son*, 2 vols. (London: Methuen & Co., 1901), vol. 1, pp. 352–53. For a comprehensive discussion, see Sheldon Rothblatt, *Tradition and Change in English Liberal Education* (London: Faber & Faber, 1976), pp. 13–74.

18. Nelly Hoyt and Thomas Cassirer, eds., *Encyclopedia: Selections* (Indianapolis: Bobbs-Merrill Co., 1965), p. 32; John Locke, *Some Thoughts Concerning Education*, ed. R. H. Quick (Cambridge: Cambridge University Press, 1913), p. 121.

19. For particularly good discussions of the traditional connections between humanistic thought, rhetoric, and taste, see Hans-Georg Gadamer, *Truth and Method* (New York: Crossroad, 1988), pp. 10–39; and Mooney, *Vico in the Tradition of Rhetoric*, pp. 84–169. Richard Lanham, in *The Motives of Eloquence: Literary Rhetoric in the Renaissance* (New Haven: Yale University Press, 1976), pp. 1–35, very accurately notes that rhetoric needs to be understood not so much as a set of rules about language but as part of a comprehensive orientation toward being. But because Lanham tries to make Renaissance rhetoricians akin to postmodern literary theorists, he misconceives what that comprehensive orientation actually was. Lanham creates (or rather borrows) rigid distinctions between "playful" and "serious" attitudes toward language that have nothing to do with actual (and flexible) traditions of civic rhetoric. Lanham's failings can also be found in the late work of Roland Barthes and the writings of Paul de Man. Again, Gadamer and Mooney are far better guides for the connection of rhetoric to personality.

20. See Fritz Caspari, *Humanism and the Social Order in Tudor England* (Chicago: University of Chicago Press, 1954); Keith Thomas, *Religion and the Decline of Magic* (New York: Charles Scribner's Sons, 1971); Natalie Davis, "Proverbial Wisdom

and Popular Errors," *Society and Culture in Early Modern France*, pp. 227–67; and Keith Wrightson, *English Society, 1580–1680* (New Brunswick: Rutgers University Press, 1982).

21. Bernard Lamy, *The Art of Speaking* (London, n.p., 1708), p. 41; George Campbell, *The Philosophy of Rhetoric* (1776; reprint, New York: Harper and Brothers, 1844), p. 165. J. M. Toner, ed., *Washington's Rules of Civility and Decent Behavior* (Washington, D.C.: W. H. Morrison, 1888), p. 27.

22. Samuel Johnson, *A Dictionary of the English Language* (London: W. Strahan, 1755), s.v. "gentleman" and "vulgar." Also see Peter Laslett, *The World We Have Lost: England Before the Industrial Revolution* (New York: Charles Scribner's Sons, 1971), p. 27; and E. P. Thompson, "Patrician Society, Plebian Culture," *Journal of Social History* 7 (Summer 1974):382–405.

23. Edward Chamberlayne and John Chamberlayne, *Angliae Notitia: or, The Present State of England*, 22d ed., (London, n.p., 1707), p. 309. In the past two decades historians have done an enormous amount of work on the separation of high and popular culture in early modern Europe. For useful syntheses, see Peter Burke, *Popular Culture in Early Modern Europe* (New York: Harper Torchbooks, 1978); and Harry C. Payne, "Elite Versus Popular Mentality in the Eighteenth Century," *Studies in Eighteenth-Century Culture* 8 (1979): 3–32.

24. On copiousness, see Thomas Sheridan, *British Education, or, The Source of the Disorders of Great Britain* (Dublin: George Faulkner, 1756), p. 143; on the "elaborated code," see Basil Bernstein, *Class, Codes, and Control* (London: Routledge & Kegan Paul, 1971).

25. Walter J. Ong, S.J., "Latin Language Study As a Renaissance Puberty Rite," in *Rhetoric, Romance, and Technology* (Ithaca: Cornell University Press, 1971), pp. 113–41; Patricia Labalme, ed., *Beyond Their Sex: Learned Women of the European Past* (New York: New York University Press, 1980); for evidence of the high reputation of Catherine Macauley among American males, see H. Trevor Colbourn, *The Lamp of Experience* (New York: W.W. Norton & Co., 1965), pp. 63, 81, 86, 128–29, 153–54, 188.

26. Linda Kerber, *Women of the Republic: Intellect and Ideology in Revolutionary America* (Chapel Hill: University of North Carolina Press, 1980), pp. 13–32.

27. Cicero, *Offices, Essays and Letters* (London: J. M. Dent & Sons, 1909), p. 57; Strachey, *Letters of the Earl of Chesterfield*, vol. 1, pp. 268–69.

28. Cicero, *De Oratore*, vol. 2, pp. 81–83; Ong, "Latin Language Study," p. 132. The best introductory discussion of arguments traditionally used to limit women's public speech can be found in Jamieson, *Eloquence in an Electronic Age*, pp. 67–89.

29. Montesquieu, *The Spirit of Laws*, 2 vols. (New York: Hafner Publishing Co., 1949), vol. 1, pp. 30, 301; George Campbell, *Lectures on Systematic Theology, Pulpit Eloquence, and the Pastoral Character* (1772; reprint, London: Thomas Tegg, 1840), p. 312. Leonard Larabee, ed., *The Papers of Benjamin Franklin*, 24 vols. (New Haven: Yale University Press, 1959), vol. 1, pp. 14–17; vol. 3, pp. 397–421.

30. Dick Leith, *A Social History of English* (London: Routledge & Kegan Paul, 1983), pp. 49–57.

31. DeWitt Starnes and Gertrude Noyes, *The English Dictionary from Cawdrey to Johnson, 1604–1755* (Chapel Hill: University of North Carolina Press, 1946); James Sledd and Gwin Kolb, *Dr. Johnson's Dictionary* (Chicago: University of Chicago Press, 1955), pp. 134–41, 172–73, 175–77.

32. Johnson prefixed a grammar to his *Dictionary* but it was only twelve pages long. After spelling, pronunciation, and the parts of speech were explained, he left only twelve short lines for syntax. English had "so little inflection," Johnson wrote, "that its Construction neither requires nor admits many rules." Grammars existed in the early eighteenth century but grammarians were often pictured not as contributors to a refined language but as nit-picking pedants.

33. Thomas Dilworth's *A New Guide to the English Tongue*, first published in 1740, typical of the earlier texts, was primarily a speller but also contained about 40 pages of grammar. Robert Lowth's 1762 grammar, on the other hand, easily the best known in the late eighteenth century, had over 130 pages of grammatical rules and examples.

34. To compile the statistics on grammars, I have used the most comprehensive bibliography of English grammars published prior to 1800. R. C. Alston, *English Grammars Written in English* (Leeds: privately published, 1965). I have added to this list one more book, Thomas Dilworth's *A New Guide to the English Tongue* (1740) which was primarily a speller but included some grammar and was often used to study grammar in the second half of the eighteenth century. The publishing history of Dilworth I have drawn from R. C. Alston, *Spelling Books* (Bradford: privately published, 1967), pp. 67–82.

35. Samuel Johnson, "Preface," *Dictionary of the English Language*, n.p.; For the shift in opinion see Murray Cohen, *Sensible Words: Linguistic Practice in England, 1640–1785* (Baltimore: Johns Hopkins University Press, 1977), pp. 88–96; Robert Lowth has often been cited by historians of the English language as someone who wished to reform usage. For an important reassessment of Lowth, see G. K. Pullum, "Lowth's *Grammar*: A Re-evaluation," *Linguistics* 137 (1974): 63–78.

36. H. Lemonie, *The Art of Speaking* (London: Lee and Hurst, 1797), pp. 25–26.

37. For the eighteenth-century status of *piece, codger, prick,* and *bloody,* see Eric Partridge, *A Dictionary of Slang and Unconventional English,* 8th ed. (New York: Macmillian Co., 1984); Anselm Bayly, *A Plain and Complete Grammar of the English Language* (London: J. Rivington, 1772), p. 43; Philip Withers, *Aristarchus, or the Principles of Composition, Containing a Methodical Arrangement of Grammatical Improprieties of Common Discourse* (London: J. Moore, 1789), p. 160; and Adam Smith, *Lectures on Rhetoric and Belles Lettres,* ed. John Lothian (Carbondale: University of Southern Illinois Press, 1963), pp. 2–3.

38. Campbell, *Philosophy of Rhetoric,* pp. 170, 173; Johnson, "Preface," *Dictionary of the English Language,* n.p.

39. *The Conversation of Gentlemen,* p. 136; *Monthly Review* 4 (1751): 365.

40. Campbell, *Philosophy of Rhetoric*, p. 247.

41. Campbell, *Lectures on Systematic Theology*, p. 142.

42. John Clive and Bernard Bailyn, "England's Cultural Provinces: Scotland and America," *William and Mary Quarterly*, 3rd ser., 11 (April 1954): 210–11.

43. Sybil Rosenfeld, *The Theatre of the London Fairs in the Eighteenth Century* (Cambridge: Cambridge University Press, 1960), p. 65. Thompson, "Patrician Society, Plebian Culture," p. 389. In the United States the separation was probably not so definitive, but colonial gentlemen too attempted to shield themselves from the commonality in the second half of the century. Virginia gentlemen stopped socializing in public. See Rhyss Isaac, *The Transformation of Virginia* (Chapel Hill: University of North Carolina Press, 1982), pp. 302–5. In the 1760s large numbers of carriages were imported to the colonies for the first time. Very wealthy Americans now rode in the privacy of their coaches. Carl Bridenbaugh, *Cities in Revolt* (Oxford: Oxford University Press, 1955), p. 341.

44. Cicero, *Three Dialogues upon the Character and Qualifications of an Orator*, trans. William Guthrie, Esq. (London: T. Waller, 1755), pp. 27, 259–60. On eighteenth-century Ciceronianism, see Wilbur Samuel Howell, *Eighteenth-Century British Logic and Rhetoric* (Princeton: Princeton University Press, 1967), pp. 75–142.

45. Blair, *Lectures on Rhetoric*, vol. 2, pp. 222–23.

46. Smith, *Lectures on Rhetoric*, pp. 52–53; Blair, *Lectures on Rhetoric*, vol. 2, pp. 206, 223. Also see Howell, *Eighteenth-Century British Logic and Rhetoric*, pp. 441, 446, 536, 545, 573, 575.

47. Over eighty pages of Hugh Blair's rhetoric were devoted to analyzing Addison.

48. *Oxford English Dictionary*, s.v. "brazenfaced," "damnable," "lingo," "flippant," and "acquaintance." Robert Lowth, *A Short Introduction to English Grammar* (Philadelphia: n.p., 1775), p. 34; On the history of *you was*, see Otto Jesperson, *A Modern English Grammar on Historical Principles*, 5 vols. (Heidelberg: Carl Winter's Universitätsbuchhandlung, 1914), vol. 2, p. 48.

49. Lawrence Stone, *Family, Sex and Marriage* (New York: Harper & Row, 1977), pp. 349–52; *The World*, no. 199, October 21, 1756; Samuel Johnson, *The Idler and the Adventurer* (New Haven: Yale University Press, 1963), pp. 39–42, 86–87.

50. J. H. Plumb, *The Commercialization of Leisure in Eighteenth-Century England* (Reading: University of Reading Press, 1973); J. H. Plumb, "The Public, Literature and the Arts in the 18th Century," in *The Triumph of Culture: 18th Century Perspectives*, ed. Paul Fritz and David Williams (Toronto: A. M. Hakkert, 1972), pp. 27–48.

51. The publishing history of Johnson shows the volume getting smaller at the same time it was being reprinted more often. The eighteenth-century editions were as follows:

|        | 1750s | 1760s | 1770s | 1780s | 1790s | Total |
|--------|-------|-------|-------|-------|-------|-------|
| Folio  | 2     | 1     | 1     | 3     | 0     | 7     |
| Quarto | 0     | 0     | 2     | 3     | 3     | 8     |

| | | | | | | |
|---|---|---|---|---|---|---|
| Octavo | 2 | 3 | 4 | 2 | 8 | 19 |
| Miniature | 0 | 0 | 0 | 0 | 8 | 8 |

SOURCE: R. C. Alston, *The English Dictionary: A Bibliography* (Leeds: privately published, 1966).

52. John Ash, *Grammatical Institutes* (London: E. and C. Dilly, 1763), p. iii.

53. Plumb, *The Commercialization of Leisure*, p. 6; Sledd and Kolb, *Dr. Johnson's Dictionary*, p. 114.

54. James Boswell, *The Life of Samuel Johnson* (New York: Modern Library, n.d.), p. 633.

55. For a pioneering essay on the spread of genteel culture and the opposition to that spread, see Leo Lowenthal and Marjorie Fiske, "The Debate over Art and Popular Culture in Eighteenth-Century England," in *Common Frontiers of the Social Sciences*, ed. Mirra Komarovsky (Glencoe: The Free Press, 1957), pp. 33–112. What Lowenthal and Fiske call "popular culture" is, I would contend, actually the diffusion of genteel culture. What people at the time (and recent historians) called "popular" was the mixture of folk and urban artisan cultures that fell below the refined. *The World*, no. 175, May 6, 1756; Withers, *Aristarchus*, pp. 160–61; The quotation from the *Ladies' Monthly Museum* is found in Stone, *The Family, Sex and Marriage*, p. 351; *The World*, no. 199, October 21, 1756.

56. Caleb Bingham, *The Columbian Orator* (1797; reprint, Boston: Manning and Loring, 1804). The Harvard oration is found on p. 32; Charles Francis Adams, ed. *The Works of John Adams*, 10 vols. (Boston: Little, Brown & Co., 1852), vol. 7, p. 249; James Burgh, *The Art of Speaking* (Philadelphia: R. Aixten, 1780), pp. 5–6.

57. Warren Guthrie, "The Development of Rhetorical Theory in America, 1635–1850" (Master's thesis, Northwestern University, 1940), pp. 84–89; David Lundberg and Henry May, "The Enlightened Reader in America," *American Quarterly* 28 (Summer 1976): 263–71. By 1813, 61 percent of libraries surveyed owned a copy of Blair. At that time still only one book was more widely owned, but, instead of Locke's *Essay*, it was Smith's *The Wealth of Nations*.

58. Alfred Young, "George Robert Tewes (1742–1840): A Boston Shoemaker and the Memory of the American Revolution," *William and Mary Quarterly* 3rd ser., 38 (October 1981): 561–62; on the Pennsylvania constitution, see Eric Foner, *Tom Paine and Revolutionary America* (Oxford: Oxford University Press, 1976), pp. 125–26, 132.

59. Quoted in Gordon S. Wood, *The Creation of the American Republic 1776–1787* (New York: W.W. Norton and Co., 1969), pp. 397, 476, 500.

60. Royall Tyler, *The Contrast: A Comedy in Five Acts* (New York: Houghton Mifflin Co., 1920), p. 54. The play was written in 1787.

61. [Mercy Warren (?)], *The Blockheads: Or the Affrighted Officers, A Farce* (Boston, n.p. 1776), pp. 10–11, 17–19. On the eighteenth-century status of the double negative see Jesperson, *A Modern English Grammar*, vol. 5, p. 123.

62. William Hill Brown, *The Better Sort: Or, the Girl of Spirit* (Boston: Isaiah Thomas and Co., 1789), pp. 12, 14, 37–38.

63. Robert Munford, *The Candidates: or, the Humours of a Virginia Election* (1770; reprint; Williamsburg: The William Byrd Press, 1948), p. 18. Jonathan Sewall, *The Americans Roused; in a Cure for the Spleen* (New York: James Rivington, 1775), p. 8; *The Blockheads; or Fortunate Contractor, An Opera as it was Performed at New York* (London: n.p., 1782), p. 23.

64. Jack Durant's assessment of the relationship between the language and character of Mrs. Malaprop is also suited to describe Mrs. Sententious and Jemima Blockhead. See Jack D. Durant, *Richard Brinsley Sheridan* (Boston: Twayne Publishers, 1975), p. 71.

65. In one 1785 play, for example, characters named Madam Brilliant, Dr. Gallant, and Mr. and Mrs. Importance call for an end to the Spartan virtues of republicanism. Their new model for deportment is a visiting French aristocrat, M. Bon Ton. Madam Brilliant complains about the "rigid manners" of the republic and hopes for "the free and easy air which so distinguishes a man of fashion, from the self formal republican. . . ." Mr. and Mrs. Importance worry about the leveling spirit that reigns but Dr. Gallant argues that the elite should not hide itself from the mob. A "particular deportment" observed in public, he asserts, "more effectually preserves preeminence than shutting oneself up from the crowd." By "assuming an appearance above the commonality, we may stamp on our characters *a superiority of rank.*" Manners are no longer the expression of respect for others but a tool of class division. At the play's close, a character called Republican Heroine condemns the party for its "British gewgaws." *Sans Souci, Alias Free and Easy*, 2d ed. (Boston: Warden and Russell, 1785), pp. 4, 9, 12.

66. For example, the character Billy Dimple in Royall Tyler's *The Contrast* (1787), Worthnaught in Samuel Low's *The Politicians Out-Witted* (1789), Strutabout in Munford's *The Candidates* (1770), Mr. Pomposity and Count Dipper Dapper in *The Gubernatorial Collection* (1779), and Mrs. Flourish in *The Motley Assembly* (1779).

67. Samuel Low, *The Politician Out-Witted* (New York: W. Ross, 1789), p. 33.

68. *Debates at the Robin Hood Society* (New York: Robin Hood Society, 1774), pp. 6, 7, 10, 12, 13.

69. Low, *The Politician Out-Witted*, p. 35; Tyler, *The Contrast*, p. 87.

70. See, for example, Noah Webster, *Sketches of American Policy* (Hartford: Hudson and Goodwin, 1785), pp. 31, 44, 47; Merril Peterson, ed., *The Portable Thomas Jefferson* (New York: Viking Press, 1975), pp. 392–95.

71. On the mid-eighteenth-century shift in British prose style, see Ian Gordon, *The Movement of English Prose* (London: Longmans, 1966), pp. 144–48.

72. *American Museum or Repository* 4 (1788): 443; Noah Webster, *Dissertations on the English Language* (Boston: Isaiah Thomas & Co., 1789), p. 367; Noah Webster, *Massachusetts Magazine* 1 (July 1789): 441; *American Magazine* (June 1788): 537; "Critical Reflections on Style," *Massachusetts Magazine* 4 (April 1792): 237–38.

73. Henry Ford Jones, *Washington and His Colleagues* (New Haven: Yale University Press, 1920), pp. 6–11; Noah Webster, *An American Selection of Lessons in Reading and Speaking* (Hartford: Hudson & Goodwin, 1789), p. 14.

74. Bingham, *Columbian Orator*, pp. 289–93. On the practice of substituting *w* for *v*, see Webster, *Dissertations on the English Language*, pp. 112–14; and David

Staniford, *A Short but Comprehensive Grammar* (Boston: Manning and Loring, 1797), in which the practice is included in a list of vulgarities at the close of the book.

75. *Columbian Orator*, p. 192.

76. Witherspoon's four essays on American English are reprinted in Mitford Mathews, *Beginnings of American English* (Chicago: University of Chicago Press, 1931), pp. 14–30; Albert Henry Smith, ed., *The Writings of Benjamin Franklin*, 10 vols. (New York: The Macmillan Co., 1907), vol. 10, pp. 75–82; *Letters and other Writings of James Madison*, 4 vols. (New York: R. Worthington, 1884), vol. 3, pp. 172; Benjamin Rush, "A Plan for the Establishment of Public Schools and the Diffusion of Knowledge in Pennsylvania," in *Essays on Education in the Early Republic*, ed. F. Rudolph (Cambridge: Harvard University Press, 1965), pp. 18–19; Robert Green McCloskey, ed., *The Works of James Wilson*, 2 vols. (Cambridge: Harvard University Press, 1967), vol. 1, p. 231; Andrew A. Lipscomb, ed., *The Writings of Thomas Jefferson*, 20 vols. (Washington, D.C.: Thomas Jefferson Memorial Association, 1905), vol. 19, p. 215.

77. *American Magazine*, (September 1788): 739–40; *Massachusetts Magazine* 3 (September 1791): 569; Warren is quoted in Lester H. Cohen, *The Revolutionary Historians* (Ithaca: Cornell University Press, 1980), pp. 172, 173; on Rush, see his letter to David Ramsey in Robert L. Brunhouse, ed., "David Ramsey, 1749–1815: Selections from his Writings," *Transactions of the American Philosophical Society*, new ser., 55 (1965): 58.

78. Samuel Eliot Morison, ed., "William Manning's *The Key of Liberty*," *William and Mary Quarterly*, 3rd ser., 13 (April 1956): 231. Robert Coram, "Political Inquiries: to Which is Added, a Plan for the General Establishment of Schools throughout the United States" (1791), in Rudolph, *Essays on Education in the Early Republic*, pp. 135–36.

79. Quoted in Wood, *The Creation of the American Republic*, p. 486.

80. Not only did the interest in grammars and dictionaries climb after mid-century, so too did academic interest in rhetoric. Yale began emphasizing English public speaking in the 1750s. In 1753 the University of Pennsylvania named Ebenezer Kinnersley the nation's first chaired professor of English and Oratory. In a series of reports written during the 1750s Harvard authorities brooded over the poor oratorical skills of their students. They in turn stiffened standards and increased course requirements. At Pennsylvania, in 1768 two assistants were hired to lighten Kinnersley's burgeoning work load. John Witherspoon arrived at Princeton in the same year and was soon giving lectures on eloquence. Rhetoric and oratory were not forced on unwilling students, either. Students in the 1760s and 1770s created speaking clubs and pronouncing societies to hone the oratorical skills that would be useful later in life. Guthrie, "The Development of Rhetorical Theory," pp. 73–78.

81. On the limits of European thinkers, see Harvey Chisick, *The Limits of Reform in the Enlightenment: Attitudes Toward the Education of the Lower Classes in Eighteenth-Century France* (Princeton: Princeton University Press, 1981); Harry C. Payne, *The Philosophes and the People* (New Haven: Yale University Press, 1976).

82. Rush, "A Plan for the Establishment of Public Schools . . ." in Rudolph,

*Essays on Education in the Early Republic*, pp. 18–19; Carl N. Degler, *At Odds: Women and the Family in America from the Revolution to the Present* (New York: Oxford University Press, 1980), p. 308; Rollo LaVerne Lyman, *English Grammar in American Schools before 1850* (Chicago: University of Chicago Press, 1922), p. 73.

83. The number of grammars printed is compiled from Alston, *English Grammars Written in English*. Both Trueman in *The Politician Out-Witted* and Doctor Quiescent in *The Father* are pedantic grammarians. Francis Hopkinson, "Speech on the Learned Languages," *American Museum or Repository* 3 (1788): 541.

84. John Harrison and Peter Laslett, *The Library of John Locke* (Oxford: Oxford University Press, 1971); John Harrison, *The Library of Isaac Newton* (Cambridge: Cambridge University Press, 1978); Harold Williams, *Dean Swift's Library* (Cambridge: Cambridge University Press, 1932); *A Catalogue of Books Belonging to the Library Company of Philadelphia* (Philadelphia: B. Franklin, 1747), p. 4; Alfred C. Potter, "The Harvard College Library, 1723–35," *Publications of the Colonial Society of Massachusetts*, 25 (Transactions, 1922–24): 1–13; *A Catalogue of Books Belonging to the New York Society Library* (New York: H. Gaine, n.d.). Later catalogues attribute this first list to the early 1770s. Geoffrey Keynes, *The Library of Edward Gibbon* (London: Jonathan Cape, 1940), p. 161; Lipscomb, *The Writings of Thomas Jefferson*, vol. 4, p. 202; James Bonar, *A Catalogue of the Library of Adam Smith* (New York: Augustus M. Kelley, 1966).

85. Daniel Drake, *Pioneer Life in Kentucky, 1785–1800* (New York: Henry Schuman, 1948), pp. 146, 152, 161–65.

86. Elias Smith, *The Life, Conversion, Preaching, Travels and Sufferings of Elias Smith*, 2 vols. (Portsmouth, N.H.: Beck & Foster, 1816), vol. 1, pp. 31–32, 46–47, 49–50.

87. The discussion of Paine is drawn from Foner, *Tom Paine and Revolutionary America*, pp. 81–87.

88. Charles M. Wiltse, ed., *The Papers of Daniel Webster*, 5 vols. (Hanover, N.H.: Dartmouth University Press, 1974), vol. 1, p. 372. Jefferson's comments on Henry were taken down by Daniel Webster in 1824. Richard R. Beeman, *Patrick Henry: A Biography* (New York: McGraw-Hill Book Co., 1974), p. 25; Edmund Randolph, *History of Virginia* (Charlottesville: University of Virginia Press, 1970), p. 179.

89. Moses Coit Tyler, *Patrick Henry* (Boston: Houghton Mifflin & Co., 1887), pp. 9, 194; Beeman, *Patrick Henry*, p. 1; Wiltse, *Papers of Daniel Webster*, vol. 1, p. 373.

90. Wiltse, *Papers of Daniel Webster*, vol. 1, p. 372.

91. Richard M. Rollins, *The Long Journey of Noah Webster* (Philadelphia: University of Pennsylvania Press, 1980), p. 30; Webster, *Dissertations on the English Language*, p. 25.

92. Webster, *Dissertations on the English Language*, p. 27. For an excellent discussion of linguistic disputes between rationalists and defenders of custom, see Christopher Looby, "Phonetics and Politics: Franklin's Alphabet As a Political Design," *Eighteenth-Century Studies* 18 (Fall 1984): 18–30.

93. Webster, *Dissertations on the English Language*, pp. 396–97.

94. Noah Webster, *A Letter to Dr. David Ramsay* (New Haven: Oliver Steele &

Co., 1807), pp. 1, 27–28; Linda K. Kerber, *Federalists in Dissent* (Ithaca: Cornell University Press, 1970), pp. 96–102.

95. Adams, *The Works of John Adams*, vol. 6, p. 185; Lipscomb, *The Writings of Thomas Jefferson*, vol. 19, pp. 213–14. Adams was most detailed: "By gentlemen are not meant the rich or the poor, the high-born or the low-born, the industrious or the idle; but all those who have received a liberal education, an ordinary degree of erudition in liberal arts and science, whether by birth they be descended from magistrates and officers of government, or from husbandmen, merchants, mechanics, or laborers; or whether they be rich or poor."

# Chapter 2

1. John Murray Cuddihy, *The Ordeal of Civility* (New York: Delta, 1974), p. 189.

2. James F. Cooper, *The American Democrat* (1838; reprint, Baltimore: Penguin, 1969), p. 174; *Boston Quarterly Review* 1 (July 1838): 372.

3. For some typical examples, see Robert Manson Myers, *A Georgian at Princeton* (New York: Harcourt, Brace, Jovanovich, 1976), p. 122; Norman E. Eliason, *Tarheel Talk* (Chapel Hill: University of North Carolina Press, 1956), p. 79; and George Cary Eggleston, *Recollections of a Varied Life* (New York: Henry Holt and Co., 1910), p. 8.

4. For some examples, see Eugene D. Genovese, *Roll, Jordan, Roll* (New York: Vintage Books, 1974), pp. 431–41; Eliason, *Tarheel Talk*, pp. 238–40; Samuel Kirkham, *English Grammar in Familiar Lessons* (Rochester: Alling, Seymour & Co., 1841), pp. 206–7.

5. Beecher is quoted in Clifford E. Clark, Jr., "The Changing Nature of Protestantism in Mid-Nineteenth Century America: Henry Ward Beecher's *Seven Lectures to Young Men*," *Journal of American History* 57 (March 1971): 834.

6. Daniel Walker Howe, "Victorian Culture in America," in *Victorian America*, ed. Daniel Walker Howe (Philadelphia: University of Pennsylvania Press, 1976), p. 14.

7. Alexis de Tocqueville, *Democracy in America* (Garden City, N.Y.: Doubleday, 1969), p. 478; David Macrae, *The Americans at Home*, 2 vols. (Edinburgh: Edmonston and Douglas, 1870), vol. 2, p. 97.

8. Henry Ward Beecher, *Yale Lectures on Preaching*, 1st ser. (New York: J. B. Ford and Co., 1872), pp. 18, 54–59, 106–17, 124, 131–32, 170, 229, 230; Henry Ward Beecher, *Oratory* (1876; reprint, Philadelphia: The Penn Publishing Co., 1901), p. 17; Lionel George Crocker, *Henry Ward Beecher's Art of Preaching* (Chicago: University of Chicago Press, 1934), pp. 13–15, 93, 94; *The New York Times* 9 June 1856. Also see Daniel Calhoun, *The Intelligence of a People* (Princeton: Princeton University Press, 1973), pp. 256–91.

9. Stephen B. Oates, *With Malice Toward None: The Life of Abraham Lincoln* (New York: Harper & Row, 1977), pp. 10–13, 20–22, 246, 249–50.

10. Frank Luther Mott, *American Journalism*, 3rd ed. (New York: Macmillan

Co., 1962), pp. 228–53; Michael Schudson, *Discovering the News: A Social History of American Newspapers* (New York: Basic Books, 1978), pp. 12–60.

11. Quoted in Frederick Hudson, *Journalism in the United States* (New York: Harper and Bros., 1873), p. 523; also see, "Good Advice from George Washington to Bushrod Washington," *New York Tribune*, 14 April 1841.

12. William Harlan Hale, *Horace Greeley: Voice of the People* (New York: Harper & Row, 1950), p. 98; Allan Nevins, *The Evening Post: A Century of Journalism* (New York: Boni and Liveright, 1922), pp. 347–49; "The American Press, No. II, Metropolitan Dailies," *Round Table* 5 (May 25, 1867): 327–28; "American Slangography," *Chicago Tribune*, 20 March 1870. Almost any issue of the *Chicago Times* was laden with sensational vulgarity. For some comments on the *Chicago Times* see Gunther Barth, *City People* (New York: Oxford University Press, 1980), pp. 97–98. The advertisement for *Arthur's Home Gazette* is from the inside back cover of the January 1852 *Peterson's Ladies' National Magazine*. The *Commercial Advertiser* ad is in *Trow's New York City Directory* (New York: Trow's Printing and Bookbinding Co., 1881).

13. It might be suggested that price and not style was the basis for popularity. This misses, I believe, the basic congruity between style and price. Cheap papers generally had a more populist tone. Expensive papers had a more refined demeanor.

14. Lawrence W. Levine, *Highbrow/Lowbrow: The Emergence of Cultural Hierarchy in America* (Cambridge: Harvard University Press, 1988), pp. 60–69, 178–84.

15. John E. Kilpatrick, *Timothy Flint: Pioneer, Missionary, Author, Editor, 1780 –1840* (Cleveland: Arthur H. Clark Co., 1911), pp. 94–95; Timothy Flint, *Recollections of the Last Ten Years* (Boston: Cummings, Hilliard & Co., 1826), p. 51.

16. "Pioneered," of course, does not mean that they invented the idiom. Eighteenth-century precursors should not be forgotten.

17. Robert Gray Gunderson, *The Log-Cabin Campaign* (Lexington: University of Kentucky Press, 1957), pp. 174–82; Sydney Nathans, *Daniel Webster and Jacksonian Democracy* (Baltimore: Johns Hopkins University Press, 1973), pp. 130–43. For examples of refined gentlemen who converted to the new style, see Bayard Tuckerman, ed., *The Diary of Philip Hone*, 2 vols. (New York: Dodd, Mead and Co., 1889), vol. 2, p. 22; and Allan Nevins, ed., *The Diary of George Templeton Strong*, 3 vols. (New York: Macmillan Co., 1952), vol. 2, p. 301.

18. Beecher, *Yale Lectures on Preaching*, pp. 51, 60, 61, 131, 172, 235.

19. "Improprieties of Speech," *Southern Literary Messenger* 3 (1837): 222; "English Language in America," *Southern Literary Messenger* 2 (1836): 111.

20. My assessment is based on the hundreds of essays, comments, and books written about the English language I have perused that were written between the mid-eighteenth and mid-nineteenth centuries. On the origin of *slang*, see the *Oxford English Dictionary*.

21. *Slang* is a word that has had many definitions, most of them far too loose to be useful for anything. Here I have followed the definitions used by the *OED*. In the eighteenth century, the word was little used because more common and more resonating words were available. Words were *vulgar* and *barbarous*, they were not *slangy*. An example of how the word shifted in meaning early in the nineteenth

century can be seen in the first two editions of Frederic Grose's *Dictionary of the Vulgar Tongue*. Published in 1785, the book was intended to be an account of low language. The word *slang* was not included. But in 1811, an unknown editor expanded the collection and published it under the name *A Dictionary of Buckish Slang, University Wit and Pickpocket Eloquence*. The slang came from all social strata.

22. See Richard H. Thornton, *An American Glossary*, 2 vols. (Philadelphia: J. B. Lippincott Co., 1912), vol. 2, p. 805; Sir James Craigie and James Hurlbut, *A Dictionary of American English on Historical Principles*, 5 vols. (Chicago: University of Chicago Press, 1940), vol. 4, p. 2138; Mitford Mathews, *A Dictionary of Americanisms*, 2 vols. (Chicago: University of Chicago Press, 1951), vol. 2, p. 1560.

23. Harry Warfel, ed., *Letters of Noah Webster* (New York: Library Publishers, 1953), pp. 521–22; Nevins, *Diary of George Templeton Strong*, vol. 1, p. 137; "Party Names," *New York Tribune*, 23 April 1841.

24. Rev. M. B. Buckley, *Diary of a Tour in America* (Dublin: Sealy, Bryers, and Walker, 1889), pp. 151–52, 223, 334–35.

25. Sarah Wentworth Morton, *My Mind and its Thoughts* (Boston: Wells and Lilly, 1823), pp. 5–6; "Plain Spoken People," *Harper's Bazaar* 1 (August 29, 1861): 690; "A Piece of One's Mind," *Harper's Bazaar* 10 (Feburary 2, 1877): 66; "Plain Speaker," *Our Boys and Girls* 11 (May 1872): 340–41; "Careless English," *St. Nicholas* 2 (January 1875): 194.

26. For examples, see Morton Keller, *Affairs of State: Public Life in Late Nineteenth-Century America* (Cambridge: Harvard University Press, 1977), pp. 247–48, Don Harrison Doyle, *The Social Order of a Frontier Community: Jacksonville, Ill. 1825–70* (Urbana: University of Illinois Press, 1978), p. 45.

27. Robert Remini, *Andrew Jackson and the Course of American Freedom, 1822–1832* (New York: Harper & Row, 1981), pp. 365–67; Nathans, *Daniel Webster*, pp. 45–46; Lynn Marshall, "The Strange Stillbirth of the Whig Party," *American Historical Review* 72 (1967): 448–50; Tuckerman, *Diary of Philip Hone*, vol. 1, p. 124.

28. James Parton, *The Life of Horace Greeley* (New York: Mason Brother, 1855), pp. 265–66.

29. "Editor's Table," *Knickerbocker Magazine* 46 (November 1855): 526–27.

30. "Editor's Table," *Knickerbocker Magazine* 34 (December 1849): 552–53; Thomas J. McCormick, ed., *Memoirs of Gustav Koerner, 1809–1896*, 2 vols. (Cedar Rapids: The Torch Press, 1909), vol. 1, pp. 335–36; also see de Tocqueville, *Democracy in America*, pp. 497–500; Thomas Hamilton, *Men and Manner in America*, 2 vols. (Edinburgh: William Blackwood, 1833), vol. 1, p. 68.

31. Richard Hurd, ed., *The Works of the Right Honourable Joseph Addison*, 8 vols. (London: T. Cardwell, 1811), vol. 2, pp. 401–02.

32. For a typical complaint against the transcendentalists, see Paul F. Boller, Jr., *American Transcendentalism, 1830–1860* (New York: Capricorn Books, 1974), p. 169. For a typical complaint against the utilitarians, see Hugh Legare, "Jeremy Bentham and the Utilitarians," *Southern Review* 4 (January 1833): 265–66.

33. H. L. Mencken, *The American Language*, 4th ed. (New York: Alfred A. Knopf, 1937), p. 302.

34. James F. Cooper, *Notions of the Americans*, 2 vols. (Philadelphia: Lea and Blanchard, 1840), vol. 1, p. 478.

35. D. H. Meyer, *The Instructed Conscience: The Shaping of the American National Ethic* (Philadelphia: University of Pennsylvania Press, 1972), pp. 65–67. Walker is quoted on pp. 65–66.

36. Hugh Blair, *An Abridgement of Lectures on Rhetoric* (Exeter: n.p., 1821), p. viii; J. C. Zachos, *Introductory Lessons in Reading and Elocution* (New York: A. S. Barnes & Co., 1857), p. ii; I. Ebbert, "The English Language," *Ladies' Repository* 1 (1841): 283.

37. "Afoot-Part III," *Blackwood's Magazine* 8 (August 1857): 210.

38. Samuel Smiles, *Character* (Chicago: Belford Clarke & Co., 1884), p. 259. Smiles went on to say that manners were very useful and should be cultivated if possible. The exact same book, word for word, was packaged for young girls under the title *Happy Homes and the Hearts that Make Them*.

39. Roy P. Basler, ed., *The Collected Works of Abraham Lincoln*, 8 vols. (New Brunswick: Rutgers University Press, 1953), vol. 1, pp. 95–100, 383–84; vol. 2, p. 56.

40. Michel Foucault has argued that Christian morality was generally conceived in terms of following specific rules instead of molding a self. Consequently, Christianity placed less emphasis on the morality of style. Michel Foucault, *The Uses of Pleasure* (New York: Random House, 1986), pp. 28–32.

41. "Conversation," *The Friend* 10 (July 9, 1837): 318–19; "Grammar or No Grammar," *The Friend* 19 (September 5, 1846): 398.

42. See the delightful comments by Henry Fairlie in "Why I love America," *The New Republic* (July 4, 1983): 12.

43. De Tocqueville, *Democracy in America*, pp. 565–67; W. MacKean, *Letters Home During a Trip to America* (privately printed, 1875), p. 114; Frances Trollope, *Domestic Manners of the Americans* (New York: Vintage, 1948), p. 99; Ernest Duvergier de Hauranne, *A Frenchman in Lincoln's America*, 2 vols. (Chicago: Donnelley and Sons, 1974), vol. 2, p. 226.

44. Hamilton, *Men and Manners*, vol. 2, p. 4; Michel Chevalier, *Society, Manners, and Politics in the United States* (Boston: Weeks, Jordan & Co., 1839), p. 433; MacKean, *Letters Home*, p. 42; Robert Ferguson, *America During and After the War* (London: Longmans, Green, Reader and Dyer, 1866), p. 21; George Jacob Holyoake, *Among the Americans* (Chicago: Belford, Clarke & Co., 1881), p. 184; Marianne Finch, *An Englishwoman's Experience in America* (London: Richard Bentley, 1853), p. 106.

45. See, for example, Hamilton, *Men and Manners*, vol. 1, p. 252; Hauranne, *A Frenchman in Lincoln's America*, vol. 2, p. 226.

46. Buckley, *Diary of a Tour in America*, pp. 291–92. Buckley's trip took place in 1870. Fanny Kemble, *Journal of Frances Anne Butler*, 2 vols. (London: J. Murray, 1835), vol. 1, pp. 111–12; Trollope, *Domestic Manners of the Americans* p. 100; Peter A. Munch, ed., *The Strange Way: Letters of Caja Munch* (Carbondale: Southern Illinois University Press, 1970), p. 30.

47. Kemble, *Journal of Frances Anne Butler*, vol. 1, p. 89; Charles Augustus

Murray, *Travels in North America*, 2 vols. (London: Richard Bentley, 1854), vol. 1, p. 102; Nevins, *Diary of George Templeton Strong*, vol. 4, p. 522; J. H. Holland, "Familiarity," *Everyday Topics: Second Series* (New York: The Century Co., 1893), p. 289.

48. Eggleston, *Recollections*, p. 214.

49. Doris Yoakam, "Women's Introduction to the American Platform," in *A History and Criticism of American Public Address*, ed. William Norwood Brigance, 4 vols. (New York: Russell & Russell, 1943–55), vol. 1, pp. 157–60; Robert Oliver, *History of Public Speaking in America* (Boston: Allyn and Bacon, Inc., 1965), pp. 438–39; the most sophisticated article on this issue, and one I have followed, is Kathleen Edgerton Kendall and Jeanne Y. Fisher, "Frances Wright on Women's Rights: Eloquence Versus Ethos," *Quarterly Journal of Speech* 60 (February 1974): 58–68.

50. Yoakam, "Women's Introduction," pp. 160–64; *The Liberator*, 20 October 1837.

51. Ibid., pp. 164–77, 184–85; on the speakers' bureau, see the *New York Tribune*, 9 September 1859.

52. Annette Shelby, "The Southern Lady Becomes an Advocate," in *Oratory in the New South*, ed. Waldo W. Braden (Baton Rouge: Louisiana State University Press, 1979), p. 211.

53. Of the 203 lyceum lecturers that the *New York Tribune* listed as available for 1859, only 12 of them were women. *New York Tribune*, 9 September 1859.

54. Hauranne, *A Frenchman in Lincoln's America*, vol. 1, pp. 281–82, 285.

55. Tuckerman, *Diary of Philip Hone*, vol. 1, pp. 308–9; George W. Burnap, *Lectures to Young Men on the Cultivation of the Mind, the Formation of Character, and the Conduct of Life* (Baltimore: John Murphy, 1841), pp. 94–95.

56. McCormick, *Memoirs of Gustav Koerner*, vol. 1, pp. 335–36.

57. Genovese, *Roll, Jordan, Roll*, pp. 268–69.

58. For excellent discussions of the relationship between speaker and audience in nineteenth-century America, see Ronald P. Formisano, *The Transformation of Political Culture: Massachusetts Parties, 1970s–1840s* (New York: Oxford University Press, 1983), p. 476; Neil Harris, *Humbug: The Art of P. T. Barnum* (Chicago: University of Chicago Press, 1973), pp. 61–89.

59. See, for example, the June 9, 1856, *New York Times* article on Beecher discussed in note 8. In chapter 3, I will discuss Romantic linguistic theory in this light. Also there see George Templeton Strong's assessment of Abraham Lincoln.

60. Rollo LaVerne Lyman, *English Grammar in American Schools before 1850* (Chicago: University of Chicago Press, 1922), p. 80; The most comprehensive single list of early-nineteenth-century grammars is found in Goold Brown, *The Grammar of English Grammars* (New York: W. Wood, 1878), pp. xi–xx. Brown lists more than three hundred grammars published in the early nineteenth century. Why Lyman ignored grammars cited by Brown is unclear.

61. Lyman, *English Grammar*, p. 81; Samuel Kirkham in "Editor's Table," *Knickerbocker Magazine* 10 (October 1837): 358. The number of Murray editions is drawn from the *National Union Catalogue*. The Cooper and Scott statistics come

from M. Francis Cooper, ed., *A Checklist of American Imprints* (Metuchen, N.J.: Scarecrow Press, 1972).

62. Elias Smith, *The Life, Conversion, Preaching, Travels and Sufferings of Elias Smith*, 2 vols. (Portsmouth, N.H.: Beck & Foster, 1816), p. 46; S. G. Goodrich, *Recollections of a Lifetime of Men and Things I Have Seen* (New York: Miller, Orton & Mulligan, 1856), p. 38; "Popular Education," *North American Review* 23 (1826): 53.

63. *Report of the Superintendent of Common Schools, Pennsylvania, 1854*, p. 4.

64. W. T. Harris, "How I was Educated," *The Forum* 1 (1886): 556; S. C. Bartlett, "How I was Educated," *The Forum* 2 (1886): 19; Eggleston, *Recollections*, p. 33.

65. Jonathan Messerli, *Horace Mann* (New York: Alfred A. Knopf, 1972), p. 12; Oates, *With Malice Toward None*, p. 20; James E. Sefton, *Andrew Johnson and the Uses of Constitutional Power* (Boston: Little, Brown, 1980), p. 11; Glyndon G. Van Deusen, *Horace Greeley: Nineteenth-Century Crusader* (New York: Hill and Wang, 1953), p. 8.

66. The American grammarians were simplifiers. With grammar a school subject, a clear, simple presentation had a market value. There was no secret to this. Many grammarians advertised that they were restating established principles in the clearest possible prose.

67. For an excellent discussion of the British version of this debate, see Olivia Smith, *The Politics of Language, 1791–1819* (Oxford: Clarendon Press, 1984).

68. Noah Webster, *Dissertations on the English Language* (Boston: Isaiah Thomas and Co., 1789), pp. viii, 27–28, 37–38, 182, 186–201; Noah Webster, *A Philosophical and Practical Grammar of the English Language* (New Haven: Brisbon and Brannan, 1807), pp. 3–13; on the inability to find the book in Boston, see William B. Fowle, *The True English Grammar, Second Part* (Boston: Munroe and Francis, 1829), pp. 15–16.

69. William S. Cardell, *Elements of English Grammar Deduced from Science and Practice* (Windsor: Simeon Ide, 1828), pp. ix, x; John Lewis, *Observations on the Objects and Progress of Philological Enquiries* (Fredericksburg: Minor, 1827), p. 5. Apart from the work of Cardell, Webster, and Lewis, the most important reform grammars were William B. Fowle, *The True English Grammar* (Boston: Munroe and Francis, 1827); Joseph Wright, *A Philosophical Grammar of the English Language* (New York: Spinning and Hodges, 1838); James Brown, *An American System of English Syntax* (Philadelphia: T. K. & P. G. Collins, 1838); James Brown, *An Appeal from the Old Theory of English Grammar* (Philadelphia: Grubb and Reazor, 1845); and Hugh Doherty, *An Introduction to English Grammar on Universal Principles* (London: Simpsin, Marshall & Co., 1841).

70. Noah Webster, *A Letter to the Honorable John Pickering* (Boston: West and Richardson, 1817), p. 10; Webster, *Philosophical and Practical Grammar*, p. 25.

71. Cardell, *Elements of English Grammar*, p. 91; Webster, *Philosophical and Practical Grammar*, p. 119; Fowle, *True English Grammar, Second Part*, p. 27.

72. Fowle, *True English Grammar, Second Part*, p. 9; James Gilchrest, *Philosophic Etymology or Rational Grammar* (London: R. Hunter, 1816), pp. 220, 207, 218, 219.

73. William S. Cardell, *Essay on Language as Connected with the Faculties of the Mind* (New York: Charles Wiley, 1825), pp. 1, 2, 28, 39; Webster, *A Philosophical and Practical Grammar*, pp. 3, 4, 13; John Lewis, *Analytical Outlines of the English Language* (Richmond: Shepherd and Pollard, 1825), pp. 16–18.

74. Fowle, *True Grammar, Second Part*, p. 25; Gilchrest, *Philosophic Etymology*, p. 207.

75. Hans Aarsleff, *The Study of Language in England, 1780–1860* (Princeton: Princeton University Press, 1967), p. 73.

76. Elias Norton, "William Bentley Fowle," *New England Historical Genealogical Register* 22 (April 1889): 109–17; Fowle, *True Grammar, Second Part*, p. 9.

77. Kirkham, *English Grammar*, p. 34; For the negative view of Joseph Wright, see *Knickerbocker Magazine* 11 (June 1838): 556–57. For other negative assessments of the reformed grammars, see "Webster's Grammar," *Monthly Review* 5 (1808): 267–77; "Correspondence," *Monthly Review* 7 (1809): 366–71; "Fowle's English Grammar," *United States Literary Gazette* 2 (June 1827): 201–8; R. G. Parker, "Reforms in Grammar," *North American Review* 25 (1827): 451–57; S. Williard, "Lewis's Outlines of the English Language," *North American Review* 23 (1826): 109–24; Asa Rand, "On Teaching Grammar and Composition," *Lectures Delivered Before the American Institute of Education* (Boston: Carter Hendee and Co., 1832), pp. 167–71; Goold Brown, "On Grammar," *Lectures Delivered Before the American Institute of Instruction* (Boston: Hilliard, Gray, Little and Wilkins, 1832), pp. 159–60.

78. For example, in the 1837 *Annual Report of the Regents of the State of New York*, twelve of twenty-eight academies discussed how to decide linguistic authority. Eleven cited reputable authors, polite custom, or standard grammars and dictionaries. Only one cited "analogy and philosophy of language" (p. 93). In 1847, all respondents cited customary usage as the standard.

79. In Massachusetts, Murray sank quickly in the late thirties. In 1837 Smith was used in 208 schools and Murray in 104. By 1840, Smith was used in 237 schools and Murray only in 54. See Lyman, *English Grammar in American Schools*, p. 86. By 1839, Smith was used in 113 schools in Connecticut. His nearest rival, Murray, was used only in 34 schools. See *Connecticut Common School Journal* 2 (June 1840): 224. On Ohio, see *Annual Report of the Secretary of State on the Conditions of Common Schools, Ohio, 1848*, p. 32. As in Massachusetts, Murray fell from favor in New York during the thirties. Whereas in 1830 Murray was used in 472 New York schools and Kirkham only in 28, by 1839 Murray was used only in 209 common schools while Kirkham was used in 427. *Annual Report of the Superintendent of Common Schools, New York, 1839*, p. 147. On Kirkham in Indiana, see Eggleston, *Recollections on a Varied Life*, p. 33. On Kirkham in Illinois, see Oates, *With Malice Toward None*, p. 20. On Vermont, see *Annual Report of the State Superintendent of Common Schools, Vermont, 1848*, p. 21; *Annual Report of the State Superintendent of Common Schools, Vermont, 1849*, p. 52. On New Hampshire, *Annual Report upon the Common Schools of New Hampshire, 1852*, 61–67.

80. The textbooks were based in varying degrees on Pestalozzian theory. What was called "object" learning was stressed, which meant learning through example rather than through memorization of rules. The spread of the new grammars is

a good indication of the Pestalozzian sentiment among common school teachers in the 1830s.

81. "Philology," *The Portland Magazine* 1 (August 1835): 349; Goold Brown, "On Grammar," *Lectures Delivered Before the American Institute of Instruction* (Boston: Hilliard, Gray Little and Wilkins, 1832), pp. 151, 159; Kirkham, *English Grammar*, pp. 205–7; Goold Brown, *The Institutes of English Grammar* (New York: n.p., 1823), p. 306; lists of "Jack Downingisms" in *Common School Journal* 1 (1839): 188, 203, 218–19, 236, 347, 361; Richard Parker, "On the Teaching of English Grammar," *The Lectures Delivered Before the American Institute of Instruction* (Boston: William D. Tickner, 1839), pp. 129–30.

82. David Simpson, in his *The Politics of American English, 1776–1850* (New York: Oxford University Press, 1986), discusses the early-nineteenth-century radical grammarians. His account is misleading, however, in suggesting that the philosophical grammars "prefigure a style and posture that would become, in various forms, much more popular from the late 1820s onward . . ." (p. 135). It is true that the grammars did have a populist tone; it is also true that a populist public rhetoric did become prevalent by the 1830s. But the radical grammars were not harbingers of the new popular idiom. Even "populist" journalists and orators studied conservative grammars.

83. Peter Bullions, *Analytical and Practical Grammar of the English Language* (New York: Sheldon & Co., 1854), p. 224; Kirkham, *English Grammar*, pp. 17, 18.

84. I have worked from the most complete bibliography of English dictionaries compiled, R. C. Alston, *The English Dictionary: A Bibliography* (Leeds, privately printed, 1966), *passim*. Emily Ellsworth Ford Skell, ed., *Mason Locke Weems, His Works and Ways*, 3 vols. (Norwood Mass.: Plimpton Press, 1929), vol. 2, pp. 169, 197, 268, 271, 275, 279, 398–99.

85. The files of the Merriam-Webster Company now in the Beinecke Library of Yale University have many unsolicited letters praising the dictionary from rural doctors and lawyers. See also, "Medical Culture," *Boston Medical and Surgical Journal* 38 (1848): 296–301.

86. On the different school and pocket dictionaries compiled by Americans, see Eva Mae Burkett, *American Dictionaries of the English Language before 1861* (Metuchen, N.J.: The Scarecrow Press, 1979), pp. 43–80. Although the *National Union Catalogue* is not reliable on the editions of dictionaries, the last listed American publication of Johnson in miniature is 1833.

87. Albert Henry Smyth, ed., *The Writings of Benjamin Franklin*, 10 vols. (New York: Haskell House, 1970), vol. 10, pp. 75–82; James Gilchrest, *Philosophic Etymology or Rational Grammar*, pp. 253–69.

88. In the introduction to the dictionary, Webster stated that Tooke's research was "very limited." "I have made no use of his writings, in this work," Webster asserted. But when discussing his orthographical reforms, Webster consistently relied upon etymology and analogy in justifying his proposed changes. Analogy, to Webster, was "the only authority from which there can be no legitimate appeal." Webster, "Introduction," *An American Dictionary of the English Language* (New Haven: Hezekiah Howe, 1828).

In an 1837 letter to the British lexicographer Charles Richardson, Webster again spoke of Tooke's many empirical mistakes, but Webster also said that the "great first principle laid down by Tooke, that a word has one meaning and one only and that from this all usages are derived, is substantially correct. . . ." Warfel, *Letters of Noah Webster*, p. 462. Webster continued to draw on the basic principles of Tooke even as he felt that Tooke's empirical research was woefully inadequate. This is not to say that there weren't differences. While Tooke had argued that the primordial unit of language was the noun, Webster asserted that it was the verb. For a very sophisticated dissection of this and other aspects of Webster's linguistics, see V. P. Bynack, "Noah Webster's Linguistic Thought and the Idea of an American National Culture," *Journal of the History of Ideas* 45 (1984): 99–114.

In my text, I am painting Webster as a linguistic "radical." Much recent scholarship has taken the opposite approach, trying to picture Webster's linguistics as essentially conservative. For examples, see Joseph J. Ellis, *After the Revolution: Profiles of Early American Culture* (New York: W.W. Norton & Co., 1979), pp. 211–12; and Richard M. Rollins, *The Long Journey of Noah Webster* (Philadelphia: University of Pennsylvania Press, 1980), pp. 123–43. These interpretations miss the specific context of early-nineteenth-century linguistic debate. When this context is unpacked, Webster clearly falls on the side of the rationalist radicals. The work of Ellis and Rollins also assumes that there must be some correspondence between Webster's conservative politics and his linguistics. There is no reason to assume this. Webster himself, in 1823, cautioned against such a connection. In an essay on education Webster argued that students should not readily question political or religious authority, but in subjects such as history, geography, *and philology*, where "it is often difficult, and sometimes impossible, to arrive at truth," students should "withhold implicit confidence in the opinions of other men however respectable; and in current tradition, however sanctioned by time and authority." Webster then went on for over thirty pages describing the errors of contemporary philological theory, including attacks on Robert Lowth and Lindley Murray. Noah Webster, *Letters to a Young Gentleman Commencing His Education* (New Haven: S. Converse, 1823), pp. 21–55. The quotations are from pp. 21–22. Those who paint Webster's philology as conservative fail to address the point so elegantly made by Linda Kerber some time back—cultural conservatives hated Webster's linguistics. See Linda Kerber, *Federalists in Dissent: Imagery and Ideology in Jeffersonian America* (Ithaca: Cornell University Press, 1970), pp. 96–102.

89. "A New Dictionary," *Boston Courier*, 28 September 1829; Lyman Cobb, *A Critical Review of Noah Webster's Spelling Book* (Albany: n.p., 1828). In 1831 Cobb expanded and republished the pamphlet under the title *A Critical Review of the Orthography of Dr. Webster's Series of Books for Systematick Instruction in the English Language* (New York: Collins & Hannay, 1831); "Webster's Dictionary and Spelling Book," New York *Evening Post*, 27 June 1829. The *New York Morning Herald* series began on July 4, 1829, and lasted until the end of August. On August 27, Sherman Converse, Webster's editor, responded to the series of articles and on September 5, the critic responded to Converse.

90. For an account sympathetic to Webster, see William Fowler, *Printed, but not Published* (privately printed, n.d.), pp. 1–8; for Goodrich's somewhat lame

defense, Chauncey Goodrich to Sherman Converse, March 1854. Both documents are in the Goodrich Family Collection, Sterling Memorial Library, Yale University. Webster's will is in the Noah Webster Papers, New York Public Library.

91. Burkett, *American Dictionaries*, p. 179.

92. "Chauncey Allen Goodrich," *Dictionary of American Biography* (New York: Charles Scribner's Sons, 1931), vol. 7, pp. 399–400; *Catalogue of the Officers and Students of Yale College, 1854–55*, pp. 36–37; Chauncey Goodrich, ed., *Selected British Eloquence* (New York: Harper and Bros., 1852); Chauncey Goodrich, "Lectures on Rhetoric and Public Speaking," *Speech Monographs* 14 (1947): 1–37.

93. Goodrich to Merriam, December 30, 1844, Goodrich File, H1844, Merriam-Webster Papers, Beinecke Library, Yale University; Fowler to Goodrich, August 19, 1845, Goodrich Family Collection, in Sterling Memorial Library, Yale University; Merriam to Goodrich, October 16, 1845, Goodrich Family Collection; Goodrich to Merriam, June 9, 1845, Goodrich File, H1845, Merriam-Webster Papers.

94. Ellsworth to Goodrich, February 16, 1846; Goodrich to Fowler, February 12, 1846; Fowler to Goodrich, February 16, 1846; Fowler to Goodrich, February 9, 1846; Ellsworth to Goodrich, July 1, 1847. Goodrich Family Collection, Sterling Memorial Library, Yale University.

95. Oliver Wendell Holmes, *The Professor at the Breakfast Table* (Boston: Little, Brown, 1893), p. 44.

96. A. Roane, "English Dictionaries, with Remarks upon the English Language," *Southern Literary Messenger* 22 (1852): 172, 170.

97. "Report of minority of committee on literature in reference to the purchase by school districts of Webster's Dictionary," [New York] *State Senate Document No. 89, 1851*, pp. 3, 7.

98. Ibid., pp. 2–3.

99. Epes Sargent, *The Critic Criticised: A Reply to a Review of Webster's System* (Springfield: G. and C. Merriam Co., 1856), pp. 15–16; Rev. John Maclay, "The Battle of the Dictionaries," *Ladies' Repository* 20 (September 1860): 519; William F. Poole, *The Orthographical Hobgoblin* (Springfield: G. and C. Merriam Co., 1859), pp. 5, 6, 11.

100. "Noah Webster's Dictionary," Boston *Daily Advertiser*, 29 July 1853; "Review of Webster's System," *United States Democratic Review* 37 (1856): 189–99; "Webster's Dictionary," *New York Home Journal*, March 19, 1859; "Worcester's and Webster's Dictionary," *DeBow's Review* 28 (1860): 566–73; "Worcester's Dictionary," *The New York Times*, supplement, 26 May 1860; "Review of Worcester," *Knickerbocker Magazine* 55 (June 1860): 636–37; and "The Two Dictionaries," *New York World*, 15 June 1860. This sample does not include literary journals published in Boston such as *The Atlantic Monthly* or the *Christian Examiner* which never failed to support Worcester.

101. Allen Walker Read, "The War of the Dictionaries in the Middle West," in J. E. Congleton et al., eds., *Papers on Lexicography in Honor of Warren N. Cordell* (Terre Haute: University of Indiana Press, 1979), pp. 3–16.

102. "Report of the committee on literature on the bill to furnish Webster's Unabridged Dictionary to common schools of this State," [New York] *State Senate Document No. 81, 1851*; George and Charles Merriam, *A Gross Literary Fraud Exposed* (Springfield: G. and C. Merriam Co., 1854), p. 10; "Webster's Unabridged Dictionary," *The American Journal of Education* 2 (1856): 517.

103. Allen Walker Read, "The War of the Dictionaries in the Middle West," in Congleton, *Papers on Lexicography*, pp. 15–16; Frank Moody Milles, *Early Days in a College Town* (Sioux Falls: Sessions Printing Co., 1924), p. 150; "Dictionaries," *Western Monthly* 3 (1870): 69.

104. The number of testimonial letters from the South in the Merriam-Webster Archives is minuscule compared to those from the rest of the country. Many of those are not unlike that of A. W. C. Cummings, president of Odd Fellows Female College in Rogersville, Tennessee, who wrote the Merriams in 1855: "When I entered upon my duties as President of this College, some months since, I was not a little surprised to find not one copy of Webster's Dictionary in the Institution, either among students or teachers." A. W. C. Cummings to Merriams, April 9, 1855; Merriam-Webster Archives, Beinecke Library, Yale University.

105. From New York, the *Evening Post, Times, World*, and *Knickerbocker Magazine* all published reviews favorable to Worcester. For examples of the more tolerant attitudes in Boston and New Haven, see untitled review, *The Atlantic Monthly* 5 (1860): 631–37; and "Worcester's Dictionary," *New Englander* 18 (1860):412–28.

106. For the standard interpretation of the dictionary war, see Ronald A. Wells, *Dictionaries and the Authoritarian Tradition* (The Hague: Mouton, 1973), pp. 67–69. Joseph E. Worcester, *A Dictionary of the English Language* (Boston: Wm. Swan & Co., 1860), pp. iii, 1–liii; "Webster's Octavo Dictionary," *Methodist Quarterly Review* 30 (January 1848): 106; and I. W. Andrews, *Webster's Dictionaries* (Springfield: G. and C. Merriam Co., 1856), pp. 4, 6. This pamphlet was first published as a series of articles in the *Marietta Intelligencer*.

107. "The War of the Dictionaries," *The New York Times*, 7 August 1860; "Worcester's Dictionary," *Christian Examiner* 68 (May 1860): 365; "Webster's Dictionary," *New Englander* 6 (January 1848): 24.

108. Levine, *Highbrow/Lowbrow, passim*; Cathy Davidson, *Revolution and the Word* (New York: Oxford University Press, 1987).

109. George Cary Eggleston, *How to Educate Yourself* (New York, G. P. Putnam & Sons, 1872), p. 23; James Parton, *Life of Andrew Jackson*, 2 vols. (New York: G. P. Putnam & Sons, 1860), vol. 1, pp. 67–68; David Crockett, *The Autobiography of Davy Crockett* (New York: Charles Scribner's Sons, 1923), pp. 17–18.

110. Frederick Douglass, *My Bondage and My Freedom* (New York: Miller, Orton & Mulligan, 1855), pp. 156–58.

111. Arda Walker, "The Educational Training and Views of Andrew Jackson," *The East Tennessee Historical Society's Publications*, no. 16 (1944): 25–26; Sefton, *Andrew Johnson*, p. 43; Oates, *With Malice Toward None*, pp. 98, 176–77, 196.

112. "Are We a Polite People? Our Gentlemen," *Harper's New Monthly Magazine* 15 (1857): 388; Macrae, *The Americans at Home*, vol. 1, p. 43; Bernard J. Stern,

ed., *Young Ward's Diary* (New York, G. P. Putnam's Sons, 1935), pp. 82, 132–33; *New York Tribune*, 8 June 1846.

113. Theodore Zeldin, *France, 1848–1945: Taste & Corruption* (Oxford: Oxford University Press, 1980), p. 315.

114. Nathan Glazer, *Affirmative Discrimination: Ethnic Inequality and Public Policy* (New York: Basic Books, 1975), p. 176.

115. "Good Manners in Journalism," *The New York Times*, 15 April 1868.

# Chapter 3

1. Wordsworth and Coleridge, *The Lyrical Ballads* (1798), ed. W. J. B. Owen (Oxford: Oxford University Press, 1969), p. 3.

2. C. C. Felton, "Review of *Hyperion*," *North American Review* 50 (1840): 148; Joel Porte, ed., *Emerson in His Journals* (Cambridge: Harvard University Press, 1982), p. 241.

3. Erich Auerbach, *Literary Language and Its Public in Late Latin Antiquity and the Middle Ages* (New York: Pantheon, 1965), pp. 31–66.

4. *The Holy Bible: 1611 Edition* (Nashville: Thomas Nelson, 1982).

5. "English Translations of the Bible," *Bibliotheca Sacra* 15 (April 1858): 286.

6. "Dr. Van Rensselaer's Reply to Dr. Vermilye's Rejoinder," *Presbyterian Magazine* 7 (December 1857): 548; R. C. Malan, *A Vindication of the Authorized Version* (London: Bell and Daldey, 1856), p. xv; Seth Adams, ed., *The Works of Fisher Ames*, 2 vols. (Boston: Little, Brown, 1854), vol. 2, pp. 406; "The Life and Writings of St. Paul," *Dublin Review* 34 (June 1853): 466. This last quote, with the reference to heresy removed, was often used by American Protestants to praise the King James Bible.

7. On Baptist sectarian translations, see my Ph.D. dissertation, "Democratic Eloquence: Language, Education, and Authority in Nineteenth-Century America" (University of Chicago, 1986), pp. 152–66; on Mormon efforts, see Robert J. Matthews, *A Plainer Translation: Joseph Smith's Translation of the Bible* (Provo: Brigham Young University Press, 1975); and Richard L. Bushman, *Joseph Smith and the Beginnings of Mormonism* (Urbana: University of Illinois Press, 1984).

8. Leicaster Ambrose Sawyer, trans., *The New Testament* (Boston: J. P. Jewett and Co., 1858), p. iii.

9. *Dictionary of American Biography*, 1935 ed., s.v. "Leicaster Ambrose Sawyer."

10. On the introduction of biblical criticism in the United States, see Jerry Wayne Brown, *The Rise of Biblical Criticism in America, 1800–1870* (Middletown: Wesleyan University Press, 1969); and Philip F. Gura, *The Wisdom of Words: Language, Theology, and Literature in the New England Renaissance* (Middletown: Wesleyan University Press, 1981), pp. 15–31.

11. J. A. Ernesti, *Elementary Principles of Interpretation*, trans. Moses Stuart (Andover: Allen, Morrill, and Wardwell, 1824); Leicaster Ambrose Sawyer, *The Elements of Biblical Interpretation* (New Haven: A. H. Maltby, 1836), pp. 34–43,

68. On Ernesti's place in German intellectual history, see Hans Frei, *The Eclipse of Biblical Narrative: A Study in Eighteenth and Nineteenth Century Hermeneutics* (New Haven: Yale University Press, 1974), pp. 247–49, 251–55.

12. As far as possible, quotations from the King James Bible will be identified in the text by chapter and verse. Footnotes will contain references only to Sawyer's version. Sawyer, *New Testament*, p. 160.

13. Ibid., p. 16. On *myths* for *fables*, compare 2 Peter 1:16 with Sawyer's *New Testament*, p. 369. On *little girls* for *damsels*, compare Matthew 5:39 with Sawyer, p. 76. On *brothers*, Leicester Sawyer, trans., *The Holy Bible Containing the Old and New Testament*, 2 vols. (Boston: Walker, Wise and Co., 1861), vol. 2, p. 381. On *persons* for *folk*, Matthew 6:5 versus Sawyer's *New Testament*, p. 76.

14. Sawyer, *New Testament*, pp. 102, 228, 311.

15. *To conceive seed*, Hebrews 11:11; Sawyer's version, *New Testament*, p. 392. On *manure* for *dung*, Luke 13:8 to Sawyer, p. 134. *Fleshly lusts*, 1 Peter 2:11; *carnal desires*, Sawyer, p. 364. *Lusts* to *inordinate desires* is 2 Peter 1:4 to Sawyer, p. 368. *Damnation* to *eternal mistake* is Matthew 3:29 to Sawyer, p. 72.

16. *Unclean* to *impure*, see Matthew 5:2 and Sawyer, p. 74. *Filthy* to *lewd*, see 2 Peter 2:7 and Sawyer, p. 369. *Uncleanliness* to *corrupt desires*, see 2 Peter 2:10 and Sawyer, p. 369.

17. *Purged* to *Purification* is 2 Peter 1:9 to Sawyer, p. 368. "For speaking extravagent words of vanity . . ." Sawyer, p. 370.

18. On Pulver and the whole eighteenth-century revision movement, see Ezra Abbott, "Versions, Authorized," in *Dr. William Smith's Dictionary of the Bible*, ed. Horatio B. Hackett, 4 vols. (Boston: Houghton Mifflin and Co., 1892), vol. 4, pp. 3438–45; Edward Harwood, trans., *The New Testament* (London: J. Johnson, 1776). Joseph Worsley, trans., *The New Testament* (London: R. Heti, 1770), title page.

19. P. Marion Simms, *The Bible in America* (New York: Wilson-Erickson, 1936), p. 231. Franklin's suggestion for Job 1:6, "And it being levee day in Heaven, all God's nobility came to court to present themselves before him. . . ." His Job 1:7 is "And God said unto Satan, You have been some time absent; where were you? And Satan answered, I have been at my country seat, and in different places visiting my friends."

20. Robert Lowth, trans., *Isaiah* (Boston: W. Hillard, 1834), p. lix; John Mason Good, *Memoirs of the Life and Writings of the Reverend Alexander Geddes* (London: G. Kearsley, 1803), pp. 195–98; John Symonds, *Observations upon the Expediency of Revising the Present English Version* . . . (Cambridge: J. Archdeacon, 1789), pp. 91–92; George Campbell, trans., *The Four Gospels translated from the Greek*, 2 vols. (Boston: T. Bedlington and C. Ewer, 1824), pp. xxix–lix; William Newcome, *An Historical View of the English Biblical Translations: The Expediency of Revising by Authority Our Present Translation* (Dublin: J. Eashaw, 1792). Also see Benjamin Blayney, trans., *Jerome and Lamentations* (1784; reprint, Edinburgh: Oliphant & Balfour, 1810); Anon., *The Reasons for Revising by Authority Our Present Version of the Bible* (Cambridge: The University, 1788).

21. Good, *Memoirs of the Life* . . . *of Alexander Geddes*, pp. 399–430; "Dr. Geddes

on the Bible," *British Critic* 4 (August 1794): 158; Ezra Abbott, "Versions, Authorized," *Smith's Dictionary of the Bible*, vol. 4, p. 3439. I do not mean that *scholarly* investigation stopped, or that translation of single books of the Bible, directed at biblical scholars, did not proceed. What ended was the movement for a new *popular* Bible.

22. Noah Webster, *The Holy Bible containing the Old and New Testaments in the Common Version with Amendments in the Language* (New Haven: Durie & Peck, 1833), p. xvi; Cecil K. Thomas, *Alexander Campbell and his New Version* (St. Louis: Bethany Press, 1958), p. 40.

23. "Revision Movement," *Southern Presbyterian Review* 10 (1858): 501–02.

24. Malan, *Vindication*, p. 228; J. W. Gibbs, "Common Version and Biblical Revision," *New Englander* 17 (May 1858): 528; Edward Gilman, "Revision of the English Bible," *New Englander* 17 (February 1859): 168, 163; "Sawyers's New Testament," *The British and Foreign Evangelical Review*, no. 29 (July 1859): 591, 597; "Does the Bible Need Retranslating?" *The Church Review and Ecclasiastical Register* 10 (April 1857): 20; *Seventeenth Annual Report of the American and Foreign Bible Society, 1854*, p. 104.

25. Robert Lowth, *Lectures on the Sacred Poetry of the Hebrews* (1753; reprint, Andover: Crocker and Brewster, 1829), p. 59.

26. Lowth, *Isaiah*, p. xxviii; Campbell, *The Four Gospels*, vol. 1, pp. 18, 20.

27. George Steiner, *After Babel: Aspects of Language and Translation* (New York: Oxford University Press, 1975), p. 266.

28. George Perkins Marsh, *Lectures on the English Language* (1859; reprint, New York: Charles Scribner's and Sons, 1874), pp. 634, 636.

29. "English Translations of the Bible," *Biliotheca Sacra*, p. 287; Alexander McClure, *The Translators Revived* (New York: Charles Scribner, 1853), p. iv; Richard Chenevix Trench, *On the Authorized Version of the New Testament* (New York: Redfield, 1858), p. 20; "Editor's Table," *Harper's Monthly* 18 (February 1859): 406.

30. Matthew Arnold, "On Translating Homer," *The Atlantic Monthly* 9 (January 1862): 144; "Bible Revision," *North American Review* 88 (January 1859): 187.

31. McClure, *Translators Revived*, p. 234; "The American Bible Society," *Princeton Review* 29 (July 1857): 537; "Dr. Curtis on a Standard English Bible," *Southern Presbyterian Review* 11 (1858): 137; "Revision Movement," *Southern Presbyterian Review*, 501; "Sawyer's New Testament," *The British and Foreign Evangelical Review*, 589.

32. "Sawyer's New Testament," *The American Quarterly Church Review* 12 (April 1859): 106.

33. A. Cleveland Coxe, *An Apology for the Common English Bible* (Baltimore: J. Robinson, 1857), pp. 12, 47.

34. Anon., *Report on the History and Recent Collation of the English Version of the Bible* (New York: American Bible Society, 1852); American Bible Society, *Historical Sketches and Records of the Proceedings of the Board of Managers in regard to the late revision of the Bible* (Philadelphia: American Bible Society, 1858); "General Assembly of 1857," *Southern Presbyterian Review* 10 (1857): 276–333; *Minutes of the*

*General Assembly of the Presbyterian Church of the United States of America, 1858*, p. 272; "The American Bible Society's Standard Bible," *The New York Times*, 30 January 1858.

35. John Pickering, "Review," *North American Review* 14 (1822): 129–30; "Anglo-Saxon Language and Literature," *North American Review* 33 (October 1831): 325–50.

36. Karl Follen, *A Treatise on Language* (1852), Maximilian Schele de Vere, *Outlines of Comparative Philology* (1852), Josiah Willard Gibbs, *Philological Studies with English Illustrations* (1857), Benjamin Dwight, *Modern Philology: Its Discoveries, History and Influence* (1859).

37. On the introduction of philology to the United States, see Adolph Benson, "James Gates Percival, Student of German Culture," *New England Quarterly* 2 (1929): 603–24; John Wilson, "Grimm's Law and the Brahmins," *New England Quarterly* 38 (1965): 234–39; Gura, *The Wisdom of Words*, passim.

38. *The Complete Writings of James Russell Lowell*, 16 vols. (Cambridge: Houghton Mifflin and Co., 1904), vol. 3, pp. 7–8.

39. "Biglow Papers," *New Englander* (February 1849): 63–64; Letter to Mary Peabody Mann quoted in Thomas Wortham, ed., *The Biglow Papers: A Critical Edition* (De Kalb: Northern Illinois University Press, 1977), p. xiv.

40. Charles Eliot Norton, ed., *Letters of James Russell Lowell*, 2 vols. (New York: Harper and Bros., 1894), vol. 1, p. 119; Sumner's reaction is recorded in Henry Cabot Lodge, *Early Memories* (New York: Charles Scribner's Sons, 1913), p. 280; On the need for Wilbur to lift the sentiments, *Complete Writings of Lowell*, vol. 3, p. 6; Lowell to Norton, September 20, 1859, Norton Papers, Houghton Library, Harvard University.

41. James Russell Lowell, "Reviews and Literary Notices," *The Atlantic Monthly* 4 (November 1859): 638, 643.

42. *Complete Writings of Lowell*, vol. 1, pp. 221, 223, 42. These essays were written in the 1860s and provide nice counterpoint to his Hosea Biglow poetry of the time.

43. William Belmont Parker, ed., *James Russell Lowell's Editorials from the National Anti-Slavery Standard* (Boston: Houghton and Mifflin, 1934), p. 232; *Complete Writings of Lowell*, vol. 2, p. 23.

44. Norton, *Letters of James Russell Lowell*, vol. 1, pp. 350–51; vol. 2, pp. 47, 65, 330; Mark DeWolfe Howe, ed., *New Letters of James Russell Lowell* (New York: Harper and Bros., 1932), p. 263.

45. See the violence of George Templeton Strong's reaction to Abraham Lincoln's using *humans* in Allan Nevins, ed., *The Diary of George Templeton Strong*, 3 vols. (New York: Macmillan Co., 1952), vol. 3, p. 146; *Complete Writings of Lowell*, vol. 3, p. 43.

46. *Complete Writings of Lowell*, vol. 3, pp. 35, 36, 44, 64.

47. Richard Chenevix Trench, *On the Study of Words* (New York: Redfield, 1853), pp. 9, 10, 13, 15–16.

48. *Complete Writings of Lowell*, vol. 3, pp. 11–13.

49. Ibid., p. 75.

50. John Camden Hotten, *A Dictionary of Modern Slang, Cant, and Vulgar Words* (London: John Camden Hotten, 1859), pp. vii, viii.

51. Alfred Elwyn, *Glossary of Supposed Americanisms* (Philadelphia: J. P. Lippincott & Co., 1859), p. iii; "Americanisms," *The New York Times*, 22 May 1870.

52. Ralph Waldo Emerson, "The American Scholar," in *The Selected Writings of Ralph Waldo Emerson*, ed. Brooks Atkinson (New York: The Modern Library, 1950), p. 61; on Emerson's interest in the popular literature of the 1830s, see Stephen Whicher and Robert Spiller, eds., *The Early Lectures of Ralph Waldo Emerson*, 3 vols. (Cambridge: Harvard University Press, 1966), vol. 1, p. 222; the final quote is in Porte, *Emerson in His Journals*, pp. 240–41.

53. Mary Kupiec Cayton, "The Making of an American Prophet: Emerson, His Audiences, and the Rise of the Culture Industry in Nineteenth-Century America," *American Historical Review* 92 (1987): 597–620.

54. Emerson, "Nature," *Selected Writings*, p. 36; on language, see pp. 14–20.

55. David Reynolds, I feel, has overstated Emerson's interest in popular literature. See his *Beneath the American Renaissance: The Subversive Imagination in the Age of Emerson and Melville* (New York: Alfred A. Knopf, 1988), pp. 4, 484–97. While Emerson did on occasion express populist sentiments, he did not do so nearly as much as Reynolds contends. Even in the passage that Reynolds cites where Emerson pays homage to Jack Downing literature, that comment is an aside amid pages mentioning Homer, Jesus, Plato, Luther, Bacon, Burke, Milton, Leibnitz, and Swedenborg. Among all this, contemporary popular literature had a very small place. See Whicher and Spiller, *The Early Lectures*, vol. 1, pp. 221–26.

56. Porte, *Emerson in His Journals*, pp. 151–52.

57. Emerson, "Manners," *Selected Writings*, pp. 381–401; Porte, *Emerson in His Journals*, pp. 520–21.

58. George P. Marsh, *Address Given Before the Graduating Class of the U.S. Military Academy at West Point* (New York: n.p., 1860), pp. 3, 7–8; Marsh, *Lectures on the English Language*, pp. 86, 118–27.

59. Ibid., pp. 127, 439–441.

60. George P. Marsh, *The Origins and History of the English Language* (New York: Charles Scribner, 1862); George Craik, *A Compendious History of English Literature and of the English Language* (London: Griffin, Bohn and Co., 1861); "New Publications," *The New York Times*, 25 January 1863; "English Language and Literature," *The New York Times*, 26 April 1864.

61. Leonard L. Richards, *Gentlemen of Property and Standing: Anti-Abolition Mobs in Jacksonian America* (New York: Oxford University Press, 1970).

62. Roy Basler, "Abraham Lincoln's Rhetoric," *American Literature* 11 (1939–40): 170; Edmund Wilson, *Patriotic Gore* (New York: Farrar, Straus & Giroux, 1962), pp. 99–130; James Russell Lowell, "Abraham Lincoln" (1864), *My Study Windows* (London: George Routledge & Sons, n. d.), p. 164. For other analyses of Lincoln's rhetoric, see Daniel K. Dodge, "Abraham Lincoln: The Evolution of His Literary Style," *University of Illinois Studies* 1 (1900): 3–58; Robert A. Ferguson,

*Law and Letters in American Culture* (Cambridge: Harvard University Press, 1984), pp. 305–17.

63. Roy P. Basler, ed., *The Complete Works of Abraham Lincoln*, 8 vols. (New Brunswick: Rutgers University Press, 1953), vol. 4, pp. 249–71. Elsewhere in the two drafts, where Seward had written the Latinate English "proceeding," Lincoln replaced it with the Anglo-Saxon "stretching." Where Seward suggested "continent" and "harmonize," both Latinate terms, Lincoln substituted "land" and "swell."

64. Garry Wills, *Inventing America: Jefferson's Declaration of Independence* (New York: Vintage Books, 1978), pp. xiv–xv.

65. See Samuel H. Monk, *The Sublime: A Study of Critical Theories in Eighteenth-Century England* (Ann Arbor: University of Michigan Press, 1960).

66. I introduced Blair's rhetoric as a neoclassical text in chapter 1; here I seem to be assimilating it to Romanticism. In fact, Blair thought that the sublime was a residual category, more apt to be found in "the early ages of the world" and the "rude unimproved state of society." According to Blair, with "the progress of society, the genius and manners of men undergo a change more favorable to accuracy, than to strength or Sublimity." Hugh Blair, *Lectures on Rhetoric and Belle Lettres*, 3 vols. (London: W. Strahan, 1785), vol. 1, pp. 76, 77.

Early-nineteenth-century Romantics, however, could take Blair's thoughts about the sublime and make it a far more important aesthetic category. This is one of the reasons why Blair remained so influential in the first half of the nineteenth century. Not only in the English-speaking world, either. Blair was translated into French in 1797 and was reissued in 1808, 1821, and in an abridged version in 1825. It was considered by French Romantics as "a manual of language and of the romantic style." Charles Bruneau, *Petite histoire de la langue française*, 2 vols. (Paris: Armand Colin, 1966), vol. 2, p. 49.

67. Blair, *Lectures on Rhetoric*, vol. 1, pp. 75–79.

68. Nevins, *Diary of George Templeton Strong*, vol. 3, p. 204; Porte, *Emerson in His Journals*, p. 521.

69. Auerbach, *Literary Language and Its Public*, pp. 58–59, 64.

70. Ibid., p. 57.

71. Ibid., pp. 65–66.

72. George Fitzhugh, *Cannibals All: or, Slaves Without Masters* (Cambridge: Harvard University Press, 1969), p. 63; Poe, "The Rationale of Verse," (1848) in *The Works of Edgar Allen Poe*, ed. Albert E. Sterner, 10 vols. (Chicago: Stone and Kimball, 1895), vol. 6, pp. 49–50; Marsh, *Lectures on the English Language*, pp. 88–89, 649; Goodrich, *Recollections of a Lifetime*, pp. 143–44; "Fowler's English Grammar," *North American Review* 89 (July 1859): 246, 245; Also see the poems lampooning grammar in *Massachusetts Teacher* 2 (1849): 288.

73. Richard Chenevix Trench, *On Some Deficiencies in Our English Dictionaries* (London: J. W. Parker and Son, 1858).

74. Trench, *On the Authorized Version*, pp. 173–84.

# Chapter 4

1. On the optimism of the highly educated in the mid-1860s, see George Fredrickson, *The Inner Civil War* (New York: Harper & Row, 1965); Morton Keller, *Affairs of State: Public Life in Late Nineteenth-Century America* (Cambridge: Harvard University Press, 1977), pp. 42–46; and Thomas Haskell, *The Emergence of Professional Social Science* (Urbana: University of Illinois Press, 1977), pp. 97–121.

2. On Arnold, see Sheldon Rothblatt, *Tradition and Change in English Liberal Education* (London: Faber & Faber, 1976), pp. 149–50. Rothblatt is very perceptive on the deep cultural echoes of Arnold's humanism. In many particulars, his account of British education parallels my own discussion of American education.

3. Historians like John Sproat and John Tomsich have called attention to the conservative and nostalgic character of postwar cultural reformers. Yet these historians have not adequately analyzed the sources of the conservatism. The moralism, patriarchy, and elitism of the reformers was derived from a way of thinking about education that was ancient. As late as the 1860s, humanistic canons of education provided the only model for *highly* educated adults in American life. The image of the "specialist" was not yet a positive one among the highly educated. To focus *only* on the nostalgia and elitism of the postwar conservative reformers, as Sproat and Tomsich do, subtly misses the cultural presumptions that underwrote their elitism and nostalgia. Sproat, for example, does not see that the term *best men* was a time-honored usage, closely associated with Cicero's *liberales*.

See John Sproat, *The Best Men: Liberal Reformers in the Guilded Age* (Chicago: University of Chicago Press, 1968); and John Tomsich, *A Genteel Endeavor: American Culture and Politics in the Guilded Age* (Stanford: Stanford University Press, 1971).

4. For some examples of this, see chapter 1, note 20.

5. L. P. Meredith, *Every-Day Errors of Speech* (Philadelphia: J. B. Lippincott & Co., 1872), pp. 13–14; Alfred Ayres, *The Verbalist* (New York: D. Appleton & Co., 1882), p. 118; Richard Grant White, *Words and Their Uses* (New York: Sheldon & Co., 1872), pp. 369, 373, 389.

6. White, *Words and Their Uses*, p. 41; William Mathews, *The Great Conversers* (Chicago: S. R. Griggs & Co., 1878), p. 43; "Contributor's Club," *The Atlantic Monthly* 45 (June 1880): 857.

7. David Swing, "A Few Thoughts on Language," *Lakeside Monthly* 9 (May 1873): 416; William Mathews, *Words: Their Use and Abuse* (Chicago: S. C. Griggs & Co., 1876), pp. 63, 65.

8. White, *Words and Their Uses*, p. 43.

9. Henry James, *The Question of Our Speech* (Boston: Houghton Mifflin & Co., 1905), p. 27; Ayres, *The Verbalist*, p. 79; White, *Words and Their Uses*, p. 211; "Contributor's Club," *The Atlantic Monthly* 45 (March 1880): 422.

10. "Thanks," *Good Housekeeping* 1 (June 13, 1885): 23–24.

11. Kurt Wolff, ed., *The Sociology of Georg Simmel* (Glencoe, Ill.: Free Press, 1950), pp. 321–22; White, *Words and Their Uses*, p. 40; Richard Meade Bache,

*Vulgarisms and Other Errors of Speech* (Philadelphia: Clayton, Remsen & Haffelfinger, 1869), p. 20.

12. White, *Words and Their Uses*, p. 42; Richard Grant White, *Everyday English* (Boston: Houghton Mifflin & Co., 1880), p. 484; Henry Alford, *A Plea for the Queen's English* (New York: Dick and Fitzgerald, 1864), pp. 261–62.

13. On deference, see Erving Goffman, "The Nature of Deference and Demeanor," in *Interaction Rituals: Essays in Face-to-Face Behavior* (Garden City, N.Y.: Anchor Books, 1967), p. 64. Josiah Gilbert Holland, "American Incivility," *Everyday Topics: First Series* (New York: Charles Scribner's Sons, 1882). The word *boss* should not be seen as a sign of deference. Early in the nineteenth century the word was borrowed from the Dutch to replace *master* in American usage. People like Holland thought workmen used *boss* to avoid the deference implied by *master*, *sir*, or *madam*. Holland called *boss* "a boorish concession to civility for the sake of trade." Holland, "American Incivility," p. 354. For another complaint about *boss*, see James Fenimore Cooper, *The American Democrat* (1838; reprint, Baltimore: Penguin Books, 1969), p. 175. Also see Sir William A. Craigie and James R. Hulbert, *A Dictionary of American English on Historical Principles* (Chicago: University of Chicago Press, 1938), s.v. "boss."

14. "Abbreviations," *The Illinois School Master* 8 (1875): 41; W. C. Brownell, "Manners in America," *The Nation* 30 (May 6, 1880): 343–44.

15. Josiah Gilbert Holland, "Familiarity," *Everyday Topics: Second Series* (New York: Charles Scribner's Sons, 1893), pp. 288–92. Etiquette books regularly abjured loud laughter, winking, gossip, and other "familiarity." Most cautioned mates not to use first names in public. See, for example, *The Habits of Good Society* (New York: Rudd & Carleton, 1860), pp. 38–51; Florence Hartley, *The Ladies' Book of Etiquette and Manual of Politeness* (Boston: J. S. Locke & Co., 1875), pp. 12–14; and Mrs. John Sherwood, *Manners and Social Usages* (New York: Harper and Bros., 1887), p. 35.

16. *Habits of Good Society*, p. 38. On the need for manners to maintain social order, see, for example, Catherine Beecher and Harriet Beecher Stowe, *American Woman's Home* (New York: J. B. Ford, 1869), pp. 199–203.

17. Ouida, "Vulgarity," *North American Review* 144 (February 1887): 149; J. P. Mahaffy, *The Principles of the Art of Conversation* (London and New York: Macmillan & Co., 1888), p. 53.

18. "Girls Don't Talk Slang." This article is in a scrapbook, in my possession, compiled by a New Jersey doctor in the 1870s. It is probably from a New York City paper, where many of the articles in the scrapbook come from.

19. See, for example, White, *Words and Their Uses*, p. 67.

20. "Slang," *Ladies' Repository* 28 (November 1868): 381.

21. "Girls Don't Use Slang." New Jersey doctor's scrapbook in author's possession.

22. Mary Kelly has stressed the ambivalence of the women writers in *Private Women, Public Space: Literary Domesticity in Nineteenth-Century America* (New York: Oxford University Press, 1984), esp. pp. 316–21.

23. White, *Words and Their Uses*, pp. 66–67.

24. "Critic," *Discriminate* (New York: D. Appleton, 1886); Edward Gould, *Good English* (New York: A. C. Armstrong & Son, 1880), pp. 61–62, 135; Lelia Bugg, *Correct English* (St. Louis: B. Herder, 1895), pp. 51–84, 140, 441.

25. Andrew Peabody, *Conversation: Its Faults and Graces* (Boston: Lee and Shepard, 1882), p. 15.

26. Meredith, *Errors of Speech*, p. 28; also see White, *Words and Their Uses*, p. 181.

27. Charles W. Bardeen, *Verbal Pitfalls: A Manual of 1500 Words Commonly Misused* (Syracuse: C. W. Bardeen, 1883), pp. 88–89; "Censor," *Don't: A Manual of Mistakes and Improprieties More or Less Prevalent in Conduct and Speech* (New York: D. Appleton, 1884), p. 66; also see *genteel* in the *Oxford English Dictionary*. Tomsich, in *A Genteel Endeavor*, p. 2, notes the derogatory implications of the word after 1850, but he does not understand that the new meaning was connected with a critique of popular culture.

28. White, *Everyday English*, p. 496.

29. Alford, *Plea for the Queens's English*, p. 44; Mathews, *Words: Their Use and Abuse*, p. 132; White, *Words and Their Uses*, p. 20.

30. Bache, *Vulgarisms*, p. 158.

31. George Calvert, *The Gentleman* (Boston: Ticknor and Fields, 1863), pp. 132–33; Henry Ward Beecher, *Lectures to Young Men*, 2d ed. (New York: J. B. Ford, 1872), pp. 237–39.

32. White, *Words and Their Uses*, p. 28; For other examples of similar discussions of vulgarity see Ouida, "Vulgarity," pp. 150–51; "Contributor's Club," *The Atlantic Monthly* 60 (August 1887): 281; "Editor's Table," *Appleton's Journal* 13 (March 20, 1875): 371–72.

33. White, *Words and Their Uses*, pp. 28–43; Alford, *Plea for the Queen's English*, p. 244; Gould, *Good English*, p. 7.

34. William E. Lecky, *History of European Morals* (1869; reprint, New York: D. Appleton, 1921), p. 131.

35. "Mr. Beecher on Newspapers," *New York Tribune*, 19 May 1879. The criticism of newspapers is voluminous and should be the subject of closer attention. A small sampling: James Fenimore Cooper, *The American Democrat*, pp. 180–86; Allan Nevins, ed., *The Diary of George Templeton Strong*, 3 vols. (New York: Macmillan, 1952), vol. 1, p. 94; "Ollapodiana," *Knickerbocker Magazine* 6 (August 1835): 123–24; "The English of Newspapers," *The Nation* 1 (December 28, 1865): 814–15; Philip G. Hamerton, "On the Reading of Newspapers," *Scribner's Monthly* 5 (January 1873): 317–19; "Newspapers and Public Opinion," *Round Table* 6 (December 14, 1867): 390–91; "Newspaperism," *Lippincott's Magazine* 38 (November 1886): 470–77; and James Parton, "Newspapers Gone to Seed," *The Forum* 1 (1886): 15–24.

36. See, for example, Philip G. Hamerton, "On the Reading of Newspapers," pp. 317–19; Lyman Abbott, ed., *Hints for Home Reading* (New York: G. P. Putnam's Sons, 1880), pp. 5–7.

37. New York *Sun*, 3 November 1870; *Chicago Times*, 12 October 1879; "Amer-

ican Politics and Education," *Chicago Times*, 16 January 1871; "The New York Times," *New York Tribune*, 18 April 1868; "Dignity in Expression," *Chicago Times*, 7 February 1871.

38. "Slang Songs in the Public Schools," *New York Tribune*, 22 March 1881. The author of the letter heard eight hundred boys in New York's most prestigious grammar school sing a song about a "Peeler" who arrested boys after a "high old night." "A Broadway Toff" was a minstrel tune: "I need not say that of girls/I'm passionately fond./And at this time it is no crime/To love an English Blonde./ And, she, I think, is rather struck/With this superior toff/And thinks, exactly like myself, that I'm immensikoff."

39. *The Lakeside Annual Directory of the City of Chicago, 1883* (Chicago: Lakeside Press, 1883), pp. 1596, 1597; David Lowe, *Chicago Interiors* (Chicago: Contemporary Books, 1979), p. 125; Karl Baedecker, ed., *The United States with an Excursion to Mexico* (New York: Charles Scribner's Sons, 1899), p. xxviii.

40. William Dean Howells, *A Hazard of New Fortunes*, 2 vols. (New York: Harper and Bros., 1889), vol. 1, pp. 1, 9, 10. The cultivated March is aware of the bombast: "Some people don't think much of the creation of man, nowadays," he says. "Why stop at that? Why not say since the morning stars sang together?" But Fulkerson misses the mild sarcasm: "No, sir; no, sir! I don't want to claim too much, and I draw the line at the creation of man. I'm satisfied with that. But if you want to ring the morning stars into the prospectus, all right; I won't go back on you" (pp. 1–2).

41. Ibid., pp. 4, 13.

42. Ibid., p. 40; vol. 2, p. 20; William Dean Howells, *The Coast of Bohemia* (New York: Harper and Bros., 1893), p. 199.

43. William Dean Howells, *The Rise of Silas Lapham* (Boston: Ticknor and Co., 1884), pp. 87–89, 507.

44. Ibid., p. 43.

45. E. L. Godkin, "The Morals of the Future," *The Nation* 9 (July 15, 1869): 45–47.

46. In forming my ideas on the critics' contradictory attitudes about their audience—whether it should be refined or mass—I owe much to David D. Hall's unpublished essay, "The 'Higher Journalism' and the Politics of Culture in Mid-Nineteenth-Century America."

47. Van Wyck Brooks, *America's Coming of Age* (1915; reprint, Garden City, N.Y.: Doubleday, 1958), p. 3; H. L. Mencken, *The American Language* (New York: Alfred A. Knopf, 1919); George Santayana, "The Genteel Tradition in America," in *Selected Critical Writings of George Santayana*, ed., Norman Henfrey, 2 vols. (Cambridge: Cambridge University Press, 1968), vol. 2, pp. 85–107; Lewis Mumford, *The Golden Day* (New York: Boni and Liveright, 1926); John Kouwenhoven, *The Arts in Modern American Civilization* (New York: W.W. Norton, 1948); H. Wiley Hitchcock, *Music in the United States: A Historical Introduction* (Englewood Cliffs, N.J.: Prentice-Hall, 1969); Michael Denning, *Mechanical Accents: Dime Novels and Working-Class Culture in America* (London: Verso, 1987), pp. 47–48. By implication, the argument is found in Daniel Boorstin's *The Americans: The National*

*Experience* (New York: Random House, 1966) and *The Americans: The Democratic Experience* (New York: Random House, 1973). Boorstin constantly stresses the irrelevance of intellectuals in nineteenth-century American life. See his comments on language norms in *The National Experience*, pp. 277–78. John Tomsich in *A Genteel Endeavor* also stresses the isolation of Gilded Age intellectuals.

48. Daniel Walker Howe, "Victorian Culture in America," in *Victorian America*, ed. Daniel Walker Howe (Philadelphia: University of Pennsylvania Press, 1976), pp. 13–14. Also Arthur Meier Schlesinger, *The Rise of the City, 1878–1898* (New York: Macmillan Co., 1933), pp. 202–87; Allan Nevins, *The Emergence of Modern America, 1865–1878* (New York: Macmillan Co., 1928), pp. 228–64; Henry Nash Smith, *Democracy and the Novel: Popular Resistance to Classic American Writers* (Oxford: Oxford University Press, 1978), pp. 8–9; Lawrence Levine, *Highbrow/Lowbrow: The Emergence of Cultural Hierarchy in America* (Cambridge: Harvard University Press, 1988).

49. Neil Harris, *The Artist in American Society* (New York: G. Braziller, 1966); Peter Marzio, *The Democratic Art: Pictures for a Nineteenth-Century America* (Boston: D. R. Godine, 1979). On the Centennial Fair and art appreciation, see "The Progress of Painting in America," *North American Review* 121 (May 1877): 451; and Josiah Holland, "American Art," *Everyday Topics: First Series*, 63.

50. Boorstin, *The Americans: The Democratic Experience*, pp. 91–100; Margaret Walsh, "The Democratization of Fashion: The Emergence of the Woman's Dress Pattern Industry," *Journal of American History* 66 (September 1979): 299–313.

51. On literacy, see Carl Degler, *At Odds: Women and the Family in America* (New York: Oxford University Press, 1980), p. 308.

52. Joseph L. Robert, *The Story of Tobacco in America* (New York: Alfred A. Knopf, 1949), pp. 173–225; Robert Sobel, *They Satisfy: The Cigarette in American Life* (Garden City, N.Y.: Anchor Books, 1978), p. 6; James Muirhead, *America: The Land of Contrasts* (New York: J. Lane, 1898), p. 201; Norbert Elias, *The History of Manners* (New York: Urizen Books, 1979), pp. 153–60.

53. Arthur Schlesinger, *Learning How to Behave: A Historical Study of American Etiquette Books* (New York: Macmillan, 1946), pp. 33–34; Schlesinger, *The Rise of the City*, pp. 67–69. On the publication of books of verbal etiquette, see the appendix.

54. On Davy Crockett, see Walter Blair and Hamlin Hill, *America's Humor: From Poor Richard to Doonesbury* (New York: Oxford University Press, 1978), pp. 143–46; On minstrelsy, see Robert Toll, *Blacking Up: The Minstrel Show in Nineteenth-Century America* (New York: Oxford University Press, 1974), pp. 134–59.

55. Harry Sunderland, "Is She a Lady?" *Peterson's Ladies' National Magazine* 12 (November 1847): 169.

56. Bache, *Vulgarisms*, p. 182.

57. Gwendolyn Wright, *Moralism and the Model Home* (Chicago: University of Chicago Press, 1980), pp. 49–50; Joseph Musselman, *Music in the Cultured Generation* (Evanston: Northwestern University Press, 1971), pp. 171–72; E. L. Godkin, "The Chromo-Civilization," *The Nation* 19 (September 24, 1874): 202.

58. "Mr. Greeley As a Gentleman," *Round Table* 7 (April 18, 1868): 244.

59. Ayres, *The Verbalist*, pp. 55–56; Augusta Hubbard, "The Significance of Trifles," *Ladies' Repository* 25 (April 1865): 237–38; Wright, *Moralism and the Model Home*, pp. 13–14. As early as the 1830s the French novelist Honoré de Balzac had predicted that details would become extremely important precisely because they were the only distinctions left. See Rosiland H. Williams, *Dream-Worlds: Mass Consumption in Late Nineteenth-Century France* (Berkeley: University of California Press, 1982), p. 117.

60. White, *Words and Their Uses*, p. 180.

61. By the 1880s, much of the debate about education and politics was not about the low status of the educated, but about why the educated would not sully themselves with politics. "Why Educated Men Have Abandoned Public Life," *Boston Herald*, 4 June 1882; "Culture in Politics, Why the American Scholar Is Not in Politics," *Boston Herald*, 11 June 1882; "Education in America," *Boston Herald*, 30 June 1882; "Popular Leadership," *Boston Herald*, 25 June 1882; "Do Highly Educated Americans Take an Interest in Politics?" *New York Tribune*, 11 January 1881.

62. Information on school programs will be presented in chapter 6. For Townsend and Hill and Chautauqua, see Arthur Bestor, *Chautauqua Publications: A Historical and Bibliographical Guide* (Chautauqua: Chautauqua Press, 1934); for mothers on trolleys, see "Contributor's Club," *The Atlantic Monthly* 47 (January 1881): 135; sample letters to the editor include "Voice of the People," *Chicago Tribune*, 5 January 1882; and "Ladies and Gentlemen," New York *Sun*, 19 March 1882. Inserted in the copy of Harlan Ballard's *Handbook of Blunders* owned by the Newberry Library in Chicago, Illinois, are numerous letters to the editor on questions of linguistic purity. Most letters are from the Boston *Daily Advertiser*. On the shift in the New York *Evening Post*, compare "Literary Tendencies," 5 February 1881, with "Ayre's Verbalist," 7 January, 1882. Both are front-page articles in the *Evening Post*. Bardeen, *Verbal Pitfalls*, 3.

# Chapter 5

1. Richard Grant White, "Words and Their Uses," *The Galaxy* 11 (June 1871): 786–800; [Thomas Lounsbury], "Words and Their Uses," *The College Courant* 8 (November 19, 1870–January 28, 1871).

2. Newman's *The Idea of a University* was completed in 1858. Spencer's essays attacking liberal education were written in the 1850s. They were published as *Education* in 1861. Dickens's *Hard Times* (1854) was a critique of utilitarian education. Arnold's report on the schools of France appeared in 1861, *Culture and Anarchy* in 1869. F. W. Farrar's edited collection, *Essays on a Liberal Education*, was published in 1867. Huxley published numerous essays on scientific education in the late sixties. The fifth chapter of Mill's *On Liberty* (1859) and his *Inaugural Address at St. Andrews* (1867) were both on the importance of liberal education. Although Mill's *Autobiography* was not published until the 1870s, the chapters criticizing his early education were written in 1861.

3. Abraham Lincoln, "Address at the Wisconsin State Fair, 1859," in *The*

*Political Thought of Abraham Lincoln*, ed. Richard N. Current (Indianapolis: Bobbs-Merrill, 1967), pp. 125–38; Horace Greeley, *An Address on Success in Business* (New York: S. S. Packard, 1867).

4. Thomas Hill, "Liberal Education," (1858) in *Representative Phi Beta Kappa Orations*, ed. Clark S. Northrup, 2d ser. (New York: The Elisha Parmele Press, 1927), pp. 140–61; F. W. Hedge, "University Reform," *The Atlantic Monthly* 18 (1866): 296–307; Francis Wayland, *Report to the Corporation of Brown University on Changes in the System of Collegiate Education* (Providence: G. H. Whitney, 1850); Henry Tappan, *University Education* (New York: G. P. Putnam, 1851); John William Draper, *The Indebtedness of the City of New York to Its University* (New York: The Alumni Association, 1853); Charles W. Eliot, "The New Education," *The Atlantic Monthly* 23 (February, March 1869): 203–20, 358–67; Noah Porter, *The American Colleges and the American Public* (New Haven, n.p., 1870).

5. Keller, *Affairs of State: Public Life in Late Nineteenth-Century America* (Cambridge: Harvard University Press, 1977), pp. 42–46.

6. Eliot, "The New Education," pp. 358–59; William Dwight Whitney, *Language and the Study of Language* (New York: C. Scribner & Co., 1867), p. 151.

7. The work of Thomas Bender and Thomas Haskell has helped me frame some key issues. Like Bender, I have seen the postwar efforts of the highly educated as a response to new forms of popular intellectual life. And like Bender, I see Henry Ward Beecher as a central figure in the new popular culture. Unlike Bender, however, I do not see anything particularly "urban" about the popular culture, unless we want to call places like New Salem or Springfield, Illinois, "urban." And unlike Bender, I do not see late-nineteenth-century professionalism as the sole response. Rather, I emphasize two different currents, the genteel critics and the scholarly philologists, each developing different ways to struggle against the new popular culture. See Thomas Bender, "The Erosion of Public Culture: Cities, Discourses, and Professional Disciplines," in *The Authority of Experts: Studies in History and Theory*, ed. Thomas Haskell (Bloomington: University of Indiana Press, 1984), pp. 84–106.

Framing the issue as scholars versus critics parallels the divisions developed by Thomas Haskell in *The Emergence of Professional Social Science* (Urbana: University of Illinois Press, 1977), a work that has helped me immeasurably. I differ, however, from Haskell in this respect—while he argues that the differences were between two different ways of being "professional," I would stress the differences in the ideals of the educated adult (really the educated *man* at this point). Following Max Weber, I find it a dispute about how to organize the self, a dispute between the ideal of the cultivated gentleman and the expert professional.

8. Of the most prominent critics, Richard Grant White was born in 1821, George Washington Moon in 1823, Richard Meade Bache in 1833, Adams Sherman Hill in 1833, and Thomas Osmun (Alfred Ayres, pseud.) in 1834. Prominent critics born before 1820 were Edward Gould (1805), Andrew Peabody (1811), Henry Alford (1817), and William Mathews (1818). The biographical information on these men mentioned in the next several paragraphs was drawn from the *National Cyclopedia of American Biography* and the *Dictionary of American Biography* with two

exceptions: material on Adams Sherman Hill came from *Who Was Who, 1896–1942* (Chicago: Marquis, 1942) and material on George Washington Moon came from *Who Was Who, 1897–1916* (London: A & C Black, 1920). The major linguists were born as follows: Francis March (1825), Fitzedward Hall (1825), William Dwight Whitney (1827), Thomas Lounsbury (1838). All material on the philologists comes from the *NCAB* and the *DAB*.

9. Hall's life reads as if he were a character in a Melville novel. He left Harvard before graduation to track down his younger brother who, upon reading Dana's *Two Years Before the Mast*, had run away to sea. Hall tracked his brother to India, but when the vessel he was traveling on was wrecked near the mouth of the Ganges, Hall was forced to spend time in India. He began studying Hindustani and Persian, and traveled through India, briefly holding a teaching post at a provincial college and then becoming a member of the British Civil Service. In 1857, during the Sepoy Mutiny, Hall was a rifleman at the fort at Saugor. He went to England in 1860, where he briefly held a teaching post, but was accused of sexual misconduct, then retired to the countryside. He became a recluse and misanthrope, and of course, one of the leading authorities on the English language.

10. "White's Everyday English," *Scribner's Monthly* 20 (September 1880): 791–93; Fitzedward Hall, *On English Adjectives in "-Able"* (London: Trübner & Co., 1877), p. 12; William Dwight Whitney, "Alford's *A Plea for the Queen's English*," *North American Review* 103 (1866): 566.

11. Whitney to Charles Eliot Norton, October 10, 1865, Charles Eliot Norton Papers, Houghton Library, Harvard University.

12. William Dwight Whitney, *Oriental and Linguistic Studies*, 1st ser. (New York: Scribner, Armstrong & Co., 1872), p. 245.

13. William Dwight Whitney, *The Life and Growth of Language* (New York: D. Appleton & Co., 1875), pp. 32–44; William Dwight Whitney, *Oriental and Linguistic Studies*, 2d ser. (New York: Scribner, Armstrong & Co., 1874), p. 168; Thomas Lounsbury, *History of the English Language* (New York: H. Holt and Co., 1879), p. 144.

14. Fitzedward Hall, *Recent Exemplifications of False Philology* (New York: Scribner, Armstrong & Co., 1872), pp. 90–91, 87; Fitzedward Hall, *Modern English* (New York: Scribner, Armstrong & Co., 1873), pp. 321–30.

15. Richard Grant White, *Words and Their Uses* (New York: Sheldon & Co., 1872), p. 24; Hall, *Recent Exemplifications*, p. 98; Edward Finegan, *Attitudes Toward English Usage* (New York: Teachers College Press, 1980), p. 70.

16. Gould, *Good English* (New York: A. C. Armstrong & Son, 1880), p. 3; White, *Words and Their Uses*, p. 395; White to Whitney, May 28, 1871, William D. Whitney Papers, Sterling Memorial Library, Yale University.

17. Hall, *Modern English*, p. 99; Hall, *Recent Exemplifications*, p. 1.

18. Stanley F. Bonner, *Education in Ancient Rome* (Berkeley: University of California Press, 1977), pp. 206–8.

19. Lord Dunsany and Michael Oakley, trans., *The Collected Works of Horace*, (London: J. M. Dent, 1961), pp. 289, 303.

20. John Locke, *An Essay Concerning Human Understanding*, 2 vols. (New York:

n.p., 1825), vol. 2, pp. 12–43; George Campbell, *The Philosophy of Rhetoric* (1776; reprint, New York: Harper and Bros., 1844), pp. 174–192.

21. Whitney, *Life and Growth of Language*, p. 1; William Dwight Whitney, "Oriental and Linguistic Studies," *Scribner's Monthly* 5 (January 1873): 396.

22. Hans Aarsleff, *From Locke to Saussure: Essays on the Study of Language and Intellectual History* (Minneapolis: University of Minnesota Press, 1982), p. 346.

23. Mark Twain, "Fenimore Cooper's Literary Offenses," in *Great Short Works of Mark Twain*, ed. Justin Kaplan (New York: Harper Torchbooks, 1967), pp. 169–81. Twain's own attitudes about language were quite complex. It is important to separate what Twain thought was appropriate language in his fictive characters from what he found acceptable elsewhere. As "Fenimore Cooper's Literary Offenses" makes clear, Twain could be as picky as the verbal critics. See Brander Matthews, "Mark Twain and the Art of Writing," *Essays on English* (New York: Charles Scribner's Sons, 1921), pp. 243–68. It is also important to see that Twain's own inconsistancies on the subject of language were rooted in the basic tension between his sense of self as a popular humorist and as a refined man of letters. See Justin Kaplan, *Mr. Clemens and Mark Twain* (New York: Simon & Schuster, 1966), pp. 145–46. Depending on how one interprets this dual personality, Twain should be seen either as a refined figure forced by popular democracy to descend to the vulgar or as an uneasy exemplar of middling culture, moving back and forth from the refined to the crude.

24. Mathews, *Words: Their Use and Abuse* (Chicago: S. C. Griggs & Co., 1876), p. 436; Hall, *Modern English*, p. 39.

25. Whitney, *Language and the Study of Language*, pp. 149–50.

26. Whitney, Lounsbury, and Hall advocated simplified spelling. March was chairman of a committee set up by the American Philological Association to pursue the goal of simplified spelling. In England, philologists like Henry Sweet and Alexander Ellis championed the cause. So too did James Murray, editor of the *Oxford English Dictionary*.

27. Whitney, *Oriental and Linguistic Studies*, 2d ser., p. 190; White, *Everyday English*, pp. 206–7.

28. Lounsbury, *History of the English Language*, p. 142; Hall, *Modern English*, pp. 161, 155; Whitney, *Language and the Study of Language*, p. 50.

29. Whitney, *The Life and Growth of Language*, p. 112; Thomas Lounsbury, "The English Language in America," *International Review* 8 (1880): 600, 603.

30. See, for example, "The People's English," a letter to the editor of the *Round Table* 4 (October 13, 1866): 172–73.

31. Whitney, *Life and Growth of Language*, p. 113; E. B. Tyler, "The Philology of Slang," *MacMillan's Magazine* 29 (1874): 502–13; Francis Andrew March, "Modern English," *The Nation* 18 (March 5, 1874): 158–59; John Russell Bartlett, *Dictionary of Americanisms*, 4th ed. (Boston: Little, Brown & Co., 1877); Lounsbury, "The English Language in America," pp. 604–5.

32. "New Publications," *New York Tribune*, 7 October 1879; also see Lounsbury, *History of the English Language*, p. 141.

33. Whitney, *The Life and Growth of Language*, p. 161; Hall, *Modern English*, pp. 23–24.

34. Francis Andrew March, "The Scholar of To-day," (1868), *Representative Phi Beta Kappa Orations*, 1st ser. (New York: Houghton Mifflin & Co., 1915), p. 127; Whitney, *Oriental and Linguistic Studies*, 1st ser., p. 389; James Taft Hatfield, "William Dwight Whitney," *Dial* 16 (June 16, 1894): 354; Thomas Lounsbury, "Words and Their Uses," *The College Courant*, November 26, 1870; Hall, *Modern English*, pp. 40–41; Whitney, *The Life and Growth of Language*, p. 113.

35. Webster argued in the introduction to his dictionary that grammar should be based on analogy, the best usage of writers, and "the authority of universal colloquial practice, which I consider as the *real* and *only genuine language*. I repeat the remark, that *general and respectable* usage in *speaking* is the genuine or legitimate language of a country to which the *written* language ought to be conformed [Webster's emphases]." Noah Webster "Introduction," *An American Dictionary of the English Language* (New Haven: Hezekiah Howe, 1828), n.p.

On Whitney and spoken language, see his *The Life and Growth of Language*, p. 2; for the connection of Whitney to Webster's "radical" linguistics, see "Linguistic Science," *Round Table* 6 (November 2, 1867): 292–93.

36. Whitney, *Language and the Study of Language*, p. 163; Whitney, *The Life and Growth of Language*, p. 178.

37. See, to choose just one of a sea of examples, Dick Leith, *A Social History of English* (London: Routledge & Kegan Paul, 1983), pp. 56–57.

38. Whitney, *Language and the Study of Language*, pp. 176–77, 471.

39. Traditional liberal culture was not necessarily hostile to practicing a profession. Cicero was a lawyer. Galen was a physician. But to the partisans of civilized culture, "mere" technical training rests below the humanizing disciplines.

40. *The Complete Writings of James Russell Lowell*, 16 vols. (Cambridge: Houghton Mifflin and Co., 1904), vol. 6, pp. 212–13; March, "The Scholar of To-day," p. 112.

41. Cicero, *Three Dialogues Upon the Character and Qualifications of an Orator*, trans. William Guthrie (London: T. Waller, 1755), p. 9; "The Art of Conversation," *Southern Review* 9 (October 1871): 827–29; White, *Words and Their Uses*, p. 356.

42. Whitney, *Language and the Study of Language*, pp. 25, 27.

43. Francis A. March, "The Future of Philology," *The Presbyterian Quarterly and Princeton Review*, new ser., 3 (October 1874): 706, 711.

44. S.v., "literature," in Webster, *An American Dictionary of the English Language*; Noah Webster, *A Dictionary of the English Language*, ed. Chauncy Goodrich (Springfield: G. & C. Merriam, 1847); Isaac Funk, ed., *A Standard Dictionary of the English Language* (New York: Funk & Wagnalls, 1895).

45. "Polite knowledge supposes in a Man, in the first place, to be a reasonable Creature, and then instructs him to rectify and enlarge his Understanding, and to Refine his Manners, so as to set off good Sense and good Qualities to the best Advantage. This is the only true Character of Politeness, and Literature, that is particularly subservient to the End, [and] is therefore eminently called *les Belles-*

*Lettres.*" John Henley, *A Course of Academical Lectures* (London: J. Mac-Euen, 1731), p. 67.

46. S.v. "belles lettres," in Worcester, *A Dictionary of the English Language* (Boston: Hickling, Swan and Brewer, 1846); William D. Whitney, ed., *The Century Dictionary: An Encylopedic Lexicon of the English Language*, 6 vols. (New York: Century Co., 1891); *Webster's Collegiate Dictionary* (Springfield: G. & C. Merriam Co., 1898).

47. Hall, *Modern English*, p. 294.

48. Ferdinand de Saussure, *Course in General Linguistics* (New York, McGraw-Hill Paperbacks, 1959), p. 76.

49. Richard Chenevix Trench, *On the Study of Words* (New York: Redfield, 1853), pp. 19, 52.

50. See, for example, Whitney, *Oriental and Linguistic Studies*, 1st ser., pp. 380–84; Francis A. March, "The Scholar of To-day" in *Representative Phi Beta Kappa Orations*, p. 127.

51. The *Transactions of the American Philological Association*, published once a year, first appeared in 1869. The *American Philological Journal* started publishing in 1880, but it contained material on everything from ancient Indian culture to modern literature to modern language to Latin and Greek. There was no journal devoted to American dialects published until 1889 and no scholarly journal devoted to linguistics published until 1924! The *Transactions* and *Publications of the Modern Language Association* first were published in 1885. In 1868, Whitney wrote to Norton asking him to publish a long article on Melville Bell's *Visible Speech*. Whitney apologized that in the absence of a decent philological outlet the *North American Review* was his only alternative. Whitney to Norton, June 9, 1868, Norton Papers, Houghton Library, Harvard University.

52. E. L. Godkin, "The New Education at Yale," *The Nation* 10 (February 3, 1870): 70–71; "The Higher Education in America," *The Galaxy* 11 (March 1871): 369; Charles Eliot, "Inaugural Address as President of Harvard, 1869" in *American Higher Education: A Documentary History*, ed. Richard Hofstadter and Wilson Smith (Chicago: University of Chicago Press, 1961), pp. 608–9, 623–24.

53. Preston E. Sherrard to Whitney, October 18, 1870; White to Whitney, May 28, 1871; Schele de Vere to Whitney, December 6, 1870. All these letters are in the Whitney Papers, Sterling Memorial Library, Yale University. They make clear that Whitney was writing to these people and in several cases what Whitney said can be inferred from the response.

54. Norton to Whitney, November 3, 1863, Whitney Papers; also see Norton to Whitney, October 17, 1863, Whitney papers; E. L. Godkin to Whitney, May 13, 1865, Whitney Papers.

55. Whitney to Norton, November 1, 1863, Norton Papers. There are frequent letters between the editors and Whitney between 1863 and the mid-seventies. Not only did Whitney direct philologists he favored to *The Nation* and *NAR*, he also told the editors whom *not* to publish. Whitney, therefore, in the sixties and seventies more than any single individual controlled the nerve center of philological study. For example, after Whitney wrote to Norton (May 11, 1867, Norton Papers)

that George Perkins Marsh was too much swayed by the fuzzy linguistics of Max Müller, Norton did not publish any more of Marsh's work. In other letters Whitney tells Norton what books to review, which he should not bother with, and which philologists are not worth mentioning in the *NAR*.

56. Eliot to Whitney, June 9, July 4, and October 20, 1869. Whitney Papers.

57. Norton to Whitney, December 20, 1875; Norton to Whitney, September 19, 1876. Whitney Papers. Whitney to Norton, September 28, 1876, Norton Papers.

58. Kermit Vanderbilt, *Charles Eliot Norton: Apostle of Culture in a Democracy* (Cambridge: Harvard University Press, 1959), pp. 70, 73–75, 146–47; Martin Duberman, *James Russell Lowell* (Boston: Little, Brown & Co., 1966), p. 358; Godkin was less convinced that pedantry or specialization was a problem, but he did have reservations. See his "The Use of Going to College," *The Nation* 37 (August 16, 1883): 133–34.

59. David F. Noble, *America by Design: Science, Technology, and the Rise of Corporate Capitalism* (New York: Alfred A. Knopf, 1977), pp. 29–32; Charles Eliot, "What Is a Liberal Education," *Century Magazine* 28 (June 1884): 203–12; Charles W. Eliot, *Education and Efficiency and the New Definition of the Cultivated Man* (Boston: Houghton Mifflin Co., 1909); "Faults in College Culture," *New York Tribune*, 31 January 1879; "The Organization of College Faculties," *New York Evening Post*, 14 March 1882; Robert McCaughey, "The Transformation of American Academic Life: Harvard University 1821–1892," *Perspectives in American History* 8 (1974): 294–314.

60. White, *Words and Their Uses*, pp. 4–5; Richard Grant White, *Everyday English* (Boston: Houghton Mifflin & Co., 1880), p. 379; Lowell, "The Study of Modern Languages," in *Complete Writings of Lowell*, vol. 6, p. 335.

61. Henry Shepherd, "Some Points in the Study of English Prose Style," *Publications of the Modern Language Association* 4 (1889): 83–85. For similar complaints, see Morton Easton, "The Rhetorical Tendencies in Undergraduate Courses," *Publications of the Modern Language Association* 4 (1889): 20–21; and James Hart, "The College Course in English Literature, How It May Be Improved," *Transactions of the Modern Language Association* 1 (1884–85): 86.

62. L. A. Stager, "Speaking as Means and End of English Teaching," *Publications of the Modern Language Association* 2 (1887): xvii–xxiv; Gilbert Tucker, "American English," *North American Review* 136 (January 1883): 55–67; James Garnett, "The Course in English and Its Value As a Discipline," *Transactions of the Modern Language Association* 2 (1886): 64–66.

63. Larzar Ziff, *Literary Democracy* (New York: Oxford University Press, 1981), p. 34; Walt Whitman, *An American Primer* (Boston, n.p., 1904), p. 16. This was originally delivered as a lecture in the 1850s. William D. Howells, "Editor's Study," *Harper's New Monthly Magazine* 72 (January 1886): 324–25; H. L. Mencken, *The American Language* (New York: Alfred A. Knopf, 1919), p. 25.

# Chapter 6

1. For some examples, see George Washington Moon, *The Dean's English* (New York: George Routledge & Sons, 1884), pp. 4, 15, 17, 23, 33; David J. Hill, *The Elements of Rhetoric and Composition* (New York: Sheldon & Co., 1878), p. 25; Theodore Hunt, *The Principles of Written Discourse* (New York: A. C. Armstrong & Son, 1884), p. 47; John S. Hart, *A Manual of Composition and Rhetoric* (Philadelphia: Eldredge & Brothers, 1869), p. 67; Brainerd Kellogg, *A Text-Book on Rhetoric* (New York: Clark & Maynard, 1880), p. 95; and George P. Quackenbos, *Advanced Course of Composition and Rhetoric* (New York: D. Appleton & Co., 1873), pp. 318–24.

2. Theodore Hunt, "Rhetorical Science," *Princeton Review* 3 (October 1874): 661; Paul Reid, "Francis J. Child: The Fourth Boylston Professor of Rhetoric and Oratory," *Quarterly Journal of Speech* 55 (1969): 269–70; E. L. Godkin, "Rhetorical Training," *The Nation* 20 (March 4, 1875): 145–46; Letter and Response, *The Nation* 20 (March 11, 1875): 171.

3. For this view, see William Riley Parker, "Where Do English Departments Come From?" *College English* 28 (1967): 339–51; and Arthur N. Applebee, *Tradition and Reform in the Teaching of English* (National Council of the Teachers of English, 1974), pp. 21–43.

4. Patrick Scott, "Jonathan Maxcy and the Aims of Early Nineteenth-Century Rhetorical Teaching," *College English* 45 (January 1983): 21–30; Dorothy Anderson, "Edward T. Channing's Teaching of Rhetoric," *Speech Monographs* 16 (August 1949): 70–84; Also see the biographical note by Richard Dana, Jr., in Edward T. Channing, *Lectures Read to the Seniors in Harvard College* (Boston: Ticknor and Fields, 1856), n.p.

5. "Review of Hart's *Rhetoric*," *Southern Review* 8 (October 1870): 483–84.

6. John Bascom, *The Philosophy of English Literature* (New York: G. P. Putnam's Sons, 1874); Alfred Welsh, *The Development of English Literature and Language* (Chicago: S. C. Griggs & Co., 1882); Henry Day, *An Introduction to the Study of English Literature* (New York: Scribner, Armstrong & Co., 1875); Theodore Hunt, *Studies in Literature and Style* (New York: A. C. Armstrong & Co., 1890); John S. Hart, *A Manual of American Literature* (Philadelphia: Eldredge & Brothers, 1873).

7. Theodore Hunt, "The Philosophical Method in the Study and Teaching of English," *Princeton Review* 5 (July 1876): 535–47; John Genung, *The Study of Rhetoric in the College Course* (Boston: D. C. Heath & Co., 1887), pp. 5, 6, 10.

8. Hunt, *Principles of Written Discourse*, pp. 67–68; Kellogg, *A Text-Book*, p. 18.

9. Alfred Welsh, *Complete Rhetoric* (Chicago: S. C. Griggs & Co., 1885), p. 1; Kellogg, *A Text-Book*, p. 13; "The Gift of Language," *Massachusetts Teacher* 24 (1871): 8–10.

10. Hunt, *The Principles of Written Discourse*, pp. 4, 11; William Mathews, *Oratory and Orators* (Chicago: S. C. Griggs & Co., 1883), pp. 9–11; Franz Thermin, *Eloquence a Virtue*, trans. William Shedd (Philadelphia: Smith, English and Co., 1859); Welsh, *Complete Rhetoric*, p. 153.

11. See George Craik, *A Compendious History of English Literature and of the English Language* (New York: Charles Scribner's Sons, 1863), pp. 22–23; 49–51; Lounsbury wrote: "The history is a history of the language, and not at all of the literature." Thomas Lounsbury, *History of the English Language* (New York: Henry Holt and Co., 1879), p. v.

12. William D. Whitney, *Language and the Study of Language* (New York: C. Scribner & Co., 1867), pp. 405, 420.

13. Francis A. March, "The Study of Anglo-Saxon," *Report of the Commissioner of Education for the Year 1876* (Washington, D.C.: Government Printing Office, 1878), p. 476; Also see James Garnett, "The Historical Method in the Teaching of English," *The Proceedings of the National Educational Association* (Philadelphia: National Educational Association, 1879), pp. 87–96.

14. Reid, "Francis J. Child," p. 274; For the evolution of March's thinking, compare Francis March, *A Course in College Philology: Literature and Language* (New York: Charles Scribner's Sons, 1865) and his "The Future of Philology," *Presbyterian Quarterly and Princeton Review* 3 (October 1874): 698–713.

15. Harold Monroe Jordan, "Rhetorical Education in American Colleges and Universities, 1850–1915" (Ph.D. diss., Northwestern University, 1952), pp. 23–24.

16. Hunt, "Rhetorical Science," p. 435; Hiram Corson, *Hand-book of Anglo-Saxon and Early English* (New York: Holt & Williams, 1871); Hiram Corson, *The Aims of Literary Study* (New York: Macmillian & Co., 1895), pp. 47, 49, 77–79; Genung, *The Study of Rhetoric*, p. 8.

17. For a sense of the eclecticism, see the survey of English programs throughout the nation in the *Report of the Commissioner of Education, 1888–1889* (Washington, D.C.: Government Printing Office, 1891), pp. 1224–93.

18. Hugh Hawkins, *Pioneer: A History of the Johns Hopkins University, 1874–1889* (Ithaca: Cornell University Press, 1960), pp. 162–68.

19. "New Publications," *The New York Times*, 20 June 1871.

20. See, for example, David J. Hill, *The Science of Rhetoric* (New York: Sheldon & Co., 1877), pp. 31–32.

21. Lounsbury, *History of the English Language*, p. 143.

22. Henry Alford, *A Plea for the Queen's English* (New York: Dick and Fitzgerald, 1864), p. xiv; M. A. Newall, "English Grammar in the Elementary School," *The Addresses and Journals of the National Educational Association, 1872*, (Peoria: B. Walker, 1873), p. 137.

23. Richard Grant White, *Words and Their Uses* (New York: Sheldon & Co., 1872), pp. 295–333.

24. "Errors in School Teaching," *The New York Times*, 1 March 1878; White published nearly thirty articles in the *Times* between May 1877 and October 1879. Before that he was an occasional contributor to the paper, and after, in February and March 1880, White published another five essays on language in the *Times*. My source is the published index of the paper. "Grammar," *Chicago Tribune*, 4 April 1875; "The Study of Grammar," *Chicago Tribune*, 21 November 1875;

"Teaching English in the Common Schools," *Chicago Tribune*, 23 December 1882; "Grammar in the Schools," *Chicago Tribune*, 31 December 1882; Emerson E. White, *The Elements of Pedagogy* (Cincinnati: Van Antwerp, Bragg & Co., 1886), pp. 255–56; Rev. Edward Thring, *Theory and Practice of Teaching* (Cambridge: The University Press, 1883), p. 228; Francis Parker, *Talks on Pedagogy* (New York: E. L. Kellogg & Co., 1894), p. 329.

25. Furness to White, June 2, 1871; June 2, 1873; White Papers, New York Historical Society.

26. "English Grammar Again," *Massachusetts Teacher* 26 (1873): 46; Francis A. March, "Methods of Teaching English in the High School," *The Addresses . . . of the National Educational Association, 1872*, pp. 240–44; William D. Whitney, "The Study of English Grammar," *New England Journal of Education* 3 (April 15, 1876): 181–82; Benjamin A. Hathaway, *1001 Questions and Answers on the Theory and Practice of Teaching* (Cleveland: The Burrows Brothers Co., 1886), p. 85.

27. This paragraph is based on my research into the school English programs of San Francisco; New York City; Chicago; Boston; Columbus, Ohio; Utica, New York; and New Haven, Connecticut. For more detailed information on this shift, see my "Democratic Eloquence: Language, Education, and Authority in Nine-teenth-Century America" (Ph.D. diss., University of Chicago, 1986), pp. 338–40. Also see John Elbert Stout, *The Development of High School Curricula in the North Central States* (Chicago: University of Chicago Press, 1921), p. 71. Between 1860 and 1865, 60 percent of the schools surveyed by Stout taught grammar; by 1876–80, that had fallen to 30 percent.

28. "The Abolition of Grammar," *The New York Times*, 25 February 1879; Florus Alonzo Barbour, *The Teaching of English Grammar* (Boston: Lee and Shepard, 1880), p. 21; *Twenty-Second Annual Report of the State Superintendent of Maine Common Schools, 1875*, p. 134.

29. Alonzo Reed and Brainerd Kellogg, *Higher Lessons in English* (New York: Effingham, Maynard & Co., 1877), p. 3.

30. White, *Elements of Pedagogy*, pp. 225–26; Parker, *Talks on Pedagogy*, p. 329; Hathaway, *1001 Questions*, pp. 83, 85; Edwin Hewett, *A Treatise on Pedagogy* (New York: American Book Co., 1884), p. 194.

31. "Popular Education," *North American Review* 23 (1826): 53; Flora Haines Longhead, ed., *Life, Diary and Letters of Oscar Lovell Shafter* (San Francisco: The Blair-Murdock Co., 1915), p. 71; Mrs. Lydia H. Sigourney, *Lucy Howard's Journal* (New York: Harper and Bros., 1858), p. 12; Margaret Barnes and Janet Fairbanks, eds., *Julia Newberry's Diary* (New York: W.W. Norton & Co., 1933), p. 32; "Errors in School Teaching," *The New York Times*, 1 March 1879.

32. *Report of the Committee on Text-Books, 1885*, School Document no. 8 (Boston: n.p., 1885), pp. 5–6; *Annual Report of the Superintendent of Schools of . . . Chicago, 1884*, p. 43; *Thirtieth Annual Report of the Public Schools, City and County of San Francisco*, pp. 61–63; *Eleventh Annual Report of the Board of Education, Rhode Island, 1881*, pp. 142–43; *Sixteenth Annual Report of the Board of Education of Rhode Island, 1885*, pp. 134–35.

33. *Thirty-Fourth Annual Report of the Board of Education of . . . New York, 1876*,

p. 241; *Twenty-Second Annual Report of the Public Schools, City and County of San Francisco, 1875*, p. 61; *Annual Report of the School Board of New Haven, 1885*, p. 29.

34. Mrs. Nelly L. Knox, *Elementary Lessons in English* (Boston: Ginn & Heath, 1880), p. x; other well-known language lesson books were those written by William Swinton: *Language Lessons: An Introductory Grammar and Composition* (1873); *Language Primer: Beginner's Lessons in Speaking and Writing* (1874); and *New Language Lessons: An Elementary Grammar and Composition* (1878).

35. The material in this paragraph is drawn from various annual reports of the school districts mentioned.

36. Applebee, *Tradition and Reform*, pp. 28–29; Thomas Shaw, *Outlines of English Literature* (London: John Murray, 1846).

37. Applebee, *Tradition and Reform*, pp. 28–29; Stout, *The Development of High School Curricula*, p. 71; Edna Hays, *College Entrance Requirements in English: Their Effects on the High School* (New York: Teachers College, 1936), pp. 1, 2, 3, 7–9.

38. Hays, *College Entrance Requirements*, pp. 15, 18, 21.

39. Richard Jenkyns, *The Victorians and Ancient Greece* (Cambridge: Harvard University Press, 1980), p. 79.

40. The disappearance of Addison might be worth some study. After nearly 150 years of having his essays touted as models of English style, he seems to have fallen from favor in the late nineteenth century. Richard Grant White included a negative discussion of Addison's prose in *Words and Their Uses*.

41. *Annual Report of the Superintendent of Schools of . . . Chicago, 1883*, p. 63.

42. William Spalding, *The History of English Literature* (Edinburgh: Oliver and Boyd, 1871), p. 4; Thomas Shaw, *Outlines of English Literature* (Philadelphia: Blanchard and Lea, 1852), pp. 62–64, 126–27, 239.

43. On Eliot, see Hays, *College Entrance Requirements*, pp. 17–18; and Elbridge Smith, "When and How Shall the English Language Be Studied?" *Massachusetts Teacher* 22 (March 1868): 80.

44. For a sense of the diversity, see Oliver T. Bright, "English Instruction for Children," *The Journal of Proceedings and Addresses of the National Educational Association, 1884* (Boston: Heath & Co., 1885), pp. 217–35; "Oratory and Vocal Culture," *Massachusetts Teacher*," 24 (1871): 131–34; W. W. Parsons, "Every Study a Language Study," *Indiana School Journal* 29 (1884): 206–8; H. R. Buckham, "English Grammar and English Speech," *The School Bulletin* 2 (December 1875): 61; and "Grammar," *Illinois Schoolmaster* 9 (June 1876): 193–96.

45. For the figures, see the appendix.

46. I have gone through the indices of *Godey's Lady's Book, Harper's Bazar, Peterson's Ladies' National Magazine*, and *Ladies' Repository*. Through the year 1885 I found nothing on scientific philology but scattered essays either citing verbal critics or in the same spirit as the verbal criticism.

47. Again, based on a search of the index, I found numerous works in the manner of the verbal critics but none following the lead of the philologists. I surveyed *St. Nicholas, Our Boys and Girls*, and *The Lutheran Sunday School Observer*

through 1885. Some examples: "Careless English," *St. Nicholas* 2 (January 1875): 194; "Don't Say," *Our Boys and Girls* 1 (1867): 299; and "Plain Speaking," *Our Boys and Girls* 11 (1872): 340–41.

48. I surveyed eight literary journals: *The Galaxy, Lakeside Monthly, Round Table* (a weekly), *Harper's Monthly, Lippincott's Overland Magazine, The Atlantic Monthly, Scribner's Monthly*, and *Appleton's Monthly*. With the two exceptions noted, all overwhelmingly favored the critics over the scholars. *Scribner's Monthly* in the mid-1870s became *The Century Magazine*. As we shall see in chapter 7, the Century Company sponsored one of the first major dictionaries to be based on philological principles. *Appleton's* also provides an interesting exception. It began in 1869 as a general interest journal of science. In that guise it included several articles on the new philology. In 1875, it was transformed into a literary journal not unlike *The Atlantic Monthly*. It then stopped printing material about philology and took a far more critical and conservative stance to the language. The magazine folded in 1881.

49. "American Slangography," *Chicago Tribune*, 20 March 1870; "New Publications," *Chicago Tribune*, 8 May 1871. William Mathews worked as financial page editor of the *Tribune* between 1868 and 1874, see *Dictionary of American Biography* (New York, 1931), vol. 12, pp. 406–7; "A New Humorist," Boston *Daily Advertiser*, 12 August 1869; "Josh Billings on Milk," Boston *Daily Advertiser*, 28 October 1869; "The Rationale of Negro Minstrelsy," Boston *Daily Advertiser*, 14 October 1869; untitled editorial, Boston *Daily Advertiser*, 29 January 1870.

50. "Philology, The Secrets of Language," *The New York Times*, 6 February 1874; "A New English Dictionary," *The New York Times*, 9 August 1879; editorial, *The New York Times*, 3 May 1875; editorial, *The New York Times*, 16 July 1875; "The Slang of Corruption," *The New York Times*, 27 November 1874; "Women and English," *The New York Times*, 19 July 1881.

51. Charles Darwin, *The Descent of Man and Selection in Relation to Sex* (New York: the Modern Library, n.d.), pp. 462, 464; Charles Sanders Peirce, *The Collected Papers of Charles Sanders Peirce*, ed. Charles Hartshorne and Paul Weiss, 8 vols. (Cambridge: Harvard University Press, 1958), vol. 4, pp. 260–73; For a useful discussion of Morgan's theories of language, see Marshall Sahlins, *Culture and Practical Reason* (Chicago: University of Chicago Press, 1976), pp. 57–64; Sir Edward B. Tyler, *Anthropology* (Ann Arbor: University of Michigan Press, 1970), pp. 27–54; and E. L. Youmans, *The Culture Demanded by Modern Life* (New York: Appleton's, 1867), pp. 45–47.

52. E. L. Godkin, "A Plea for the Queen's English," *The Nation* 2 (March 15, 1866): 340–41; W. P. Atkinson, "The Moon-Alford Controversy," *The Nation* 2 (June 22, 1866): 791. By the next year, however, Whitney, Hall, and March are writing for *The Nation*. The tone becomes extremely hostile to verbal critics. See [William D. Whitney], "G. W. Moon's Bad English," *The Nation* 7 (December 10, 1868): 482–83; "Vulgarisms and Other Errors of Speech," *The Nation* 6 (May 21, 1868): 415–16; and E. L. Godkin, "The Odium Philologicum," *The Nation* 17 (November 13, 1873): 318–19.

53. Mrs. Eliza B. Duffey, *The Ladies and Gentlemen's Etiquette* (Philadelphia:

Lippincott & Co., 1877), p. 41; *The Bazar Book of Decorum* (New York: Harper and Bros., 1874), p. 129.

54. James McCabe, *The Household Encyclopedia of Business and Social Forms* (Philadelphia: National Publishing Co., 1881), pp. 17–52; Julia McNair Wright, *Practical Life* (Boston: D. L. Guernsey, 1881), pp. 139–40.

55. See the appendix.

56. John Harvey Kellogg, *Ladies' Guide in Health and Disease* (1882; reprint, New York: Harper and Bros., 1888), pp. 210–11.

57. I have surveyed eight newspapers, four aiming at refined audiences, four more popular in tone. The four refined papers were the Boston *Daily Advertiser*, *The New York Times*, the New York *Evening Post*, and the *Chicago Tribune*. The four popular papers were the *Boston Herald*, the *New York Tribune*, the New York *Sun*, and the *Chicago Times*. I looked through each of these papers for the years 1871 and 1882 and also dipped into them randomly at other points. Since *The New York Times* published an index, my survey of that paper was more systematic. So too with the *New York Tribune*, which began publishing an index in 1876. For the change at the *Tribune*, see Harry W. Baehr, Jr., *The New York Tribune since the Civil War* (New York: Dodd, Mead & Co., 1936), pp. 67, 74, 83–84, 137–38, 143. The publication of the index beginning in 1876 was still another attempt to turn the paper into a high-culture endeavor. The project was suggested to Reid by Charles Francis Adams, Jr. (Baehr, pp. 140–41). At that time, only two English newspapers, *The London Times* and *The New York Times*, published indexes.

58. Edwin M. Bacon, *King's Directory of Boston* (Cambridge: Moses King, 1883), p. 225; Albert P. Pangtry, ed., *Metropolitan Boston: A Modern History*, 4 vols. (New York: Lewis Historical Publishing Co., 1929), vol. 2, pp. 567–70. By the mid-1880s, the managing editor of the Boston *Daily Advertiser* was commenting that journalistic vulgarity had vanished in Boston. See Frank Luther Mott, *American Journalism: A History*, 3rd ed. (New York: Macmillan Co., 1962), p. 453.

59. Clarence Stone, *Dana and the Sun* (New York: Dodd, Mead & Co., 1938), pp. 33, 34, 53.

60. Compare "Servant-hunting," New York *Evening Post*, 18 March 1882 with "The Sort of Education They Need," New York *Sun*, 7 May 1882.

61. Circulation figures were notoriously inaccurate, but everyone agreed that those papers I have called "popular" sold far more copies than gentlemen's papers. For example, while the New York *Sun* in 1880 printed about a hundred thousand copies each day, *The New York Times* circulated thirty thousand. Stone, *Dana and the Sun*, p. 382; Elmer Davis, *History of the New York Times* (New York: The New York Times, 1921), p. 118.

62. William H. Hills, "Advice to Newspaper Correspondents," *The Writer* 1 (June 1887): 50; Stone, *Dana and the Sun*, pp. 389–91; also see the *Chicago Times*, 28 May 1882.

63. "The Devil's Chapel," *The New York Times*, 1 January 1874.

64. *Boston Herald*, 4 June 1882; Baehr, *New York Tribune since the Civil War*, p. 83; "Education in Politics," *Chicago Tribune*, 21 June 1882; "John Bright on American Literature," *Chicago Tribune*, 16 June 1882.

65. See in the *Sun*: "Wedding Garments, Table Manners, and the Privileges of the Engaged," 26 March 1882; "Common Sense in Car Travel," 28 March 1882; "Shall He Study Medicine," 23 July 1882; "How He Looks on the Ministry," 24 July 1882; and "The Sort of Education They Need," 7 May 1882.

66. "What Books Shall He Read?" New York *Sun*, 6 August 1882; "The Queen's English," *New York Tribune*, 30 July 1883; "Titles in Republics," *Chicago Tribune*, 20 March 1882; editorial, *Chicago Tribune* 28 May 1882; "New Publications," *Boston Herald*, 15 January 1882.

67. Altina L. Waller, *Reverend Beecher and Mrs. Tilton* (Amherst: University of Massachusetts Press, 1982), *passim*.

68. On Irish women becoming refined, see Hasia R. Diner, *Erin's Daughters in America: Irish Immigrant Women in the Nineteenth Century* (Baltimore: Johns Hopkins University Press, 1983), pp. 140–42. Lawrence W. Levine, *Black Culture and Black Consciousness* (New York: Oxford University Press, 1977), pp. 144–49, and esp. 153–54.

69. A copy of this advertisement is in the author's possession.

70. See chapter 1, note 95.

71. Robert Darnton, *The Great Cat Massacre* (New York: Basic Books, 1984), p. 140.

72. "Vulgarity and Gentility," *The New York Times*, 9 March 1879; "Editor's Chair," *Peterson's Ladies' National Magazine* 68 (September 1875): 220; R. Gilsan, *Journal of Army Life* (San Francisco: A. L. Bancroft & Co., 1874), pp. 451–53.

73. "Vulgarity and Gentility," 9 March 1879; J. A. K. Thomson, trans., *The Ethics of Aristotle*, (Baltimore: Penguin, 1953), pp. 30–31.

74. Robert DeMaria, Jr., *Johnson's Dictionary and the Language of Learning* (Oxford: Clarendon Press, 1986), pp. 221–27. Johnson's quote is from Richardson's *Clarissa*: "Professional, as well as national reflections are to be avoided."

75. S.v. "professional" in Sir William A. Craigie and James R. Hulbert, eds., *A Dictionary of American English on Historical Principles* (Chicago: University of Chicago Press, 1938); Mitford M. Mathews, ed., *A Dictionary of Americanisms on Historical Principles* (Chicago: University of Chicago Press, 1951).

76. "Good Manners in Journalism," *The New York Times*, 15 April 1868; "Useless Knowledge," Boston *Daily Advertiser*, 14 August 1869.

77. Henry Ward Beecher, *Yale Lectures on Preaching* (New York: J. B. Ford and Co., 1872), p. 231; the promotional literature from John Hopkins is quoted in Lawrence Veysey, "Higher Education," in Nathan O. Hatch, ed., *The Professions in American History* (Notre Dame: University of Notre Dame Press, 1988), p. 26.

78. On the history of *profession* and *professional*, see the *Oxford English Dictionary*.

79. On "professional schools," see Mathews, *Dictionary of Americanisms*; James is quoted in the *Supplement to the Oxford English Dictionary*, s.v. "professional."

80. "The World of Amusement," *Chicago Tribune*, 1 May 1870; "Manners on the Road," *Harper's Bazar* 2 (October 16, 1869): 658; "What Is a Gentleman," *The New York Times*, 23 February 1875; editorial, *The New York Times*, 29 August 1879; "Living Like a Gentleman," *The New York Times*, 9 November 1879.

81. "Table Talk," *Appleton's Journal* 6 (July 27, 1871): 134; "Table Talk," *Appleton's Journal* 6 (September 9, 1871): 302–3; Henry Ward Beecher, "The Christian Use of the Tongue," *The Original Plymouth Pulpit Sermons of Henry Ward Beecher*, 10 vols. (Boston: The Pilgrim Press, 1873), vol. 10, pp. 397–98; "No 'Middle Class' Here," *Peterson's Ladies' National Magazine* 83 (March 1883): 260.

82. "Lady and Gentleman," New York *Sun*, 19 March 1882.

83. John Tomsich, *A Genteel Endeavor* (Stanford: Stanford University Press, 1971), p. 193.

84. On eighteenth-century Europe, see chapter 1; Ramsay MacMullen, *Roman Social Relations* (New Haven: Yale University Press, 1974), pp. 30–32; Hans H. Gerth and C. Wright Mills, eds., *From Max Weber: Essays in Sociology* (New York: Oxford University Press, 1946), pp. 434–41; Clifford Geertz, *Local Knowledge* (New York: Basic Books, 1983), pp. 59–61.

85. After the Civil War, it was common to pose the self-made man and the college-bred man as alternative cultural models. According to the highly educated critics, "self-made" implied a personality without the accumulated wisdom of Western Civilization, that is, a man literally made by himself. For examples of the opposition, see "Classical Culture in America," *Round Table* 8 (November 7, 1868); C. C. Nott, "American Colleges and Legislators," *The Nation* 17 (August 28, 1873): 141–42; and E. L. Godkin, "Educated Man in Centennial Politics," *The Nation* 23 (July 6, 1876): 5–6.

86. New York *Evening Post*, 12 February 1881; 7 January 1882; *Boston Herald*, 15 January 1882.

87. "Voice of the People," *Chicago Tribune*, 5 January 1882.

88. Joseph Medill, *An Easy Method of Spelling the English Language* (Chicago: n.p., 1867). This pamphlet is a populist attack on traditional, obfuscating spelling customs. Later editorials in the *Tribune*, however, freely used the authority of the scholarly linguists. See, "Spelling Reform," 29 December 1878; "Spelling Reform," 2 May 1880; and "Spelling and Pronunciation," 25 July 1880.

# Chapter 7

1. The list of members is in Phillip Schaff, *A Companion to the Greek Testament and the English Version* (New York: Harper and Bros., 1892), pp. 571–77.

2. Anon., *Historical Account of the Work of the American Committee of Revision* (New York: Charles Scribner's Sons, 1885), pp. 46–56.

3. The differences in age were especially striking in the New Testament companies. Seventeen of the British members were born before 1816, twelve were born after, and one date is unknown. Of the Americans working on the New Testament, six were born before 1816, thirteen were born after. The American New Testament committee fought hardest to modernize the Bible. For the birth dates of the revisers, see Schaff, *A Companion*, 571–77.

4. Samuel Hemphill, *A History of the Revised Version of the New Testament* (London: Elliot Stock, 1906), p. 67.

5. Ibid., pp. 43–65; Arthur Fenton Hort, *The Life and Letters of Fenton John Hort*, 2 vols. (London: Macmillan Co., 1896), vol. 2, pp. 236–38.

6. Howard Crosby, "The Coming Revision of the Bible," *North American Review* 131 (1880): 450.

7. *The Holy Bible* (Cambridge: Cambridge University Press, 1885), p. vii; Schaff, *A Companion*, p. 455.

8. Talbot Chambers, *A Companion to the Revised Old Testament* (New York: Funk & Wagnalls, 1885), p. 17; Phillip Schaff, "The Old Version and the New," *North American Review* 132 (1881): 435; Marvin Vincent, "Notes on the Revised New Testament," *Presbyterian Review* 2 (1881): 684; Crosby, "The Coming Revision of the Bible," p. 448.

9. Timothy Dwight, "The Revision of the Authorized English Version of the New Testament," *New Englander* 38 (July 1879): 409.

10. Coxe quote from *Chicago Tribune*, 15 February 1880; George Perkins Marsh, "The Proposed Revision of the English Bible," *The Nation* 11 (October 13, 20, 27, 1870): 238–39; 261–63; 281–82.

11. Schaff, *A Companion*, p. 452.

12. Ibid., p. 186.

13. "The Revised Version of the New Testament," *Edinburgh Review* 154 (July 1881): 177.

14. Matthew Arnold, *Isaiah of Jerusalem in the Authorized English Version with an Introduction* (London: Macmillan and Co., 1883), p. 3; Chambers, *A Companion*, p. 138.

15. Hemphill, *A History of the Revised Version*, p. 85.

16. David Schaff, *Life of Phillip Schaff* (New York: Charles Scribner's Sons, 1897), p. 378.

17. Charles Robinson, "The Bible Society and the New Revision," *Scribner's Monthly* 21 (January 1881): 450.

18. Ferenc Morton Szasz, *The Divided Mind of Protestant America 1880–1930* (University: University of Alabama Press, 1982), pp. 19–20.

19. This evidence, and much more, is presented in Schaff, *A Companion*, pp. 403–11.

20. *The New York Times*, 22 May, 30 September, 13 November, 21 November 1881; "The Bible Revision Among the People," *Scribner's Monthly* 22 (August 1881): 624–25.

21. Elias Riggs, "Some Reasons in Favor of Retouching the Revised English Version of the Scriptures," *Presbyterian Review* 9 (1888): 32; John Fulton, "Why the Revised Version Has Failed," *Forum* 3 (June 1887): 354, 363; George Washington Moon, *The Revisers' English* (New York: Funk & Wagnalls, 1882), p. 84; Theodore W. Hunt, "The English Bible and the English Language," *New Englander* 47 (October 1887): 259.

22. Daniel Goodwin, *Notes on the Late Revision of the New Testament Version* (New

York: Thomas Whittaker, 1883), p. 11; "Editor's Table," *Appleton's Journal*, n.s., 11 (July 1881): 90–91; E. L. Godkin, "The New and the Old Version," *The Nation* 32 (July 9, 1881): 401–2; Hunt, "The English Bible and the English Language," pp. 260–66; Fulton, "Why the Revised Version Has Failed," pp. 357–58; Matthew Arnold, *Literature and Dogma* (London: Smith, Elder & Co., 1873), *passim*; Matthew Arnold, *God and the Bible* (London: Smith, Elder & Co., 1875), *passim*.

23. Francis Bowen, "An Early American Version of the Scriptures," *Princeton Review* (1883): 19–45; Many of the revisers came to this opinion in later years, for example, Brooke Foss Westcott, *Some Lessons of the Revised Version of the New Testament* (London: Hodder and Stoughton, 1897), pp. 7–8.

24. On the Baptists, see *The New York Times*, 12 June 1883; *Minutes of the General Assembly of the Presbyterian Church in the United States of America, 1887*, p. 72; *Minutes of the General Assembly of the Presbyterian Church, 1889*, pp. 80–81; *Minutes of the General Assembly of the Presbyterian Church, 1892*, p. 178.

25. Rev. John Chadwick, "The New Old Testament," *Arena* 7 (February 1893): 298; Episcopal minister quoted in "How Shall the Church Utilize the Revised Version?" *Methodist Review* 80 (January 1898): 131–32; James M. Whiton, "The American Revision of the Bible," *Outlook* 58 (February 12, 1898): 416; "The Use of the Revised Version," *Methodist Review* 79 (March 1897): 303.

26. George Steiner, *After Babel: Aspects of Language and Translation* (New York: Oxford University Press, 1975), p. 315.

27. Washington Gladden, "The New Bible," *Arena* 9 (February 1894): 295–304; For the best discussions of the importance of late-nineteenth-century ritualism, see T. J. Jackson Lears, *No Place of Grace: Antimodernism and the Transformation of American Culture 1880–1920* (New York: Pantheon, 1981), pp. 184–215; also see Daniel Bluestone, "Landscape and Culture in Nineteenth-Century America" (Ph.D. diss., University of Chicago, 1984), pp. 135–39; on the Church Congress, *The New York Times*, 27 and 28 October 1881.

28. Some examples of this are C. J. H. Ropes, "The Revision and Its Cambridge Critic," *New Englander* 42 (September 1883): 690; Chambers, *A Companion*, p. 35; "Editor's Easy Chair," *Harper's New Monthly Magazine* 63 (August 1881): 465–66; G. C. McWhorster, "Revision of the English Bible," *Appleton's* 9 (January 25, 1873): 142–43; and Frank Ballard, *Which Bible to Read—Revised or Authorized?* (London: Allenson, 1897), p. 39.

29. Matthew Brown Riddle, *The Story of the Revised New Testament: American Standard Edition* (Philadelphia: Sunday School Times Company, 1908).

30. Frederick F. Bruce, *The English Bible* (London: Lutterworth Press, 1970), pp. 153–66; Ira Price, *The Ancestry of Our English Bible* (New York: Harper and Bros., 1949), pp. 292–94.

31. These figures are compiled from the published index of the *Times*.

32. In fact, *no* Bible, not even the Revised Standard Version, could come remotely close to generating the interest that the Revised Version did in the 1880s. See Barry Hoberman, "Translating the Bible," *The Atlantic* 255 (February 1985): 45.

33. "The Bible in Sunday Schools," *Century Magazine* 29 (November 1884): 147; "The Bible in English—Biblical Theology," *Methodist Quarterly Review* 68 (July 1886): 591.

34. Robert K. Leavitt, *Noah's Ark: New England Yankees and the Endless Quest* (Springfield: G. & C. Merriam Co., 1947), p. 81; William D. Whitney, ed., *The Century Dictionary: An Encyclopedic Lexicon of the English Language*, 6 vols. (New York: The Century Co., 1889–1895), vol. 1, p. v; Isaac Funk, ed., *A Standard Dictionary of the English Language*, 2 vols. (New York: Funk and Wagnalls Co., 1895), vol. 1, p. vii; Robert Hunter, ed., *The American Encyclopaedic Dictionary*, 4 vols. (1894; reprint, Chicago: W. B. Conkey Co., 1896), vol. 1, p. 9.

35. K. M. Elizabeth Murray, *Caught in the Web of Words: James A. H. Murray and the Oxford English Dictionary* (Oxford: Oxford University Press, 1977), p. 266.

36. *The American Encyclopaedic*, vol. 1, p. 10; *A Standard Dictionary*, vol. 1, p. vii.

37. Noah Porter, ed., *Webster's International Dictionary of the English Language* (Springfield: G. & C. Merriam Co., 1895), "Statement of Publishers;" "Preface," pp. iii–iv.

38. Ibid., "Preface," p. iii (written by Noah Porter); "Statement of Publishers."

39. For the gradual inclusion of experts into the Webster's production, see Leavitt, *Noah's Ark*, *passim*. The quote from the *Springfield Union* is from Leavitt, p. 60.

40. Thomas R. Lounsbury, "Part Third of the New English Dictionary—II," *The Nation* 45 (August 25, 1887): 155–56; the comments from *The American Encyclopaedic* and *Standard Dictionary* are both from the title page.

41. *A Standard Dictionary*, vol. 1, p. vii; *The Century Dictionary*, vol. 1, p. vi.

42. "Worcester's Dictionary," *New Englander* 18 (1860): 416; For Johnson's attitude toward technical vocabulary in relation to earlier British lexicography, see DeWitt Starnes and Gertrude Noyes, *The English Dictionary from Cawdrey to Johnson, 1604–1755* (Chapel Hill: University of North Carolina Press, 1946), p. 185.

43. *The Century Dictionary*, vol. 1, p. vi.

44. *Webster's International*, p. iii.

45. *Webster's International*, "Statement of Publisher"; *A Standard Dictionary*, vol. 1, p. viii; *The Century Dictionary*, vol. 1, p. vi.

46. Joseph E. Worcester, *A Dictionary of the English Language* (Boston: Hickling, Swan and Brewer, 1860), p. v.

47. *A Standard Dictionary*, vol. 1, p. xiii; *The American Encyclopaedic*, vol. 1, p. 12.

48. Murray, *Caught in the Web of Words*, pp. 221–23.

49. *Poop* was included in Funk and Wagnall's *Standard Dictionary* and in Robert Hunter's *The American Encyclopaedic*.

50. See *The Century Dictionary* and *A Standard Dictionary*.

51. *The American Encyclopaedic*, *The Century*, and *A Standard*.

52. The *Standard* and *American Encyclopaedic* labeled *red-eye* "slang," *The Century*

called it "low." *The Century* and *A Standard* included *eye-opener*. *The Century, American Encyclopaedic*, and *A Standard* all included *moonshine*. *Webster's International* called *moonshiner* "cant." The complete list of liquor synonyms was drawn from Richard Harwood Thornton's *American Glossary*, 2 vols. (Philadelphia: Lippincott, 1912).

53. *The American Encyclopaedic* and *The Century* sanctioned the word. The *Standard* labeled it an Americanism. Only the conservative *Webster's International* called it "low." Earlier dictionaries routinely condemned the word if they included it. The 1886 *Worcester's*, for example, called it "vulgar" and the 1873 *Webster's* called it "colloquial and vulgar."

54. The three dictionaries that included *sheeny* were *A Standard, The American Encyclopaedic*, and *The Century*.

55. S.v. "slang" in *Webster's, The American Encyclopaedic*, and *A Standard*.

56. S.v. "slang" in the *Century*.

57. William Dean Howells, *Criticism and Fiction* (New York: Harper and Bros., 1891), pp. 2, 134–40, 187–88.

58. "The Century Dictionary," *The New York Times*, 13 July 1890; also see "Contributor's Club," *The Atlantic Monthly* 54 (1884): 428.

59. "The Latest Triumph of American Lexicography," *The New York Times*, 21 January 1892; "A Sign of the Times in Lexicography," *Century Magazine* 28 (August 1884): 636–37; Melville B. Anderson, "The New 'International' Webster," *The Dial* 11 (November 1890): 189–90; "The Century Dictionary," *The New York Times*, 1 March 1891.

60. W. A. Mowry, "Good English Crystallized," *Education* 11 (1890): 115; "A Standard Dictionary," *The Atlantic Monthly* 76 (September 1895): 417; Thomas R. Lounsbury, "The New English Dictionary," *The Nation* 38 (April 24, 1884): 368; "The Standard Dictionary Completed," *The New York Times*, 19 May 1895.

61. William H. Wells, "Encyclopaedic Dictionaries," *The Dial* 4 (October 1883): 124; untitled editorial, *The Writer* 8 (September 1895): 133.

62. Richard Grant White, *Words and Their Uses*, (New York: Sheldon & Co., 1872), pp. 365–66, 368–69.

63. Theodore W. Hunt, "English Lexicography," *New Englander* 55 (September 1891): 208–10.

64. Fitzedward Hall, "The English Philological Society's Dictionary," *The Nation* 50 (March 6, 1890): 200–201.

## Chapter 8

1. Arthur C. Champneys, *History of English* (New York: Macmillan & Co., 1893), p. 2.

2. George Phillip Krapp, *Modern English: Its Growth and Present Use* (New York: Charles Scribner's Sons, 1909), pp. 10–11.

3. Oliver F. Emerson, *A Brief History of the English Language* (New York: Macmillan Co., 1896); Thomas Lounsbury, *A History of the English Language*, rev. ed., (New York: Henry Holt and Co., 1894).

4. See William Morton Payne, ed., *English in American Universities* (Boston: D. C. Heath & Co., 1895), pp. 41, 71, 84, 46.

5. H. G. C. Jagemann, "Philology and Purism," *Publications of the Modern Language Association* 15 (1900): 74–96; E. S. Sheldon, "Practical Philology," *Publications of the Modern Language Association* 17 (1902): 91–104. What is striking about this debate is how little of it there actually was.

6. See, for example, Albert Cook, "The Province of English Philology," *Publications of the Modern Language Association* 13 (1898): 185–204.

7. I mean here to contradict those scholars who equate the teaching of English with the creation of English departments. Exponents of that view include Don Cameron Allen, *The Ph.D. in English and American Literature* (New York: Holt, Rinehart and Winston, 1968), pp. 10–11; William Riley Parker, "Where Do English Departments Come From?" *College English* 28 (1967): 339–51; Arthur N. Applebee, *Tradition and Reform in the Teaching of English* (National Council of the Teachers of English, 1974), pp. 21–43.

8. E. L. Godkin, "The Growing Illiteracy of American Boys," *The Nation* 63 (1896): 284–85.

9. W. P. Garrison, "English at Harvard and Elsewhere," *The Nation* 55 (1892): 299–300; William Brewer, "English at College," *The Nation* 63 (1896): 327.

10. For a sample of the voluminous debate: Theodore W. Hunt, "The Place of English in the College Curriculum," *New Englander* 45 (February 1886): 108–23; George Beardsley, "Teaching English for a Livelihood," *The Dial* 23 (November 16, 1897): 270–72; "Contributor's Club," *The Atlantic Monthly* 71 (May 1893): 656–62; "Contributor's Club," *The Atlantic Monthly* 72 (August 1893): 284–85; Horace E. Scudder, "The Educational Law of Reading and Writing," *The Atlantic Monthly* 73 (February 1894): 252–62; Horace E. Scudder, "The Academic Treatment of English," *The Atlantic Monthly* 74 (November 1894): 688–93; W. H. Johnson, "The Deterioration of College English," *The Dial* 22 (May 1, 1897): 271–72; George Beardsley, "English Literature at the Colleges and Universities," *Educational Review* 16 (1898): 185–91; "English in the Preparatory Schools," *The Nation* 55 (November 24, 1892): 388–89; E. L. Godkin, "College English," *The Nation* 61 (September 26, 1895): 219–20; W. W. Goodwin, "School English," *The Nation* 61 (October 24, 1895): 291–93; "School English," *The Nation* 61 (October 31, 1895): 309–10; and "College English," *The Nation* 65 (November 4, 1897): 351–52.

11. Joan Hoff Wilson, *Herbert Hoover: Forgotten Progressive* (Boston: Little, Brown and Co., 1975), pp. 10–11.

12. James Morgan Hart, "Cornell Course in Rhetoric and English Philology," *The Academy* 6 (1891): 188.

13. Albert Raymond Kitzhaber, "Rhetoric in American Colleges, 1850–1900" (Ph.D. diss., University of Washington, 1953), p. 101; James A. Berlin, *Writing Instruction in Nineteenth-Century American Colleges* (Carbondale: Southern Illinois University Press, 1984), p. 60; Payne, *English in American Universities*, p. 52.

14. Berlin, *Writing Instruction*, pp. 77–92; Donald C. Stewart, "Two Model Teachers and the Harvardization of English Departments," in *The Rhetorical Tra-*

*dition and Modern Writing*, ed. James J. Murphy (New York: Modern Language Association, 1982), pp. 118–29.

15. Arlo Bates, *Talks on Writing English* (Boston: Houghton Mifflin Co., 1896), pp. 43, 18–19; Edwin Woolley, *Handbook of Composition* (Boston: D. C. Heath & Co., 1907), p. 2; also see Henry Pearson, *The Principles of Composition* (Boston: D. C. Heath & Co., 1897), p. 142; and Alphonzo G. Newcomer, *Elements of Rhetoric: A Course in Plain Prose Composition* (New York: Henry Holt & Co., 1898), pp. 197, 228, 306.

16. William Cairn, *The Forms of Discourse* (Boston: Ginn & Co., 1896), p. 17; Woolley, *Handbook of Composition*, p. 3.

17. Kitzhaber, "Rhetoric in American Colleges," pp. 131, 134.

18. Ibid., pp. 143–44, 327, 333; Pearson, *Principles of Composition*, p. ix; Bates, *Talks on Writing English*, p. 20. For other defenses of the new composition approach, see "Briefs on New Books," *The Dial* 8 (January 1888): 226; "Briefs on New Books," *The Dial* 20 (February 1899): 129–30; Martin Sampson, "Teaching the Art of Writing," *The Dial* 20 (February 1896): 108; "Notes," *The Nation* 60 (January 31, 1895): 91; "English Composition," *The Atlantic Monthly* 69 (January 1892): 129–33; and "Language Before Literature," *Century Magazine* 54 (July 1897): 469–70.

19. John Genung, *The Study and Practice of Rhetoric in the College Course* (Boston: D. C. Heath & Co., 1892); Theodore Hunt, "The Study of English in American Colleges," *Educational Review* 12 (1896): 140–50; also see "English Rhetoric and Composition," *The Nation* 64 (March 4, 1897): 167–68; and "Two Ways of Teaching English," *Century Magazine* 51 (1896) 793–94.

20. Kitzhaber, "Rhetoric in American Colleges," p. 191.

21. John Genung, *The Practical Elements of Style* (Boston: Ginn & Co., 1886), p. xii; Newcomer, *Elements of Rhetoric*, p. iii; Kitzhaber, "Rhetoric in American Colleges," p. 154. Kitzhaber blames the post–Civil War rhetoricians like Genung, Hart, Hunt, and Adams Sherman Hill for starting the drift toward utilitarian composition. That view is correct, but there is a difference in the pre-1885 rhetorics and the later composition texts. The later teachers did not conceive composition as a character-forming subject. For evidence of the rhetoricians' views, see chapter 6.

22. Payne, *English in American Universities*, pp. 25, 42, 92, 124.

23. Percival Chubb, *The Teaching of English* (New York: Macmillan Co., 1902), pp. 1–2.

24. Along with Chubb's book were Burke A. Hinsdale, *Teaching the Language Arts* (New York: D. Appleton and Co., 1896); and George Carpenter, Franklin Baker, and Fred Scott, *The Teaching of English in the Elementary and Secondary School* (New York: Longmans, Green and Co., 1903).

25. Chubb, *The Teaching of English*, pp. 378, 382–83, 319, xx–xxi.

26. Chubb complained of formalism and spoke of the importance of developing good habits instead of teaching rules of conduct. Chubb also cited contemporary psychologists as authorities, although he also suggested that the teaching methods of the new experts were misguided. Chubb, *The Teaching of English*, pp. 238–43, 360–62, 376–77.

27. S. S. Laurie, *Lectures on Language and Linguistic Method in the School* (New York: Cambridge University Press, 1890), pp. 6–16. Laurie taught the History of Education at the University of Edinburgh.

28. Hinsdale, *Teaching the Language Arts*, p. 132; Laurie, *Lectures on Language*, p. 6.

29. These generalizations are based on readings of the 1890s school reports of New York City; Utica, New York; Columbus, Ohio; Chicago, Illinois; Boston, Massachusetts; and San Francisco, California. For documentation of these claims, see my dissertation, "Democratic Eloquence: Language, Education, and Authority in Nineteenth-Century America" (University of Chicago, 1986), pp. 467–68.

30. John Mantle Clapp, *The Place of English in American Life* (Chicago: National Council of the Teachers of English, 1926), esp. p. 46. Also see Charles S. Pendleton, *The Social Objectives of School English* (Nashville: privately published, 1924); J. W. Swearson, "Meeting the Public Demand," *English Journal* 10 (June 1921): 327–31; "Out of School Uses of English," *English Journal* 22 (June 1933): 466–71; and F. H. Lumley, "The English Teacher and Radio Broadcasts," *English Journal* 33 (June 1934): 478–85.

31. Carpenter, Baker, and Scott, *The Teaching of English*, pp. 58, 244–50, 235.

32. Ibid., p. 18 for the quote; also see pp. 54–55, 193–94.

33. Applebee, *Tradition and Reform*, pp. 81–91, 139–62.

34. Samuel Thurber, "English in Secondary Schools," *School Review* 2 (1894): 472; Mary A. Dean, "English: A Word of Protest," *School Review* 14 (1906): 686–89.

35. Benjamin Ide Wheeler, "Art in Language," *The Atlantic Monthly* 86 (December 1900): 912; Woodrow Wilson, *Mere Literature, and Other Essays* (Boston: Houghton Mifflin Co., 1896), pp. 1–27; also see "Corruption of Language," *New York Tribune*, 26 November 1895; "The English Language and Others," *New York Tribune*, 15 March 1900; Thomas Lounsbury, *The Standard of Usage in English* (New York: Harper and Bros., 1908); and *Casual Essays of The Sun* (New York: Robert Grier Cooke, 1905), pp. 205–65.

36. Brander Matthews, *Parts of Speech: Essays on English* (New York: Charles Scribner's Sons, 1901), p. 71; Brander Matthews, *Essays on English* (New York: Charles Scribner's Sons, 1921), p. 43; "Man in the Street as Grammarian," *Living Age* 185 (May 24, 1890): 510.

37. Woodrow Wilson, *Mere Literature, and Other Essays*, pp. 1–27; Theodore W. Hunt, *Studies in Literature and Style* (New York: A. C. Armstrong & Son, 1891), pp. 7–25.

38. Norris quoted in Larzer Ziff, *The American 1890s* (New York: Viking Press, 1966), p. 251.

39. The best discussions of the new magazine style are Ziff, *The American 1890s*, pp. 120–32; Christopher P. Wilson, "The Rhetoric of Consumption: Mass-Market Magazines and the Demise of the Gentle Reader, 1880–1920," in *The Culture of Consumption: Critical Essays in American History, 1880–1980*, ed. Richard Wrightman Fox and T. J. Jackson Lears (New York: Pantheon Books, 1983), pp. 41–64.

40. Edward Bok, *The Americanization of Edward Bok* (New York: Charles Scribner's Sons, 1920), p. 296; Page quoted in Wilson, "The Rhetoric of Consumption," p. 49; Robert Underwood Johnson, "The Responsibilities of the Magazine," *The Independent* 73 (December 19, 1912): 1487–90; "Wanted: A Style for the Times," *The Nation* 75 (September 4, 1902): 185–86.

41. Lorenzo Sears, *The History of Oratory* (Chicago: Scott Foresman & Co., 1896); Henry Hardwicke, *The History of Oratory and Orators* (New York: G. P. Putnam's Sons, 1896).

42. William Jennings Bryan, ed., *The World's Famous Orations*, 10 vols. (New York: Funk & Wagnalls, 1906); David Brewer, ed., *The World's Best Orations*, 10 vols. (St. Louis: Fred P. Kaiser, 1899); Thomas R. Reed, ed., *Modern Eloquence*, 15 vols. (Philadelphia: John D. Morris & Co., 1900); Chauncey Depew, ed., *The Library of Oratory: Ancient and Modern*, 15 vols. (New York: The International Society, 1902); Guy Carleton Lee, ed., *The World's Orators*, 10 vols. (New York: G. P. Putnam's Sons, 1900); Mayo Hazeltine, ed., *Orators from Homer to William McKinley*, 24 vols. (New York: P. F. Collier & Sons, 1902).

43. Thomas Reed, ed., *Modern Eloquence*, 10 vols. (Chicago: George L. Shuman Co., 1900), vol. 1, p. v.

44. Cleveland Frederick Bacon, "Itinerant Speechmaking in the Last Campaign," *Arena* 85 (1901): 410; Curtis Guild, Jr., "The Spellbinder," *Scribner's Magazine* 32 (November 1902): 561.

45. Barnet Baskerville, *The People's Voice: The Orator in American Society* (Lexington: University of Kentucky Press, 1979), pp. 129–31, 133–34; Bacon, "Itinerant Speechmaking," p. 414.

46. Richard Murphy, "Theodore Roosevelt," in *A History and Criticism of American Public Address*, ed. Marie Kathryn Hochmuth, 4 vols. (New York: Russell & Russell, 1955), p. 359; for Roosevelt's training at Harvard, see p. 329.

47. Oscar King Davis, *Released for Publication—Some Inside Political History of Theodore Roosevelt and His Times* (Boston: Houghton Mifflin Co., 1925), p. 213; Masters is quoted in Murphy, "Theodore Roosevelt," p. 360.

48. Hermann Hagedorn, ed., *The Works of Theodore Roosevelt*, National Edition, 20 vols. (New York: Charles Scribner's Sons, 1926), vol. 18, p. 447; vol. 19, p. 19; William Griffith, ed., *Newer Roosevelt Messages* (New York: Current Literature Publishing Co., 1919), p. 1073.

49. William Bayard Hale, " 'Friends and Fellow-Citizens'—Our Political Orators of All Parties, and the Ways They Use to Win Us," *The World's Work* 23 (April 1912): 676.

50. Henry Cabot Lodge, ed., *Selections from the Correspondence of Theodore Roosevelt and Henry Cabot Lodge*, 2 vols. (New York: Charles Scribner's Sons, 1921), vol. 1, p. 95.

51. Murphy, "Theodore Roosevelt," pp. 345–46.

52. Ella Winter and Granville Hicks, eds., *The Letters of Lincoln Steffens*, 2 vols. (New York: Harcourt, Brace & Co., 1938), vol. 1, p. 152.

53. Henry Steele Commager, *The American Mind* (New Haven: Yale University Press, 1950), p. 347.

54. Kathleen Hall Jamieson, *Eloquence in an Electronic Age: The Transformation of Political Speechmaking* (New York: Oxford University Press, 1988), pp. 84–89.

55. Lodge, *Correspondence of Theodore Roosevelt and Henry Cabot Lodge*, vol. 1, p. 95; Bacon, "Itinerant Speechmaking," p. 414.

56. On newspapers in the 1890s, see Michael Schudson, *Discovering the News: A Social History of American Newspapers* (New York: Basic Books, 1978). See *The New York Times* editorial of August 18, 1896, announcing the new style. It reads like a preface to one of the new college composition texts.

57. John Higham, "The Re-Orientation of American Culture in the 1890's," in *Writing American History* (Bloomington: University of Indiana Press, 1973), pp. 73–102; T. J. Jackson Lears, *No Place of Grace: Antimodernism and the Transformation of American Culture, 1880–1920* (New York: Pantheon, 1981), pp. 97–139; Beth Bailey, *From Front Porch to Back Seat* (Baltimore: Johns Hopkins University Press, 1988), pp. 16–19; Gwendolyn Wright, *Building the Dream: A Social History of Housing in America* (New York: Pantheon Books, 1981), pp. 171–72; Lewis Erenberg, *Steppin' Out: New York Nightlife and the Transformation of American Culture, 1890–1930* (Westport, Conn.: Greenwood Press, 1981); Lary May, *Screening Out the Past* (Chicago: University of Chicago Press, 1980); Arthur M. Schlesinger, *Learning to Behave: A Historical Study of Etiquette Books* (New York: Macmillan Co., 1947), pp. 49–61.

58. John H. Vivian, "Spelling an End to Orthographical Reforms: Newspaper Response to the 1906 Roosevelt Simplifications," *American Speech* 54 (Fall 1979): 163–74.

59. "Editor's Study," *Harper's Monthly* 112 (April 1906): 801.

60. For some very perceptive comments on the *Ladies' Home Journal*, see Wilson, "The Rhetoric of Consumption," pp. 53–55; and Walter Hines Page, "The Cultivated Man in the Industrial Era," *The World's Work* 8 (July 1904): 4980–85. It might be noted how Page's definition of the "new" cultivated man differed from that of Charles Eliot, who was concerned with the same issue at the same time. Eliot's *Education and Efficiency and the New Definition of the Cultivated Man* (Boston: Houghton Mifflin) was published in 1909. Eliot, in keeping with the ideas of the previous generation of "specialists," hoped to merge gentlemanly cultivation with some expertise. Page, on the other hand, felt no such compulsions. Eliot, for example, hoped the new expert would also have some "literary and linguistic culture" (p. 44). Page, however, just noted the "old" cultivated man spoke elegantly: "He talked well . . . He had distinguished manners. . . . Perhaps his chief pleasure was got from political oratory" (p. 4981). (Page's *got* here was perhaps a deliberate slap at the old cultivated man.) Page did not speak of any linguistic attainments of the new cultivated man, he rather focused respect for science.

61. "Announcement," *McClure's Magazine* 1 (June 1893): 94–96.

62. For example, Matthews, *Parts of Speech*, pp. 53, 103–4, 129, 132, 207, 219, 232–34.

63. Edward Jones, "Education and Industry," *Popular Science Monthly* 64 (March

1904): 431–44; R. H. Thurston, "Education for Professions," *Popular Science Monthly* 62 (May 1902): 441–52; "Political Gentlemen," *The Nation* 62 (June 11, 1896): 450–51; Eliot, *Education and Efficiency*, pp. 44–45.

64. Ephraim Emerton, "Gentleman and Scholar," *The Atlantic Monthly* 85 (June 1900): 773, 777, 778; for other examples see L. B. R. Briggs, "Some Old-Fashioned Doubts about New-Fashioned Education," *The Atlantic Monthly* 86 (October 1900): 463, 467; Henry Calderwood, "Risks and Responsibilities of Specialism," *Presbyterian Review* 6 (1885): 91–100; Arthur Reed Kimball, "The Social Menance of Specialism," *Century Magazine* 54 (July 1897): 475–76; Victor Walker, "The Reign of the Specialist in Our Schools," *Methodist Review* 76 (May 1894): 442–47; James Russell Lowell, *The Complete Writings of James Russell Lowell*, 10 vols. (Cambridge: Houghton Mifflin Co., 1904), vol. 7, p. 211.

65. Rollo Ogden, "The Decay of Professional Mannerisms," *The Nation* 54 (March 31, 1892): 245.

66. The change in college students in the late nineteenth century has been well documented. Literary societies collapsed and students became preoccupied with sports. Joseph Kett, *Rites of Passage: Adolescence in America* (New York: Harper Colophon Books, 1977), p. 182. A good discussion of the phenomenon can be found in an untitled editorial of the New York *Evening Post*, 18 February 1895. At the University of Indiana, oratory was more popular than sports as late as 1890. When "progressive" educators attempted to disband the Indiana Oratorical Association in 1887, students and public clamored for its survival. The association sponsored an oratorical contest for students in colleges throughout the state. As late as 1891, the contest was closely followed by Indiana's press. By 1900, however, campus literary societies and public interest in oratory were almost nonexistent. Thomas D. Clark, *Indiana University: The Early Years*, 3 vols. (Bloomington: Indiana University Press, 1970), vol. 1, pp. 246–49.

67. Eliot quoted in New York *Evening Post*, 26 January 1895; E. L. Godkin, "Football and Manners," *The Nation* 59 (December 27, 1894): 476; Eliot, *Education and Efficiency*, pp. 39–45.

68. Sara Norton and M. A. DeWolfe Howe, eds., *Letters of Charles Eliot Norton*, 2 vols. (Boston: Houghton Mifflin Co., 1913), vol. 1, p. 300; Kermit Vanderbilt, *Charles Eliot Norton: Apostle of Culture in a Democracy* (Cambridge: Harvard University Press, 1959), p. 221.

69. Arthur Reed Kimball, "The Invasion of Journalism," *The Atlantic Monthly* 86 (July 1900): 121.

70. See William L. Riordon, *Plunkitt of Tammany Hall* (New York: E.P. Dutton & Co., 1963), pp. 46–47, 52–53.

71. James Bradstreet Greenough and George Lyman Kittredge, *Words and Their Ways in English Speech* (New York: Macmillan Co., 1901), pp. 16, 27; H. L. Mencken, *The American Language* (New York: Alfred A. Knopf, 1919), p. vii.

72. Greenough and Kittredge, *Words and Their Ways*, p. 27.

73. For an excellent summation of Krapp's work, see Edward Finegan, *Attitudes Toward English Usage: A History of a War of Words* (New York: Teachers College Press, 1980), pp. 82–86.

74. For some later expositions and refinements of the thesis: George Phillip Krapp, *The Knowledge of English* (New York: Holt, Rinehart and Winston, 1927), pp. 55–76; Charles C. Fries, "What Is Good English?" *English Journal* 14 (1925): 685–97; S. A. Leonard and H. Y. Moffet, "Current Definitions of Levels in English Usage," *English Journal* 16 (May 1927): 345–59; John Kenyon, "Cultural Levels and Functional Varieties of English," *College English* 10 (October 1948): 31–36; Martin Joos, *The Five Clocks* (New York: Harcourt, Brace & World, Inc., 1961).

75. Krapp, *Modern English: Its Growth and Present Use* (New York: Charles Scribner's Sons, 1909), pp. 330–31; also see Krapp's review of Lounsbury's *Standard of Usage in English* in *Educational Review* 36 (1908): 195–200.

76. George Arditi, "Role As a Culture Concept," *Theory and Society* 16 (1987): 565–91.

77. Anselm Strauss, ed., *George Herbert Mead on Social Psychology* (Chicago: University of Chicago Press, 1964), p. 207.

78. William James, *The Principles of Psychology* 2 vols. (Cambridge: Harvard University Press, 1981), vol. 1, pp. 279–379.

79. Alisdair MacIntyre, *After Virtue: A Study in Moral Theory* (Notre Dame: University of Notre Dame Press, 1981), p. 31.

80. James Greenough, "The English Question," *The Atlantic Monthly* 71 (May 1893): 656–62; see generally, Gerald Graff, *Professing Literature: An Institutional History* (Chicago: University of Chicago Press, 1987), pp. 113–18.

81. David Starr Jordan, "The College of the West," *Popular Science Monthly* 65 (May 1900): 31–32; Herbert Croly, *The Promise of American Life* (New York: Macmillan Co., 1909), pp. 427–41.

82. Thorstein Veblen, *The Theory of the Leisure Class* (New York: Penguin Books, 1967), pp. 398–400.

# Epilogue

1. William Faulkner, *As I Lay Dying* (New York: Cape and Smith, 1930), pp. 463–64.

2. For a similar thought, see Ernest Hemingway, *A Farewell to Arms* (New York: Charles Scribner's Sons, 1929), p. 196.

3. On advertising, see Geoffrey N. Leech, *English in Advertising* (London: Longman, 1966), esp. p. 75; on American politics, see Kathleen Hall Jamieson, *Eloquence in an Electronic Age: The Transformation of Political Speechmaking* (New York: Oxford University Press, 1988), *passim*.

4. Michael McGerr, *The Decline of Popular Politics: The American North, 1865–1925* (New York: Oxford University Press, 1986), pp. 138–83; Robert Westbrook, "Politics as Consumption: Managing the Modern Election," in *The Culture of Consumption: Critical Essays in American History, 1880–1980*, ed. Richard Wrightman Fox and T. J. Jackson Lears (New York: Pantheon, 1983), pp. 143–74.

5. Dale Carnegie, *Public Speaking* (New York: Pocket Books, 1926), p. 94; on Carnegie's career, see Daniel Boorstin, *The Americans: The Democratic Experience* (New York: Random House, 1973), pp. 467–69.

6. For examples, see Harvey C. Mansfield, Jr., "The Forms and Formalities of Liberty," *The Public Interest* 70 (Winter 1983): 121–31; and Allan Bloom, *The Closing of the American Mind* (New York: Simon & Schuster, 1987), pp. 68–81. Bloom argues for the debilitating effect of rock and roll. According to Mansfield, "In our democratic age, overflowing informality is a source of tyranny and rebellion" (p. 123).

7. Jules Henry, *Culture Against Man* (New York: Vintage Books, 1963), pp. 47–54, 90–93.

8. William Strunk, Jr., and E. B. White, *The Elements of Style* (New York: Macmillan Co., 1959), p. 55; on college entrance exams, see Edna Hays, *College Entrance Requirements in English: Their Effects on the High Schools* (New York: Teachers College, 1936), pp. 72–91, 116, 119–21; Claude M. Fuess, *The College Board: Its First Fifty Years* (New York: Columbia University Press, 1950), pp. 85, 115, 129–32.

9. For an argument that the plain style of "objective" newspaper reporting is a way to reach a diverse audience, see Herbert J. Gans, *Deciding What's News* (New York: Pantheon, 1979), p. 186; on the colloquial as a rhetoric of conciliation for a mass audience, see Jamieson, *Eloquence in an Electronic Age*, pp. 51–53.

10. *The New York Times*, 11 July 1885.

11. *The New York Times*, 28, 29, and 31 July 1869.

12. I am skeptical of Thomas Haskell's claim that professional social science became decisively authoritative in the twentieth century. See Thomas Haskell, *The Emergence of Professional Social Science* (Urbana: University of Illinois Press, 1977), pp. 235–40. This would require more empirical evidence than Haskell offers. My own reading of linguistics is that the situation was far more complicated than he suggests. For a useful discussion of how professional historians did not win the authority they coveted, see Peter Novick, *That Noble Dream: The "Objectivity Question" and the American Historical Profession* (Cambridge: Cambridge University Press, 1988), pp. 185–97, 368–77.

13. John Durham Peters, "Democracy and American Mass Communication Theory: Dewey, Lippmann, Lazarsfeld," *Communication* 11 (1989): 199–220; John Durham Peters, "Satan and Savior of Democracy: Mass Communication in Progressive Thought," *Critical Studies in Mass Communication* 6 (September 1989): 247–63.

14. This is a story that has been told many times. For a useful overview, see McGerr, *The Decline of Popular Politics*.

# Selected Bibliography

## Manuscript Sources

James Russell Lowell Papers. Harvard University.
Goodrich Family Collection. Sterling Memorial Library. Yale University.
Merriam-Webster Archives. Beinecke Library. Yale University.
Noah Webster Papers. New York Public Library.
Richard Grant White Papers. New York Historical Society.
William Dwight Whitney Papers. Sterling Memorial Library. Yale University.

## Newspapers

*Boston Herald*
*Chicago Times*
*Chicago Tribune*
*Daily Advertiser* (Boston)
*Evening Post* (New York)
*The New York Times*
*New York Tribune*
*Sun* (New York)

# Selected Books and Articles

Aarsleff, Hans. *The Study of Language in England, 1780–1860*. Princeton: Princeton University Press, 1967.

———. *From Locke to Saussure: Essays on the Study of Language and Intellectual History*. Minneapolis: University of Minnesota Press, 1982.

Allen, Don Cameron. *The Ph.D. in English and American Literature*. New York: Holt, Rinehart & Winston, 1968.

Alston, R. C. *English Grammars Written in English*. Leeds: Privately published, 1965.

———. *The English Dictionary: A Bibliography*. Leeds: Privately published, 1966.

———. *Spelling Books*. Bradford, England: Privately published, 1967.

Applebee, Arthur N. *Tradition and Reform in the Teaching of English*. National Council of the Teachers of English, 1974.

Auerbach, Erich. *Literary Language and Its Public in Late Latin Antiquity and the Middle Ages*. New York: Pantheon, 1965.

Beecher, Henry Ward. *Lectures to Young Men*. 2d ed. New York: J. B. Ford, 1872.

———. *Yale Lectures on Preaching*. 1st series. New York: Howard and Hulbert, 1872.

———. *The Original Plymouth Pulpit Sermons of Henry Ward Beecher*. 10 vols. Boston: The Pilgrim Press, 1873.

Blair, Hugh. *Lectures on Rhetoric and Belles Lettres*. 3 vols. London: W. Strahan, 1785.

Bledstein, Burton. *The Culture of Professionalism*. New York: Norton & Co., 1976.

Bluestone, Daniel. "Landscape and Culture in Nineteenth-Century America." Ph.D. diss., University of Chicago, 1984.

Brown, Goold. *The Grammar of English Grammars*. New York: W. Wood, 1878.

Burkett, Eva Mae. *American Dictionaries of the English Language Before 1861*. Metuchin, N.J.: Scarecrow Press, 1979.

Campbell, George. *Lectures on Systematic Theology, Pulpit Eloquence, and the Pastoral Character*. London: Thomas Tegg, 1840.

———. *The Philosophy of Rhetoric*. New York: Harper and Bros., 1844.

Cicero. *Three Dialogues Upon the Character and Qualifications of an Orator*. Translated by William Guthrie, Esq. London: T. Waller, 1755.

Cohen, Murray. *Sensible Words: Linguistic Practice in England, 1640–1785*. Baltimore: Johns Hopkins University Press, 1977.

Crocker, Lionel. *Henry Ward Beecher's Art of Preaching*. Chicago: University of Chicago Press, 1934.

de Saussure, Ferdinand. *Course in General Linguistics*. New York: McGraw-Hill Paperbacks, 1959.

Eliot, Charles W. *Education and Efficiency and the New Definition of the Cultivated Man*. Boston: Houghton Mifflin Co., 1908.

Finegan, Edward. *Attitudes Toward English Usage*. New York: Teachers College Press, 1980.

Gerth, Hans, and Mills, C. Wright, eds. *From Max Weber: Essays in Sociology*. New York: Oxford University Press, 1946.

Goffman, Erving. *Interaction Ritual: Essays in Face-to-Face Behavior*. Garden City, N.Y.: Anchor Books, 1967.

Goodrich, Chauncey. "Lectures on Rhetoric and Public Speaking." *Speech Monographs* 14 (1947): 1–37.

Gould, Edward. *Good English*. New York: A. C. Armstrong & Son, 1880.

Gray, Hanna. "Renaissance Humanism: The Pursuit of Eloquence." *Journal of the History of Ideas* 24 (1963): 497–514.

Greenough, James Bradstreet, and Kittredge, George Lyman. *Words and Their Ways in English Speech*. New York: Macmillan Co., 1901.

Gura, Philip F. *The Wisdom of Words: Language, Theology, and Literature in the New England Renaissance*. Middletown, Conn.: Wesleyan University Press, 1981.

Guthrie, Warren. "The Development of Rhetorical Theory in America, 1635–1850." Master's thesis, Northwestern University, 1940.

Hall, Fitzedward. *Recent Exemplifications of False Philology*. New York: Scribner, Armstrong & Co., 1872.

———. *Modern English*. New York: Scribner, Armstrong & Co., 1873.

———. *On English Adjectives in "-Able."* London: Truebner & Co., 1877.

Haskell, Thomas. *The Emergence of Professional Social Science*. Urbana: University of Illinois Press, 1977.

Hays, Edna. "College Entrance Requirements in English: Their Effects on the High School." Ph.D. diss., Columbia University Teacher's College, 1936.

Howe, Daniel Walker, ed. *Victorian America*. Philadelphia: University of Pennsylvania Press, 1976.

Howell, Wilber Samuel. *Eighteenth-Century British Logic and Rhetoric*. Princeton: Princeton University Press, 1971.

Hurd, Richard, ed. *The Works of the Right Honourable Joseph Addison*. 8 vols. London: T. Cardwell, 1811.

Jamieson, Kathleen Hall. *Eloquence in an Electronic Age*. New York: Oxford University Press, 1988.

Jesperson, Otto. *A Modern English Grammar on Historical Principles*. 5 vols. Heidelberg: Carl Winter's Universitatsbuchhandlung, 1914.

Johnson, Samuel. *A Dictionary of the English Language*. London: W. Strahan, 1755.

Jordan, Harold Monroe. "Rhetorical Education in American Colleges and Universities, 1850–1915." Ph.D. diss., Northwestern University, 1952.

Kitzhaber, Albert Raymond. "Rhetoric in American Colleges, 1850–1900." Ph.D. diss., University of Washington, 1953.

Krapp, George Phillip. *Modern English: Its Growth and Present Use*. New York: Charles Scribner's Sons, 1909.

———. *The Knowledge of English*. New York: Holt, Rinehart and Winston, 1927.

Laurie, S. S., *Lectures on Language and Linguistic Method in the School*. New York: Cambridge University Press, 1890.

Leith, Dick. *A Social History of English*. London: Routledge & Kegan Paul, 1983.

Lewis, John. *Observations on the Objects and Progress of Philological Enquiries*. Fredericksburg, Virginia: Minor, 1827.

Lounsbury, Thomas. *A History of the English Language*. New York: Henry Holt and Co., 1879.

————. *A History of the English Language*. Rev. ed. New York: Henry Holt & Co., 1894.

————. *The Standard of Usage in English*. New York: Harper and Bros., 1908.

Lowth, Robert. *A Short Introduction to English Grammar*. Philadelphia: n.p., 1775.

————. *Lectures on the Sacred Poetry of the Hebrews*. Andover, Mass.: Crocker and Brewster, 1829.

Lyman, Verne. *English Grammar in American Schools Before 1850*. Chicago: University of Chicago Press, 1922.

MacIntyre, Alasdair. *After Virtue: A Study in Moral Theory*. Notre Dame, Ind.: University of Notre Dame Press, 1981.

March, Francis. *A Course in College Philology: Literature and Language*. New York: Charles Scribner's Sons, 1865.

————. "The Future of Philology." *Presbyterian Quarterly and Princeton Review* 3 (October 1874): 698–713.

Marsh, George Perkins. *The Origins and History of the English Language*. New York: Charles Scribner's Sons, 1862.

————. *Lectures on the English Language*. New York: Charles Scribner's Sons, 1874.

Mathews, William. *Words: Their Use and Abuse*. Chicago: S. C. Griggs & Co., 1876.

————. *The Great Conversers*. Chicago: S. C. Griggs & Co., 1878.

————. *Oratory and Orators*. Chicago: S. C. Griggs & Co., 1883.

Matthews, Brander. *Parts of Speech: Essays on English*. New York: Charles Scribner's Sons, 1901.

————. *Essays on English*. New York: Charles Scribner's Sons, 1921.

Mencken, H. L. *The American Language*. 1st and 4th eds. New York: Alfred A. Knopf, 1919, 1937.

Moon, George Washington. *The Revisers' English*. New York: Funk & Wagnalls, 1882.

————. *The Dean's English*. New York: George Routledge & Sons, 1884.

Mott, Frank Luther. *A History of American Magazines*. 2 vols. Cambridge: Harvard University Press, 1938.

————. *American Journalism*. 3rd ed. New York: Macmillan Co., 1962.

Nevins, Allan, ed. *The Diary of George Templeton Strong*. 3 vols. New York: Macmillan Co., 1952.

Parker, William Riley. "Where Do English Departments Come From?" *College English* 28 (1967): 339–51.

Partridge, Eric. *A Dictionary of Slang and Unconventional English*. 8th ed. New York: Macmillan Co., 1984.

Pocock, John. *The Machiavellian Moment: Florentine Political Thought and the Atlantic Republican Tradition*. Princeton: Princeton University Press, 1975.

Sawyer, Leicaster. *The Elements of Biblical Interpretation*. New Haven: A. H. Maltby, 1836.

————, trans. *The New Testament*. Boston: J. P. Jewett and Co., 1858.

————, trans. *The Holy Bible Containing the Old and New Testament*. 2 vols. Boston: Walker, Wise and Co., 1861.

Schaff, David. *The Life of Phillip Schaff*. New York: Charles Scribner's Sons, 1897.

Schaff, Phillip. *A Companion to the Greek Testament and the English Version*. New York: Harper and Bros., 1892.

Schudson, Michael. *Discovering the News: A Social History of American Newspapers*. New York: Basic Books, 1978.

Seigal, Jerrold. *Rhetoric and Philosophy in Renaissance Humanism: The Union of Eloquence and Wisdom, Petrarch to Villa*. Princeton: Princeton University Press, 1968.

Simms, P. Marion. *The Bible in America*. New York: Wilson-Erickson, 1936.

Sledd, James, and Kolb, Gwin. *Dr. Johnson's Dictionary*. Chicago: University of Chicago Press, 1955.

Smith, Adam. *Lectures on Rhetoric and Belles Lettres*. Edited by John Lothian. Carbondale: University of Southern Illinois Press, 1963.

Starnes, DeWitt, and Noyes, Gertrude. *The English Dictionary from Cawdrey to Johnson, 1604–1755*. Chapel Hill: University of North Carolina Press, 1946.

Steiner, George. *After Babel: Aspects of Language and Translation*. New York: Oxford University Press, 1975.

———. *Language and Silence: Essays on Language, Literature and the Inhuman*. New York: Atheneum, 1977.

Stone, Lawrence. *The Family, Sex and Marriage in England 1500–1800*. New York: Harper & Row, 1977.

Thornton, Richard Harwood. *American Glossary*. 2 vols. Philadelphia: Lippincott & Co., 1912.

Tomsich, John. *A Genteel Endeavor: American Culture and Politics in the Gilded Age*. Stanford: Stanford University Press, 1971.

Trench, Richard Chenevix. *On the Study of Words*. New York: Redfield, 1853.

———. *On Some Deficiencies in Our English Dictionaries*. London: J. W. Parker and Son, 1858.

Warfel, Harry, ed. *Letters of Noah Webster*. New York: Library Publishers, 1953.

Webster, Noah. *Sketches of American Policy*. Hartford: Hudson & Goodwin, 1785.

———. *An American Selection of Lessons in Reading and Speaking*. Hartford: Hudson & Goodwin, 1789.

———. *Dissertation on the English Language*. Boston: Isaiah Thomas & Co., 1789.

———. *A Philosophical and Practical Dictionary of the English Language*. New Haven: Brisbon and Brannan, 1807.

———. *A Letter to the Honorable John Pickering*. Boston: West and Richardson, 1817.

———, trans. *The Holy Bible Containing the Old and New Testaments in the Common Version with Amendments in the Language*. New Haven: Durie & Peck, 1833.

White, Richard Grant. *Words and Their Uses*. New York: Sheldon & Co., 1872.

———. *Everyday English*. Boston: Houghton Mifflin & Co., 1880.

Whitney, William Dwight. *Language and the Study of Language*. New York: Charles Scribner's Sons, 1867.

———. *Oriental and Linguistic Studies*. 1st series. New York: Scribner, Armstrong & Co., 1872.

———. *Oriental and Linguistic Studies*. 2d series. New York: Scribner, Armstrong & Co., 1874.

———. *The Life and Growth of Language*. New York: D. Appleton & Co., 1875.

Wilson, Woodrow. *Mere Literature, and Other Essays*. Boston: Houghton Mifflin Co., 1896.
Worcester, Joseph. *A Dictionary of the English Language*. Boston: Hickling, Swan and Brewer, 1860.
Ziff, Larzer. *The American 1890s*. New York: Viking Press, 1966.

# Index